Pragmatic
Group Leadership

Pragmatic Group Leadership

Jeffrey A. Kottler
Oakland University

Brooks/Cole Publishing Company
Monterey, California

Brooks/Cole Publishing Company
A Division of Wadsworth, Inc.

Printed in the United States of America
10   9   8   7   6   5   4   3   2   1

Library of Congress Cataloging in Publication Data:
Kottler, Jeffrey A.
    Pragmatic group leadership.

    Bibliography: p.
    Includes index.
    1. Group counseling.   2. Group psychotherapy.
    3. Leadership.   I. Title.
    BF637.C6K68   1982   158'.3   82-17895
ISBN 0-534-01254-X

Subject Editor: Claire Verduin
Manuscript Editor: Barbara Burton
Production Editors: Joe Guzaitis, Jane Stanley
Interior Design: Vernon T. Boes
Cover Design: Vernon T. Boes
Illustrations: John Foster
Typesetting: Boyer and Brass, San Diego, California

To Cary Jay Kottler

Dr. Jeffrey Kottler has studied at Oakland University, Wayne State University, Harvard University, the University of Stockholm, and received his Ph.D. from the University of Virginia. He has worked as a group therapist in a variety of settings including the following: a mental health center, a crisis center, a university, nursery school, a corporation, a hospital, a municipal department of human services, and in private practice.

Dr. Kottler is the author of the books Ethical and Legal Issues in Counseling and Psychotherapy *(with William Van Hoose) and* Mouthing Off—A Study of Oral Behavior, Its Causes, and Treatments. *He has served as Chair of the Ethics and Professional Standards Committee of the Association For Specialists in Group Work and has been guest editor of their journals and a member of the editorial board.*

Kottler has recently returned from a 5-month tour in Peru where he served as a Fulbright Scholar and Senior Lecturer in group therapy at Inca Garcilaso de la Vega University and Catholic University in Lima. He has now resumed his duties as Adjunct Professor at Oakland University and Clinical Director of Huron Valley Counseling Services in Farmington Hills, Michigan.

Preface

This book is designed for the student who is already familiar with the theory and research of group counseling and therapy, who understands the basic mechanisms by which change occurs in a group setting, and who has had some experience as a participant or leader in a therapeutic group. It is assumed that the reader is motivated to upgrade current levels of expertise and to supplement existing skills and knowledge.

Pragmatic Group Leadership is for counselors and therapists who wish to integrate interdisciplinary knowledge, a wide range of useful skills, and a plethora of accepted theories into a universal model of helping people in groups. This philosophy permits the student or practitioner to imprint his or her own personal style and therapeutic preferences into a pragmatic experience base wherein the meaning of an idea or strategy is viewed in terms of its practical consequences. In short, this book is about successful intervention in clients' lives, using anything and everything that clinical research has demonstrated to be reliably helpful.

Why Group Leadership?

It is interesting to speculate about who has chosen to advance his or her knowledge as a group leader and about why such a decision was made. There are, of course, both altruistic and selfish reasons for entering the helping professions. Some people wish to save the world while others wish merely to save themselves. From melancholy? From angst or self-pity? From boredom or mediocrity? No matter. We all need saving from something. While it could have been an accident that we became full-fledged therapists or counselors, it is no quirk of fate that we end up spending most of our time helping people in groups while our colleagues scornfully stick to their couches. It takes a special kind of person with unique traits and skills to survive the slings and arrows of group interaction, let alone to direct the course of its action consistently. Few sound persons would choose to train for leading therapeutic groups unless they had many broadly based motives.

We become group leaders because such an arena is considerably more challenging to the therapist than seeing individual clients. It carries more responsibility, and it requires continual concentration. It is impossible to finish a two-hour group session without sweat. The focus of sessions is totally unpredictable, and so fickle is client behavior that the group leader must function in a state of confused ambiguity. It is easy for events to get out of control: one minute there is placid goodwill; the next minute there is ruthless civil war. When such an event concludes, the leader is left to sort out the mess, figure out what happened, and make meticulous plans to ensure that such an explosion doesn't recur.

Yet in spite of colleague ridicule, media distortion, and extra stress and strain without additional compensation, there are many reasons supporting our infatuation with a helping structure that at times seems to have almost magical effects on clients. Above all, there is the firm conviction that groups offer the best means of helping the greatest number of psychologically suffering people. There is also, of course, the greater efficiency, economy, and cost-effectiveness of seeing many clients simultaneously.

Then there are the personal reasons why we have chosen to lead groups. If we are honest, we realize that it is much more fun working in the dynamic, spontaneous company of diverse people than in seeing clients on an individual or an assembly-line basis. Leading groups energizes the leader's spirit and tests endurance and hubris. The group leader must quicken reflexes so as to respond more spontaneously to conflicts as they arise. A sense of humor must be honed to razor sharpness to enliven sessions and diffuse tension. And with the more rigorous training that is required, there is also more sustained growth for the therapist. Most group sessions offer us insights and reflections that are of immense personal use. In the course of a single group meeting, clients deal with a variety of issues that still reverberate in the practitioner's brain a year later: the fear of going crazy, the search for parental approval, the complexities of extramarital relationships, feelings of career entrapment, stagnation, and loneliness, the burden of neurotic ambition, as well as the difficulties of child rearing. Although we are careful to maintain objective detachment and avoid self-indulgence during sessions, a portion of our mind keeps noting personally meaningful material for later integration.

Finally, we may choose to be group leaders for more perverse reasons. Short of politics, there is no better way to pursue Sartre's Soul of Human Ambition—to be God—than to lead groups. The homage, adulation, respect, and deference from clients are potentially never-ending. The group leader is omnipotent, in some cases a model to be worshiped. Who among us does not enjoy as well as fear the awesome power we wield in influencing others? The group setting can be a more fertile environment for change than the individual therapy session. No doubt that is why irresponsible religious fanatics have had such success in brainwashing their disciples. For whatever reasons a therapist chooses to work in groups, this young profession offers fulfillment on a scale matched by few others.

Anatomy of This Book

What to include in this book became an exciting decision process. Chapter outlines were repeatedly revised. Everything, it seemed to me, in the fields of sociology, psychology, political science, linguistics, philosophy, history, even physiology, had some bearing on what I wanted to include.

I knew that I would first have to deal with theory and all that philosophy means for group leaders in their search for truth. The first section of the book includes some of the philosophical threads that help bind our profession together. In spite of the differences between practitioners, there is common agreement as to certain assumptions that we believe to be true. Chapter 1 summarizes this "glue" that holds our nucleus of truth together.

In Chapter 2 I present a case for pragmatism, a hallowed "native born" philosophical position in America. Such a philosophy of operation, a philosophy of thought out of which operations materialize, is fundamental to effective action on the part of any group worker.

If the desired outcome of counseling or therapy groups is positive behavioral change for each member, it seems imperative that group leaders have a thorough understanding of why, when, and how people change. Chapter 3 addresses the question of how people change. What are the processes, the intervention strategies in groups, that result in new learnings in individuals or in new decisions that permit or cause new feelings and actions? Chapter 3 also includes an interdisciplinary outlook, wherein theoretical propositions are formulated from which operational directions and intervention strategies can be drawn. When a leader does anything or permits anything in a group to begin or continue, what theoretical behavior-change rationale will support such action?

The second part of the book includes the most significant dimensions of group leadership. Chapters 4 through 8 discuss the most appropriate rules, attributes, and reasoning processes of the pragmatic group leader.

Traditionally, the concept of modeling has been centered largely in the language of the social learning theorist or the psychodynamic concept of identification. It is my premise that the way group leaders act, the personal characteristics they demonstrate, and the force of their personalities significantly influence successful group member performance. Regardless of actual approach or leadership style, those who exhibit dimensions of personal mastery in their own lives tend to be more effective group leaders. Chapter 4 includes specific suggestions for expanding the roles of therapeutic modeling in groups, examining such factors as appropriate self-disclosure, semantic modeling, role reversals, and "groupside manner."

Because spoken language is the chief medium through which group work occurs, a leader's expertise depends in large measure on how language is employed. It befits the group worker to become a psycholinguist, a semanticist, a student of what is linguistically current as well as of what idioms are peculiar to various ethnic and age groups. Chapter 5 makes a strong case for avoiding certain words, phrases, concepts, and structures that are confusing, obstructive, or not suited to the outcome goals of the individuals in a group. These include technical terms that constitute the special jargon of the therapy and group field; sexist or class-discriminating terms; terms that reinforce erroneous concepts about the nature of thought and emotional processes; and terms that reinforce directions, attitudes, values, or goals that are inimical to positive behavioral change on the part of individual members. Replacement terms and concepts are offered and discussed, and suggestions are made for determining how messages are received.

Chapter 6 takes up the crucial area of diagnostics: understanding the make-up of individuals and diagnosing what is going on in the group as a whole, including the formation of subgroup coalitions. The process of productive labeling, and how it is therapeutically beneficial, is also discussed here. The goal is to provide the advanced group leader with a comprehensive framework for understanding what is happening in the group and within the members at any given time. As part of the process involved in macro- and microdiagnosis, certain predictable problems and critical incidents will occur in most groups. Chapter 7 focuses on the most typical, presenting case examples and suggestions for handling them.

As marriage, family, and sex therapists have known for years, there

are numerous advantages for members and leaders alike when partners lead a group in tandem. Leaders can depend on one another to
provide support, demonstrations, or to monitor more effectively the
reactions of group members. Teamwork is an essential part of effectively breaking in a less experienced leader. There are considerations
involved in the pairing of leaders that may militate against or promote smoother operation—issues such as ideological differences,
training variances, division of labor, differences in skill levels, personality types, and experiential backgrounds. Then, too, some group
techniques and structures are more suitable for use when leader-
pairs conduct the group sessions. Chapter 8 focuses on the important issues and nuances of co-leadership.

The third section of the book focuses on specific techniques and
strategies for the pragmatic group leader who wishes to augment a
base of traditional skills. These chapters may be seen as only examples of the types of creative advancement that are possible.

Whether one is initiating or ending a relationship, making a career
or lifestyle change, practicing novel behavior, confronting a significant person, or disclosing personal history, there are always risks
accompanying pursuance of the unknown, the untried. Chapter 9
considers risk taking in depth and discusses how group leaders can
invite more constructive risk taking among participants. Chapter 10
illustrates these principles in action.

Group leaders have no technological hardware to aid in helping
people. We have only our minds and our skills of communicating
what is in them. The more refined and expert group leaders become
in their use of language, the better they will become at making telling
interventions. Chapter 11 focuses on the use of metaphors and images that can facilitate insight and motivate growth. Though the clinical application of verbal images in groups is emphasized, much of
the material here is borrowed from all the communication disciplines, including literature, philosophy, the sciences and humanities, even children's stories.

Participation in a therapeutic group can be intensely serious,
laden with conflict and tension. Frequently the only laughter heard
is the nervous giggling that is the telltale sign of anxiety. Yet the
important tasks of a therapeutic group need not be compromised by
the leader's effort to bring humor into the setting. With all the hard
work involved in the process of changing, comic relief promotes a
more relaxed, natural, desirable atmosphere. Humorous anecdotes
are used throughout Chapter 12 to describe how group leaders can
make their sessions more enjoyable. Although virtually everything

worth learning in life tends to be painful or difficult, no one has ever said that a spirit of fun cannot accompany it.

Chapter 13 provides an impetus for advanced group leaders to increase their range of possible intervention choices. Described are creative group structures such as subgrouping, spatial interventions, thinking on one's seat, and other therapeutic strategies which only the experienced practitioner could make work.

Chapter 14 moves into adjunct structures. It is not what clients say and do in group sessions that makes a definitive difference; it is how they act in the outside world. Limitless resources are available to the creative group leader who wishes to supplement scheduled sessions with opportunities for further client growth. Many practical adjunct strategies are described that allow the group leader to stimulate progress toward client change between sessions. Among other structures, I discuss environmental programming, people monitoring, journal keeping, and psychological homework.

Chapter 15 draws together the separate strands of the book and touches on a number of areas under the topic of ethics. I look to the future of group work, where I see the field headed, and to the future of group leaders.

This overview of the book's contents make certain themes evident. The principal emphasis is on integrating existing knowledge in the field, bringing together diverse approaches into a format that is useful for the practitioner.

Jeffrey A. Kottler

I wish to acknowledge the following professionals for their assistance and guidance throughout the preparation of this book: specifically, Dr. Anita Lancaster for her early dialogues with me in helping to conceptualize the contents of the book; Dr. John Vriend for his friendship, his many critical suggestions, and his help in co-authoring the first chapter; Dr. Gerald Corey, Dr. Allen Dye, Dr. Stephen Feit, and Dr. George Gazda for offering many helpful suggestions; Claire Verduin of Brooks/Cole for her oasis of trust, confidence, and expertise in a sometimes barren publishing world; Barbara Lukas and Joe Guzaitis, also of Brooks/Cole, who helped production to run smoothly and enjoyably; and Ellen Kottler, for editing and typing progressive drafts of the manuscript.

Contents

PART 1

The Threads That Bind Group Helping Systems

Among the skirmishes and conflicts between group leaders, dialogues between theoreticians and researchers, there is an unspoken consensus as to the most effective means to promote change. There is general agreement in the field about certain underlying assumptions of leader behavior, about explaining how group members learn, and hence change, and about the philosophic orientation that ought to be part of a therapist's or counselor's diagnostic and treatment process. Pragmatism permits the practitioner to function as a philosopher-scientist, inductively and deductively weaving the most stable threads of all helping systems into a comprehensive model of group treatment.

CHAPTER 1

Group Work as a Synergistic Modality*

It is midsummer, hot and muggy in the cavernous meeting room of the old Atlantic City Hotel. The room is high-ceilinged, echoey. Large-bladed fans hang from the ceiling and rotate lethargically. Floor-to-ceiling windows span one long side of the rectangular room, the drapes open, midafternoon light spilling in. On the opposite side, floor-to-ceiling mirrors cover the entire wall, broken only by the massive doors open to welcome more air.

More than 100 people sit in concentric circles on folding chairs around a demonstration counseling group of 12 members and the co-counselors. Most of the observers are fanning themselves with their workshop programs, straining to hear all that goes on in the "fishbowl" group, cooperating uncommonly under the conditions, striving not to scrape their feet or move their chairs, being careful to avoid side-talk. The counseling group has been in session for an hour, one-half of its scheduled time. The interpersonal interaction has grown meaningful to several of the members. The level of counseling has gotten vital, even profound, rapidly. The in-group participants are 90% oblivious to the horde of friendly and interested observers, absorbed with, focusing on the concerns of May, Joe, and Miranda who have plunged into personal revelations about their current life situations and struggles, who are sensing that they can receive help from this experience, inviting it.

Suddenly, from who knows where, a sparrow flies through the open doors and circles the room, perching briefly on a chandelier, then exploring a way out, again circling the room.

One of the counselors says, "A bird has just entered this room. Normally this would be an unusual and interesting distraction, and any one of us might be tempted to break our concentration and attend to the bird. But we didn't come all the way to Atlantic City to watch a bird, did we? It has been hard for each of you to shut out all

*co-authored with John Vriend

the observers, to forget them and work hard at making this experience worth your while. But everyone seems to have managed that. Now, let's also try to ignore the bird and work at using this time in the way we agreed to do. Is there anyone who feels that she or he cannot do that?"

Some discussion ensues about whose responsibility it is to take care of the bird. All decide it is someone else's. After a few minutes the group grows intensely absorbed in the counseling process. The bird is ignored. The observers, too, take their cue from this.

The bird, for the next half-hour, grows more confused. It flies against the large window panes, falls to the floor stunned several times. Next it smashes into the mirrors reflecting the outdoors from the windows. It falters in flight, once perching on the head of an observer. Finally it rests bewildered under a chair. When the fishbowl ends, someone captures the bird and releases it into Atlantic City's outer world.

It is the final meeting of a counseling group that has gone through twelve sessions. The co-counselors have conferred and plan to end the group with an evaluation and feedback exercise, one that includes reinforcement of past group goals and future plans for each client-member. They work well together. They have co-led many groups over thousands of hours. Philosophically and strategically in tune, they complement one another in interventionistic style. It is an early morning meeting.

One of the counselors, the previous evening, received a telephone message from one of his grown daughters that her older sister has cut her throat with an electric knife. She has given herself a tracheotomy and is hospitalized, under sedation. This is the third and most serious attempt she has made on her own life. She lives across the continent. Dad feels helpless, disturbed, depressed.

In the morning he arrives at the counseling room early and writes on the blackboard:

> This is the way the group ends,
> This is the way the group ends,
> This is the way the group ends,
> Its throat gets cut with an electric knife.

His co-counselor arrives, reads the message, and asks, "Don't you think that's a bit strong?" Dad shares his story. "Are you going to be

OK? Do you want me to take over the group?" asks his partner. "No. I'll be OK. Just be sensitive to what I'm carrying in my breast, and confront me if I fade from the business at hand."

Members arrive, buzz back and forth over the stark image, and the group begins with a focus on the jolting effects of separation, the abruptness and finality of closure. The image, as catalyst, works. "Dad," in his professional role, has not denied his personal reality or feelings. He integrates what is internally heavy into his actions to the members. There is no self-disclosure to the members. After the group, he and his partner process his internal and group dynamics.

The counseling group has met for 9 out of a scheduled 12 sessions. Everyone has exchanged, shared, used the group time to focus on personal concerns, set goals, and work on these between the weekly sessions, everyone except Junellen, who has not uttered a word. She has never smiled, though there is lively conviviality and humor in the group, much laughter, session after session. The group is cohesive. All the members have a sense of belonging. They have become a family, except for Junellen, who is the "outsider." The others begin to resent her.

Earlier sorties to include Junellen were ignored. She would look down at her lap when any attention came her way. The group leader's one or two attempts to include her had made no difference.

After the third session she confided privately to the group leader that she just couldn't bring herself to participate; she wanted to drop out. Learning of her lifelong fear of being in small groups, the details of her personal struggle, the counselor agreed to meet with her between sessions to discuss her thoughts and feelings—what she experienced during group sessions—and vowed to support her against other group members in her silence or whatever stance she wanted to take. He was convinced that the group experience was more important for her than for any other participant. It was in the "laboratory" that she needed to work through her lifelong anxiety/avoidance pattern of behavior.

During the ninth session the critical incident occurred. Members talked to one another about her, discussed asking her to leave unless she made some effort to say something to them, to give some explanation for her standoffishness. Many, if not every one of the 13 other members, directly confronted her. The group leader said nothing but watched her closely and sat next to her to give her physical support. Tears came. She found it hard to breathe. The counselor rested his hand on her arm and asked, "Junellen, do you want me to answer them?" Long pause. Heavy sighs. "No—I will." Then she talked.

"I like all of you. But I can't help myself that I'm not like you." More tears. Wads of paper tissue emerge from her purse. "I—want to talk—Oh, it's so hard!" Finally she got going. It poured out. What was happening in her life had nothing to do with any of them. She went on to say how important to her was each piece of private information she had garnered from particular members. Once her story had gushed out, the members were by turns contrite, then sympathetic, then realistically helpful. The ninth session ended with two-thirds of the members going for coffee afterward to relate to her, to welcome her and solidify her entry into the fold.

Experienced therapeutic group leaders could relate many similar anecdotes. The key word is *experienced.* Once we have been trained, conquered our initial caution, acquired confidence in our abilities and leadership role, developed a repertoire of behaviors and structures, and *permit* existential phenomena to happen, we learn that almost anything can and does happen. We are never certain what form a particular group session will take. Every new round of group sessions differs from previous ones because members are always unlike previous members. Plus, the mixture always changes.

In short, human beings are endlessly different, endlessly fascinating in their variability. Although there is such a phenomenon as mob psychology in which humans tend to act in concert in a predictable way, the small group organized to help individuals in their lives outside the group hardly ever fits such a mold. Thus, conscientious group leaders, those who have chosen this professional specialty as their primary area of expertise tend not to suffer from "burnout" in their group leader roles and actions. Burnout comes as a result of repetition, and it is virtually impossible to repeat a group experience.

The three sketches introducing this chapter were chosen to illustrate that three categories of distraction are paramount, three possible areas wherein the experienced leader might be tested and called on to perform in uncharted waters. First, there are environmental distractions. Second, there are distractions internal to the leader. Third, there are distractions that arise in any given group member. There are other categories as well, but in considering what these others might be, none held the status relegated to these three. By identifying these three areas, I am trying neither to oversimplify nor to stress their weightiness. I am calling to attention the unpredictability of so much that occurs in group work and pointing to the three primary sources of group events for which a leader cannot formulate a blueprint for action or reaction in advance.

The professional development of a group leader never ends. The consummately competent leader is an ideal, understood and sought after but unattainable in a single lifetime. The more one knows about leading groups, the more humble one is likely to become and the more open to sources for professional growth. Having gone through the spirited surge of training and early accomplishment and won one's spurs as an effective professional, having immersed oneself in the literature to search for new ideas, structures, exercises, interventions, strategies, points of view, and how-to-do-it reports from other practitioners, all with diminishing returns, where does one go for further enlightenment? Beyond one's experiential discoveries, where else but to further searching?

A SYNERGISTIC MODALITY

Synergy denotes a whole greater than the sum of its parts. It is a term that can be applied in a number of social contexts as well as in the physical sciences. Synergism implies cooperation among discrete agents to produce a cumulative effect greater than any independent unit. What better concept than this to name the uniqueness of what happens in small group work, where a kaleidoscopic mixture of human interactions and complex influences helps to generate positive behavioral change for each participant.

Research into the nature of the human mind and how it works has accelerated in the past decade, but the more facts scientists corral into the realm of the known, the more vast the realm of the unknown appears to be. We often fail to appreciate just how complex each individual human being is and how difficult it is to know ourselves. And when we interact in groups, the complexity—the mystery, even—that is present in the cross-fertilization may be said to be compounded potentially to the nth power. We strive to make our way by reducing the complexity to what we have found works according to normatively effective operating principles, but we are uncertain and baffled a good deal of the time. The fact that we so frequently follow hunches, that we respond intuitively to stimuli, makes us no less scientific or desirous of more reliably effective ways to function: we are simply in unmapped territory.

The first anecdote at the head of this chapter, presenting a distraction in the environment, is relatively simple to deal with. Somehow all that is nonhuman is less complex and more subject to understanding and manageability, easier to make decisions about than, for example, that which churns up within the group leader. The distractions that occur within the group leader are in turn less complicated than those that arise within individual members because the group leader can take the time to review and study these more easily and can exercise a greater measure of control. What goes on within a member and how this affects other members has the highest degree of complexity because every other member is at once a product and the carrier of all his or her past. Finally, I might have referred to a category of distractions that exist "within" the group, as though such happenings were located in a plurality rather than within a given person, but this would be inconsistent with a point of view that will be reinforced throughout this book.

What, then, are we being invited to acknowledge here? First, that practitioners who lead small groups are constantly being reminded by circumstances that there are limits to their knowledge, repertoire of skills, training, and experience. They are constantly endeavoring to provide service to members in fuzzy contexts in which uncertainty about "right" action tends to be the norm. Second, that leading a group is more of an art, in which creativity and on-the-spot ingenuity are called for as a matter of course, than it is a science in which cause and effect operate along predictable lines. Leading a group is always a chancy business. Third, that enough is known by the results produced to validate the worth of the endeavor. Fourth, that one cannot account for the whole by an examination of the parts. Fifth, that we who are determined to be professionally competent are still discoverers, bravely voyaging in uncharted waters we see as holding promise.

Of course we know, or have faith in, some things that keep us sailing. Already shelved in libraries around the land is enough evidence to sustain our faith: we are not fools or blind do-gooders. As group clinicians we are drawn together because of the commonalities we share rather than our differences. Whether seasoned veterans or struggling neophytes, we can subscribe to the concept of synergism, and this includes having a synergistic perspective about what exists in the literature: let contributions from every quarter help the whole be greater than the parts.

UNIFYING ASSUMPTIONS

In less than 30 years (if one does not take into account the pioneering research of sociologists who made earlier discoveries in group dynamics) the technology of helping people in small groups has become a formidable discipline. Following World War II, the group work field enjoyed a growth period that came into full flower in the 1960s and early 1970s, similar to what the fields of gerontology and human sexuality are undergoing today. Small groups were being tried in every social arena. The encounter group became familiar to the aware layperson. Brainstorming groups, rap groups, conscious-ness-raising groups, and peer-counseling groups became familiar designations especially to mental health and allied professionals. Psychotherapy and counseling-group literature swelled with new discoveries, learnings that poured forth from experimenters in dis-similar contexts—from marathon group enthusiasts, from Esalen, from Synanon, from the family counseling movement, from psycho-drama, from schools, hospitals, churches, community agencies. This growth has now leveled off on a plateau where what is known is being consolidated through the publication of numerous books that are repetitive in their offerings.

This means that group work has become institutionalized, vali-dated. More mental health workers, through training, professional organizations, and licensing procedures, are being required to know about therapeutic group procedures in order to effectively lead groups to achieve positive treatment outcomes for their clients or patients. Professional organizations have developed training stan-dards and guidelines, as well as ethical codes concerning group work. The Association for Specialists in Group Work and the Ameri-can Group Psychotherapy Association are two of the most viable organizations seeking to promote the profession through respected journals and sponsored training workshops among their other ac-tivities. They typify the visibility and respectability that group work-ers, small group structures, and the group process are accorded in mental health and educational circles and by society at large.

The diversity of professionals who identify themselves as group leaders makes it understandably difficult to create a singular image of the field. Disciplines as wide-ranging as management science, sociology, social work, medicine, education, nursing, psychology, and counseling have spawned theoreticians, researchers, and prac-titioners who have made significant contributions to the body of knowledge about group work. It is increasingly evident that the sys-tematic and effective practice of group leadership will require profes-sionals with an education that bypasses and bridges the arbitrary divisions of academic curricula. Yet such a generalist must also have some fairly specialized training in the techniques unique to group practice.

In addition to the range of professional labels that group leaders use to describe themselves—psychiatrists, psychologists, social workers, nurses, educators, counselors, human relations specialists, management consultants, therapists, facilitators—further differences are manifested through theoretical affiliations. Thus, a Gestalt leader is of quite a different breed from a behaviorist; likewise, a psychoanalytic practitioner appears to have little in common with a colleague who practices out of a rational-emotive orientation. Then there are the varied settings in which group leaders deliver their services: schools, prisons, hospitals, industry, community agencies, universities, mental health centers, and private practice.

The interaction among disciplines, training programs, theoretical orientations, and settings would not appear to be conducive to agreement among this group of professionals. Notwithstanding that we all tend to work in circles, use a high frequency of "you seem to be saying" statements, and are impassioned about the subtle complexities of human interaction, what concepts are most group leaders likely to agree with, regardless of implicit individual differences? What consensus can we reach about the nature of group leadership based on current research, theory, and practice?

As a means of synthesizing and summarizing the current state of the art, ten assumptions are here presented which represent a foundation on which to build more advanced group work knowledge. They provide us with a sense of continuity and cohesion for the field and collectively serve as an integrative statement for most practitioners.

Ten Assumptions

1. *There are different kinds of groups for different purposes.* Though the generic term *group work* describes the therapeutic process of helping people to learn about themselves for the purpose of making constructive behavioral and life changes, there are specific varieties of group treatment that are uniquely geared for special goals, situations, and client populations. There is, however, enough confusion in the field as a result of trying to distinguish *counseling* from *psychotherapy* without adding the complexities contained in the taxonomy of various group strategies.

Betz, Wilbur, and Roberts-Wilbur (1981) attempt to clear up the confusion surrounding the various group processes by creating a structural blueprint of group modalities. The Task Group Cluster (composed of committees, meetings, and conferences), the Socio-Process Cluster (guidance and discussion groups), and the Psycho-Process Cluster (therapy and counseling groups), which comprise the principal focus of this book, are distinguished by several distinct variables. Depending on group size, stated objectives, leader behaviors, member expectations, duration of sessions, length of treatment, participant composition, and techniques employed, the various forms of group work may be delineated into fairly discrete categories (Vriend & Dyer, 1973(D); Corey & Corey, 1977).

Guidance groups, counseling groups, T-groups, task groups, rap groups, discussion groups, sensitivity groups, human potential groups—all bring to mind a particular image of group work in action. If group members act somewhat unorthodoxly and are wearing pajamas, we are probably watching a therapy group with hospitalized patients. If members are wearing business suits and taking notes on clipboards, we may be witnessing a discussion group. In fact, the varieties of group work can themselves be grouped on a continuum according to their status on certain variables. Essentially, the more severe the client's difficulties and the longer the treatment the more likely the group will follow a medical mode; an educational model more appropriately fits groups that are structured and task oriented.

2. *Group work has certain advantages and disadvantages in comparison with individual treatment.* Group work has several distinct advantages over individual treatment. Practitioners can reach many persons in a group setting within a specific block of time. The built-in support system is conducive to more serious commitment on the part of clients, and the nurturing environment makes group members more willing to explore and try out new ways of thinking, feeling, and behaving. Further, a group setting more closely parallels the social milieu of the client's real world. It allows participants to improve their interpersonal skills at the same time they are working in specific problem areas. Then there is the vicarious learning and identification process that inevitably occurs as a result of observing individuals receive specific help.

The collective experience of so many assistant helpers available in a group and the high-intensity interaction also make the learning process more potent. Therapeutic groups act as safe laboratories in

A Continuum of Group Work Styles

Discussion group	Group guidance	Human potential group	Counseling group	Group therapy with neurotics	Group therapy with psychotics

EDUCATIONAL MODEL	MEDICAL MODEL
Cognitively oriented	Affectively oriented
Task oriented	Process oriented
Short term	Long term
For normal functioning persons	For those with problems in reality testing
Identification of goals	Use of differential diagnosis
Focus on upgrading skills or knowledge	Focus on personality restructuring
Use of readings and homework as adjunct structures	Use of medication and individual therapy as adjunct structures

which to experiment and rehearse new behaviors for the outside world; they enable participants to learn success skills for surviving in a world of groups. Participants gain an unusual and cherished opportunity to receive honest and constructive feedback, more accurate mirroring of their attitudes, beliefs, biases, feelings, and behaviors, perhaps the most valuable aspect of group work.

Even with the zeal that typifies those of us who are committed to group work as the preferred mode of helping, however, these advantages are counterbalanced by some disadvantages that are difficult to ignore. Potential problems seem directly proportional to the number of persons we attempt simultaneously to help. In a group, the leader has less situational control than in individual counseling or therapy; more things can go awry. Difficulties are more likely to develop if the group leader cannot effectively balance the need for freedom versus the need for structure (Lieberman, Yalom, & Miles, 1973).

Each client receives less attention in a group because there seems always to be a shortage of available time. Confidentiality is more difficult to mandate and virtually impossible to enforce because group members are not bound to ethical codes or to the therapist's promises (Davis & Meara, 1982). The coercion and peer pressure toward conformity that are part of every group process operate at intense levels in a therapeutic group, subtly shaping individuals toward accepted norms and dangerously curbing individual initiative. This factor must be explored more closely.

3. *Therapeutic groups can act as coercive influences to stifle individual autonomy.* Case examples abound of the power that groups wield in corrupting individuals far beyond a point where they never believed their value systems would allow them to go. The news media predictably disclose their continuing astonishment when apprehended assassins disclose that they were raised in ordinary middle-class families. The fact remains, however, that after a few months in a terrorist training camp or of radical religious indoctrination, a great many ordinary people are turned into murderers. Jim Jones and the People's Temple are examples of mutant group forces at work. In this instance, hundreds of people were induced to renounce their possessions and then their lives at the whim of a powerful group leader. Although their goals may be dissimilar, the Moonies, est, Ku Klux Klan, and Hare Krishna are also highly proficient in group brainwashing techniques that maximize cohesion, solidarity, and peer pressure.

People tend to conform to group norms, however inappropriate, illogical, or distorted they may be. The shared reality of persons in a group may take precedent over individual perceptions. In his classic experiment illustrating the effects of group behavior on the conformity of an individual, Asch (1951) discovered that a person will actually "see" distortions in perceptual reality if others in the group claim such common experience. In judging the length of a line or the passage of time, people will ignore their own intuitions in favor of majority opinion.

Milgram (1965) placed a subject with two confederates in a group situation and found that peer pressure induced the subject to inflict more pain on an innocent victim than was otherwise likely. Festinger's concept of *deindividuation* is also noteworthy in this context (Festinger, Pepitone, & Newcomb, 1952). A person attempts to reduce internal cognitive dissonance by submerging the self in the group, thereby (1) reducing inner restraints, (2) liberating deviant norms, (3) diffusing responsibility, (4) facilitating anonymous participation, and (5) reducing the likelihood of negative consequences for any individual. This lynch mob mentality can temporarily make intelligent, responsible, moral people capable of suspending their personal standards to commit atrocities (Shaw, 1981).

In group situations, people attempt to enhance their status by appearing more as risk takers (Brown, 1965). Also, because responsibility is diffused and multiple authorship of a decision is shared among members, people in groups tend to make collectively riskier decisions than they would make alone (Stoner, 1968; Runyan, 1974; Spector, Cohen, & Penner, 1976).

More "spectatoring," self-judgment, and self-evaluation occur in the presence of others. People tend to make more comparisons about how they stand up to their peers. This "pacing behavior" ranges from comparing neighborhood lawns to comparing infant development (my baby has three teeth and is crawling, and *he* is only six months old). The mere presence of others enhances well-memorized performances, such as reciting standard social lines like "what I do for a living," but hinders performances that involve trying out new behaviors (Markus, 1978; Baron, Moore, & Sanders, 1978).

Groupthink (Janis, 1972) occurs when group members experience such cohesion, loyalty, and uniformity that they deteriorate in their individual capacities for reality testing, logical analysis, and moral judgment. Shaw (1981) lists several other consequences of the groupthink phenomenon:

1. Group members rationalize their loss of personal identity.
2. Moral consequences of actions are more often ignored.
3. Stereotypic views of others are perpetuated.
4. There is an unwillingness to say or do anything to destroy the perceived happy balance.
5. There is an emergence of gestapo-type "mindguards" to ensure that complete stability is maintained.

Jeffries (1973) views counseling groups as vehicles for deradicalizing minority and creative children. Kids who demonstrate mannerisms not approved by "the System" are yanked out of class—for backtalking, for being funny or disruptive, or merely for being different from the rest—and are sent to the school counselor for appropriate disciplinary tactics to stamp out the subversive elements. In spite of the fact that the greatest thinkers of our time have been troublemakers in school, we continue to treat such delinquents as threats to the status quo.

In their classic study of eminent thinkers, Goertzel and Goertzel (1962) discovered, after feeding the biographical information of our 100 greatest personalities into a computer to sort out commonalities, that the majority of these great scientists, politicians, artists, and writers had had serious school problems. Bertrand Russell, Albert Einstein, and Sigmund Freud would all have ended in their counselor's office as precocious, unruly discipline problems, pressured to give up their disruptive behaviors in favor of preserving the peace of conventional students and teachers.

> Thus, group counseling serves as a potent vehicle for the counselor to use a knowledge of peer group pressure to help large numbers of children conform and maintain the status quo.
>
> It is important to deradicalize people while they are in the developmental stages of childhood and incarcerated in the schools.
>
> If they escape the process, they may grow up to push toward real change in the established institutions of society (Jeffries, 1973, p. 115).

Although the negative effects of the Many on the One have less to do with therapeutic groups than with those that are task oriented, the contamination is still active in diluted forms. A silent group member or dissenting participant is prodded to conform to the norm. In fact, the following episode is predictable in the course of every group.

"I don't know about the rest of you, but I'm tired of spilling my guts in here and having Sandra stare at me as if I'm some animal in a cage."

(After having been directed to speak directly to Sandra.)

"It's true. You always sit there with that smile on your face, as if you're better than the rest of us. Why don't you ever say anything? How come you never participate? I don't think you belong with us unless you start acting right."

Such confrontations do produce results. Sandra will burst into tears, mumble apologies, and promise to do better. And, in fact, she will *appear* to *perform* better. She will memorize her lines, recite her speeches, say the correct things at the appropriate times. Everyone will feel better, including the leader, now that Sandra is *cooperating*.

It is only after reading the process journals of the participants that we will learn that Sandra had been growing the most of all members in the group. Although behaving shyly in the group, her life outside the group had turned around. She had been searching desperately for an identity, a self apart from her parents and husband who constantly pressured her to conform. In the group she had experimented with deliberately stifling approval-seeking comments. She had decided that until she could truly speak her own mind, reasonably certain that she was not playing her usual games, she would keep quiet. Now her journal entries reflected the recent surrender to her peers' preferences. After all, she had had lots of practice at mimicry; she could be the superstar of the group in delivering what was expected. Similarly, some of the most well behaved, talkative, cooperative members of the group were among those who changed the least. Their journal entries tended to take the form of lecture notes, memorized phrases, shallow comments, and stereotyped jargon.

The pragmatic group leader intuitively understands the deceptions of appearance, the implicit booby traps in groups that make them such powerful places to change, for better or for worse.

4. *Group work is the treatment of choice for some therapeutic situations and is contraindicated for others.* Group work is not for everyone. Because of the reflexive interaction that occurs among clients, one person in a group may strangely affect the experiential outcomes of the others. If a particular client is aggressively domineering, irresponsibly abusive, extraordinarily passive, hostile, or devoid

of reality-based orientation, such characteristics may block growth for others. People prone to manipulating, monopolizing, rambling, intellectualizing, approval seeking, dependency, and game playing, or who tend toward vulnerability, present varying degrees of handling difficulty for group leaders although they are not necessarily candidates for exclusion from a group experience since they may in fact make dramatic progress in mitigating or eliminating their self-defeating behaviors as a result of the confrontive feedback (Ohlsen, 1977; Corey & Corey, 1977).

On the basis of available research, Yalom (1975) also concludes that group work should not be used with persons who are paranoid, brain damaged, suicidal, acutely psychotic, sociopathic, hypochrondiacal, or narcissistic. On the other hand, those who have moderate intelligence, a cooperative attitude, the ability to communicate fluently, high expectations for positive change, and a degree of extraversion are considered to be prime candidates for group work (Giedt, 1961; Heslin, 1964; Yalom, 1975; Trotzer, 1977). Group membership implies the right to influence, and to accept the influence of, others in that group. If prospective clients are appropriately screened to ensure that only reasonably suitable individuals are admitted, many of the disadvantages can be minimized.

5. *Members have equal status in a therapeutic group.* Equality of status for all members of a therapeutic group is an important "given," one that knowledgeable professionals work at maintaining throughout the life of the group experience. This means that no member has more importance than any other; that each member has an equal right to make use of the group time and available help; and that variables such as age, sex, ethnic origin, vocation, wealth, and educational attainment, which account for inequality of position or status in the community at large, are put aside during group sessions. Inequality of role status outside the group—as when agency directors are members alongside secretaries or supervisees in a group composed of those who work together—frequently poses a condition that must be transcended before genuine help can be extended to all participants in egalitarian terms.

6. *Many public fears and myths are associated with the practice of group work.* All human beings seem to harbor a deep desire for belonging. Gregarious creatures by nature, we have a long evolution-

ary history of group membership going back to our Neanderthal cave-group days. In our literature, Robinson Crusoe stories are rare. When from Guam on 25 January 1972 a press release reported that Sergeant Shoichi Yokoi of the 38th Infantry Regiment of the World War II Japanese Imperial Army had finally surrendered to American soldiers after living alone in the jungle for 28 years, the world was flabbergasted. The awe and admiration of people worldwide was focused not so much on his survival techniques as on how he could have made it without the company of others. Short of killing, the severest forms of punishment are solitary confinement, banishment, exile, being marooned, or becoming a shipwrecked castaway, cut off from all company and communication with other people.

6a. *Groups are enclaves for brainwashing.*

Belonging is so potent a drive that most humans are perpetually ready to trade personal freedom for group membership. Knowing this, both benevolent and malevolent group leaders use a variety of methods to lock followers into place. Many groups are homes or family circles that dispense love and protection, provide a spiritual meaning for being alive, enlist the lonely wanderer into service for a just cause, and help the recruit to feel enlarged, transcended, important beyond the boundaries of self. Members acquire worth and status as a result of belonging.

Preparing athletes to function at maximum limits depends on team spirit, esprit de corps, and coaches work overtime to build loyalty to the team into each player. Military organizations use group methods of indoctrination to shape recruits into willing warriors, willing to kill or be killed, to see other humans in the black-and-white categories of friend or foe. Street gangs, the Ku Klux Klan, the Black Panthers, fraternities, the Mafia—all build a "one for all and all for one" spirit into each initiate through the promise of communally sharing the wealth, power, and gains of the group. Dissenters are weeded out. Once an initiate is sworn into full status, the penalty for unorthodoxy, nonconformity, or disobedience ("a chain is only as strong as its weakest link") is ostracism, excommunication, disbarment, and not infrequently death.

In therapeutic groups, confidentiality is a mild form of bonding through secrecy: only the privileged know what goes on in the inner sanctum. The leader says it at the beginning:

"What goes on in this group belongs only to us. It's our business and no one else's. If someone in here relates personal material and someone else in here reveals such information to someone outside of this group, harmful consequences can occur. If anyone of us believes that what is revealed here will leave this room, none of us will feel safe enough to talk about personal concerns. Does everyone understand this? Is there anyone in the group who cannot subscribe to this, who feels she or he won't be able to respect this idea and live by it?"

It would be difficult to convince any adult today that his or her fears are not justifiable over the potential dangers a psychologically sophisticated villain might cause. Adolf Hitler, after all, was a brilliant tactician of group dynamic factors, using peer pressure, authority, cohesion, dress coding, rituals, ingroup identification, even group goals that promised world dominance for the chosen ones. Charles Manson knew instinctively how to get his "family" of crazy killers to do his bidding by using principles of group norms, social reinforcement, transference, sexual bonding, modeling, and programming. The public has also seen religious leaders manipulating disciples to donate all their worldly possessions, as well as their rational minds, to an elusive cause.

It is not difficult to translate the actions of a few irresponsible zealots, who have used groups of confused searching minds for their personal playgrounds, to the practice of group therapy by trained professionals. This connection is the more apparent when supposed experts in our field, famous psychiatrists or psychologists, disclose their personal approaches to group leadership as if they were representative of what all practitioners do. Martin Shepard, for instance, has produced several widely read books in which he describes his rather erotic style of group therapy.

> "I have an encounter game I'd like to play, if you're all willing. It's called the Truth Game. What we do is go around the room and say truthfully what is on our minds..."
>
> After everybody had their tediously profound say concerning man's fate, the French girl's turn came.
>
> "I can't really think of anything," she said, looking bored and uninterested.
>
> Just as I was considering going home, her husband hit the nail squarely on the head.
>
> "I'm thinking that if the orgy doesn't start in five minutes, I'm leaving..."
>
> "Well," I said, "if an orgy's going to start, we might as well take

our clothes off," and with that I began to undress (Shepard, 1972, pp. 94 – 95).

In a significant contribution to our field, Rowe and Winborn (1973) identified 50 articles critical of group work that appeared in professional journals and popular publications. Through careful content analysis they were able to identify 37 different specific fears.

Most professional group practitioners are aware of, and sensitive to, a negative press that has alarmed the public to potential dangers and spend a good part of their therapeutic energies ensuring that members are not coerced into doing anything they do not feel would be in their best interests. While it is true that many subtle forms of psychological pressure arise in groups, these factors contribute significantly to the safe accepting and trusting climate that clients find so invigorating. In most therapeutic groups, participants are not forced to do anything against their wills except perhaps to confront self-deceit.

6b. *Groups are for sickies.*

Why is it that we must open our initial group sessions with an impassioned speech similar to the following?

"I applaud your decision to join this group. Many people don't have the courage to admit that they are less than perfect, that they could substantially profit from a group experience in which honest self-analysis is the order of the day. Although most of you don't necessarily have serious problems, you do recognize that there are ways that you can improve the quality of your life. You need not exhibit pathology, mental illness, psychotic or even neurotic symptoms to get help from a group such as this. The very fact that you're here says that you are far ahead of most people who are content with a mediocre, lackluster existence. This group is a place where, regardless of your current level of behavioral functioning, you can become more masterful in your life."

Most clients seem defensive about their membership in a therapeutic group, as if preferring to get help with their concerns means they are not in charge of their worlds, that they are psychologically or socially dysfunctional in some pathological ways. Though we know that such an assumption is invalid, the general public image of group work nevertheless inaccurately portrays participants as being inadequate, just as, in about the same measure, subjects who go for individual psychotherapy are generally seen to be.

C. *The group is a living being.*

Many myths about group work are perpetuated in the professional literature as well as in the public media. Such violations of reality impede therapeutic effectiveness by distorting language. One such myth is the unfounded notion that a group is a living, breathing creature with a mind of its own. Typical of the writing style prevalent in books about the subject are such phrases as the following (Corey & Corey, 1977, p. 107):

> "When a group seems very resistant ..."

> "... the group is avoiding doing meaningful work ..."

> "... we challenge the group to assess its own processes ..."

What is this mysterious creature called the *Group?* It thinks. It feels. It judges. It sets goals. It resists. It processes. It even changes. Is it really possible to counsel the Group, to help it identify its self-defeating behaviors for the purpose of making constructive altera- tions? If so, what happens when the Group disbands?

The Group is nothing more or less than a collection of individual clients. Each group member has a different set of goals, expectations, interests, feelings, and needs. There are no group goals, only indi- vidual goals. There is no collective consciousness in which state- ments like "their attitudes," "they believe," "the group's feelings," can speak for everyone alike, yet these phrases continually crop up in group leader speeches in absurd ways. The therapist naively begins a session by asking: "How does the Group feel today?" And each member thinks: "Nope. She isn't talking to me. My name isn't Group."

It is not surprising that consumers are captured by the wizardry of group treatments in view of how we describe what we do. In the face of ambiguous, inflated, esoteric-sounding jargon, how can the public do otherwise than to create its own formulation of what constitutes therapeutic dynamics? Scholarly articles state that groups help people to become more self-actualized (whatever *that* means), and group leaders explain their goals in terms of increasing levels of tolerance, acceptance, self-respect, caring, and sensitivity. Clients nod their heads pretending that they really understand what these abstractions have to do with their suffering.

"How's your group going?"

"Oh, just fine. In case you haven't noticed, I'm becoming more self-actualized."

These myths and fears, among scores of others, are part of the legacy with which all group leaders, regardless of their theoretical orientation, must contend.

7. *Associated with therapeutic group work is a specialized technology of intervention strategies which lead to real-life problem resolution.* Among such strategies, to list a mere half-dozen, are:

A. Receiving feedback from members
B. Acting out conflicts in psychodramatic structures
C. Receiving support in an atmosphere of mutual trust
D. Committing oneself aloud to attain self-declared goals
E. Expressing one's feelings and thoughts more fluently and honestly
F. Producing growth through information processing which predictably occurs as the result of interaction among diverse people in their exchange of ideas

8. *If a group is considered to be a collectivity, there are successive and predictable stages in its development.* If one wishes to abstract sequential-process components that occur in every group, though the number, titles, and order are open to debate, one can easily find support in most group-work literature. Rogers (1970) talks about stages like "milling around" and the "cracking of facades." Hansen, Warner, and Smith (1980) use such terms as "conflict stage" and "cohesiveness," while Foley and Bonney (1966) prefer labels such as "transition stage" and "establishment stage." Whatever the names used, it is confusing to figure out when one process component ends and another begins: "Each stage of the group is like a wave that has momentary identity as it crests but whose beginning and demise are swallowed up in the constant movement of the sea" (Trotzer, 1977, p. 52).

Most group-work theoreticians would concede that every therapeutic group has a beginning wherein participants persist, adjust, and explore; a middle during which they develop insight into their concerns and interact intensely; and an end when they attempt to incorporate their learnings into some form of action beyond the tenure of the experience.

9. *Participation in a therapeutic group involves personal risks related to potential life changes.* Insofar as the overall goal for most

participants in therapeutic groups is to help themselves to formulate and make constructive changes in their lives, there are always risk factors involved. All clients hear echoing in their brains throughout the duration of every session: "Is this *really* a safe place? Will these people keep to themselves what I reveal to them? Can I *really* trust them? Should I tell them how I feel right now? Maybe I should just leave well enough alone; my life isn't *that* bad." Most often they tell themselves "this hurts" or "I'm scared."

Professional group leaders would agree that developing a productive therapeutic atmosphere is crucial to making the inherent risk taking in groups more safe. In large part, the intensity and depth of client disclosures, risk-taking gestures, and stated concerns are determined by the cohesion levels that have been created. More eye contact, disclosed concerns, and client improvement occur in sessions where a cohesive atmosphere is prevalent (Flowers, Booraem, & Hartman, 1981). Thus, pains are taken to enforce confidentiality and to promote intimacy, trust, openness, and cohesiveness. It is only after such conditions exist that people develop a sense of safety, acceptance, and the confidence that enables them to take risks they would not ordinarily take in individual therapy (Yalom, 1975; Guttmacher & Birk, 1971).

10. *Therapeutic groups are effective means for helping people to change.* It goes without saying that we believe in our therapeutic service delivery in groups even if positive results cannot clearly be supported by research findings. Outcome studies on group treatments, while by no means demonstrating overwhelming evidence that every type of group setting and leader style produces positive results, still indicate that we are not wasting our time.

There has always been some disharmony between skeptical scientists and zealous practitioners. Scientists maintain that until empirical evidence can substantiate hypotheses scrupulously adherent to formal research methodology about group work, it is no more precise or valid than the practice of witch doctors. Pragmatic clinicians counter with claims that they *know* they are making a difference in their clients' lives. They see emotionally wounded and desperate people walk into their groups, and a few months later watch them leave appearing to feel cured of their suffering. "What other proof is necessary?" they cry.

Considering that about 85% of all research investigations on group counseling deals exclusively with outcome variables, there seems to be a consistent trend toward empirically demonstrating effectiveness (Gazda, 1978). While the debate continues as to whether group treatment—or, for that matter, *any* form of therapeutic help—is really of any lasting value, group leaders go about their work doing the best they can. An impressive body of evidence indicates that certain aspects of a group setting are much more likely than other settings to produce desired outcomes. For instance, groups that are structured to allow for constructive, supportive feedback focusing on specific member behaviors tend to be more profitable than those that do not (Jacobs, Jacobs, Feldman, & Cavior, 1973; Jacobs, 1974; Ohlsen, 1977; Stockton & Movran, 1980).

It seems virtually impossible to design research investigations demonstrating conclusively that certain process or treatment variables are consistently effective or ineffective, given the variability of individual differences among people and the infinite possibilities that exist when different combinations of individuals are coalesced for a therapeutic group experience. No two groups are ever alike. No two leaders function in exactly the same way. Replication studies are thus difficult to conduct without gross error margins. Pragmatic practitioners therefore see the tools of research scientists as currently inadequate to validate or invalidate what they do, and rely instead on their own critical judgment based on their own experiences, or on the judgment of trusted and insightful colleague consultants, to help themselves determine how and when to modify and upgrade their professional skills.

Many additional assumptions could have been added to the ten in this assortment. Although a majority of group leaders might agree in principle with any further selections, some would take exception, perhaps vehemently, to any listing. Take, for example, the assumption that the leader's role is mainly that of a counseling expert and chief behavioral model but *not* that of a group member. Although I strongly support this notion of professional responsibility, there are those operating from a "group facilitator" orientation, who see themselves as "player/coaches," and they would feel handicapped by the restrictions placed on their options for spontaneous involvement. And if it were more specifically mandated that, in their roles as experts, group leaders should have a defensible rationale for every instance in which they intervene, the opportunity for gut-level, spontaneous leader behavior would be further curtailed.

One of the purposes of including a list of underlying assumptions that almost every group leader could support is to concentrate on

what our field has established as a foundation. The preceding statements provide just such a skeleton on which to hang the viscera that
are the core of our profession, the nervous system that facilitates
intercommunication between varied colleagues, and the muscular
system which mobilizes synergistic progress in a group movement
that is becoming more identifiable as a behavioral science field and
as a discipline that is becoming more integrated and professionally
accepted.

CHAPTER 2

The Group Leader as Philosopher-Scientist

Imagine a room filled with persons in a circle like a wagon train about to be attacked by a band of hostiles. From nowhere a deafening silence emerges, leaving only the sound of shuffling feet. You wait patiently, knowing from theory and experience that people need some quiet time in which to ponder and process previous happenings. After a few minutes you begin to notice squirming movements and other nonverbal cues that lead you to conclude, on the basis of a particular theory, that people are anxious and uncomfortable.

You decide to wait them out, let them squirm a little. After all, isn't there a theory somewhere that says group members must take responsibility for their progress? In the flash of the next few seconds you survey a list of other explanations for the collective behavior. They're resisting. No, they're relaxing. No, they're confused. Finally in desperation, you throw theory to the winds and ask someone what is going on.

"Regina, I notice that everyone seems a bit quiet. Do you have an explanation?"

"Well," Regina replies, "I can't speak for anyone else," (you feel proud—she remembers the importance of speaking only for herself) "but I don't have anything to say right now."

Well, of course! They're waiting for some direction.

No one can say this group leader did not operate from a fairly organized set of propositions about the nature of the world. Indeed, within this brief span of time, theories of metaphysics, logical relationships, ethics, human behavior, motivation, learning, and development all came into play.

In the words of Argyris and Schon (1974, p. 29), a theory of action was applied wherein "In situation S, if you intend consequence C, do A, given assumptions $a_1 \ldots a_n$." In creating the major premises and minor concepts that guide the choice of interventions, the practitioner functioned as a philosopher. By making observations, drawing inferences, formulating hypotheses, predicting outcomes, testing assumptions, and evaluating results, the practitioner functioned as a scientist. In fact, all effective group leaders, transcending their self-categorizations, tend to operate as pragmatists. Whatever we do that produces desirable results we will tend to do again in similar circumstances. If a procedure doesn't work, even though a theory says that it is supposed to, we abandon it or (more likely) make it work in the future by adapting it to our unique situation.

PHILOSOPHY, THEORY, AND ACTION

A group leader never operates out of a vacuum. Somewhere deep within the smoky recesses of the brain, motives are formulated, underlying attitudes and values are constructed, interpretations of the world are made, and a philosophy is articulated in the hope of answering life's ultimate questions. The philosopher-scientist critically explores puzzling questions to make sense of confusion and to guide professional behavior (Russell, 1961). "Philosophers desire ultimately to have an overall view of the world so that every event can be explained in terms of general principles and the occurrence of other events" (Glossop, 1974, p. 5). The philosophy guiding therapeutic practitioners is thus responsible for their unique set of beliefs about the world, about clients, and about how clients can change in a world of groups.

The theoretical preferences of group leaders are chosen or created on the basis of consistency between personal philosophy and primary postulates of a theory of action. If a group leader believes in the intrinsic healing powers of the human system, prefers to view the environment as an extension of each individual, and sees client concerns as manifestations of a sick soul, it is likely that a theory will be adopted that is compatible with these personal convictions.

Similarly, specific therapeutic interventions will sprout from one's theoretical orientation, just as theory will arise from one's underlying philosophies regarding the mechanisms of the universe. The group leader's actions, including *any* intervention, from a complex psychodramatic scenario to a simple nod, are direct extensions of a systematic philosophy known as the *scientific method* wherein: (1) observations are made of situation-specific behaviors, (2) operating assumptions are formulated regarding their actions, (3) problems are clearly identified and related hypotheses stated, (4) possible solutions are generated which are likely to alleviate the problems, (5) probable consequences are deduced and desired outcomes predicted, (6) some action is taken, and (7) results are evaluated in the light of preferred outcomes. There is, of course, an obvious similarity between this systematic application of philosophy/science to the method that all group leaders follow. Reichian, Rational-emotive, Rolfing, Reality, or Rogerian practitioners will all use the same basic format even if their philosophic preferences differ radically.

Ambrose Bierce (1911, p. 99) facetiously described philosophy as "A route of many roads leading from nowhere to nothing," but practitioners, from architects to group leaders, would be rendered helpless without it. Practitioners are more than applied engineers; we must think. More than gathering data, we must integrate it. More than noting observations, we must make inductive generalizations. We must contemplate the meanings behind what we do, reflect on our actions in retrospect, and from such conceptual analyses a philosophy is born, an internally consistent set of propositions that leads to an *espoused theory of action.* This theory of professional intervention includes both a body of scientific postulates as well as a series of philosophic criticisms (Bolan, 1980).

The espoused theory, to be distinguished from an *action-theory-in-use,* comprises the knowledge and overt intentions to which the practitioner will publicly claim allegiance, even though the latter will more accurately guide behavior (Argyris & Schon, 1974). A profession's body of knowledge, methods of practice, and code of ethics, as well as such normative structures as the law, accreditation, training, institutional policies, colleague approval, and situational cues, will thus be arranged by each individual group leader into a fairly well-organized philosophy, which in turn leads to an espoused theory and later to an action-theory-in-use that will steer specific professional episodes (Bolan, 1980; Argyris, 1976).

The fields of psychology, education, and medicine have been dominated by empirical epistemology for the past several decades. Before that, we pondered metaphysical questions. Just in the past century, in the practice of therapy, widely divergent philosophical trends have influenced practitioner action. We have moved from Intuitionism and Structuralism to Functionalism and Logical Positivism, then to Subjectivism, Existentialism, Phenomenology, and finally to Cognitivism, Behaviorism, Interpretive Dialecticism, Hermeneutics, and Integrationism.

After analyzing these philosophical trends, Royce (1975) concluded that only *constructive dialecticism* can maintain the tension between opposing theoretical forces while elaborating their limitations, assets, and paradoxes and resolving the contradictions. There are no simple solutions. For the pragmatic group leader there is no choice but to become thoroughly familiar with the different branches of philosophy so as to create an action-theory-in-use that is consistent, congruent, and comprehensive.

> Once we have opened the Pandora's box of "total man," that is, seeing man as unconscious as well as conscious, man as irrational and emotive as well as rational, man as cognitive as well as conditionable, man as motivated, curious, creative, and contemplative, and man's "being" as well as his "doing"—once we go beyond simplistic conceptions of "behaving" to the complexities of "mind"—it seems ridiculously obvious that we will be forced into more sophisticated philosophic-conceptual analyses of what we are doing and why (Royce, 1975, p. 2).

Metaphysics

What constitutes science and what is more legitimately a part of philosophy is a muddled distinction that was never even considered until the mid-19th century. Plato, Archimedes, Newton, and Harvey were grouped as philosophers. America's first psychologist, William James, taught in a department of philosophy. Even laboratory implements like Bunsen burners were called "philosophical instruments." With the publication of Kant's *Critique of Pure Reason* (1781), however, the stage was set for a parting of philosophy and science, a separation that has only become reconciled with the disciplinary collaborations so necessary to our field. The therapist today must garner knowledge from any conceivable source—from textbooks and from the streets—to create a working model of how the world works, a model that can be readily explained to clients in their search for metaphysical answers.

To clients who ask "Why?" the group leader must respond as a philosopher, helping the seeker to find an approximation of personal truth. While science tests hypotheses that can be confirmed on the basis of experimentation, philosophy works with untestable hypotheses, those that cannot be verified even though they have universal interest. The group leader is a composite of both worlds. The group therapist attempts to instruct through challenge, discourse, philosophic inquiry, and scientific hypothesis testing. That scientific

Theoretical and Philosophical Influences on Group Leader Behavior

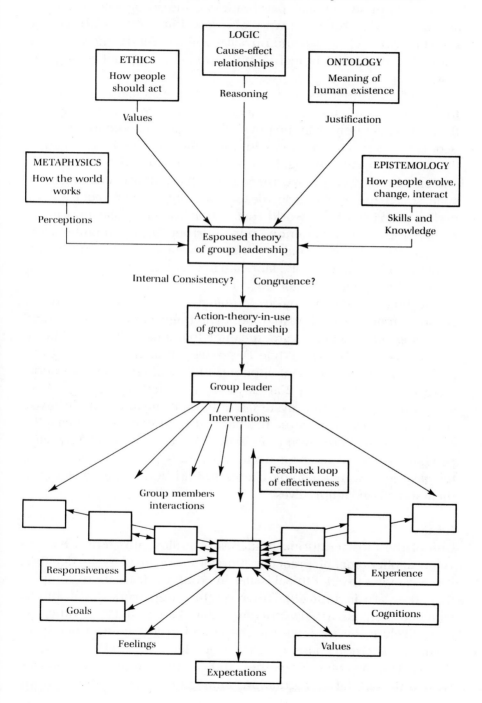

training is necessary for the effective functioning of group leaders is no great surprise. Medical, psychological, and social work programs are top-heavy with course work of a scientific nature—physiology, statistics, research, social and physical science. Yet the therapist also applies every distinct branch of philosophy to the practice of group work.

Metaphysics attempts to describe the universal features of reality. In the process of change, such as the dissolution of a marriage, do the same laws apply as in the physical change of a liquid to a gas? Are people's lives predetermined with the same inevitability that causes the earth to rotate in regular cycles? Is the process by which a person becomes depressed the same process that elicits anger? In such speculations, the group leader attempts to construct a comprehensive view of the world that will allow for application in explaining any single phenomenon. Further, group members are helped to develop personal schemata of metaphysics when they are challenged to define reality, fabricate a meaning for their actions, or discern the essence of their lives.

One branch of metaphysics, *ontology*, is particularly useful for group members struggling to understand themselves. To understand our Being, our essence, to give meaning to our existence is the legitimate scope of ontology. While Descartes found his thoughts to be proof of his existence, contemporary philosophers such as Gabriel Marcel, Jean-Paul Sartre, Karl Jaspers, and Martin Heidegger have looked deeper into the mysteries of what it means to Be, to exist. "Ontology seeks to discover the basic structures of existence—the structures which are given to everyone at every moment" (May, 1969, p. 112). Naturally, much of what constitutes psychotherapy is ontological in nature—helping clients to find underlying meaning in their sometimes empty lives.

Ethics
One of the most enduring branches of philosophy, ethics has become a phenomenal preoccupation of group leaders in deciding how we ought to act. Ethical issues in group work are more complex than they are in individual therapy. In group work, for example, confidentiality is virtually unenforceable. Verbal abuse of others is more likely to occur since the therapist has less control over proceedings. There are also quacks in our field who take a bottle of Wesson Oil, strip off their clothes, and call themselves professionals. With little legislative regulation, ambiguous laws, watered-down

ethical codes, and greater risks, group leaders have no choice but to become ethical philosophers.

What should we do when we discover a colleague having sex with his or her clients? How should we handle coercion from a supervisor demanding to know the content of group sessions? What should we do if our negligent actions result in substantial damage to group members? These are the larger ethical issues, but there are also small voices nagging:

"Was my last self-disclosure really necessary or was I just trying to impress them with my experience?"

"Was it fair for me to try out this new technique in the group before I tested it in a safer situation?"

"Is it alright for me to lie a little, exaggerating the services I can provide but knowing that I'm being helpful by setting up favorable expectations?"

"Am I being negligent by not following up on my group members' re-entry problems?"

"Am I seeing these clients longer than is absolutely necessary because I need the income?"

Group leaders are in good company pondering such issues. To whom we are ultimately responsible for our actions has preoccupied philosophers from Plato and Epictetus to Hobbes, Hegel, and Mill. Do we answer primarily to our clients, to the parents of the young, to our supervisor, to the Constitution, to the Ten Commandments, to God, or to ourselves? Questions of moral obligation, values, responsibility, duty, conscience, rights, good and bad, right and wrong plague the group leader at every turn. The methodology of ethical inquiry requires the use of both philosophical and scientific principles to produce explicit imperatives for action.

It is fitting that John Dewey, the eminent American philosopher, should be primarily responsible for developing the problem-solving method that is the basis for scientific investigation. This decision-making process, adapted for ethics by Van Hoose and Kottler (1977), has been considerably expanded for use by group leaders in applying philosophy and science to the resolution of conflicts.

Ethical Decision Making for Group Leaders: What Ought I to Do?

1.0	Theoretical Inquiry
	What values do I wish my clients to learn?
1.1	Scientific Methodology
1.11	What verifiable hypotheses are plausible?
1.12	How may they be experimentally tested?
1.13	What effects will this intervention have to the greatest benefit of the most participants?
1.101	Hypothetical Imperative
	If I want these group members to exhibit honesty I must model these traits.
1.2	Philosophical Methodology
1.21	What a priori moral propositions do I know to be true for most group members?
1.22	What obligations as a group leader do I have for the welfare of my clients?
1.221	Categorical Imperative
	Abusive language should not be allowed in this group.
2.0	Practical Inquiry
	What ought I do in this situation?
2.1	Initial Recognition of Ethical Conflict
2.11	How do I know this is a conflict?
2.12	What variables and issues are involved?
2.13	Must I consider this issue?
2.14	What are the consequences of avoiding the conflict altogether?
2.141	Procrastination
2.142	Repression
2.143	Denial
2.144	Rationalization
2.145	Ignore conflict
2.15	Decision to confront ethical conflict
2.2	Description of Conflict
2.21	Who is involved?
2.22	What are the participants' expectations?
2.23	What variables are involved?
2.24	What are the predicted consequences?
2.25	What goals are desirable?
2.26	What factors are blocking the goals?
2.3	Description of Alternatives

Logic

In the systematic process of problem solving, in the diagnosis of client symptoms, in making ethical decisions, or in effectively coordinating group behavior, the branch of philosophy known as *logic* comes into play. Since most psychopathologies and self-defeating behaviors involve disorders in reasoning, much of what group leaders do constitutes the application of deductive and inductive logic—the former conclusions based on valid arguments, the latter conclusions established by degrees of probability.

Logical analysis, like psychotherapy, is less concerned with matter than with the form it takes. It makes not the slightest difference whether a group member wishes to work on controlling temper tantrums or losing weight; similar logical processes of change are involved in developing impulse control. The logical flaws in the client's reasoning are identical: "Because I have acted this way before, I must continue to act that way in the future."

The Aristotelian syllogism becomes the cornerstone for rebuilding shaky logical foundations. While there is little that can actually be proved within the ambiguous nature of group work, therapists nevertheless wish to formulate operating assumptions that can withstand critical scrutiny. Arguments must not only be convincing in their delivery but sound in their underlying propositions and concepts. The group leader must often systematically refute invalid client premises such as, "If I open up in this group, I will only get hurt as I have every other time before," and counter with inductive explanations that have a greater probability of being true:

"First, you confuse terms and definitions. You have never actually opened up before, since engaging in small talk about how much money you make doesn't exactly involve being open. From observing your behavior in this group, I believe that you misinterpret 'openness' to mean spilling all your darkest secrets at once. Also, the people you have previously chosen to be open with, such as strange women in bars, do not qualify as being potentially responsive candidates.

"Second, you imply that there is a causal relationship between self-disclosure and vulnerability, which is only true in circumstances of obvious inequality. In this group situation, where everyone is open, there is actually a clearer relationship between disclosure and intimacy. The more open you become, the more likely others will gravitate toward you.

"Third, you assume that you can be hurt by other group members.

Aside from any physical interaction, which is not permitted, it is impossible for anyone to wound you psychologically unless you allow it. In fact, you can't 'get hurt' although you may certainly decide to 'hurt yourself' after you're done hearing my little speech.

"Finally, you make a value judgment that being open, vulnerable, hurt, intimate are signs of weakness, which they are in your cutthroat business world of high finance. But those assumptions are not necessarily generalizable to this situation, in which the rules and goals are quite different."

Epistemology

The nature and limits of knowledge and belief are part of *epistemology*, the branch of philosophy concerned with inferring truth. With the often radical discrepancies between clients' experience and reality, the epistemological group leader has much work to do in the role of passionate truth seeker.

In an autobiographical anecdote, Bertrand Russell describes how he first became infatuated with philosophy at age 11. Tired of tenuous truths, tentative discussions, and inconsistent knowledge, young Russell discovered geometry because someone told him it could prove things. Pure mathematics is perhaps the only discipline in which an epistemologist may feel comfortable. He therefore begged his brother to teach him geometry so that he might experience the joys of true knowledge.

> My brother began at the beginning with the definitions. These I accepted readily enough. But he came next to the axioms. "These," he said, "can't be proved, but they have to be assumed before the rest can be proved." At these words my hopes crumbled. I had thought it would be wonderful to find something that one could *prove*, and then it turned out that this could only be done by means of assumptions of which there was no proof. I looked at my brother with a sort of indignation and said: "But why should I admit these things if they can't be proved?" He replied: "Well, if you won't, we can't go on" (Russell, 1956, pp. 56–57).

Each branch of philosophy, each component of the critical thinking process, acts as a catalyst for group leader behavior. If the world is believed to be essentially a safe place, clients will be encouraged to venture forth, experimentally testing new behaviors that may be risky. If guilt is seen as a useless, destructive emotion, efforts will be made to wipe it out. If the principal purpose in life is to live each moment to its fullest potential, group members will be taught to appreciate the fragrance of a thorn bush. If it is believed that human emotional suffering is the result of unresolved, unconscious conflicts of the past, interventions will be designed to facilitate awareness of these disguised maladies. In each case a specific philosophic assumption guides the practitioner's actions.

Unfortunately, philosophy and theory are as often mutated to limit effective behavior as they are used to enhance productivity. When philosophy becomes rigid, stagnant, and dogmatic, it ceases to function as an aid to critical thinking and acts as a blocking force toward further development.

Tenuous Truths

Counseling philosophy is intended to help group leaders make sense of the world. It should be a guide for producing change and a structural basis for measuring progress (Hansen, Warner, & Smith, 1980). It aids in prediction by providing a schematic representation of relevant information (Shertzer & Stone, 1974). Group counseling philosophy and theory should be a blueprint (without all the lines penciled in) for any action the leader takes. Notions about how the world works, what is good for clients, and how best to help clients find what is good for them are all part of this proposed theory (Geis, 1973). A conception of how people learn, how their personalities are constructed, how they develop, what obstructs growth, and how groups work are also part of any useful theory.

Yet, in the face of the human need to wipe out ambiguity and uncertainty, to replace the unknown with delusional security, we buzz around like worker bees with a single motive in life: to make sense of the things around us. The 3-year-old child has a burning curiosity to know why the moon is following her. We only wish to understand why people do what they do.

There is no certainty about knowledge except that it will evolve. Just 15 years ago it was part of our theory of truth that children were advised: (1) "Don't go in the water until you've waited at least an hour after you eat or you'll get stomach cramps and die," (2) "I don't care how hard you're playing, you can't drink water during strenuous exercise. You can gargle the water, but spit it out." Now experts tell us that it is important to eat a light meal before going in the water so that our body temperature can be maintained. One explanation of why so many sports records have been broken in recent years is that athletes now have permission to drink as much liquid as they can hold.

The logical question, then, is, what truths do we accept today as part of group counseling theory when in just a few years we will look back and laugh at our primitive efforts? It wasn't so long ago, after all, that our ancestors in group therapy conducted stake-burnings and bloodlettings as the treatments of choice for the mentally afflicted. One popular group treatment of its time, trial by water, involved throwing "clients" into a deep lake with their hands and feet bound. The theory suggested that persons who sank and drowned must have been innocent of any emotional problems, while those who floated were to be burned at the stake as witches. A hundred years from now, what will they say about "active listening?"

THE WHOLEY WARS

For the beginning group leader, the concepts of *philosophy* and *theory* had a fairly narrow personal meaning. Some time after the practicum started but before it was over, students were expected to fully articulate their theory of choice. The most intelligent choice under the circumstances was to select an existing theory, *any* theory, though it was advantageous to select the one your instructor followed. This shotgun wedding between therapist and theory continues to be a monogamous relationship long after the practicum ends; and it really *does* feel like cheating if the delicious fruits of another point of view are sampled.

At a more advanced level, flexibility is the order of the day. Rigidly following the tenets of a particular theory can eventually become as much of a handicap as an aid. The theory becomes a closed system that forces conformity and compliance. Characteristic of perceptual input systems in human beings (group leaders included), we look for things that confirm what we already know, ignore things that contradict our beliefs, selectively interpret the world to fit our expectations, and vehemently refute those things that jeopardize the stability of the theory.

Freud set the precedent. Whenever his disciples became too feisty, independent, or critical (as did Jung, Adler, and Rank), he would throw them out of his group. He also set up a brilliant organizational defense mechanism in claiming that to criticize psychoanalysis legitimately, one had first to undergo the experience. If on completing the analysis the critic persisted in his attacks, obviously the psychoanalysis had been unsuccessful.

It has often been observed that Sigmund Freud, Carl Rogers, Albert

Ellis, Fritz Perls, Eric Berne, and the rest of the therapy field's leaders were all effective clinicians. Each theory that the respective high priest represents has an impressive body of evidence demonstrating that it is the true heir to the throne of Truth. In fact, however, *all* theories seem to work in some situations, depending on who is practicing them. Each has proven utility in helping people, even though radical divergencies in philosophy, therapist role, techniques, and other factors attest to their differences. Thus, that Jungian patients dream in Jungian symbols, that Freudian patients all seem to have transference/oedipal/defense mechanism problems, and that Gestalt patients all have fragmented souls speaks more for the effective indoctrination of the jargon systems than as actual proofs that these concepts are universally true.

Any client who has ever shopped for a therapist must have felt bewildered by the friends, acquaintances, and other experts who enthusiastically endorsed a particular helping approach as the only legitimate path toward enlightenment. Whereas in an earlier decade the choice had been limited to perhaps a psychoanalytic Viennese type or a behavioristic laboratory sort depending on one's financial resources and social position, there now exists a smorgasbord of alternatives. You can be Rolfed, Erharded, primally screamed, encountered, existentially analyzed, or thorazined, to name but a few of the choices.

So habitual is our tendency to categorize people that we have our own diagnostic schemes for one another. Whereas in college years the magical question, What is your major? was purported to unlock the secrets of a person's soul, now we have graduated to classifications determined by our theoretical orientations. Thus, one conversation among professionals at a convention might be typified by the following.

Group Leader A: (wearing a tweed vest and jacket, bow tie, Bermuda
     shorts, barefooted, smoking a pacifier):
          "I'm a neo-Freudian sub-Adlerian with some Phenomenological
          leanings and Rogerian sympathies. What are you?"
Group Leader B: (wearing a simply cut outfit in black leather and
     chains):
          "I'm into bondage."

The competition among diverse therapy approaches to recruit disciples is intensifying with a fervor that rivals a Holy War. Each therapy argues persuasively that it has The Answer to solving today's problems. With their public relations networks, touring superstar leaders, and a "Bible" instructing the congregation on appropriate behavior, these academic theories are becoming more and more like religions. All group members, regardless of their personalities, interaction styles, experience, particular problems and needs, are expected to conform to the group leader's conception of reality (as dictated by her or his theory).

Nothing is more amusing than to watch a client who has spent years in a psychoanalytic group discussing countertransference, ego defense mechanisms, and anal stages, in the same group with a veteran of encounter groups who can express feelings like a pro, and a behaviorally oriented leader who is talking in the language of goals, outcomes, and reinforcements. None of the people can communicate with one another, though their vocabularies contain similar concepts with different labels.

The alternative to single-theory allegiance, with its disadvantages of restricting freedom of choice and perpetuating rigid thinking, is to develop a personal, flexible style of operation, a multi-modal approach that is solidly based in principles of scientific inference and that focuses on practical, useful intervention strategies (Lazarus, 1981). Such a posture—the practice of pragmatic group leadership—combines a complex, individually designed philosophy of human existence with unlimited therapeutic technology adapted from every known sphere of human knowledge.

PRAGMATISM

The philosophy of pragmatism is a distinctively American invention credited to physicist, logician, and historian Charles Peirce (1839 – 1914). Stressing the importance of logical inference in dealing with contemporary problems, Peirce created the Metaphysical Club, a diverse group of Harvard thinkers, to critically examine such significant unresolved issues as Darwin's (then novel) theories of evolution. Chauncey Wright, William James, John Fiske, Oliver Wendell Holmes, and John Dewey, among the greatest minds of their era, coordinated their efforts to build a new practical philosophy.

In this new philosophy, all courses of action were to be examined in terms of their likely consequences. According to James, the pragmatist "turns away from abstraction and insufficiency, from verbal solutions, from bad a priori reasons, from fixed principles, closed systems, and pretended absolutes and origins. He turns toward concreteness and adequacy, toward facts, toward action and toward power" (James, 1907). Pragmatism, then, is an active rather than a contemplative philosophy. It deals with facts and their outcomes. It is concerned with observable consequences of human action. The sum of all possible consequences constitutes the action's meaning.

I. S. Cooper, in his personal account of life as an experimental neurosurgeon, graphically demonstrates the pragmatic spirit as applied to medicine. While demonstrating his new technique of chemopallidectomy for treating the symptoms of Parkinson's Disease, he was queried by an eminent colleague about exactly where in the brain he inserted his surgical probe. X rays were taken to observe the results. Cooper, a brash youth who was revolutionizing the field of neurosurgery with his flexible disregard for the accepted theories of his day, responded with the basic guiding principle of his distinguished career.

> It doesn't really make any difference, . . . his tremor is gone. The rigidity too. He can move his arm and leg. The patient can speak and is unharmed. The X ray was a means—not an end. If we don't find out for a hundred years where the tip of the probe is, what difference will it make? Eventually we will know (Cooper, 1981, p. 91).

As it happened, Cooper was off by a few centimeters in his theory, even though the execution of his technique was stunningly effective.

> We are not operating to produce an X ray, but to produce a clinically rewarding result. When I interpreted the X ray erroneously, it was a stupid mistake. Fortunately, I learned a great deal from this and no one was harmed. Happily, that day in December of 1953 was really the birthday of thalamic surgery for movement disorders (Cooper, 1981, pp. 95 – 96).

Similarly, group leaders are not operating to produce an X ray or elegant theory "but to produce a clinically rewarding result." It would seem that all great discoveries were made by pragmatic scientists who were bound by neither their existing theories nor their limited visions but who struggled to combine compatible elements into novel procedures. The basic tenets of a pragmatic philosophy are already a part of the methodology of most group leaders. The logical reasoning that allows a practitioner to consider several possible courses of action, systematically projecting likely outcomes, rejecting unsuitable alternatives, and finally electing the intervention most likely to produce desirable consequences is one such example.

Pragmatism, however, is *not* synonymous with eclecticism, which focuses on choosing the best technique from diverse sources and systems (Dimond, Havens, & Jones, 1978). An underlying philosophy becomes a hindrance to such a style because the emphasis is solely on collecting problem-solving techniques without regard to their origins. The eclectic approach has sometimes been criticized as being evasive, wishy-washy, and as operating from a philosophic desert with little theoretical grounding.

Indeed, there are problems in any field for a professional who has memorized a lot of gimmicks and techniques to solve problems but who doesn't understand how conflicts arise or the theory behind making systematic change efforts. And so every therapist, regardless of what theoretical label is used for purposes of simple classification, has a uniquely personal idea of how people develop emotional/ behavioral problems and how they are best treated.

Theories are not to be casually discarded as obstacles to dynamic action. The only theory that restricts freedom is the one invented by someone else and swallowed before it was cleaned, deboned, and simmered a bit. While the eclectic shuns theory, the pragmatist uses it in creatively applied ways: "Pragmatism unstiffens all our theories, limbers them up, and sets each one at work" (James, 1907, p. 46).

Pragmatism and Group Work

Historically, group work arose from the need to provide therapeutic learning experiences that closely parallel experiences in the real world. As such, experimentation, creative innovation, and the scientific application of practical intervention strategies have always lent themselves particularly well to group settings. Helping structures that have been traditionally designed and restricted to a solo instructional system are becoming increasingly flexible in their application to groups as well.

A few years ago, for example, it was inconceivable that the treatment of sexual dysfunctions could ever have been done in groups. Because clients experience such embarrassment discussing their sexual problems and because the therapy takes a fairly individualized, prescriptive form, it was never imagined that a group could be an appropriate place for treatment. But resourceful and pragmatic practitioner/researchers have been particularly flexible in adapting sex-therapy strategies to the group treatment of premature ejaculation (Kaplan, Kohl, Pomeroy, Offit, & Hogan, 1978) and orgasmic dysfunctions (Schneidman & McGuire, 1978). Similarly, behavioral science literature is making increasing reference to the use of groups with a strange variety of purposes, goals, and populations The group leader unrestricted by the bounds of a parent discipline, or even by the walls of an office, ventures out into the world prepared to help its inhabitants on their own territory.

There is great historical precedent for the marriage between the philosophy of pragmatism and the practice of group work. Kurt Lewin, J. L. Moreno, and many of the founding parents of the group movement were incredibly flexible and open in their orientations. Counselors and therapists operating on the front lines know that the cardinal rule in running any group is to come armed with an agenda for action but prepared to throw it out if circumstances change. There are too many unpredictable variables and individual needs to have a plan for The Group. You pay attention to what has been going on—the dynamics and interaction. You do your homework and preparation, anticipate potential problems, develop strategies for handling them, rehearse your opening lines, and then—*Blam!* Before there is a chance to pick up where you left off last week or to get a progress report from clients, a crisis arises that needs immediate attention. So much for the agenda.

Recently, rigid adherence to a theoretical affiliation has been decreasing in the newer publications such as those by Wachtel (1981) and Marmor and Woods (1980). However, it appears to be even less prevalent in the writings of therapists practicing in groups. Perhaps the luxury of operating from a closed system that restricts available choices and interprets all behavior in terms of a unique jargon is not affordable when many people are being helped at the same time. Perhaps the theories of group treatment are not yet as elegant as their individual cousins. Whatever the reason, group leaders must be flexible and open in their approach, aware of subtle changes and responsive to them.

What if, as scientist/practitioners, we could formulate a philosophy that can change to fit the requirements of the job?

Basic Premises of a Pragmatic Approach

1. *There is a distinction between absolute truth and relative truth.* Absolute truth is an ideal to be pursued, a life goal that can never be reached. All theory is regarded as tenuous; human constructions are subject to constant revision in light of further data. The only truth we may be absolutely certain about is the inevitability of death. Nevertheless, a pragmatic group leader would find it crippling to make sweeping generalizations about human behavior. While it may

be relatively true that *some* people's problems stem from a faulty self-concept or that *some* people suffer from irrational beliefs while *other* people are victims of environmental manipulations, it would be a gross oversimplification of reality to believe that any single factor is the absolute contributor.

Are there any absolute truths about conducting therapeutic groups? One basic rule that might come to mind is that nonverbal attending behaviors are crucial to developing rapport, thus creating the cardinal maxim for practice: always maintain eye contact with group members. Always? This principle of interpersonal communication could conceivably be reversed for maximum therapeutic benefit. A group leader may deliberately *avoid* eye contact as a way to extinguish approval seeking in a particular group member. Even the most basic so-called universal truths of the profession—such directives as "never give advice"—are relative to time, place, and circumstances. They are no more static than the rest of Dr. Einstein's universe.

2. *Pragmatism is concerned only with useful knowledge that can be applied directly to practical situations.* Theorizing about physiological indices of stress may be a fascinating study of the human condition, but unless the group leader can put such information to clinical use, its functional utility is worthless.

Following hours of group observation and equipped with the results of research available on the subject, the astute pragmatist can distill useful information to aid his or her work. Diagnostically, the therapist could note frequency of eyeblinks as a measure of member anxiety (Stern, Bremer, & McClure, 1974) or use eye-movement patterns to determine whether a client would respond better to visual, kinesthetic, or auditory imagery (Bandler & Grinder, 1979). The group leader who systematically collects useful data and stores it for later execution would continuously monitor all perceptual input systems, asking the crucial question, How can I use this?

Books, films, television, parties, any possible source of information about how people function in groups is a legitimate building block in the pragmatic approach. All personal experiences are valid shapers of professional effectiveness, especially in psychological helpers. The group leader who can draw on past associations of feeling shy and socially inept will find such empathic experiences valuable in helping clients to open up in groups. The group leader who has made a systematic study of interpersonal approach patterns in shopping malls can apply such data toward promoting group intimacy more effectively. All group leaders could profit from a more systematic application of pragmatic philosophy, studying the world to find what it can teach.

3. *The use of pigeonhole diagnostics that categorize clients into discrete cells is to be avoided.* Terms such as *normal, neurotic, schizophrenic, involutional melancholic,* and *cyclothymic personality* have little functional value for the pragmatist except to fill out spaces on insurance forms. Human beings are much too complex and behaviorally variable to distill the essence of their functioning into a single label. Does a person who is schizophrenic act like a schizophrenic in *all* situations of life? Is a passive-aggressive personality one that *always* acts out a destructive pattern? Does a shy person act shy with everyone?

The pragmatic group leader uses differential diagnosis but only as a means of helping group members to identify self-defeating behaviors they wish to change. Thus, the phrase "classroom bananas behavior" will probably have much more personal meaning for a kid who acts up in school than calling him the proud owner of an "antisocial personality disorder." The former label implies behavior that can be changed in the group; the latter bespeaks an unalterable condition. It is useful for the child to think in terms of "acting bananas," or being out of control, because this realization is necessary before he can take charge of himself again. It can only be destructive for him to believe that he has a condition that gives him an alibi for continuing to act inappropriately.

4. *Pragmatism is an empirically based philosophy, steeped in the scientific method yet immune to much experimental research.* Knowing that there is a statistical difference in trust dimensions (as measured by frequency of "I feel" statements) between groups that received a particular treatment and groups that didn't is a wonderful piece of news, particularly if you need significant results to get a dissertation completed or an article published. But such studies are of minimal value to the group leader confronted by the angry stares of ten skeptics who believe that confidentiality is hogwash.

The philosopher/scientist is interested in useful research that allows him or her to make accurate predictions about the likely consequences of any action. The group leader is also interested in what can safely, reliably, and effectively be used to help a client reach a specific goal or to create a special climate in a given group. One way to accomplish those ends is to become familiar with what tends to work with most people in similar situations. Large sample research is an excellent source of data for such purposes. But another way of reaching situation-specific goals is to collect data for that given set of circumstances, predict the desired outcomes, create an intervention that is most likely to produce desired results, implement the strategy, and assess its impact.

This systematic study of micro- rather than macrochange is the foundation for intensive design research. It is ideally suited for the pragmatist in that the best features of humanism and behaviorism are melded into a form of practical experimentation. The strategy is distinctly behavioristic in flavor with its strong emphasis on specificity, observability, and measurability; yet it is also solidly humanistic because of its in-depth study of a single case. Graphs, anecdotal material, or changes in the slope or acceleration of plotted lines are relied on in the analysis instead of parametric statistics.

Ironically, single-subject design research originated in B. F. Skinner's experimental assessments of intervention effects (Frey, 1978). While it is a primary tool of the behaviorist interested in measuring change over time, it is the antithesis of what has become traditional well-controlled group-based research. Instead of large random samples comparing their behavior with the behavior of those who have received no treatment and then making inferences to a single case, intensive research studies an *N* of 1 and makes inferences to people in general.

The pragmatic group leader, the practitioner in the field whose only interest in traditional research is to skim the professional journals, may nevertheless structure important studies in his or her own backyard. The most significant research is that which is most impactful. If a clinician reads about an experimental study that produced relevant, useful data, the best possible way to put the results to work is to replicate the study as intensive design research with his or her own groups. Likewise, case study investigations become the pilot programs for more massive research efforts at a later date.

5. *Pragmatism is above all pluralistic in its orientation.* "American pragmatism has fostered an *empirical* respect for the complexity of existence requiring a *plurality* of concepts to do justice to the diverse problems of mankind in its evolutionary struggles" (Wiener, 1949, p. 191). Critical common sense is used as a basis for operational,

piecemeal analysis of how things and people work. The method is adopted to the subject matter until tests of verifiability can determine the meaning of an idea.

The use of any technique is sanctioned, regardless of its theoretical origins, but within the context of an articulated philosophical rationale that is flexible, encompassing, useful, and personally designed. Milton Erikson, the virtuoso therapist and hypnotist, believed passionately in the pragmatic approach.

> You need to extract from the various techniques the particular elements that allow you to express yourself as a personality. The next most important thing about a technique is your awareness of the fact that every patient who comes to you represents a different personality, a different attitude, a different background of experience. Your approach to him must be in terms of him as a person with a particular frame of reference for that day and the immediate situation (Haley, 1968, p. 530).

For one particular group situation, a soft manner, quiet voice, low-key leader role, and lots of reflection might produce the most responsive involvement. For the same clients at another time (or a completely different group composition), the most advantageous strategy might be the use of direct confrontation, dramatic role plays, an authoritarian leader role, and behavior modification technology.

6. *The group leader formulates a defensible rationale for every intervention used.* Since the goal of therapeutic groups is to help clients make constructive changes in their lives, therapists are interested in developing reliable tools for facilitating such progress. The key to any systematic attempt at group leadership is the consistent replicability of the tools that are used.

Just prior to any therapeutic action—whether an attempt to focus counseling content, to disperse conflict, to offer support, or to facilitate insight—the group leader would internally ask three questions: What exactly appears to be happening? What specifically do I wish to accomplish? How will the intervention I'm about to use meet my desired goals? If the answers are abstract, vague, or reduced to elusive intuitions, the group leader will closely scrutinize personal motives. Preferably, such an assessment is done as the process occurs; more likely it will be done during the convenience of an after-group autopsy.

Such a detailed analysis of so-called gut realities will help to make them more precisely implemented at future times but will also help to stifle leader self-indulgence. Before using self-disclosure, for instance, to build trust or model openness, the leader can ask himself or herself: Am I doing this to help a group member or to make myself look good? Am I telling this anecdote to illustrate a specific point (if so, which one?) or to entertain myself? Am I confronting this client because he is genuinely disruptive to the group process or because he irritates me? ·

In addition to censoring inappropriate verbalizations, defining rationale for action allows the leader to accumulate a wider choice of strategies by filing away for retrieval those that have consistently worked before in similar circumstances. It also allows the practitioner to reveal the mechanisms by which change occurs in the group. Since group members often function as assistant leaders and are also committed to learning how therapy works so that they can change themselves in the future without having to return to the group, it is advantageous to share with them the reasoning behind a mysterious action.

If the group leader were spontaneously to stand up and dance around the circle of chairs, tapping each person on the shoulder while offering feedback, it would probably be helpful to share the rationale for doing so: "I am attempting to breathe some life into this group. People are acting bored and lazy. By varying my vocal pitch and nonverbal movements, I immediately captured your attention. Notice that you are all sitting up straight now with animated expressions on your faces."

7. *The pragmatist is versed in an interdisciplinary perspective of his/her chosen profession.* The advanced group leader, in addition to being familiar with the theory and research of psychology, education, and related social sciences, would also have a broadly based understanding of the various branches of philosophy. Since the pragmatic group leader would be reluctant to embrace any single theoretical construct as the exclusive heir to truth, he or she must know the mechanics of personal theory building so that relevant and useful principles may be systematically collected from the universe of knowledge.

The sequential development of a theory-in-use that is applicable to group work usually commences in a fairly narrow adherence to an existing theory that has several attractive variables. The practitioner learns the necessary behaviors without thoroughly understanding their conceptual base and can readily apply the "party line." After this single theory is thoroughly accommodated into an existing philosophical framework, the group leader next moves toward bilingualism, or the ability to split allegiance among several attractive systems (Lancaster, 1981). The experienced group leader struggling for professional identity would next seek to explore higher levels of theoretical structure as the result of intrapsychic conflicts that are irreconcilable at the practitioner's present level of primitive thinking.

As in the developmental sequences of all stage theories, like those of Freud, Piaget, Kohlberg, Erickson, Havighurst, Perry, and Loevinger, the group leader's philosophical progression moves in an orderly fashion toward higher levels of sophistication. As the pragmatic group leader begins to feel increasingly frustrated and restricted by the limitations of single-theory allegiance, more complex group dynamics, client concerns, and intervention problems will stimulate growth toward the next developmental stage in philosophic refinement. If an orthodox rational-emotive group leader, for instance, runs up against a client who is rational to the point of inhibiting spontaneity, the situation will call for borrowing strategies from other group-work theories that more effectively facilitate the desired behaviors.

Once group leaders begin a systematic investigation of alternative helping strategies, a cognitive process begins to integrate this new knowledge into a unified system. At first, this multidimensionality will increase cognitive dissonance, thereby encouraging the reduction of ambiguity into a more concrete, pragmatic structure that will allow for the efficient selection of appropriate techniques. "If . . . then" strategies help the group leader to make simple decisions: *if* these conditions exist, these behaviors are demonstrated and these goals are indicated; *then* I need to do these three things.

In the final stage of professional development, the group leader moves from a multimodal posture to the creation of a new system of order. From previous observations of group behavior, inquiry into existing theoretical explanations, integration of relevant knowledge, and testing of inductively reasoned hypotheses, eventually a new, personally designed philosophy will be deduced (Cattell, 1966).

The logic of this discovery process has been all but ignored by philosophers and scientists alike except for the early work of pragmatists such as Charles Peirce. Royce (1958) has drawn parallels between logical discovery, the final stage of professional development, and the methodology of multivariate statistics such as factor analysis. The spiral loops of identifying meaningful factors that account for the maximum variance among a number of diverse variables makes factor analysis a suitable model for explaining how complex constructs evolve from the insightful progression of blurred covariation.

Constructive dialecticism permits group leaders to create their own pragmatic philosophies. Conceptual pluralism, synergism, relativism, probabilism, secular democratic individualism, eclecticism—these are the new watchwords of our profession. The basic tenets of philosophy and the operating principles of science can be effectively merged to create for each individual practitioner a truly functional pragmatic theory to guide leader behavior.

CHAPTER 3

How People Change in Groups

Franz Kafka begins his surrealistic tale *Metamorphosis* with a haunting description of powerlessness.

> As Gregor Samsa awoke one morning from uneasy dreams he found himself transformed in his bed into a gigantic insect. He was lying on his hard, as it were armor-plated, back and when he lifted his head a little he could see his dome-like brown belly divided into stiff arched segments on top of which the bed quilt could hardly keep in position and was about to slide off completely. His numerous legs, which were pitifully thin compared to the rest of his bulk, waved helplessly before his eyes (Kafka, 1948, p. 67).

Some of the same feelings must confront hard-working clients on discovering that they, too, are undergoing a metamorphosis. Seemingly overnight, new skills have grown like uncoordinated appendages. A new shell replaces its molted predecessor. New antennae have sprouted, sensitizing the being to levels of awareness that previously had been impossible. When this transformed creature views its strange image in the mirror, it must indeed appear alien: where has the old Me gone?

PLUS ÇA CHANGE

Human learning, an elusive and complex process that involves metamorphic adaptation, has been viewed essentially as a survival function of the central nervous system (Anthony & Thibodeau, 1979). In the face of a constantly changing external world, the body's internal environment labors to maintain a delicate homeostasis. Various neurophysiological and biochemical processes in the brain coordinate their actions to gather, record, code, store, organize, and retrieve information about the external world. The organism then uses these data to better adapt to changing circumstances.

The same might be said about how and why people change in groups. No person ever really wants to change. A client with a happy marriage doesn't casually get a divorce, a perfectly satisfied employee doesn't quit a job, and a person who has discovered successful strategies for handling anxiety doesn't spontaneously throw them out the window just to learn new, improved coping mechanisms.

Group members *say* they want to change. ("I'm so unhappy, I wish I could be someone else." "I hate myself the way I am." "I really do have to start acting differently.") But what they really mean is that they want their group leaders to change them so that they don't have to do the hard work. The human organism does not voluntarily correct psychological imbalances; it is *ordered* to change because the host body and mind are too uncomfortable with the way things are going. In terms of energy expenditure and emotional investment, it is no longer economically feasible to continue chugging along at current unproductive levels. It hurts too much *not* to change. The person feels demoralized, hopeless, desperate. Something must be altered.

So much for one hypothesis about why people change. But an equally fascinating and more relevant question for therapists who attempt to promote change is, how and when does change occur?

A collection of persons enters a strange room, each with a different set of expectations. They spend a few hours together in a circle, talking but mostly listening. They are not hooked up to electronic gadgetry, given pills to swallow, or subjected to surgical procedures to remove the offending problem. They simply spend time in one another's company, and somehow they feel better as a result. What is this magic that cures people of their suffering?

Any "normal" science can discover cause-effect relationships by isolating single variables that are suspected catalysts, subjecting them to intensive scrutiny and systematic manipulation, and then drawing inferences about their probable actions. The cataloguing of neurotransmitters within the brain is an example of such an activity, one so significant that it usually results in annual Nobel Prizes as rewards. From such investigations theories are born. The scores of substances that have already been identified, such as dopamine or norepinephrine, have scarcely scratched the surface of what is still left to learn. Current theories about the mechanisms regulating neurophysiology are so primitive that their authors are apologetic. Yet in our science of producing psychological changes—an infinitely more complex process than the anatomy of a single hormone or neurological system—theories of change flourish like hungry bacteria.

One theory claims that all group members make changes in their lives as the result of resolving childhood conflicts by working them through with surrogate family members. Another theory tells us that it is the "atmosphere" in a group that becomes the central healing force, as if air rich in oxygen, nitrogen, or empathy helps people to breathe more easily. Other theories claim that groups have "reinforcers" which, like traffic cops, tell clients when to stop and go. Still another approach says that within a group of 10 people there are really 30 people who all act like their own parents or kids or other grownups. Apparently these 10 or 30 people (depending on your perspective) all want to play games with one another, but the leader won't let them.

Theories have been advanced that say change occurs when group members, who are broken into pieces like shattered glass, become whole again. Another states that clients should talk to themselves more often like the people who wander around the streets of New York (which is where the author of the theory is from). Other change theories recommend that group members chant mantras, take off all their clothes, eat brown rice, roll into a ball, have their feet massaged, stick needles in their ears, pray for deliverance, take hot baths, or do nothing at all.

Unfortunately, all the existing theories that attempt comprehensively to explain how people change in groups are in some way negligent. They all reflect the biases of their inventors (Palmer, 1980), who were blind to the work of others (Smith, 1975). They exhibit denominationalism (Stein, 1961), academic tribalism (DiLoreto, 1971), parochialism (Wolberg, 1954), cultism (Thorne, 1973), and religiosity (Ford & Urban, 1963).

It shows a gross misunderstanding and disrespect for the individuality of each person in a group to assume that all are there for the same purpose, that all relate to the world in precisely the same way, that all learn and change by identical processes. Each client comes to a group with a different set of experiences, backgrounds, personality styles, goals, and cognitive patterns. People are so extraordinarily different from one another, even in their biological equipment, as to virtually defy classification.

Hence, any theory of human change, whether it is concerned with molecular alterations or behavioral metamorphoses, ought to be wide-ranging in scope. Fortunately, there is a growing movement among therapy researchers to examine the process of psychological change within the context of shared features among diverse approaches (Goldfried, 1980). No longer can a single theory adequately explain the intricate mechanisms of therapeutic action, particularly since the majority of practicing clinicians in the United States follow no single orientation exclusively (Garfield & Kurtz, 1976; Kelly, Goldberg, Fiske, & Kilkowsky, 1978). The trend for the future is not toward further diversification of therapeutic schools but toward closer allegiance, eclectic theory, and pragmatic action.

Every theory appears to be an adequate explanation for the actions of its creator. It is probably true that a sizable part of the population does change as the result of expressing honest feelings, while another group of people (or perhaps even the same people) can change by altering their thought patterns, confronting their repressed desires, or structuring their environments. These multiple factors responsible for facilitating change may be isolated from the literature.

VIVE LA DIFFÉRENCE!

No two individuals are precisely the same. Ask any shoe manufacturer, dentist, or fingerprint expert about the differences in human beings. "Typical" hearts, stomachs, kidneys, and other organs exhibit a staggering diversity of shapes, sizes, and levels of function. In the nervous system—the main mechanism of perception and communication, containing all that may be described as consciousness—there are also many individual differences. In a comprehensive study of human physiological differences, Williams (1967) concludes there really is no "average" person. The sensations of sight, hearing, taste, hunger, the needs for sleep and stimulation, the experiences each person has of the world are quite different phenomena.

If people are so different in the specific chemical compositions of their bodies, why should they be any more alike in the ways they learn, change, or grow? Is it any more valid to assume all people learn by modeling, or by reinforcers, or unconscious motives, or catharsis, or feeling expression, than it is to erroneously believe that all people have the same "normal" body temperature, react the same to medications, have a 30-gram thyroid, engage in sex 3 times per week, or perhaps think identically?

THE MATRIX FOR CHANGE

Many researchers, writers, theoreticians, and practitioners think in terms of the conditions and therapeutic factors conducive to change in groups rather than in terms of any single school of thought. This *facilitative factors approach*, which seeks a fuller explanation of how and why group members change, has been advanced by several authors attempting to reconcile contradictory points of view. Though it is highly unlikely that any one of the following variables adequately explains how and why people change in groups, it is probable that most of them are quite influential. The matrix for change depicted here includes those factors that researchers and practitioners have found maximally to create and maintain the conditions that contribute to change.

The statistical science of factor analysis was spawned to provide mathematical models for explaining psychological theories (Harmon, 1967). Simplification of complex human processes is the goal of factor analysis, which describes meaningful categories by determining the principal factors that maximally account for the variance (communality plus uniqueness) of a contributing variable to its total model. A *factor* is a condensed statement of linear relationships between relevant variables that represent the actual reality of a complex psychological phenomenon (Eysenck, 1967). Factors are true variables that stand for the underlying theoretical constructs of human action (Royce, 1967). The sum of all possible factors would thus constitute a perfect explanation of how several different variables are related to one another.

In the process of human change, there are a number of plausible factors that account for its action. If most of these "parts of the whole" could be gathered together to describe how change occurs in groups, a geometric model could probably be constructed in which the factors could represent all known variables mathematically as well as symbolically. Gorsuch (1974), for example, describes an orthogonal component model in which variables are graphically plotted as points, and then two factors can be optimally added to the cluster as the best attempt to account for their relationships.

In the case of variables that lead to change in groups, several points can be graphically displayed according to their relationship to two primary dimensions. Factor A represents "Level of Insight" versus "Level of Action"; Factor B describes a continuum of "Cognitive" versus "Affective" response styles. These quadrants were originally developed by Frey (1972) and later adapted by Hansen, Warner, and

Factor Matrix for Change Variables in Groups

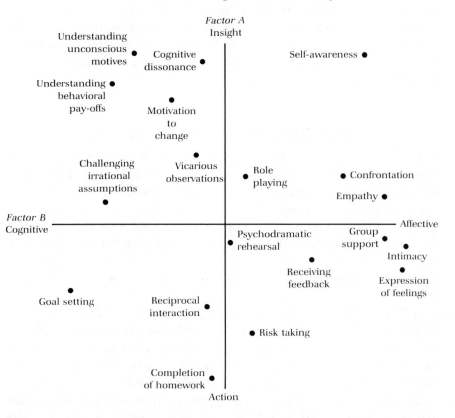

Smith (1980) for explaining group counseling theory. In this context they are used as examples of how two factors can be portrayed as a basis for explaining the inter-relationships between all relevant variables. Unfortunately, the process of change in groups is considerably more complex than can be adequately described by only two factors. Even a dozen factors could not account for all variance in the equation.

The factor analysis approach is consistent with the overall theme of this book, which attempts to integrate from various sources the major principles that best account for therapeutic change. Just as the preceding chapters have presented assumptions with which most practicing group leaders could agree despite their theoretical differences, this chapter presents a global view of change that is both generally applicable and specifically delineated.

In any model, however, no matter how comprehensive and detailed, a generalized overview of change in groups may not apply to any single case. Client change often involves exchanging the logical for the unreasonable. At other times, the 15 discrete steps in this model may all occur within a few seconds. Finally, no matter how confident and strong the collective human mind may feel, do we ever have the capacity to fully understand something as complex as how people change?

OVERVIEW OF CHANGE IN GROUPS

The following outline delineates five general change stages sub-divided into discrete, sequential steps beginning in Stage I with pre-treatment variables that operate in clients' heads before they ever enter a therapeutic group. The client's initial mind-set, for example, will be influenced by such predisposing variables as genetic deter-minants, physiological functioning, developmental stages, and frus-tration tolerance. Precipitating factors, catalytic events, characteristic thinking patterns, and expectations are all part of pretreatment vari-ables.

An exploration phase (Stage II) is part of any helping system, al-though its length will depend on whether the group leader is psychodynamically or behaviorally inclined. After self-defeating be-haviors are defined, they enter Stage III, understood as to their payoffs, consequences, and other insight variables. Stage IV factors involve formulating and applying an action plan of intervention that will be evaluated and modified in Stage V. These identical process components, although labeled differently by individual helping sys-tems, nevertheless have more in common than has previously been acknowledged.

STAGE I: PRETREATMENT

1. Origin of Concern
   A. Predisposing Variables
   B. Precipitating Factors
   C. Catalytic Events
2. Mind-Set
   A. Cognition
   B. Affect
   C. Behavior
3. Development of Symptoms
4. Initial Recognition of Difficulty
5. Decision to Seek Help

STAGE II: EXPLORATION

6. Client Expectations for Cure Formulated
7. Discomfort Intensified
8. Scene Setting
9. Placebo Planted for Favorable Prognosis
10. Trust Building
11. Leader-modeled Disclosure
12. Risk Taking
13. Exploration of Client World
14. Catharsis
15. Group Support and Initial Feedback
16. Mutual Identification, Sharing, and Spectatoring

STAGE III: INSIGHT

17. Challenge Irrational Assumptions
18. Confrontation with Inconsistencies
19. Realization of Hidden and Unconscious Motives
20. Understanding Behavioral Payoffs and Consequences
21. Reassurance and Peer Support
22. Generalization to Other Behaviors

STAGE IV: ACTION

23. Motivational Support
24. Decision to Change
25. Commitment to Group
26. Brainstorming of Alternative Courses of Action
27. Information Giving and Guidance
28. Goal Setting
29. Formation of Plan
30. Reality Testing
31. Rehearsal
32. Constructive Feedback
33. Psychological Homework
34. Commitment to Action
35. Closure
36. Real World Practice

STAGE V: EVALUATION

37. Progress Report
38. Additional Input and Modifications
39. Reinforcement
40. Finger on the Pulse

Stage I: Pretreatment

1. *Origin of concern.* A disaster occurs: an earthquake, a war, a famine, a flood, a cosmic accident. People die. The landscape is irrevocably altered. Some of the victims are crushed both literally and figuratively. The survivors clear their vision; they attempt to cope with the consequences. Some will shrug indifferently while others will wail in helpless misery.

Why is it that people react so differently to identical crises? A death in the family can cripple some mourners for an agonizing decade of grief, while others bounce back after a weekend of hard crying. One woman will be driven to the brink of suicide over the shame of rape, while another will think of the episode as a distasteful inconvenience to be reckoned with. A divorce, a loss of income, an illness, a sexual dysfunction, or an exploded dream catalyze major negative consequences for some people; others find ways of constructively using such concerns as growth forces.

It appears that each individual's unique constitution acts as a predisposing variable for reaction to personal troubles. Depending on the body's chemistry, hormonal balance, genetic determinants, and physiological functioning, a person is more likely to react to certain stimuli in certain ways than in others. Although no conclusive evidence supports the notion of "alcoholic genes," "depression DNA molecules," or "schizophrenic neurons," there is growing data for the hypothesis that much of human behavior may be controlled by underlying biological processes. At this time it would be very difficult to determine whether a bad temper is caused by predisposing "anger genes" (such as those popularly believed to accompany red hair) or by environmental influences. It is nevertheless significant to note that a wide range of reactions is possible to the same stressful situation.

Genetics and physiology may indeed play a causative role in client concerns, just as developmental stages probably exert their influence. An adolescent who is struggling through Piaget's period of formal operations, Kohlberg's stage of conventional morality, and Erickson's conflict of identity versus role confusion is likely to react to a crisis situation very differently from a man living through Levinson's Age-50 transition in middle adulthood. All these factors, including other relevant predisposing variables, such as one's characteristic frustration tolerance and stable personality traits, will dramatically affect performance under fire. Even sleep patterns, energy level, body image, and self-concept will influence the total behavioral scheme.

A person's readiness to change is another important predisposing factor. The life work of Jean Piaget, Jerome Bruner, Arnold Gesell, and other developmental theorists indicates that people must reach a certain point in their personal-problem evolution before change can readily occur. Self-discovery depends not only on people's conscious willingness but on their capacity to change. Bruner (1963) believed, however, that readiness could be taught by providing the client with prerequisite skills necessary for higher order functioning.

In a group led by two beginning leaders it was evident that a volunteer willing to use group time was not immediately forthcoming. The leaders felt uncomfortable waiting for someone to volunteer, but they didn't quite know how to select an appropriate member on whom to focus. It hadn't occurred to them that they could search their memories for past content areas elicited from each client during preliminary exercises, nor could they think of a rationale for choosing any particular client with whom to explore. Instead they determined to let fate decide who would have the first honors, and so they randomly focused on a group member who had been silent. Dick, a very accommodating young man, dutifully responded to the query with the statement that he had had a problem but that it was now worked out. The co-leaders decided to pursue their quarry, mistakenly believing that he wanted help but was too shy to ask for it.

Dick felt hurt because a friend had ended their relationship as a result of a solitary incident over which he had had no control. An hour was spent attempting to help Dick express his resentment, rehearse a confrontation scene, and get reactions from other participants. Throughout the counseling, Dick patiently repeated that he felt his problem was already resolved, although it was evident to others that there was much residual frustration. The problem was isolated, a plan was formulated, everything was taken care of except one thing: Dick didn't feel ready yet to confront the issue head-on.

Since he had been involuntarily selected, Dick had no power to control his progress. He knew that change would eventually become necessary, but he needed more time to mobilize his resources, build his energy, heal wounds, and only then bid for group time. Because he had been forced to participate before he was ready, Dick's forward momentum was stalled; he backed farther into his shell. The other group members also left the session feeling frustrated because they perceived that valuable time had been wasted and that given enough of a chance, several of them would have volunteered to work on concerns that needed more immediate attention.

2. *Mind-set*. The human mind perceives and responds on a number of different levels: thinking, feeling, and acting. In addition to catalytic events, predisposing variables, and precipitating factors, the client's initial mind-set will strongly determine how she or he responds to a crisis. Individual group members who prefer to reason and think analytically will *act* differently from those who prefer to feel intensely and emote spectacularly. Bandler and Grinder (1979) have made some stunning observations on the unique perceptual mind-set of persons who may prefer to relate to the world from primarily an auditory, visual, or kinesthetic mode.

Persons who believe that their feelings must be spontaneously expressed before they can find relief will respond to their personal concerns a bit more dramatically than those who view their behavior as the logical product of environmental and intrinsic reinforcers. Likewise, a group member who believes that behavior is caused by feelings which are in turn caused by thoughts will naturally focus on cognitive aspects of the situation.

The human mind, notwithstanding the sameness of its physical components, is managed differently according to individual style and mind-set. There appears to be a relationship between anticipatory cognition and subjectively experienced disappointment if expectations are not met. Thus, a person who dwells endlessly on a future goal, whether a desired job or an important date, will be more disappointed than a person who minimizes anticipatory thoughts and feelings. If circumstances don't turn out as hoped, a high-expectation mind-set will program a drastic emotional response—depression, anger, anxiety. A person who avoids unrealistic expectations will therefore experience less emotional trauma.

Though cognitive style contributes greatly to the development of behavioral symptoms, alterations in mood also affect stressful situations. When a person is having a bad day or is short of patience, it takes far less to ignite the fuse. These obvious factors, combined with physiological, developmental, and psychological processes, all interact to produce the first signs that change is imminent.

3. *Development of symptoms*. The first indicators of underlying emotional distress show themselves as symptoms. Before potential group members ever begin to realize that a presenting problem is severe enough to seek outside help, they will notice the occurrence of certain physiological and behavioral changes. Dilated pupils, rapid heart rate, nausea, diarrhea, dizziness, stomach cramps, and cold

feet may accompany feelings of anxiety; depression may cause insomnia, loss of appetite, lethargy, or loss of sex drive (Bockar, 1976).

Symptoms signal that something is wrong, just as pain tells us of possible physical injury. Whether the group leader is inclined to treat behavioral symptoms (such as drug abuse) as the "real problem" or views them only as surface cues of some underlying pathology, the client will initially notice feelings of discomfort and will be highly motivated to reduce their level of intensity.

4. *Initial recognition of difficulty.* Excerpt from a group member's journal:

> "In my former work situation as a salesman among a jungle of aggressive peers and complacent clients, my task was to apply appropriate ass-kissing behaviors as I deemed necessary to attain a particular client's "friendship", and hence business. I worked with peers I despised as whimsical prostitutes willing to do or say anything for money. I worked under supervisors who knew less than I about human nature and with clients who suck the blood from those who call on them. To compound matters, I had a strong psychological dependence on my boss—my own father. I felt totally alien and apart from those I worked with—.
>
> "I gave in to the security, to the future, to the financial rewards of my work. I felt drugged senseless by outside forces that I allowed to control me. I looked around me at all of my working peers and their deluded bliss and realized that I could no longer hide from the inevitable—as much as I dreaded making changes, for the first time, I understood that *something* would have to happen."

When a symptom becomes unbearable and the person cannot discover ways to keep things under control, there is realization that a problem will not go away by itself. The change process begins with the first recognition that some alteration is necessary. Whistling in the dark won't dissolve the monster, procrastination and avoidance won't stop it from recurring.

Tristan has noticed that the more he tries to gain on all the tasks he feels he must accomplish, the farther he falls behind. He cannot decide between using his Sunday afternoon to winterize his house, visit his mother, finish his school reading, complete a report for work, or catch up on his correspondence. So instead he watches a football game on television, though feeling very guilty that he will now never finish what he needs to do.

The lists he has created make him feel even worse; he gets a stomachache every time he sees the schedule taped to the refrigerator door. Tristan's frustrations build, his symptoms of distress grow, affecting his friendships, his enjoyment of leisure time, and his self-concept. The difficulties multiply like malignant cells out of control, polluting every aspect of his life with which they come into contact.

5. *Decision to seek help.*
- "I can't afford it."
- "Why am I so weak that I can't solve my own problems?"
- "Other people will think I'm crazy."
- "I don't have the time."
- "I can't open up in front of a bunch of strangers."

Yet Tristan decides to join a therapeutic group anyway because his level of desperation and desire for relief outweigh his apprehensions. He is nervous, excited, fearful, optimistic, worried, reluctant, confused, skeptical, determined, and relieved all at once. Fluctuating in his decision to seek help, he consults friends and family and finally decides there is no use postponing what must be done. It is time to stop peering over the edge; the tiger, chasing him in circles, is catching up. "Perhaps a group experience will be the answer I've been looking for," he ponders, "but, I doubt it."

Stage II: Exploration
6. *Client expectations for cure formulated.* Before clients arrive at the therapist's door, they have formed an impression of what they believe will happen. Because most group leaders know the dangers of ignoring expectations for treatment, they usually start intake interviews by exploring client perceptions. This fishing expedition is often amusing in the strange, diverse, and unrealistic comments it elicits. The layperson generally knows little about how groups work except from the distortions of gossip, sensational literature, and the media. Assuming that clients agree to be completely honest regarding their intentions for attending a group, we might hear responses such as the following:

Rose: I don't feel so good. I don't have any friends. I'm lonely. I want you to wave a magic wand so that my life will be perfect. Guys will start calling. Someone will offer me a good job. Please make me happy.

Donald: I'm horny. I haven't gotten laid in seven months. I was hoping to meet some hot women here since I heard everyone take off their clothes and gets down to it at these group things.

Randolph: My mother made me come. She says I got problems. I'm hoping you can convince her that there is nothing wrong with me.

Terry: My doctor says he won't give me any more drugs unless I come to this silly group. That's cool. I don't mind. As long as he keeps the pills coming. I'll sit here forever. What? You want to know what I think will happen? That's easy. You'll talk a lot. We'll pretend to listen, then we'll make up a bunch of garbage to tell you. And you'll act real pleased, but you couldn't care less if we live or die.

Lynn: I guess I'll tell you my problems and then you'll tell me what to do.

Fran: We'll play games and stuff. Tell stories. It'll be real fun. I can't wait to give massages.

7. *Discomfort intensified.* As participants wait for the group to get going, their levels of tension, anxiety, and perceived threat will rise. Fortunately, these are precisely the conditions that lead to further dissatisfaction with the self in its present state. The more uncomfortable a person becomes with recurrent self-defeating behaviors, such as shyness, fear of taking risks, or hesitance to open up and trust others, the more willing that person will be to do something to change the status quo. Withdrawal and passivity are certainly viable options, but, under the effective leader's direction, the cognitive dissonance can be reduced through constructive action.

The initial discomfort that group members invariably feel when confronted with the prospect of interacting with strangers acts as a further motivating force to ensure that they will follow through on their decisions to change. Unless anxiety reaches too far, in which case panic reactions may significantly inhibit any progress, intensified discomfort will often make clients more ready to take necessary risks to restore psychological equilibrium.

8. *Scene setting.* The group leader begins to set in motion a series of planned actions that are likely to facilitate desired changes in clients. Logically, the first task is to establish ground rules that will lead to efficient performance. Issues of confidentiality are usually discussed. Rules are explained pertaining to fees, breaks, smoking, and attendance.

Most therapists also make a great effort to describe what is likely to happen in the group, and what appropriate roles are both for the leader and participants. The therapeutic process is often explained in reassuring terms, giving clients an overview of how change occurs. This preliminary description often acts as a predictor, in confident terms, of what will happen and how exactly it will occur. Since client expectations have already been elicited, it is now time for the leader to give realistic predictions.

9. *Placebo planted for favorable prognosis.* The expectation of success is a strong healing force. The repeated testimony of others reporting how greatly they have been helped, coupled with the leader's confidence and positive expectation, sets the stage for maximum potential change in a group.

Jerome Frank (1961) draws a compelling analogy between the change forces that operate in contemporary therapeutic groups and those of a past era. The primitive faith healers were readily able to persuade large crowds to have conversion experiences by instilling powerful expectations of what could happen. Jefferson Fish (1973) has capitalized on this faith inspiration by describing a procedure of "placebo therapy" that structures group members' beliefs to maximize the sense of drama and impending magic that will occur. The charisma of an astute leader creates a powerful religious fervor in the flock; the faith of the people around each client acts as a social norming mechanism.

Most practicing physicians have to sometimes practice deliberate deceit when a patient cries for unneeded medication. Giving the person in pain a sugar pill while commenting "I know this will make you feel better" has helped millions of sufferers to find relief. The ethical considerations involved in deliberately misleading a patient are believed by some to be relatively less important than providing the unneeded medication or sending the person home empty-handed.

Nonmedical group leaders don't have to wrestle with ethical conflicts related to the use of placebo drugs, but we do make use of the same psychological principles when we plant a favorable prognosis: "This group is a great place to be. You made a very intelligent decision when you chose to come here. In fact, you are well on your way to making progress already as evidenced by your commitment to work on yourself in this group. I have helped many people, just like yourselves, work on resolving their concerns. I believe I can help you as well." If we are worthy of the trust that clients place in our hands, we can deliver what we claim.

10. *Trust building.* Erik Erikson believed that the struggle between trust and mistrust is the first hurdle the newborn human must overcome. If the infant experiences security and continuity in receiving parental love, is allowed to flourish in feeding, sleeping, and elimination patterns, then a lifelong sense of trust will be developed (Erikson, 1963). In group work we attempt to simulate the kind of nurturing environment that facilitates growth in the child. Carl Rogers (1970) describes this greenhouse as a safe place for exploration, where façades fall off, true feelings and total acceptance emerge, and participants feel a sense of closeness that they haven't experienced since their days at their mother's breast.

All group leaders, from the radical behaviorist to the Chairman of the Board, attempt to create an atmosphere of trust, knowing that it is crucial to eliciting maximum productivity from participants. Many exercises have been designed to allow clients to feel optimally trusting in a situation that appears dubious. Would clients in their right minds actually *believe* the statement about confidentiality until it is proved beyond a shadow of a doubt? Introductions are thus structured to initiate the trust-building process by having members declare their reasons for attending the group. To change. A common bond is established.

Initially, client change efforts are made to please others—the leader, other members, a lover, or a friend: "I'll become different to make *them* happy." But such an attitude is only one step removed from a previous strategy that had worked even less efficiently: "If only my mother/spouse/pet gerbil would change, then my life would be fine!" We then respond: "Swell. Sounds great. Next week, instead of your coming to the group, send everyone else in your life who is causing you suffering. Don't forget your boss, the launderer who ruined your shirt, and, oh yes, send an invitation to the U.S. Congress. We'll counsel *them*, and then *you* will get better. Right?"

Eventually most group members work through their self-defeating approval seeking into a more internally based motive. Until that occurs, however, it is important that each client perceive other group members as attractive and trustworthy (Cartwright, 1951; Cartwright & Zanders, 1968). Ohlsen (1977) recommends that group leaders increase their group's attractiveness by screening members to include those who communicate effectively and are nonjudgmental and by dealing initially with client problems that imply that relatively healthy, well-adjusted, prestigious persons participate in group work.

11. *Leader-modeled disclosure.*

"I dare you."

"Double dares go first."

A person asked to try something risky is unlikely to take your word that nothing disastrous will happen. Any intelligent human being, before taking a plunge into a strange pool, is going to do several things: (a) test the temperature with an exploratory toe, (b) scan the surface for dangerous obstructions, (c) check out the bottom for jagged rocks, (d) estimate the depth, and (e) watch others go first to see whether they're attacked by sharks. Only then will the cautious person take a few deep breaths and jump.

Group leaders usually pacify preliminary fears by initially demonstrating that risk taking is necessary and even attractive. In an introductory exercise by which the therapist wishes to elicit personal information without the usual nonsense people reveal at first encounters, it is advantageous to model the kinds of disclosures that are most helpful.

"As the leader of this group, I will not use your valuable time to meet my own needs. Any time I share something about myself, I will deliberately do so to illustrate a point or to make it easier for you to respond. For instance, in this introductory exercise it is *very* important that we hear honest self-descriptions that will help us all to know you well enough so that we can get down to the work at hand. This involves some risk, and so naturally you will want to hedge your bet by introducing yourself in the safe way you would at a cocktail party—telling us your age, marital status, occupation, place of birth, and other meaningless details we will learn anyway as a function of being around you. Instead, I would like you to introduce yourself in a uniquely personal way, perhaps sharing how you intend to use this group, what most people don't understand about you, or how you got to be who you are. Let me show you what I mean.

"I am basically a happy person, not because I was born this way but because I've worked hard on myself over the years. Actually, my progress began in a group very similar to this one when I was having incredible problems overcoming feelings of dependency on my father, trying to separate what I wanted to do with my life as opposed to what he wanted me to do. Since that time I have lived through some hard times—the deaths of several people I love, setbacks in my work, and I still do a lot of approval seeking to get people to like me. I am pretty good at identifying these concerns in myself whenever they crop up, and I know what to do to work them through. It's just that sometimes I feel too lazy. In this group I hope to teach you similar skills for changing the parts of yourself that you don't like."

Jourard and Jaffee (1970) and Egan (1975) found that in a group setting, participants tend to follow the leader in sharing self-revealing remarks. Other evidence suggests that, when timed appropriately, leader-modeled self-disclosure tends to encourage similar behavior on the part of clients (Cozby, 1973; Mann & Murphy, 1975; Thase & Page, 1977; Simonson, 1976; Halpern, 1977). Cormier and Cormier (1979) also suggest that when counselors verbally share information about themselves, they directly influence clients' change levels and indirectly create a more open atmosphere.

12. *Risk taking.* The first major step toward change is to encourage group members to get their feet wet. The risk taking that usually occurs during the exploratory phase of group work involves a public commitment in which (a) vulnerabilities are admitted, (b) helplessness is shared, (c) the desire for a new way of being is declared, (d) intimate thoughts are revealed, (e) preliminary intercommunication is begun, and (f) dreams for a better life are disclosed.

During this critical stage we attempt to disguise how difficult risk taking can be. We pretend that revealing oneself is about as natural as clamming up, and so we deliberately act casual to put people at ease: "You want to kill yourself and take everyone else with you? No problem." We gear up our optimal levels of acceptance, respect, unconditional positive regard, warmth, and empathy to make participant risk taking appear to be easy. It's a good thing, too. Taking risks *is* synonymous with change.

13. *Exploration of client world.* What is the minimum amount of data that needs to be collected from a given client in order to begin therapeutic interventions? At the very least, this exploration of the presenting concerns, how they are specifically manifested, and how they affect the group member's total functioning is systematically accomplished. Some group leaders need more information, others favor personal digging strategies which they feel best elicit valuable data. Everyone wants to get a firm handle on exactly what the client-in-focus feels is most disturbing.

Data might be collected on childhood traumatic experiences, relationships to parents, or developmental crises. Other group leaders might focus on mental status examination variables, such as assessing intellectual functioning or reality testing. Medically trained group leaders may want to check out urinary frequency, weight loss, fatigue, constipation, and appetite disturbances.

Every group leader has favorite exploratory questions on a variety of relevant issues. "When were you first aware of this problem?" "What would you guess is behind this conflict?" "What have you tried to do so far to work on this concern?" "How are you feeling right now?" "What are your favorite defensive strategies when you feel threatened?" "How do you believe we could best help you?" Some therapists don't find it necessary to gather any information at all— just a clear statement of the presenting problem. In any event, before change efforts can be accurately aimed, a preliminary target must be set up. Although the initially stated concern rarely ends up being the real problem, it is a starting point for further investigation.

14. *Catharsis.* It was Freud's original intent that his "talking cure" would form the basis for a new therapy of the mind. The ego and its defense mechanisms form a protective barrier, an immunological system, that fights off undesirable elements from releasing psychic energy stored up in the unconscious and the repressed id. Today, the orthodox psychoanalyst, as well as most forms of group treatment, agree that Aristotle's concept of *catharsis,* or purging of the spirit, serves a useful purpose for clients, although it can sometimes be used as a ready excuse for therapists who don't know how to do anything else.

Haley (1980) cynically advises therapists who understand the scientific basis of diagnosis and research, know the theories of personality, development, and general systems, understand how to pass licensing or school tests, but cannot figure out how to cause change in clients: when in doubt, cathart. "The general procedure used by most experienced therapists who don't know how to cause change is to encourage the client to talk and talk on the gamble that this will cause improvement" (Haley, 1980, p. 386). Strangely enough, this *does* appear to have beneficial effects in a great many cases. As soon as group members begin to share their concerns, immediately the fears diminish and warm feelings of relief wash over.

When group members share in great detail the disturbing elements of their lives, their frustrations and disappointments, or their self-defeating behaviors, the group leader will inevitably rely on therapeutic interventions such as active listening to encourage the full expression of these thoughts and feelings. And it is true that an expression of serenity often accompanies release of this previously stifled bile. Finally, whether it is used in the Rogerian sense of clarifying and expressing feelings to other group members or in the Freudian sense of releasing psychic energy, catharsis is nevertheless timed to occur during appropriate intervals. "Ventilating one's feelings in an empty closet or in a group of strangers is hardly helpful" (Yalom, 1970, p. 72).

15. *Group support and initial feedback.* It is just after an intense verbal barrage that a group member most needs to be reinforced for taking interpersonal risks and disclosing difficult material, and it is at this point that structures for providing feedback are ordinarily employed. Clients receive supportive messages (and sometimes constructive suggestions) that their teary-eyed behavior was both appropriate and productive. Nonverbal confronting gestures often come into play for the first time, though certainly this critical incident is also a time for reflection. The group-member-in-focus sighs in relief with the realization that the first great obstacle has been surmounted.

Carin feels better, not only because she finally told caring people about what has been plaguing her all these months, but because she has had the first definite signal that help is forthcoming. The other group members did not laugh. On the contrary, they indicated great warmth, kindness, and empathy, even unrestrained admiration because she had taken a great risk by disclosing her personal feelings. Carin beams, gathering strength for the next round of tension. But the other group members begin to squirm because they realize that Carin had been speaking for them as well.

16. *Mutual identification, sharing and spectatoring.* Human beings seem to have a morbid fascination for watching others in trouble. In the Roman Coliseum as in the Superdome, we pay extravagantly to support gladiators in real or mock fights. Spectators get vicarious thrills imagining that they are the heroes struggling in a land-acquisition game like football or in a soap opera that makes our own troubles seem minor. Our expressways get clogged when accidents occur, not so much from wrecked cars as from curious onlookers who slow down hoping to catch a glimpse of blood.

In therapeutic groups, the thrill in watching members with conflicts comes not from the attitude "better you than me" but from the powerful realization that we all share similar concerns. Cohesion develops during this phase. People start feeling closer to one another, lose their sense of alienation, as they identify with a common issue. After all, what person has not had problems controlling negative oral habits, fears of failure, sexual fantasies, and other prevalent themes?

Every time a person makes a statement, shares a fear, or is addressed by the leader, everyone else internalizes the implicatons, asking: What does this have to do with me? Do I have a similar concern? How can I apply similar principles to my own life? It is strange that by watching other people change, we in turn change as well. When exploration of any client concern is completed, every person in the group has identified similar issues, shared them aloud, and offered support to the client struggling to change.

Stage III: Insight

On the matrix for change presented earlier, the opposite ends of the theoretical pole are represented by group strategies that emphasize "Insight" or "Action." Many group leaders unconditionally accept this dichotomy, aligning themselves with either an approach that focuses on plans, techniques, and other action strategies or an approach that encourages self-awareness, discovery, exploration, and self-understanding. The insightists assume that knowledge of the problem will make it go away. On this issue, David Viscott comments:

> Understanding how and why you are a rat won't change the fact that you're a rat who irritates the hell out of people, unless you do something about it. Some patients who use therapy to get a complete understanding of everything in their life and still don't change can and often do use therapy as a weapon (Viscott, 1972, p. 114).

The compromise position taken in this book, and emphasized in the following stages, is that *insight is a necessary but insufficient condition alone to produce change.* By teaching group members a set of practical skills without helping them to understand how and why they work, we deprive them of the opportunity to create their own strategies for handling new concerns in the future. Insight strategies, on the other hand, may be wonderfully enlightening in that they provide a form of relevant education; however, they may, at best,

merely waste time and, at worst, disorient and confuse. If the pragmatic group leader incorporated only as much functional insight as
is necessary for clients to understand how and why they are having
difficulties and then focused on practical action strategies for changing specific behaviors, a perfect balance would be achieved.

17. *Challenge irrational assumptions.* As a starting point, it is sometimes helpful to highlight the underlying self-sabotaging assumptions that result in undesired behavior. Albert Ellis (1977a) identified
many of the themes that pervade irrational thinking, such as exaggerating reality, demanding that the world be different, or judging
others or oneself according to absolute standards. Whether sympathetic to the methods of rational-emotive therapy (RET) or not, one
cannot be blind to the usefulness of adapting parts of the theory to
promoting self-understanding. Ellis (1974), for instance, identifies
several crucial insights that he believes group members must have
before permanent change can occur. Clients are thus helped to understand that it is their thoughts that are triggering unwanted feelings and that these may be altered by challenging the underlying
irrational assumptions.

While the RET clinician makes deliberate, repeated, and systematic
interpretations of certain irrational assumptions, all group leaders do
essentially the same thing, though less rigidly. When a group member
talks of being consistently late because his job keeps him from punc-
tuality, we begin to question the validity of this faulty assumption.
When another client complains that she can't help being promiscu-
ous because she has Italian blood on her father's side, we challenge
that assumption. And when a group member expects everyone else
to devote unlimited time every session to working on a single concern, that unrealistic assumption is examined. The fact is that all
practitioners have a favorite list of recurrent assumptions that they
are fond of challenging to initiate the process of insight.

18. *Confrontation with inconsistencies.* The self-understanding
process that begins with an analysis of illogical thinking patterns
continues when discrepancies in behavior are pointed out. With
great diplomacy, clients are helped to examine their statements
within the context of other messages they have communicated. The
skilled Gestalt group leader is fond of isolating examples in which a
client's words say one thing while body language communicates
quite another. Other times, group members will contradict previous

statements with verbalizations that are inconsistent. In any case in which group members act, think, or feel in ways that appear to be shallow or deceiving, the therapist will attempt nonthreateningly to bring such behaviors to conscious awareness.

There are, of course, distinct differences between how people see themselves, how others see them, how they believe others see them, and how they really are. Internal congruence, consistency between internal and external behavior, and authenticity are the universal goals for most group leaders working with clients. Yet when interactional inconsistencies enter the picture, demonstrating discrepancies between what people say, what they really mean, what other group members believe they heard, and what was actually said, the potential for exhibiting congruence and consistency is significantly reduced. Joseph Heller's *Catch-22* presents a hilarious dialogue typical of interpersonal incongruence.

Clevinger one day stumbled during a march and the next day found himself confronting a court martial charged with "mopery, ...being a smart guy, listening to classical music," among other things (Heller, 1955, p. 77). The following vignette, with all its comic absurdity, is only slightly exaggerated compared to some of the communication styles we encounter in groups. Clevinger, attempting to defend himself before the tribunal, finds an interpersonal logic different from what he is used to.

> "Just what the hell did you mean, you bastard, when you said we couldn't punish you?"
>
> "I didn't say you couldn't punish me, sir."
>
> "When?" asked the colonel.
>
> "When what, sir?"
>
> "Now you're asking me questions again."
>
> "I'm sorry, sir. I'm afraid I don't understand your question."
>
> "When didn't you say we couldn't punish you? Don't you understand my question?"
>
> "No, sir. I don't understand."
>
> "You've just told us that. Now suppose you answer my question."
>
> "But how can I answer it?"
>
> "That's another question you're asking me."
>
> "I'm sorry, sir. But I don't know how to answer it. I never said you couldn't punish me."
>
> "Now you're telling us when you did say it. I'm asking you to tell us when you didn't say it."
>
> Clevinger took a deep breath. "I always didn't say you couldn't punish me, sir" (Heller, 1955, p. 79).

Only after such gross inconsistencies are confronted can group members and the client-in-focus hope to proceed toward deeper levels of mutual self-understanding and then move on to the action stages of change.

19. *Realization of hidden and unconscious motives.* We are again indebted to the work of Freud for popularizing the role of the unconscious mind in conscious actions. The human brain is so mysterious, who can really claim to understand its complex modus operandi? Who really knows just how important the unconscious motive (if there is such a thing) is in creating problems or affecting change? It is better to be safe than sorry.

Milton Erickson had little tolerance for dynamic techniques of interpretation that bring repressed material to the surface, but he did have great respect for the power of the unconscious mind to promote necessary changes. He would therefore bypass the alert brain and speak instead to its dormant counterpart, sometimes producing magical effects. For patients resistant to hypnosis, Erickson might tap the unlimited powers of the unconscious by asking it direct questions and getting answers.

"Does your unconscious mind think that you can go into a trance?" Further elaboration is offered: "Consciously you cannot know what your unconscious mind thinks or knows. But your unconscious mind can let your conscious mind discover what it thinks or understands by the simple process of causing a levitation of either the right or left hand. Thus your unconscious mind can communicate in a visibly recognizable way with your conscious mind. Now just watch your hands and see what the answer is. Neither you nor I know what your unconscious mind thinks, but as you see one or the other of your hands lifting, you will know" (Erickson, 1967, p. 37).

This pragmatic application of therapy for the unconscious often produces dramatic results, though it still doesn't provide conclusive evidence for the existence of surreptitious motives tucked deep in the cerebral cortex. If, however, we pretend that hidden and disguised motives *do* exist, then we would be well advised to spend some time helping to make these thoughts and feelings more explicitly understood.

20. *Understanding behavioral payoffs and their consequences.* From medical literature we learn of a phenomenon known as *secondary gains* that describes the indirect advantages of a patient's illness

(Stern, 1964). As every hypochondriac well knows, sick people get a lot of attention and pity. They have a ready-made excuse for procrastination, bad temper, any abusive behavior. They can't help it, they're sick; they have a right to feel bad.

In the therapeutic self-understanding process, clients are introduced to the concept that *all* their behaviors have secondary gains, positive as well as negative consequences (Greenwald, 1973; Dyer, 1976). These payoffs create a vicious cycle that make the job of changing that much more difficult to accomplish. In theory, the idea of teaching clients to understand the payoffs of their behavior is fine. In practice, however, the execution can be a bit more complicated.

In a group, a father was on the brink of tears describing a letter from his daughter informing him that she was dropping out of college to get a job. The daughter explained that she was sick and tired of being told what to do with her life and wished to be left alone. The father was riddled with guilt. Conceivably, he could be feeling proud that his daughter had the courage to do this difficult thing, but both pride and his daughter were the furthest things from his mind. He was playing back the record of his encounters with her and all the things he had done wrong. He shouldn't have pushed her so hard. He should have spent more time with her. He shouldn't have gotten the divorce or let her go so far away to school. It was all his fault; he had ruined her life, and now he would have to suffer for these unpardonable sins.

The group leader implemented a strategy in which he asked the father to repeat the stem sentence "The great thing about feeling guilty is. . .," and members of the group would help him list possible payoffs that prevented him from changing his feelings (Dyer & Vriend, 1980).

The great thing about feeling guilty is:
- you can torture yourself for errors you feel you made and hope that this suffering wipes the slate clean.
- you can bloat your sense of self-importance. After all, you are totally responsible.
- you can avoid thinking about *your* problems as long as you focus on your daughter's.
- you can convey to others how much you care for your daughter in being so willing to take the blame for her actions.
- you can feel like a victim betrayed by an ungrateful child.
- you can get lots of sympathy from others because you act like this tragedy happened to *you*.

In this group, the technique worked flawlessly. When I had the opportunity to practice it at a later date, however, it happened to be during counseling with an individual client. She was duly educated about how and why payoffs work and could readily see how important it was to understand them. But when it came time to finish the stem sentence and the client was predictably speechless, I nervously looked over my shoulder for help from group members and recalled that, alas, we were alone. It was then that I determined to learn the common behavioral payoffs for every self-defeating action.

Basically, most examples of client suffering exhibit five common themes which therapists can isolate to facilitate the process of self-understanding (Kottler, 1979). These themes are:

- procrastination
- avoiding risks
- retreating from the present
- avoiding responsibility for one's actions
- avoiding work or having to change

By making hidden secondary gains more explicit, we essentially rob group members of their well-worn excuses for resisting efforts to change.

21. *Reassurance and peer support.* Along with the gift of insight is the associated pain of self-revelation. It hurts to discover how blind we have been, how ignorant and unaware of ideas that now appear obvious. In addition, understanding how and why personal troubles have been so persistently bothersome leads inevitably to the conclusion that some action must be taken. There is no longer any place to seek refuge. Excuses for avoiding change now sound so feeble that not even the client believes them. Before panic can set in and the flight impulse becomes too strong, the group's support system once again takes prominence. Members draw on their vast reservoir of concern and empathy to offer reassurance to their peer who is struggling with novel learnings.

22. *Generalization to other behaviors.* One final twitch of insight is necessary before the change process moves forward toward concrete action. Most behavior is representative of a theme prevalent throughout a client's total being. If Fred has difficulty developing intimacy with other group members, he probably has similar problems of mistrust in other relationships. He avoids taking risks in his

job, preferring predictable routines to more innovative productivity. He rarely deviates from his usual paths of travel while driving. He avoids unfamiliar parts of town, reasoning that if he had car trouble he would be stuck without help.

In short, Fred realizes that his drive for self-reliance and avoidance of any possible vulnerability, such as his behavior in the group attests, is altogether typical of his style. The knock-out punch! Fred not only gains insight into the self-defeating mechanisms that keep him hanging back in the group but learns that he engages in similar behavior throughout his life. The same irrational assumptions, closed-circuit traps, behavioral payoffs, and hidden motives that sabotage his efforts to change within the group hold true for actions outside the group as well.

Stage IV: Action
23. *Motivational support.* The transition between insight and action change processes, however discreetly they are implemented, will inevitably produce ambivalence and resistance in the client. With the realization that there is no turning back to the previously ineffective coping strategies, coupled with the increased self-knowledge as to why the self-defeating behaviors have persisted, the client understands that a great many things will have to change. As attractive as the new order of thinking appears, however, the client also wistfully reminisces about the old self being left behind. There is also the significant prospect that what lies ahead will involve excruciatingly difficult efforts to put the accrued insights to work.

The group leader attempts to be helpful by being more nurturing and supportive, acting as the coach to a dozen cheerleaders who simultaneously cry "You can do it!" After a while, even the client will begin to believe it.

24. *Decision to change.* Just as much energy is expended to *evade* making decisions as in dealing with them, no matter how impending, crucial, or how dire the consequences may be (Janis & Mann, 1977). And no wonder: there is always so much to lose. No matter what decision is made, there is always the possibility of committing the eighth deadly sin—making a mistake.

The decision to change ought to be the logical conclusion of the previous group work stages, which involved a sort of brainstorming. This problem-solving procedure, originally developed for use in industrial settings by Clark (1958) and Osborn (1963), has been found to be an optimal strategy for increasing productivity and creativity (Bayless, 1967; Parnes, 1967). Brainstorming, which has been used to invent such consumer products as the flashcube, has wide implications for the decision-making that occurs in therapeutic groups. The accepting, open environment, high motivation of participants, and emphasis on free thinking provide a perfect setting for committing oneself to constructive action.

25. *Commitment to group.* There is nothing like a public statement to commit oneself to a course of action. With the possible exception of politicians, who give themselves permission to change their minds according to where their support is coming from, most people find that by verbally disclosing their intentions they will find it difficult to deviate from their course of action. The motive to change increases proportionately with the magnitude of commitment. If a group member tells many people vehemently that she intends to quit her job and try a new career, it is unlikely that she will be able to avoid that path should she change her mind in midstream. Too many people are watching.

Before clients commit themselves to change, they must be reasonably certain that they are doing so for themselves rather than to please significant others. At this stage in the change process, the commitment usually takes the form of a client voicing the results of his decision making in a way similar to the declaration of commitment that took place earlier when group participants shared the concerns they were having trouble coping with.

In one group, before Aaron had the opportunity to formulate a systematic plan of attack, he spontaneously decided to declare that he was going to make some changes in his life. After absentmindedly attending to a session dealing with another client, he blurted out in the middle of a reflective pause that he would have some good news to report the following week. The group leader redirected the focus to the original client, promising to get back to Aaron's outburst but never had the time to do so. Nevertheless, the next week, in spite of getting no specific help Aaron made his dramatic report.

"You may not believe this, but in the last week my whole life has changed. I decided that I had had enough of living a sham, being dependent on people around me. After the last group meeting I wanted to back down but realized that I had already committed myself to act, even if you didn't know exactly what I was going to do. At the time, I didn't either. Anyway, today you are looking at an unattached, unemployed, but *very* happy person. This week I broke my engagement, quit my job, sold all my possessions, told my parents to leave me alone, and decided to start my life over again."

26. *Brainstorming of alternative courses of action.* In the process of change, group members help one another to expand the choices available to them. All therapists attempt to remove obstructions that limit a client's perceived options in the world. While these obstructions may include distorting reality, "disasterizing," lack of confidence, impoverished perceptual fields, unrealistic expectations, or inhibiting destructive emotions, the goal of all psychological treatment is to give clients alternatives to their self-defeating strategies.

A group setting is particularly facilitative in this regard because the collective experience of a number of individuals is sure to generate viable options. Group members are trained to think scientifically when asked to reason through the decision-making process in an analytic way. Janis and Mann (1977) go so far as to specify seven major criteria that should be considered in "high-quality" decisions. The client should:

   A.   review the widest possible range of alternatives available, initially including even far-out choices in the hope that they could turn out to be feasible

   B.   examine the desired objectives and the implications of each alternative for the client's personal value system

   C.   systematically consider the positive and negative consequences that could conceivably result from each choice. Goldfried and Goldfried (1980) further recommend looking at both the personal and social consequences of each action as well as proposed short-term and long-term effects.

   D.   explore any relevant information that might shed light on alternatives

   E.   integrate new information

   F.   reexamine the consequences of each alternative

   G.   develop contingency plans to cope with known risks and hazards

Many group members experience a liberating feeling just knowing that other choices exist. There is a great difference between choosing to stay in a frustrating job or marriage and feeling trapped as if there were no other viable option. Bateson's (1956) concept of the "double-bind" that drives kids into schizophrenia is an extreme example of the *logical* results of a lack of perceived choice.

Okun and Rappaport (1980) describe one possibility of this trap: A family consists of a girl, her mother, and father. The parents constantly nag the daughter about not showing them enough affection. Whenever she attempts to show affection, the parents scream at her for invading their privacy. When she retreats to show consideration for their privacy, she is berated for ignoring them and not showing affection. The girl is only 10 years old and so cannot leave the home. What choice is there for her except schizophrenia? When group members feel similarly trapped, we teach them that their own limiting state of mind creates the problem. By expanding the range of possible alternatives we free clients from the slavery of the status quo.

27. *Information giving and guidance.* When E.G. Williamson, C.G. Wrenn, and Donald Super were in their prime, group work was synonymous with giving advice and instruction. For educational and career planning, there were few better ways to impart useful information than in a group setting in which discussion could take place.

In most therapeutic groups today, there comes a time when the leader and members offer constructive guidance to one another. If a member is seriously considering going to law school, it would be appropriate for relevant information, such as potential job opportunities, to be imparted. If a recently married person who is having conflicts in her relationship is seriously considering divorce, it would be helpful for her to understand what the process will involve.

Group guidance can be particularly valuable in the area of sexual dysfunction. In the instance of one couple, the wife felt frustrated because the husband was perfectly content until she complained. One day while watching the "Phil Donahue Show" the woman heard a sex expert casually mention the topic of female orgasm. The woman was dumbstruck: "Women have orgasms too? Oh my God, there's something wrong with me. I better get some help."

Reluctantly, the husband accompanied his distraught wife to the therapeutic group and eventually their problem came out. When questioned about what sex was like for them, the woman replied with embarrassment: "I don't know. Just like everyone else, I guess. Usually I'll be doing housework, watching TV or something, and he will clear his throat and point his finger toward the stairs. Then, you know, I pull down my pants and he undoes his zipper and puts it in me. How long does the whole thing take? Quite a long time, sometimes even a few minutes." When the laughter subsided, then stopped abruptly as group members realized she was serious, helpful information was provided on the importance of foreplay (including the revelation that such an activity exists). Simply revealing some tenets of basic sex education was enough to resolve their problem.

28. *Goal setting.* When all possible courses of action have been narrowed to a few viable options, the client's goals are specified according to his/her value system, constitution, and desired consequences. Again, the development of an appropriate goal involves the interactive contributions of all participants. It is to be hoped that this goal represents the logical culmination of all previous therapeutic efforts. Ideally, it should be as realistic as possible so that the client may have the greatest probability of success in reaching desired outcomes.

The formulated goals also function as a pre-test for evaluating the relative success of the treatment plan. For this reason, group member goals should include a systematic format in which the overall group goals are specifically defined as individual subgoals for each participant, behavioral objectives are defined, priorities are ordered, and incomplete objectives are eliminated (Ryan, 1973). The group leader's task at this juncture is to ensure that momentum is carried forth to accomplish the stated goals (Krumboltz & Potter, 1973).

29. *Formulation of plan.* As a direct result of the previous decision making, alternative generating, and goal-setting procedures, group members are now prepared to aid in the formulation of a therapeutic plan designed to resolve the stated concerns. Such a blueprint might take the form of skill acquisition, structured risk taking, response decrement, environmental alterations, cognitive restructuring, or response increment (Gottman & Leiblum, 1974). In any case, the clients determine the strategy that is most likely to lead to a satisfactory conclusion.

After considering several viable options, Angela has decided that confronting her boss with a complaint will do no good since this supervisor has not responded well in the past to even the gentlest of constructive criticism. Going above her supervisor's head would probably only make things more tense. Practicing assertive skills in the group, confronting other members in a nonthreatening manner, would be good practice, but Angela is already an accomplished confronter. Finally it is determined that the best strategy would be to focus on Angela's internal behaviors—her unrealistic expectations, demanding attitude that others live by her rules, and perfectionistic standards. Angela decides that she could profit by learning to relax, to calm herself down when she feels herself losing her cool with the boss. She could practice dealing with her supervisor in the same manner she has so far but *feeling* differently about the experience.

30. *Reality testing.* As an extra check on the plan's suitability, Angela and her co-members critically pick apart the program's components. They predict the likely consequences; they determine risks, short- and long-term benefits. In this process of reality testing it is discovered that at weekly departmental meetings it would be unrealistic for Angela to keep her mouth shut and concentrate instead on doing her own excellent work; she feels morally bound to try to change aspects of the work situation that are not in the employees' best interests. It is not realistic for her to be exclusively concerned with her own frustrations because she feels a sense of responsibility to help her less articulate colleagues who would suffer even more without her support. These reality-testing dialogues enable group members to make some necessary revisions.

31. *Rehearsal.* The greatest overall benefit of group work is the emphasis placed on the realistic practice of self-enhancing behaviors. As an experimental laboratory with controlled conditions, the group setting provides clients with structured rehearsal sessions. Criticism and other self-indulgent practices are minimized. Attempts are made to make these therapeutic simulations as like the real world as possible.

In psychodrama and role-playing techniques, the group leader acts as director, setting the stage, helping the client to cast antagonists and to write the script (Moreno, 1964). Group members are allowed spontaneously to confront their real conflicts in a reasonably safe situation; their performances may later be analyzed by their understudies and director.

Rehearsal of internal behaviors, such as of Angela's goals, may also be practiced before the client is thrown to the wolves. Participants may keep a journal to practice thinking in new ways, internalizing novel ideas, and to combat inhibiting fears. One group member used her journal as a vehicle for imagery rehearsal, practicing what she would say to herself and to her husband when they met in divorce court.

32. *Constructive feedback.* Rehearsing new skills is meaningless unless group members can learn how well or badly they performed and how their behaviors may be made more effective in the future.

Feedback is used to reinforce desirable actions while extinguishing those, such as yelling, that consistently create problems. Rehearsed feedback is also helpful for providing data on the effects the client has on others when certain behaviors are used. It motivates group members to continue trying the things that tend to work.

Feedback from the group leader or other members should follow certain guidelines.

A. It should be clearly expressed in terms and language to which the client-in-focus can best relate.

B. It should be expressive and personalized so that it does not come across as a cliché or stereotype.

C. It should be concise, reducing the essence of a message into efficient words.

D. It should be as specific as possible, labeling the target behaviors and supporting them with examples.

E. It should be given as soon after the rehearsed behaviors as possible to maximize reinforcement principles.

F. It should be given with a specific rationale in mind; i.e., to point out an inconsistency or offer a suggestion.

G. It should be honest, avoiding watered-down truths, predictable statements, or comments designed to score approval-seeking points.

H. It should be diplomatically confrontive, straightforward without being needlessly provocative. The delivery of the message is at least as important as its content.

I. It should be sensitively expressed, capitalizing on empathy variables like kindness, respect, and acceptance.

J. It should include both constructive criticism *and* constructive support rather than being given in a context of positive and negative.

The use of feedback in groups is limitless. It is one of the best services provided throughout the sessions and various therapeutic stages because it is so rare to get helpful, honest feedback in the real world. Perhaps the most difficult task is for the group leader to elicit constructive feedback that meets the above criteria.

33. *Psychological homework. Homework* is an unfortunate word evoking images of forgotten assignments, teachers' red-marked corrections, and repetitive busy work. It is not unknown for a group member to flush in indignation when a careless therapist comments:

"That's an area you could work on. Why don't you do that as a homework assignment for next week?" Just as students "forget" to hand in their papers or recklessly scribble some half-hearted last-minute effort, some clients act similarly, usually because of a lack of commitment to complete something that another person has authoritatively assigned. When assignments are mutually determined and the reasons behind the work are clearly understood, the successful completion of tasks is more likely.

We are well aware of the intrinsic difficulties in practicing group work: that our clients often become dependent on us or become group junkies; that they learn to perform like zoo animals, acting only when there are spectators throwing peanuts; that the hard-fought effects of therapy are short-lived. To counteract these problems, the therapist attempts to structure ingenious ways to get clients working on their own time, practicing in their worlds, where it counts, what they have learned in the group. "Thus, practice leads to improvement, and improvement leads to increased practice" (Palmer, 1980, p. 174).

To facilitate the transfer of learning from the group situation to the client's world, group members are helped to create and follow through on homework of a special kind. These assignments should be self-initiated (Cormier & Cormier, 1979), mutually negotiated with the therapist and other members (Dyer & Vriend, 1977), and involve fairly attainable and realistic tasks. They should contain a "do statement" specifying what the task is to be, and a "quantity statement" declaring how often the behavior will be practiced (Shelton & Ackerman, 1974).

34. *Commitment to action.* Once insight is gained into the concern, goals are set, a plan of action is established, relevant skills are rehearsed, and outside work is determined, a final commitment is made in the group to follow through with stated intentions. Mutual support and discussion usually result in several other members making silent or public commitments to initiate desired changes. Clients who are competitive by nature, or who constantly compare themselves to others as a yardstick for measuring their own self-worth, will now use their neurotic drives for productive purposes:

"What a boring group tonight. I've been sitting here for the past two
    hours talking to myself just like this. I can't believe Nadine is
    finally going to get off her butt and read her husband the riot act.

So he is selfish, demanding, spoiled, and insensitive. Big deal. I wonder if she realizes what a good thing she's got going? I wouldn't take that crap if someone treated me that way. Except from my mother. So she gets a bit carried away sometimes. It's not so bad. I can live with it. I'd just love to see a weakie like Nadine try and tell off my mother when she gets in one of her moods. Actually, it might be quite a show. Nadine has fire in her eyes that has never been there before. Well, hell, if she can do it, so can I. Maybe it's time for me to finally tell my mother to get off my back."

Aloud: "Yea, I have something I could work on too."

35. *Closure.* Closure comes next—end of session. We learn in graduate school that closures should be perfectly timed and paced. First we tie up loose ends, then elicit summary statements from clients concerning what they learned and what they will work on between sessions. After the debriefing and gradual decompression adjustment to re-entering the real world, we give our final speech, timing its end with the sweep of the second hand so that members leave the group with a sense of completion.

Inadvertently, however, we have also discovered advantages to another form of closure: none. Because we forgot to watch the time and a crowd of people is clamoring to use our room, we are forced to interrupt interaction in the middle with an apology: "I'm sorry, folks, but we seem to be out of time. We'll pick up with this next week." The clients, of course, grumble; they feel as if they've been left hanging on a hook. But then a strange thing happens: as dissonance rises, group members think about the group proceedings more often than usual during the week. They must resolve their own closure in the face of many dangling ends that don't fit together.

There is thus a rationale for choosing a method of closure, depending on intended goals. Tying things in a neat package or deliberately programming a healthy amount of chaos may both serve clients well.

36. *Real world practice.* This, the most important part of therapy, does not occur in the group. The rehearsal is over, and the live performance begins before an intensely critical audience. If preparation has been sufficient, the clients will successfully complete their therapeutic tasks, internalize novel ideas, apply their newly acquired skills, and practice thinking in more fully functioning ways. The use of adjunct structures, such as those described in Chapter 14, are also helpful at this stage.

Stage V: Evaluation

37. *Progress report.* Before any new business is taken up, the group leader will check out and evaluate the progress of group members who previously received counseling time. Clients will report what they have worked on, to what degree they have met their objectives, and how they feel about their experiences. "Are you on the right track?" "Which parts were most difficult for you?" "What unexpected problems did you encounter?" "How do you feel now about what you have done?" "What do you plan to do next to follow up on this progress?"

38. *Additional input and modifications.* Seldom do things go according to plan, no matter how meticulous the preparations. Unexpected variables always crop up. People never seem to co-operate as they are supposed to. At this stage, the leader and group members briefly offer input and elicit client reactions to departures from the intended path. "Just how effective were the planned interventions in light of your goals?" "Are your goals still the same?" "What modifications in your plan are necessary?"

Ordinarily, a transition will be made from this externally framed evaluation pattern to a self-monitoring orientation in which group members may now independently follow and control their own progress. Gottman and Lieblum (1974) favor the use of tools like "The Annotated Record," studying concomitant variations in graphic displays, Stewart Charts, or even calculating autocorrelations to determine the specific impacts of planned interventions. Group leaders less behaviorally inclined will devise similar strategies to ensure that group members follow through on their initial work.

39. *Reinforcement.* In addition to the self-satisfaction that results from accomplishing a difficult task, group members receive healthy doses of peer respect and praise. Sometimes it is just the anticipation of how great it will feel to tell group members about how well you performed and to acknowledge their laudatory comments that act as a final impetus for implementing difficult changes. The reward-enriched milieu of a group allows the "cure" to be maintained throughout subsequent sessions.

40. *Finger on the pulse.* Subsequent sessions will provide numerous additional opportunities for group members to refine and practice the behaviors they are working to master.

That Kafka's Gregor Samsa became metamorphosed into an insect, never adjusted to his group norm, and finally died to avoid becoming a burden to those around him attests to the complex issues involved in the alteration of a single organism. From a human being understood and approved to an alien creature, an insect, Gregor symbolizes all that is mysterious and unknown about the process by which people change.

Chapter 3 has aimed at integrating the most prominent and useful learning theories into a comprehensive, flexible explanation of how people change in groups. The action-theory-in-use is no more or less than a functional description of what most group leaders do in their groups. It is not itself a static, stable concept but a metamorphic phenomenon. When group leader personality variables, training experiences, goals, and unique group member needs and interests are added to the formula, the theory of change takes on quite a different surface structure, with its own language, techniques, and preferred strategies. But the underlying structure of most group approaches remains the same. This final chapter of Part One completes discussion of the interwoven threads that bind group helping systems together.

PART 2

Dimensions of Group Leadership

There are certain attributes of the leader, specific reasoning processes and appropriate roles, that are more likely to promote desired outcomes. Therapists who are effective models, who capitalize on imitative learning processes, who skillfully use their bodies, language, and the ways they live their lives as examples of a masterful existence, will, ultimately, enhance the power of their interventions. The specific ways in which leaders communicate their modes of thinking and reasoning, their methods of dealing with problems and conflict, their styles of interacting with clients or colleagues, will also provide groups with a more therapeutically charged atmosphere.

CHAPTER 4

Following the Leader

A tribal ritual among certain South American societies is literally to eat the brains, therefore the spirit, of enemies defeated in battle. They believe that consuming the courage and knowledge of their vanquished foes enhances their prowess as warriors. In modern Western society, we worship our heroes instead of eating them. Recording artists, movie stars, athletes, and writers are paid seven-figure yearly salaries to act as heroes for us. We seek their autographs, pay homage to them, and glorify them to a level above our own. To select and follow heroes or mentors appears to be a human drive.

A *mentor* is a wise adviser, a guide, a sponsor, a teacher of the protégé, a transitional figure who encompasses the virtues of competence, wisdom, ethics, and success. Levinson believes the mentor relationship to be crucial to an individual's development through the seasons of life: "The relationship enables the recipient to identify with a person who exemplifies many of the qualities he seeks. It enables him to form an internal figure who offers love, admiration, and encouragement in his struggles" (Levinson, 1978, p. 334).

THERAPEUTIC MODELING

The importance of the roles that significant models play in people's lives cannot be underestimated. While reductionist learning theorists would have us believe that the human race is shaped by satisfiers, reinforcers, need hierarchies, antecedent determinants, or all varieties of different stimuli-response chains, many other powerful forces facilitate human growth and development as well. In addition to the genetic scripts that program how humans evolve and the sequential stages of cognitive reasoning of which developmental theorists are so fond, there are other, intuitive answers to the question, How did I get to be who I am?

We are all constantly on the lookout for new people to admire, to learn from, to study and imitate. Merchandisers, fashion specialists, and marketing personnel understand this, playing up to the compelling attractiveness of models in the media who are deliberately created to exhibit the dimensions of power that Bandura (1977) has found most seductive. Thus, models displaying their nurturance capabilities attract attention to aspirin or laxatives. Paid actors dress up in white lab coats with an assortment of pencils in their pockets, a stethoscope around their necks, and proclaim "Tests in a major hospital found—". However silly their appeal, we *do* buy their products. Models who exhibit striking physical or sexual power command even more attention and influence.

In a narrow sense, therapeutic modeling in groups can be regarded as an extension of social learning theory. The group leader attempts to maximize attentional, retentional, and motor reproduction processes that occur in imitative learning mechanisms. Once a client has been motivated to observe the modeled behavior, is helped to retain the image and to rehearse it symbolically, the pathway is cleared for actual execution of the duplicated behavior in real-life situations. This paradigm is familiar to the group helping model since members are regularly encouraged to experiment with new skills they have witnessed within the safety of the group. Psychodrama and role playing aid rehearsal efforts; support and feedback from peers act as reinforcers to perpetuate the imitated behaviors and to facilitate the internal cognitions necessary for generalization and integration to occur.

It is no less one-dimensional to think of therapeutic modeling as a collection of philosophically compatible techniques that produce similar outcomes. No doubt the clinical technology that has emerged from social learning theory has produced significant advances in the practitioner's repertoire. The techniques of covert modeling (Cautela, 1976), symbolic modeling (Reeder & Kunce, 1976), vicarious reinforcement (Bandura, 1969), vicarious desensitization (Ritter, 1968), participant modeling (Bandura, Jeffrey, & Gajdos, 1975), self-modeling (Hosford & de Visser, 1974), and emotive imagery (Lazarus & Abramowitz, 1962) have helped to make the group leader's job much easier when introducing novel concepts to clients who need them.

Historically, every therapeutic pioneer from Hippocrates to Freud has made systematic use of his personality as a means of encouraging mimicry by patients. The use of anecdotal material so common to the psychoanalyst, of self-disclosure by the Rogerian, of semantic demonstrations by the rational-emotive group leader are all examples of explicit modeling in action. Regardless of theoretical affilia-

tions then, all group leaders today tell "therapeutic" stories, construct metaphors, and relate successful encounters showing that
their methods work. Most group leaders rely on role playing as a
major strategy, demonstrating appropriate skills for effective living,
hoping that group members will incorporate the strategies by having
observed them. They also believe in one of the principal strengths of
group work: while one client is receiving specific help, most of the
others are learning by watching.

That group members make constructive changes in their lives
merely as the result of observing others doing so seems to be a very
tenuous assumption. Yet we notice that often it is the participants
who say the least that grow the most. While one client tearfully
relates her struggle to break free of her husband's dominance, the
others sit quietly. She promises to make some changes during
the coming week—to assert her independence, confront the insensitive spouse, to think differently about her situation—yet she returns
having had only minimal success. The real magic of the situation lies
in what the other clients have to report:

"Well, at the time, last week seemed incredibly tedious to me. I
kept wandering and drifting, looking at my watch, hoping the session would end. It wasn't until I got home that I realized how closely her situation parallels mine. I guess I was afraid to pay attention
because while you were talking to her, you were talking to me, too.
Well, anyway, I sat down with my wife and straightened some things
out. I'm tired of being pushed around, too!"

Strangest of all is that we take these incidents for granted. The
veteran is seldom surprised when people on the right make an
about-face though the leader is talking to someone over on the left.
Putting therapeutic modeling to work in groups has become auto-
matic. The group leader rarely makes a conscious decision to model
a little here or model a little there. The subtle and spontaneous
aspects of one's personality, the personal effectiveness that is displayed by one's characteristic style, are as much facilitative forces as
the most deliberate technical intervention.

A FULLY FUNCTIONING MODEL

The single thread that binds together all effective group practitioners
is certainly not their unanimous allegiance to a particular theoretical
approach. At first glance, master group leaders such as Fritz Perls,

Eric Berne, Carl Rogers, and Albert Ellis would appear to have little in common. Their therapeutic goals, favorite techniques, underlying philosophies, and leader roles contradict one another. Yet they all project to their clients an image of a formidable individual who is fully in charge of his personal world. They exude self-confidence, expertise, worldly experience, and serenity.

Carl Rogers is the prototype of a warm, sensitive, caring, and genuine human being, precisely the characteristics he considers to be crucial to the therapeutic relationship. Albert Ellis walks around rationally engrossed, the epitome of an internally controlled, logical person who can cure himself of any emotional suffering. Freud, Adler, and Perls were also incredibly dynamic personalities, scientists who took great pains to practice what they preached. Their legacy to contemporary group practice is found in the behavior of every pragmatic group leader. Behind every exciting, beneficial group experience is an energetic, knowledgeable, skilled, and enthusiastic leader.

There is surprising agreement among writers who have sought to list the attributes considered to be crucial to the ideal leader-model. The themes of self-awareness, emotional stability, neutrality, flexibility, and similar variables reappear again and again. The list of group leader characteristics offered in this chapter comprises a composite portrait of the ideal model. Each dimension of personal mastery represents a specific behavior that every group leader is in the process of upgrading. This composite conception has been constructed from the writings of Maslow (1954); Kottler, Vriend, and Dyer (1974); Corey and Corey (1977); Trotzer (1977); and Kottler (1978).

Personal mastery is a relative concept, one that takes into consideration the potentialities, goals, expectations, resources, and limitations of any given individual, although there is a consistent image regarding what constitutes the characteristics of such a person. The personally masterful group leader is one who has attained a state of fluid movement through life, who works toward higher levels of proficiency in every human action, who is always involved in a process of formulating goals to work toward. This group leader is the kind of person toward whom others gravitate because of a reservoir of inner strength, quiet competence, and compassionate spirit.

What is personal mastery but the development of skills necessary for a happy existence? A personally effective human being is in control of his life, goals, dreams, and destiny. This is what Abraham

Maslow (1954) meant by the term "self-actualized," what Fyodor Dostoyevsky (1864) described as a person of "acute consciousness," and
what Ambrose Bierce (1911) defined as a "fool":

> A person who pervades the domain of intellectual speculation and
> diffuses himself through the channels of moral activity. He is om-
> nific, omniform, omnipercipient, omniscient, omnipotent. It was
> he who invented letters, printing, the railroad, the steamboat, the
> telegraph, the platitude, and the circle of sciences. He created
> patriotism and taught the nations war—founded theology,
> philosophy, law, medicine, and Chicago . . . In the morning of time
> he sang upon primitive hills, and in the noonday of existence
> headed the procession of being. His grandmotherly hand was
> warmly tucked in the set sun of civilization, and in the twilight he
> prepares Man's evening meal of milk-and-morality and turns down
> the covers of the universal grave. And after the rest of us shall have
> retired for the night of eternal oblivion he will sit up to write a
> history of civilization (Bierce, 1911. pp. 43 – 44).

Personally masterful therapists are busy persons, intensely concerned with their well-being and that of their fellow humans. They
are action-oriented truth seekers who pursue the unknown and take
productive risks in the search for a more satisfying life. Most important, they are in a continual state of improved change, ever working
to become more personally masterful.

In addition, there are some corollary assumptions implicit in the
personal mastery model.

1. The more personally skilled group leaders become, the more
professionally effective they become.

2. The group leader is in a constant state of change, as are all
group members. Each client concern and interaction conflict forces
the leader to look inward, asking the question, Have I worked this
problem through for myself? While using group time to work through
personal struggles is clearly unethical, the group leader cannot help
but use the time between sessions to personalize relevant struggles
to bring them toward successful closure.

3. The more effective group leaders become at solving personal
problems, the better teachers they can be at facilitating such outcomes in clients. The group leader should have learned ahead of
time how to work through any concern with which a group member
may have difficulty.

4. No mere human has ever reached perfection. Every group
leader ought to be engaged in a rigorous self-training process aimed

at teaching higher levels of personal mastery. Identifying behaviors in need of improvement is the first step in making constructive changes. The following list of characteristics will aid group leaders in self-evaluation.

Self-Confidence
Group leaders who have faith in their therapeutic powers transmit this contagious attitude to their observant clients. Therapy takes place between two believers (Fish, 1973). Before group members can realistically hope for progress, they must fervently believe in the leader's skill. A level of self-assurance balanced by realistic modesty seems necessary to gain and keep a client's confidence. The group leader should therefore feel a strong sense of mission in this work, an attitude reflected in personal style. Introducing a technique with "I believe this will help you considerably" will produce more dramatic results than a hesitant alternative such as, "I'm not sure, but I hope this will work—if we're lucky."

Risk Taking
Because all change involves risk, a good portion of time spent in groups is centered on activities designed to facilitate risk taking in a safe, secure atmosphere. Sharing personal secrets, giving feedback, committing oneself to a goal, or (for some clients) even talking aloud results in accelerated heartbeats. For a group leader to expect clients to unburden their troubles or undrape their vulnerabilities without being a world-class expert in this difficult life skill is to practice hypocrisy. A person skilled in risk taking welcomes the mysterious and unknown, actively initiates new relationships, abjures superficial communication, and willingly experiments with new behaviors. Such group leaders are admirably equipped to help clients take the plunge because they actively practice constructive risk taking in every facet of life, from discovering new roads for travel to higher levels of intensity in love relationships.

Humor
The person who can create and bring humor to life is one committed to joy. Therapeutic groups are notoriously serious places, full of tears, gut-wrenching pain, and the molted skins of people struggling to become who they are not. The group leader who can appreciate the folly of human existence, the silliness of so many human actions, the sublime and ridiculous in his or her own behavior as well

as in other people's behavior is well-prepared to lighten the load of client suffering. To appreciate what is funny is one thing, to laugh at oneself is still more admirable, but actively to create humor in groups is crucial to helping people keep their problems in perspective.

Flexibility

The flexible mind is one without a vested interest in retaining any attitude, value, thought, feeling, or behavior. Such a mind argues only with itself, is open to all possible alternatives, and has no desire to convince other minds of its rightness. Its possessor will try any means available (as long as it is morally responsible) to accomplish a goal, and, if no acceptable solutions to a problem readily occur, it becomes a matter of routine to create a new pathway to truth. The flexible mind does not worship strategies that have worked previously but is constantly searching for more efficient and effective means for solving life's problems.

Creativity

Albert Einstein described creative people as those who are unable to understand the obvious. They are continually searching for original paths to take. They are intellectually playful, exploring ideas for their own sake or to see where they lead. Creative persons are more sensitively attuned to their environment, more perceptually aware of subtle events around them. Nonconforming individuals frequently refuse to play by conventional rules but are constantly experimenting with novel approaches to making their lives more efficient. They are rebels, sometimes "troublemakers," because of their persistence in pursuing truth to its conclusion regardless of the consequences. Creative group leaders leave every session bathed in sweat, having squeezed their brains to find new ways of energizing, motivating, and facilitating client growth.

Internal Discipline

The psychologically independent person is one free of conventional schedules. Since there are too few moments in the day to enjoy life to its fullest, sleep becomes an enemy to such a person. Sleep is practice for death, and boredom is just another way that people sleep through their waking moments.

The internally disciplined individual is totally absorbed in work and play and is capable of resisting approval-seeking behaviors or any dependency on a person, routine, or habit. This person is in charge of his or her body, telling it what it may eat, when it may sleep, and how it must perform despite destructive temptations. The capacity to resist enculturation and societal demands that are not personally meaningful are other components of internal discipline, as are the ability to get things done and the dedication to pursue productive activities in the face of seductive distractions.

Flow

When a person becomes so immersed in the present moment as to lose the sense of time and of self, experiencing floating action without thought, heightened awareness without effort, that is *flow* (Csikszentmihalyi, 1975). Between boredom and anxiety, between relaxation and alertness, lies the capacity to flow, to experience each waking moment to its fullest. Maslow, who described such intrinsically satisfying moments as "peak" experiences, noticed that self-actualized persons release their creative spirit during periods of special wholeness. The Oriental understands this concept as *Ki*; the Western mind thinks of it in terms of living totally in the present moment. For clients who escape into a past of guilt, trauma, or self-defeating patterns or who "futurize" with worry and fantasy, the group leader can be a powerful model of someone totally centered in the here and now.

Free of Negative Emotions

Group leaders must be experts at helping clients to rid themselves of self-defeating emotions such as anger, depression, shame, jealousy, guilt, worry, self-pity, and frustration. The internally controlled person is immune to the panicky fluctuations of mood to which the helpless are afflicted. Neither the weather nor other externally caused events and human actions affect the balanced emotional stability of one who is in charge of thoughts and feelings. Freedom from extreme negative emotions means continual internal ruddering to make certain that personal conflicts are worked through and that active steps are taken to keep a realistic perspective in focus. Negative emotions are not foreign to the personally masterful, but such persons have the skill to ensure that upheavals are mild and short-lived.

Logic

Logic is the systematic application of reasoning to interpret and make sense of the world. With the human heritage of belief in magic and spiritualism, the subjective nature of perceptual systems, and the wide range of individual differences, very few people reason in the same way. Nevertheless, the group leader, above all else, must be a clear thinker and systematic problem solver who can sort through the confusing maze of human action to isolate relevant segments for scientific analysis and intervention.

Honesty

An adjective that often precedes the noun *honesty* is *brutal.* Outside the confines of a therapeutic group, people are little interested in hearing the truth. They prefer to be slightly deceived, subtly misled, or told a few white lies because the truth usually hurts. It is difficult to be direct, to tell people exactly how they come across. It is even more difficult to be diplomatically confrontive. The scrupulously honest person feels compelled to speak his or her mind but can do so with enough sensitivity to avoid triggering defensiveness. But the honest person refuses to dilute the truth, even if it means listeners will not like what they hear.

Energetic Enthusiasm

In a study of eminent thinkers of the past century, Goertzel et al. (1978) found a striking pattern among the world's great scientists, writers, artists, and politicians: none of them slept very much. They had unbounded energy to pursue their goals, taking time out for rest only when their bodies were driven to exhaustion. The zest with which one pursues a vocation, the excitement that one feels for living, the enthusiasm and energy evident in one's voice and manner are the most compelling evidences of an effective model. This excitement is transmitted like electricity vibrating in the atmosphere, seducing others to tap greater energy resources.

Compassion

While Rogers and Carkhuff restrict their discussions of therapist personality to clinical dimensions, such as empathy, unconditional positive regard, acceptance, and genuineness, a far more important characteristic is evident in dedicated helpers. Compassion is that uniquely human quality of feeling an affinity for all others in the world. A concern for others' welfare, a love for all people, a respect for individual rights, an individually principled concept of morality, and a great sensitivity to the suffering of others are all part of what it means to be compassionate. A compassionate person offers aid for internal satisfaction rather than for monetary gain or to win points in heaven.

MODELED MESSAGES

There are a number of ways in which a group leader capitalizes on modeling influences as therapeutic tools. It can even be argued that everything a group leader does is an example of covert modeling. From the deliberate use of self-disclosure to the more subtle forms of cued reinforcement, the therapist communicates the force and power of his or her personality. Though most modeling occurs on unconscious levels, the group leader is nevertheless studiously observed and imitated by attentive protégés. We would therefore be well advised to spend far more time and energy attempting to make such learning mechanisms more explicitly pointed. Following are a sampling of group leader techniques that capitalize on modeling effects.

Watch Me

In psychodramatic role reversal, the group leader alternates between demonstrating effective interaction strategies and providing supervised experience for the client to practice new skills. According to the prescribed formula, a client is given an opportunity to recount relevant background information, such as the exact nature of the conflict, accompanying trepidations, previous experimental outcomes, capsulized portraits of antagonists, even details regarding where the confrontation might occur, including the most realistic arrangement of a stage set.

Next, the client-in-focus, who (let us say) is consistently trapped into arguments during every family visit, selects the players who will act out a representative conflict situation. The client may be asked to choose group members who most resemble her mother-in-law, husband, and other characters, or volunteers may be recruited for these parts. In either case, the scene is set, positions are taken, and the action begins.

Client: Hello, Mother. I hope we're not late?

Mother-in-law: As a matter of fact, you are. I just know the roast is burned. I knew I shouldn't have trusted you again.

Client: But Mother, I told you—.

Father-in-law: Never mind. Let's sit down to eat.

Client: But I tried to explain—.

Mother-in-law: Explain? There's nothing to explain. My son was never late until he married you.

Client: As a matter of fact, the reason we're late is because your son decided he had to watch the end of the football game.

The destructive interaction pattern between the client and her in-laws is already evident. After group members conduct an autopsy, offering suggestions, analyzing motives, and exploring client feelings, the group leader proposes that characters assume their parts once again, this time with the client watching the proceedings as an observer.

Client (played by therapist): Hello, Mother.

Mother-in-law: You're late again, you know.

Therapist: Yes, actually I do realize we're 15 minutes past the time you expected us. That's why I gave you an estimated time of arrival.

Mother-in-law: You gave me no such thing! Hubert, did she tell *you* that?

Father-in-law: Not that I remember, dear.

Therapist: Mom, Dad, this seems to be getting out of hand, and we've only just walked in the door. I wonder if I might talk to you both for a moment?

Mother-in-law: Well, what about? I'm very busy. The roast is already ruined. I don't know what I'll serve for dinner.

Therapist (stepping out of role and addressing client): What did I do that was different from your approach?

Client: For one thing, you didn't lose your cool. You also didn't get defensive or try to hurt her back.

Therapist: Yes, and I also set her up to confront the issue head-on instead of playing games. Why don't you jump in now and deliver the speech you've been practicing all along? Say the things you've always wanted to tell her. But remember, stay calm as you saw me do. Don't let her ruffle your feathers.

The psychodramatic encounter is now programmed to allow for further role reversals. Each time, the group leader can highlight a particularly effective behavior that can be used to defuse an explosive conflict.

Specific personally masterful behaviors pervade the group leader's style. The message "watch me" is communicated whenever the leader steps in to redirect the focus of counseling content. When intervening with the statement "Perhaps you could be a bit more concise in giving us this background," group members may be thinking to themselves, "I must remember to do that more myself when people start rambling." When the leader interrupts a member who, in sharing his feelings repeatedly uses the pronoun *we*, by asking, "Are you speaking for every person in this room?" the modeled message gets clearly understood by others who may realize that they too can use this technique to stop their spouses from speaking for them without their consent.

Other "watch me" messages include memorable verbalizations such as the following:

- "That's an excellent question. Would anyone care to answer it? *(To be used when you can't or don't want to answer the question yourself.)*
- "You say you don't know what you would do. Well, what would you guess you might do?" *(To be employed when a person refuses to take a stand on an issue.)*
- "Who says life is fair?" *(To be asked of a victim of self-pity.)*
- "What do *I* think of you? How does that make a difference?" *(To be used to short-circuit approval seeking.)*

Clients will tend to remember and use the responses their leader uses effectively in the group. Through osmosis they become more proficient at important life skills such as "keeping the ball in the other person's court" or never feeling ashamed about something in oneself that is impossible to change.

There is, of course, much more to the imitative learning approach than committing a few magic words to memory. Nonverbal gestures of self-confidence, tranquility, and competence are also transmitted. Group members attempt to resolve their initial discomfort and anxiety by creating a semblance of structure in what appears to be a chaotic situation. They become possessive about their physical space (their chair), exercising a territorial imperative. They also look to the leader for appropriate cues, imitating posture, language, even gestures. Shapiro reports on one group

> led by a colleague who had a habit of rhythmically stroking her long hair during periods of silence and high tension. By the fourth week of the group all six of the female group members were stroking their own hair the same way. This was even true for one woman who had short hair and who in effect was stroking hair which would not be long enough for years! (Shapiro, 1978, p. 130).

One of the distinct advantages of group work is that it allows clients to receive training as helpers at the same time that they are working through their personal concerns. One of the best possible ways to learn a skill such as reflecting one's feelings is by watching a master demonstrate the behavior and then to have readily available opportunities to practice it. A therapeutic group provides just such a workshop atmosphere.

Both unconsciously and deliberately, group members learn communication skills that are part of the leader's repertoire—to use confrontation nondefensively, to simplify the complex, to summarize, to describe things concretely, and to interpret the meanings of behavior. It is the group leader's "chairside manner," the cool, calm style, that keeps clients intrigued enough to keep learning. Once the group leader has earned the group members' respect as an invaluable resource person and consultant, modeling strategies fall easily into place.

Since what a client does outside the sessions is far more important than what goes on within the group, the therapist can use modeling capabilities to structure beneficial homework assignments. Modeled demonstrations in the field act as transitional learnings to form a bridge between group work and the real world. Milton Erickson was an absolute wizard when it came to programming therapeutic incidents for his clients. He had been known on several occasions to take his clients by the hand and lead them through forays into the "combat zone." Whether to a bar, restaurant, party, or a walk through the park, Erickson would creatively structure situations that allowed him to model appropriate behaviors and then to prod his clients to try them out.

There are a host of possible field trips that the creative group leader may incorporate into the treatment plan. A group of chronic overeaters may be taken to a tempting restaurant to demonstrate useful strategies for ordering healthfully from the menu. The group leader can model the pace of the meal, emphasizing a slow, savoring approach to eating. Overeaters learn by observation to be more selective about what they put into their mouths.

A group of shy participants may be taken to a social gathering, asked to observe the leader approach strangers and deal calmly with rejection, and then encouraged to initiate conversations themselves. A group of 4-year-old kids can be led to a local playground and taught the basic concepts of sharing and respect for property by modeled demonstrations.

Whether in the group or in the field, the modeling group leader indirectly offers this advice: "Watch me. Words lie but actions don't. Observe what I do and how I act. What you see in me is the best I have to offer you. Reject the aspects of my behavior that you find counterproductive. But watch carefully. Those skills I have that you admire, those things I do that you wish you could apply, those behaviors that you want to adopt for yourself—take them! They're yours for the asking."

Listen to Me

The theoretical works of Ellis (1977a), Meichenbaum and Goodman (1971), and Bandler and Grinder (1975) have focused largely on the language people use to describe events. Meaning is derived from an interpretation of objective occurrences by subjective internal sentences. The ways in which people talk to themselves and the language they use to communicate with others predispose them to think in rational or irrational patterns. This cognitive-based approach to explaining emotional suffering has helped even the psychoanalyst, existentialist, and humanist to pay a lot more attention to the structure of syntax, choice of vocabulary, and semantics, regardless of their avoidance of the rational philosophy and technique.

A great deal of semantic modeling occurs in any group in which clients spend time listening to their leader. Characteristic speech patterns, favorite expressions, and even vocal intonations are unconsciously imitated. The group leader concerned with logical precision of language is careful to speak in terms consistent with reality-based constructs, thus modeling effective ways to think aloud. If members of a group are particularly uncommunicative, uncooperative, and resistant during a session, the leader may choose, instead of an angry, scolding outburst, to demonstrate by choice of words that he or she is constructively working on the inner frustration:

"At first I really *made myself feel* upset at all of you because I felt that my time was being wasted. Then I *said to myself,* these people are not here to please me; I'm here to help them. *I told myself* to stop feeling self-pity and to get busy trying to initiate some action. *I helped myself* to feel more relaxed by realizing that your actions are not part of any conspiracy against me; this is a problem *I created for myself* by distorting what actually happened."

The language-sensitive group leader corrects exaggerations of reality that are prevalent in client speech. What group members say indicates how they characteristically think about their life situations. In response to the statement "My lover puts so much pressure on me that I am trapped in the relationship," the group leader might ask, "Don't you mean 'I am putting so much pressure on myself that I am trapping myself in the relationship'?"

Ellis and Harper (1975), Bandler and Grinder (1975), and other writers offer several specific incidences in which other modeling language interventions might be appropriate.

Client: I feel awful.
Therapist: I want you to say instead: "I feel awful when I don't get what I want."

Client: But if I do assert myself, I will surely hurt her feelings.
Therapist: You will hurt her feelings, or *she* will hurt her own feelings?"

Client: This is just so depressing.
Therapist: This is so depressing, or are you making yourself feel depressed over this situation?

Client: I'm shy.
Therapist: You mean: I act shy whenever I am with a group of strangers who are older than I am.

Client: I really should buy her a present.
Therapist: Should? Who says you should?

Client: I must finish whatever I start.
Therapist: Must? You will die if you don't?

Client: I have to get this job.
Therapist: I don't recalling seeing that among the Ten Commandments. Perhaps you mean: I would *prefer* to get this job, but if I don't I guess that will be another example of something I wanted but couldn't get. Oh, well.

Client: Obviously, this is a waste of time.
Therapist: To whom is it obvious?

Client: I can't just move out of the house.
Therapist: You *can't* or you *choose* not to at this time?

Client: It is terrible that this happened to me.
Therapist: Is it really *terrible* or only inconvenient?

Client: I'm just no good at asking girls out on dates. I've always been that way.

Therapist: You've got date-inhibiting genes? Don't you mean instead: Until now I have never learned to ask girls out on dates, but I may decide to learn that skill in the future?

Self-Disclosure

The use of self-disclosure in groups is probably the single most abused therapeutic intervention. Group leaders who like to hear themselves talk, who, because of ego deficiencies, attempt to impress clients with their prowess, or who use group time to meet their own needs are acting unethically. Yet every leader is periodically guilty of sharing personal information or a story that is really not to help clients feel more comfortable but to help him or herself feel more at ease. In answer to the internal question, "What do I hope to accomplish by sharing this with members of the group?" We sometimes have no defensible rationale.

All self-disclosure involves the sharing of personal information, but there are a number of specific intentions for initiating this modeling technique (Cormier &. Cormier, 1979). Leader self-disclosure can be used to facilitate client personal sharing on the same level or to develop better rapport by reducing the psychological distance between therapist and clients. It can be used to create a more open group atmosphere, to convey warmth, genuineness, and empathy or to change client perceptions about their behavior. It can be employed as a morale booster to convey messages such as: "I'm OK, you're OK," "Be like me!" "You can do it, too!" or "This really works."

In any capacity in which self-disclosures are used to model appropriate behaviors, leaders ought first to ask themselves: Whom will I help by sharing this? How will it help them? Is there another intervention that might accomplish the same goal without focusing on me? Such self-monitoring activities will ensure that the leader will be spotlighted only in the specific instances when this is effective for promoting client change.

Ain't I Great?

"I am an extremely happy person. You'll almost always see me smiling because that's how I feel inside. I rarely get angry, feel depressed or frustrated, sad or jealous, or experience negative emotion. I make things happen in my life rather than waiting for relationships or events to come to me. I am very productive, sleep only about 5 hours a night, and yet know how to feel relaxed and forgive myself when I don't complete all self-assigned tasks.

"I am constantly searching for areas of my behavior to improve. For instance, I am too impatient, and sometimes I push people a little too much. But I have the skills and knowledge to work through virtually any personal concern. I know how to make depression or boredom go away. I can appreciate privacy but am rarely lonely. I am always in some stage of goal setting for myself to work toward.

"I used to be a pitiful creature: helpless, dissatisfied, and depressing to be around. But then I went to work on myself. I practiced new skills I'd learned in the group, worked on new behaviors between sessions, talked to myself in my journal, in my head. I worked hard to get where I am now. It's no accident, act of fate, or coincidence that I feel as good as I do. I am the one responsible. So can you be responsible for your growth!"

The preceding introduction illustrates how a group leader uses self-disclosure to transmit some powerful modeled messages. By candidly and confidently revealing personal strengths and successes, the group leader clearly communicates "I did it! So can you. I dare you to be like me." Positive self-disclosure conveys the image of a group leader in charge of self. The dimensions of power in modeling that Bandura (1977) felt were crucial to successful learning transfer are strongly implied in positive statements about oneself that exude expertise, competence, confidence, and nurturance.

I'm Human, Too

Negative self-disclosures can also be therapeutic, although they rely on an opposite strategy. To develop rapport with group members, to close the psychological distance between master and disciple, to increase the sense of perceived similarity between client and therapist, it is important to model messages that emphasize the essential humanity of the group leader. It is crucial for clients to understand that their leader is a victim of error, failures, mistakes, and miscalculations just as they are.

Shame, for example, is easier to bear when a person whom you admire and respect shares something apparently shameful without embarrassment: "Yes, I was once caught stealing as a child. I got a job in a drugstore so that I could requisition some birth control devices that I was too young to purchase. When they caught me I wanted to die."

The group leader is as error-prone as the rest of the human race. Acknowledging past mistakes while at the same time highlighting acceptance of one's limitations is an instructive attitude to demonstrate for group members. The fear of failure is a crippling self-defeating behavior that sabotages any attempt at experimentation or risk taking.

"I approached the first waitress for a date, and she immediately turned me down. It didn't hurt as much as I thought it would. What the heck, what did I have to lose? So I walked up to another attractive waitress, who also declined a date but was a little more diplomatic. I then realized for the first time that no one could ever reject me again. To refuse a date is not to reject me as a person. Only I am capable of rejecting me because that is more a state of mind than of circumstances. I felt so freed that I approached two more waitresses, both of whom also said no. The funny thing is that when I walked out of that restaurant, dateless after four attempts, I never felt better in my life!"

The group leader gives permission for others to feel vulnerable or admit weaknesses by demonstrating that such behavior is not incompatible with pride. It is perfectly all right to cry, to hurt, or to be confused.

I'll Give You a Cookie
The spectator effects of group work make it ideally suited for emphasizing the social aspects of reinforcement. Observers tend to increase the frequency of behavior that they see being reinforced in others.

> To cite but a few examples from laboratory studies, people will adopt high performance standards that reduce self-gratification, they will select non-preferred foods, they will sacrifice material goods, they will divulge personal problems, and they will pursue formerly resisted courses of action more readily if they see models praised for exhibiting such conduct than if models receive no recognition for their actions (Bandura, 1977, p. 119).

Since the principal object of therapeutic groups is to get people experimenting with new behaviors that they previously have been inhibited from trying, vicarious reinforcement is among the best tools available to the group leader. Participants can be clearly rewarded for engaging in socially approved ways: "Sam, it was fantastic watching you in action. I really respect the courage it must have taken to share that with us."

Socially undesirable behavior may also be vicariously extinguished through the use of modeled punishment. Particularly in beginning group sessions, when clients are learning ground rules and acceptable behavior, leaders will rely on subtle forms of shaping procedures to help facilitate a fully functioning group. After a group member offers unsolicited advice to another, the leader may intervene: "Dana, how was it helpful to you to hear Kevin tell you what he would do in your shoes? Oh? It wasn't helpful? You resented him for taking the focus off you, and, besides, hearing his advice doesn't help *you* to think for yourself?"

When one client becomes verbally abusive to another, vicarious punishment will act as a deterrent to future transgressions. Modeling of this sort provides indirect information to observers about how they may and may not act. While it does not work quite as effectively as more experiential forms of modeling, vicarious reinforcement will motivate people to persist in their change efforts, even in the face of failure, when they witness others being similarly rewarded. Bandura (1977) also believes that vicarious reinforcement can reduce group members' inhibition levels and increase their influenceability potential. Observing a peer undergo threatening confrontations without adverse consequences, even producing favorable results, increases the probability that others will imitate this modeled behavior.

Once Upon a Time

Many group members feel stuck in a rut with little hope of ever stopping their wheels from spinning. Some come from economically and culturally deprived backgrounds while others come from homes in which there was little emphasis on the stuff from which dreams are made. With underestimated potential, underdeveloped goals, and an overall attitude of indifference, it is difficult to make significant progress toward desired achievements. Kids who get off to a bad start, with a poor record of academic achievement and/or behavioral problems, want to give up; adults with physical/psychological disabilities tend to succumb to self-pity. Group leaders are hard-pressed to invent ingenious ways of pulling the unmotivated out of the muck.

One energizing force involves recruiting models from the past. Throughout history, people have overcome long odds to make significant contributions to humankind. The lives of these admired people may be effectively displayed so that group members can profit from the inspiration. That a creative genius like T. S. Eliot was the victim of depressive bouts that forced him into seclusion, or that Al Jolson, Muhammad Ali, Bob Dylan, Ingmar Bergman, and Babe Ruth were all budding juvenile delinquents, has instructive value for people trying to overcome similar problems. Tennessee Williams recovered from a year-long illness only to develop a debilitating shyness that lasted the duration of his childhood.

These and other testimonies from famous people act as a powerful means of modeling effective behavior. The hero worship of celebrities that goes on in our society makes it even more difficult for the average citizen to be content with an ordinary existence. We are trained from an early age to pay homage to the wealthy and famous, and our heroes become our models.

It is often helpful to point out the fallibility of those we admire. It makes them more approachable, easier for us to relate to. From a systematic study of biographical literature, the group leader may select the life of a famous person, a powerful model, to hold up as a blueprint for group members to emulate. Thus:

• A group member who acts extremely withdrawn and shy in the group can be told of Albert Einstein's reluctance to circulate among strangers. This man, the first to be nominated as prime minister of Israel, fought a lifelong battle to learn even the most basic social rituals.

• Bertrand Russell's struggle with the meaning of love throughout his 98–year life offers a potent example of someone who took personal responsibility for his happiness, juggling relationships, affairs, and marriages to satisfy his longing for a compassionate, sensual companion.

• Charles Darwin, perhaps the most radical and independent scientist in recorded history, experienced such guilt when trying to sever his emotional dependence on his father that he was prepared to cancel his voyage on the *H.M.S. Beagle* as a naturalist and become a country clergyman if that was his father's preference.

• To the young person entering a new profession with many obstacles, the group leader may mention the tribulations of Vincent Van Gogh: "Here was a man who had the dedication and commitment to pursue a career in which he never once received emotional support. He stood alone, suffering day after day of isolation, never once selling a painting in his lifetime. And you've just used 15 minutes to lament that a whole week went by without your having made a single sale."

Ernest Hemingway's bouts of alcoholic depression, Sigmund Freud's stoic tolerance of chronic pain, Andre Gide's search for his homosexual identity—all can be brought out as models of attempts to cope with difficult problems. If history has any real value, it is for us to learn from the lives of those who have gone before us. How have the self-actualized heroes of the past coped with their personal handicaps? What can they teach us today?

It is not enough for the advanced group leader to remain current only with the literature of counseling and psychotherapy. Professional journals and new texts have much to teach us about theoretical innovation, improvements in behavioral intervention technology, research in group dynamics, and refinement of group techniques; but group leaders belong to a profession whose relevant knowledge transcends academic demarcation.

The study of philosophy allows the group leader to reason critically and to investigate issues carefully. The different branches of philosophy—logic, ethics, ontology, epistemology, metaphysics, and kineology—all help the trained mind to approach the sensitive problems of human existence with clarity. Philosophy helps the group leader to select the best questions to ask, even if it provides few answers.

The social sciences, humanities, human physiology, linguistics, even the performing arts all help to make group leaders more worldly in running groups. The more experience they collect, the wider the range of knowledge from which to choose the best intervention. Dedicated group leaders who travel around the world are exposed to different cultures and customs. The skilled traveler learns to communicate on a variety of levels, to initiate helpful relationships, to appreciate the subtle complexities of the environment, and to adapt readily to changing circumstances. Even tourist photography trains one to pay attention to detail and composition, to examine the world through a sensitive, artistic eye. All such life experiences make a group leader better able to relate to a variety of persons and to understand a broader range of human problems.

In a sense, we have been in a continual state of rigorous training for our profession since birth. We remember and know how to use the critical incidents of our childhood. We recall our significant learnings vividly and are able to pass on valuable insights. The first bicycle ride without training wheels, the first kiss, the first stay away from home, and other critical incidents give us the background to understand the personal meaning of such events for others.

Voracious reading is another means by which pragmatic group leaders pursue their education. Novels, poetry, plays, biographies and other nonfiction give us glimpses into the motives and thinking processes of distressed characters. Dostoyevsky teaches us about existential suffering, Salinger instructs us in adolescent development, Doris Lessing helps us to understand depression. Films and television add visual and auditory stimuli to the study of human conflict. In short, the more intensely group leaders experience life, the better they become in dealing with intensity in others. By studying the lives of famous people in addition to in-depth analyses of their own lives group leaders can help clients to select models more intelligently.

CHAPTER 5

The Power of Language in Groups

Whereas neurologists, cardiologists, internists, and surgeons have electroencephalograms, blood tests, biochemical analyses, and biopsies to aid in their diagnoses, group leaders have nothing but their sense organs and a few primitive psychometric devices. There are no technological aids to bail us out of trouble. We have our minds, our training, our intuition, and a propensity for the masterful manipulation of language. We are neither technicians nor scientists; we are communicators. We cure with the power of language.

Language is both a formal system of verbal expression and a description of behavior in flux. Since its birth in the fifth century A.D. the English language has continually changed to reflect new thinking and more modern concepts. Language evolves as words are manufactured, borrowed, assimilated, and blended from other sources.

Language is phenomenally responsive to change. The language of Chaucer bears little resemblance to that of the contemporary Hollywood street person cruising Sunset Strip. Through mispronunciation of words, short-cut speech patterns, or even blends (*clap + crash = clash; flame + glare = flare*), our language changes. We readily swipe words from other languages and call them our own. *Tycoon* comes from Japanese; *rocket* from Italian; *salt* from Old Norse; *emotion* from French; *boss* from Dutch; and *skunk* from Algonquian Indian (Farb, 1974).

Syntactical aspects of different languages are indicative of underlying cognitive principles unique to each national heritage. When learning a Romance language, for instance, one of the most difficult concepts for English speakers to grasp is the subjunctive mood which changes the tense of subordinate clauses ("It is necessary *that you pick me up*," or "*I wish that you would come*"). In cases of expressed doubt, desire, denial, negation, emotion, preference, insistence, regret, or impersonal situations, respect for logical relationships is indicated by implying that because we wish something to occur doesn't necessarily mean that it will occur. In English, the subjunctive is becoming extinct. Except following the words *may* or *might* ("that he may live forever") or expressing conditions that are contrary to fact ("If I were a rich man"), this tense has been abandoned. One wonders what impact these omissions have on our thinking processes.

Perhaps our language is contributing to the prevalence of externally controlled people, avoiders of responsibility, and psychologically dependent individuals. Whereas in English it is common to hear illogical utterances such as "he made me so angry" and "she worries me to death," indicating speakers who are not in charge of their emotional states, Spanish makes use of reflexive verbs for similar statements. This linguistic structure forces speakers to take responsibility for their own internal processes and self-initiated actions, turning passive actions in English into active states in Spanish. The verbs *to be angry* and *to worry*, for example, are expressed quite differently in Spanish reflexive verbs. *Enojarse* literally means "to get yourself angry"; *preocuparse* means "to worry yourself." Quite legitimately, responsibility for these internally manufactured states is placed within the sphere of the speaker's ultimate control.

Many English-speaking group members could profit by thinking reflexively or subjunctively—that is, by abdicating unrealistic expectations for controlling other people's behavior and taking more responsibility for one's own. Subjunctive tenses could express more logical ideas:

"If I were only a man *(but I'm not)*, I wouldn't take so much flak."
"I prefer *(but I'm only expressing my preference)* that you visit me
    tomorrow."
"I insist *(but I can't make you)* that you stop calling me for help."

Reflexive verb uses could also be used to focus responsibility more legitimately:

"*I frustrated myself* when I didn't get the job."
"*I woke myself up* at 6:00, *worried myself* about being late, and then
    made myself cry because I couldn't *make myself remember*
    where I was going."

THE LOGIC OF LANGUAGE

Language is a means of communicating thoughts by symbols that have a degree of permanence in time and a discreteness in space. According to Bertrand Russell (1961), this utility is both indispensable and dangerous, for language, unlike mathematics, is relatively imprecise. It describes objects with definitions that are unsupported by the laws of physics. What precisely are *time* and *space?* Can they be seen or touched? How do we know they really exist?

We speak of "time," apparently understand its meaning, even pretend it exists in the world. But we often forget that such abstractions are created within the human mind. They help to ease our intolerance for ambiguity, the frustrations of the unknown. In a sense, then, we invent our realities through language. We speak of things like cohesion, trust, norms, power, relationships, dynamics. We invent ideas like "super-ego," "mind," "personality," "neurotic," and wear them like the emperor's new clothes.

> Language continually asserts by the syntax of subject and predicate that "things" somehow "have" qualities and attributes. A more precise way of talking would insist that "things" are produced, are seen as separate from other "things," and are made "real" by their internal relations and by their behavior in relationship with other things and with the speaker (Bateson, 1979, p. 67).

Language represents only one aspect of reality—a symbolic map of the territory, the coding into words of actual things-in-the-world. This verbal portrayal may be consistent and logical or may exhibit dimensions that are quite unreal.

Bandler and Grinder (1975, 1979) distinguish between the deep structure and surface structure of a person's communications, suggesting that verbalizations seldom convey accurately their intended messages. For instance, a group member might say "I'm sick and tired of people laying a bunch of crap on me all the time," when what he really means is "I don't like it when my wife constricts my freedom by giving me orders about how I should spend my time on Sundays." The concepts "people," "bunch of crap," "all the time" not only fail to convey the real meaning behind the communication, but they don't specifically provide a useful perspective on reality.

Words are the symbols we use to express ideas, which are in turn abstractions of our thought and feelings, which are the result of how we perceive the world. There is thus a funneling effect which converts the nature of reality into a more progressively diluted form, each step in the conversion losing a degree of accurate representation from its predecessor.

Nature of Reality
Perceptual Input
Sum Total of Retrievable Experience
Cognitions
Linguistic Capacity
Actual Verbalizations

Good old active listening, the main mode of helping, is a process of ignoring surface statements and discerning their underlying affective messages. By decoding or interpreting what people say aloud to mean something quite different, we help them to become more "whole" (in Gestalt language), more "congruent" (in Rogerian terms), better "ego-integrated" (in psychodynamic jargon), more "rational" (in the cognitive-behavioral system) or operating from a "less impoverished model" (in neurolinguistic programming language). These therapeutic goals, and the labeling processes used to reach them, can be substantially diverted from course if the group leader forgets that the "language map" is not the same as the "territory" it represents.

Unfortunately, a cursory review of major group work texts produces a consistently illogical, reified style of language in which logical principles are violated (*reification* means treating an abstraction as if it were a concrete material object). Though people are actual objects in reality, The Group is an abstraction used to describe a collection of such individuals. Observe the use of this abstraction in the literature:

- "It seems that when a group accepts a goal those who most strongly accept the goal display a strong need to have the group achieve its goals" (Napier & Gershenfeld, 1981, pp. 211–212).
- "The concept of the group as a genuine, organized, and dynamic organism in its own right, comparable to the integrity of the individual personality, was and probably still is difficult for many people to accept . . ." (Shaffer & Galinsky, 1974, p. 5).
- "When the group permits the doubtful to remain on probation, the counselor must help them state precisely what their new expected behaviors will be to remain and achieve full membership again" (Ohlsen, 1977, p. 127).

- "What are the kinds of procedures a group undergoes in attaining its goals within a social environment?" (Goldberg & Goldberg, 1973, p. 106).
- "Before the group can move from the transition phase to the working phase, the participants need to test the group leader, the other members, and themselves" (Corey, 1981, p. 37).
- "If the group does not seem to be moving and is apparently unproductive, it is imperative for the leader to examine self, style, and techniques" (Hansen, Warner, & Smith, 1980, p. 500).

The Language of Family Therapy

A special class of group workers, marital and family therapists, have a language of their own for describing the processes they witness— and conceptions about who exactly is being helped in family therapy have lately become a bit muddled. What was once an abstraction denoting a collection of persons engaged in human behavior has become a living entity, a creature with a mind of its own, that exists nowhere except in the therapist's brain. Excerpts from a representative issue of the *Journal of Marital and Family Therapy* (January 1980) reveal a consistent pattern of language used to describe the therapy process in this specialized group treatment. In their article about how families behave, for example, Palazzoli, Boscolo, Cecchin, and Prata (1980) explain: "The smiling family; this is usually a courteous, good-humored family, without the least anxiety...," and elsewhere in the article we find: "the reaction of the family," "the family will do anything," "the motive which has led the family into therapy)" [pp. 4, 5].

So far we have an image of The Family as a thing capable of experiencing emotions, a creature with a single motive who can react, smile, laugh, and do practically anything else. Later in this journal, Charney (1980, p. 37) elaborates by wondering "how it can be that so many people and families are disturbed"; Andolfi (1980, pp. 29–36) notices "the endless game played previously by the family," and later, "the family will feel itself relieved." But can The Family be a living being with a heart, brain, and soul? Can The Family be changed? Is it possible to counsel a Family, a Marriage, a Group, or a Committee? Can one address The Family as a unity? "Well, Family, what is your main problem and how may I help you?"

However illogical such descriptions of people may be, there is a consensus among professionals to refer to marriages, families, and groups as if they do exist in the world as living creatures. In the process, individual clients are depersonalized, their behaviors are distorted, and their collective feelings and thoughts are generalized to be part of a total system.

Such labeling violates reality because a family or group cannot actually feel, think, or breathe; it also leads to counterproductive thinking of another sort. If a group leader conceptualizes a gathering of clients as a homogeneous unit and operates from this assumption, distortions can occur that will lead the therapist to underestimate the individual motives, goals, and feelings of each member.

The business of marital and group therapists is to help individual people, not The Family. Families don't come for counseling; people do. While it is often advantageous to view and treat a particular client's distresses within the context of family interactions and through interventions that actively involve all members of the family unit, this does not mean that the collection of persons making up the unit becomes a single entity with a spirit of its own.

Group Leaders as Language Coaches

Group therapists must upgrade professional speech to the level of current research and clinical expertise. Imprecise language not only indicates faulty reasoning on the therapist's part but can lead clients to deny responsibility for their actions because "The Family" is at fault.

It can be therapeutically beneficial to help clients see themselves as unique individuals within their larger family systems. Speaking about what "we believe" or what "our family feels" can be corrected by determining whether the speaker is expressing the true beliefs of all persons present with their consent. Interventions such as the following might be implemented.

Therapist: Hector, your father just said that all of you are dissatisfied with the way things have been going lately. Is he speaking for you, too?

Therapist: Cynthia, I notice that you keep using the pronoun *we* and glancing at your husband each time I ask you a question. I wonder how *you* feel, compelled to include his opinion with yours, and how he feels having you answer for him.

It would also be advantageous for therapists to obliterate "we-oriented" thinking from their own conceptual vocabulary. Avoiding the reduction of individual persons into categories or labels would keep the focus of therapy on treating people and not just their relationships. A marriage, family, or group exists to serve the needs of the people in them. Once the relationships become destructive and self-defeating, a therapist can intervene to enhance the quality of communication among people, teaching each person either to act in a more fully functioning manner with family members or to make decisions regarding reduced quantity of interactions. In either case, the family or group does not change; the individual people do.

It must be said that many implicit rules of therapeutic groups are conducive to fakery, and first among them is the unique language system.

Bertha: I experience you as hostile.
Irving: Oh, yeah? You're just projecting.
Leader: I hear you both saying that you're angry.

This jargon often gets in the way of honest, natural communication since group members, before they can "spontaneously emote," must first translate their naked feelings into suitable clothing.

Clem: I think you're full of ostrich manure.
Leader: Don't you really mean: I *feel* you're full of ostrich manure?

Alan Watts (1966) lists seven basic rules that can be adapted by group leaders.

> "A double-bind game is a game with self-contradictory rules, a game doomed to perpetual self-frustration—like trying to invent a perpetual-motion machine in terms of Newtonian mechanics, or trying to trisect any given angle with a straightedge and compass. The social double-bind game can be phrased in several ways:" [p. 67]

"The first rule of this game is that it is not a game."
The group leader perpetuates this contradiction with the statement "Let's pretend this is real." Group members then imagine that others are their mothers or boss, and speak to them *as if* they were. They play feeling games and interaction exercises all the while they pretend that they aren't really playing games at all.

"Everyone must play."
It doesn't matter if the clients are convicted murderers serving six consecutive life sentences, or students who are "encouraged" by

their teachers to participate in the program, or parents who threaten their kids with a choice of solitary confinement or a group, let's pretend we all want to be here. Since everyone is here anyway, I would like to ask you all to share your perceptions of one another. But, of course, you don't have to participate unless you want to.

"You must love us."
We're all such nice people, so caring. We really like you a lot. We have empathy, unconditional positive regard, acceptance, respect, and genuineness. You must love us, too.

"You must go on living."
Isn't life grand? It is so full of freedom and choices. Even when your body is riddled with cancer or your mind is preoccupied with depression and pain you must go on living.

"Be yourself, but play a consistent and acceptable role."
If you can't act naturally in this group, where can you feel comfortable? Right? Just be yourself . . . as long as we can predict what you're going to be and approve of that self.

"Control yourself and be natural."
Smile into the camera. That's right. Look like you're having a good time; or, at least, learning something. Wipe away those tears; they're ruining your make-up. OK now, ready?

"Try to be sincere."
Even if you don't know how to act sincere, fake it. We'll never know the difference.

Group members as well have created unique linguistic structures to represent their thinking symbolically. Clients thus believe in abstractions like "shyness," "trauma," and "depression" and allow these words to influence how they think, feel, and act. Rather than acting as elected delegates to represent ideas, words *become* ideas. Group members speak of their "unassertiveness" as if it were a genetically transmitted disease. They ascribe their problems to "fate" or the "unconscious," but what these abstractions mean depends entirely on the user's perceptions. We may, in fact, apply any number of verbal labels to our observations, each the product of perceptual/cognitive/effective processes.

Ellerbroek (1978), for instance, was interested in the psycho-dynamic effects of language on acne. Because the names we choose to call a thing are optionally determined, acne can be called a "disease," a "normal condition," a "sign of stress," a "dermatological problem," "a curse," or "a kind of chosen behavior." Ellerbroek explained to his patients that acne results from a *feeling* of being picked on, a depressive reaction, a psycholinguistic pattern and was therefore able to treat pimples psychologically.

A. J. Ayer, the logical positivist, attempted to dispel fuzzy thinking and communication by bringing language under the umbrella of empiricism. By applying the criteria of verifiability to test the genuineness of statements, Ayer (1952) was able to distinguish three types of propositions in the world of discourse, all of which can be considered as nothing more than probable hypotheses. All statements made, whether analytic, synthetic, or judgmental, are factually significant only to the extent that they may be verified by any given person. This linguistic assumption fits well within the philosophy of pragmatism and the practice of group work. All statements may be formulated in different linguistic patterns and may be interpreted in the unique language of each client.

Acting essentially as a language coach, teaching clients to change the descriptors they use of the world (Shands, 1970), the therapist must be particularly concerned with the precise use of language and its power to influence. The philosopher Ludwig Wittgenstein believed that the problems of philosophy (and therefore of the world) are essentially confusions in the use of language. One goal of therapy, then, is to clear away defective linguistic usage in communication processes (Chessick, 1977).

THE LANGUAGE OF EMOTIONAL EXPRESSION

In discussing the affective dimensions of language in social contexts, Hayakawa (1964) describes the power of several communication devices to exaggerate, to command attention, or to send a message more forcefully. The group member may hide in a forest of abstraction or venture forth in a web of allusion. For the group leader, the tasks of language sensitivity are twofold: first, to diagnose affective messages hidden in the content of discourse: second, to communicate subtle verbalizations by means of a variety of delivery modes.

The use of *metaphor*, for example, is the bread and butter of group interaction language. At the most elementary level, it is the most powerful of affective descriptors: "I'm so sick of this crap I could die!" First cousin to metaphor, but less confrontive in demonstrating parallels between unrelated subjects, the *simile* also carries much emotional weight in its descriptions: "Can't you take charge of your life? You're acting like a half-fucked fox in a forest fire."

What of the shock value of so-called dirty words? (a metaphoric value judgment in itself). Words, of course, have no emotional valence except that which the listener reads into them. The shock value of certain scatological terms arises from their taboo. Their utility derives from their emotionally descriptive implications.

For group leaders, the first problem of emotionally descriptive language is the presence of discrepant experiences in the use of obscenities. Some group leaders claim that the prolific use of such language is therapeutic because it enables the therapist to speak to clients as they speak to themselves. After all, a person who drops an anvil on his foot is unlikely to think: "Oh, gee whiz. What a shame. I just smashed my foot into a bloody pulp." But group leaders prone to the use of swear words may alienate clients so offended by the medium that they can't hear the message. And for group leaders who themselves find such words distasteful, there is the risk of communicating nonacceptance to group members who pepper their talk with an occasional expletive.

Several other linguistic devices of emotional expression affect a person's relative perspective. These include *personification* ("This school system really pisses me off with its self-righteous rules") and *allusion*, an abbreviation of images. For more complex feelings, language can create incongruent comparisons to deal with shades of affect or ambiguous arousal. The use of irony, pathos, and humor are helpful in this context.

There are also many cases of language abuse in therapeutic groups as the result of emotional factors. Since we are often unaware of how we speak, our language can act as a hidden obstacle to effective thinking. We respond unconsciously to certain words, depending on our prior experiences with them. "Shirt," for example, seems an innocuous word unless one has prior experience with Hitler's "Brown Shirts." So, too, words like kike, nigger, Communist, or psychotic have other than neutral connotations.

Huppe and Kaminsky (1962) identify several common language errors that occur in forms of emotional communication to which therapeutic group work is highly susceptible. Clients will rely on emotional but illogical language practices as resistance tactics. Unless these emotional arguments are countered by group leaders who are skilled at recognizing and disputing them, it is unlikely that lasting changes will occur.

Abusive Uses

The first in a series of language errors that result from emotionality is *character assassination*. While previously this has involved questioning race, religion, or profession as an invalidating factor, group settings commonly evoke the misuse of psychological jargon: "How can *you* tell *me* what to do; you're the one with the inferiority complex."

Group members may defensively attempt to destroy one another's views by criticizing their origins. In the *genetic fallacy*, the content of a perceived attack is ignored while focus is placed on distracting variables. The client can therefore totally refute any validity in a threatening statement: "No wonder you're off base, look where you got your information."

Any of several emotional appeals can also be used. In *appeal to the people*, a client may seek to gain validity for expressed ideas by consensual methods. If group member unity can be swayed to support the deviant position, the client reasons that arguments will carry greater weight. "We all know this. We've seen you do it." In the *appeal to pity*, the speaker uses arguments topheavy with emotional seductiveness. Sympathy is aroused by appealing to listener emotions: "You just *have* to help me. I can't do it all myself. Just do it this time to get me started."

Appeal to a higher authority is among the most tenaciously resistant arguments to counterlogic by the therapist. "But my minister says—" "But Freud didn't believe that—" "But that directly conflicts with the Bible—." Finally, the *appeal to force* is a favorite tactic of childhood, as when a youngster threatens "I won't be your friend if you don't loan me your bike." In groups, the threat takes a similar form: "Maybe I won't come back next week unless—."

Faulty generalizations are evident when group members base all-inclusive assumptions on a sample of one, erroneously believing all cases to be identical: "My Aunt Minosa got better by trying this idea; I don't know why you won't try it, too."

The *"post hoc ergo propter hoc" fallacy* involves a confusion in causal relationships in which, for example, recency is assumed to exercise the most important effect on behavior. Skinner has explained how superstitions develop through precisely this same mechanism. If one happens to do well on an exam using a particular pen, the pen takes on lucky qualities.

Client: My wife ran out on me just because I quit my job.
Group Leader: Sure, one event happened to occur right after the other. However, it appears that your wife left you because you've been a drunk for the past two years.

A favorite stall tactic is the use of *circular reasoning.* To the child who asks why little girls don't have babies, the mother replies "Because they're little girls, honey. That's why."

> Sometimes an argument is quite complex and then it is more difficult to check for circularity: "Freud claims that we are often frustrated because our sex drives are blocked and they become blocked because we are thwarted in our desires." The circularity here may be difficult to discover until "frustrated" is seen to have the same meaning as "thwarted in our desires" (Huppe & Kaminsky, 1962, p. 202).

Another filibuster maneuver is the one of *irrelevance*—that is, the speaker attempts to cloud the issue by bringing in distracting variables. "Maybe what you say is true, but I don't see how it can be proved. I remember once when I saw Buckley on TV—have you ever seen this guy? He's got this style that's fantastic—."

In the use of *imperfect analogy,* verbal reasoning goes something like this:

1. "You and I are similar."
2. "When I had problems in school, so did you."
3. "Just before my latest divorce, my wife started complaining about not having enough freedom."
4. "Your wife is now asking for more freedom."
5. "Therefore, you're going to end up with a divorce, too."

The *misused metaphor* relies on inappropriate pictorial phrases and vivid language to presume parallels between unrelated things. For instance, based on only two of a person's qualities, she or he is called "a monster."

All these abusive uses of language appeal to emotional factors in communication. They form incomplete representations, semantic deletions, and impoverished surface structures. They violate the linguistic rules of well-formedness and semantic relationships (Bandler & Grinder, 1975).

In the course of evolution, the intonations of phonemes (as heard, for instance, in infant babbling) have become associated with various emotions rather than with any content (Lacan, 1968). When emotion becomes intentionally directed toward an object, the child is born into language. "The relation of language and emotion thus constitutes an evolutionary advance: to use language—the abstraction of underlying systems—to change those systems" (Kellerman, 1979, p. 258).

The relationship between emotional states, their representative cognitions, and expressed language has become the foundation for two quite popular approaches to therapy. In neurolinguistic programming, group participants are taught to attend more consciously to the deeper structures of language. Syntax and logical semantic relations are formed to represent true experiences more accurately. By avoiding semantic deletions, distortions, ambiguity, nominalizations, generalizations, and other illogical linguistic structures, group members are able to change their models of the world, hoping to introduce more options and choices into their repertoire (Bandler & Grinder, 1975).

In rational-emotive therapy, group members are also instructed to eliminate irrational language from their internal vocabularies. According to this theory, the language that people use in their self-talk as well as in communications reflects an underlying pattern of emotional/cognitive disturbance (Ellis, 1977). Illogically based statements like "I can't stand it," "I must do it," "I'm a louse," and "He made me angry" are therefore altered to reflect more accurate representations of concepts: "I can stand this but I don't like it," "I choose to do it," "I've done a few lousy things," "I made myself angry over what he did."

Such theories have brought about the precise phrasing of therapeutic comments to imply that impending changes among group members are not only possible but likely.

Guidelines for Group Leaders

"Just as a mechanic carries around a pair of pliers and a screwdriver for use in an emergency—just as we all carry in our heads tables of multiplication for daily use—so can we all carry in our heads convenient rules for extensional orientation" (Hayakawa, 1964, p. 314). Hayakawa's introduction to the rules of logical communication offers the group leader a mind-set for applying the guidelines of effective semantics. To ground us in reality, to prevent mindless behavior, to avoid illogical verbal solutions, the following rules are suggested.

1. *Words are not things.* Alfred Korzybski was among the first philosophers to help untangle the confusion between thoughts and their symbolic codings in language. His famous dictum "the map is not the territory" suggests both the incompleteness of the spoken word, in that it does not represent *all* the nuances of a thought, and the assurance that some parts of the whole will inevitably be lost in the coding and transformation from an abstract image into a concrete medium.

Language is therefore a convenient approximation of an idea, a classification or naming such as a map represents but is not itself the territory it describes: "It is necessary to be quite clear about the universal truth that whatever 'things' may be in their pleromatic and thingish world, they can only enter the world of communication and meaning by their names, their qualities, and their attributes" (Bateson, 1979, p. 68).

Group leaders must therefore use their symbols well, employing precise, descriptive language to convey their ideas. Group members, too, speak in symbols of their thoughts, often saying much more or less than they mean. They may follow counterfeit maps, hastily scribbled, expecting to reach a destination that is impossible given the limitations of their internal cartographers, who may draw what they *see* but not see what they draw.

Jean Piaget observed that children operate from false maps and attempted to explain why they consistently experience perceptions inconsistent with reality (as *we* know it). Children can cheerfully describe the moon following them over their shoulders or how a nickel can be worth more than a dollar because it is heavier.

Clients, too, use their language to inadequately describe the territorial images in their brains. We dutifully attend to these communications, yet never assume that they are anything more than approximations of the intention. The meanings that words have for us are not necessarily the meanings *in* clients. The high frequency of clarifying and restating leader interventions attests to this sensitivity.

2. *Meaning is determined by context.* The phenomenology of an individual's background and unique perceptions determine the precise meaning of a verbalization. The statement "you're bad" can have quite different meanings with only the minority status of the speaker

rotated as the independent variable. A black adult or Catholic priest could thus intend two very different interpretations of this moral judgment—the former, highly favorable in its recognition of "coolness;" the latter, an indictment of sin and moral transgression.

3. *Distinguish differences in "truth."*

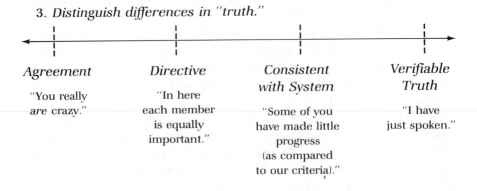

Agreement	Directive	Consistent with System	Verifiable Truth
"You really are crazy."	"In here each member is equally important."	"Some of you have made little progress (as compared to our criteria)."	"I have just spoken."

Wachtel (1980) suggests that communicators should encourage clients to think in terms of unlimited choices and alternatives for the future. He compares the difference between static confrontations such as "you are a person who has difficulty speaking" and interventions such as "sometimes you talk more easily than at other times." This principle can be taken several steps farther in groups by ensuring that interpretations and confrontations include the following elements:

A. The assumption that most behavior—emotional, cognitive, and motor—is varied and inconsistent. Not: "You are passive" but "Occasionally in the presence of threatening persons like myself, you *act* passively."

B. The assumption that actions do not have a life of their own but are the result of people's deliberate or unconscious intentions. Group members are responsible for what they think, feel, and do. Not: "What you just said made me angry!" but "I just made myself angry over what you just said."

C. Interventions include *specific* data regarding the target behaviors. The difference between "Sometimes you talk more easily than at other times" and "Whenever Francine has finished talking or she glares at you, you inhibit yourself from talking" is that the latter feedback provides useful, specific information that can be acted on.

D. The assumption that verbalizations have a specific rationale. While shooting from the hip sometimes produces the most dramatic effects, almost all interventions have specific rationales in a group leader's head, *whether they can be articulated or not.* It is a good idea to encourage group members to query leader interventions whenever they are confused—both to expose the apparent magic of actions and to train clients to think analytically. The message to them is: *before* you do or say something likely to bring about mushroomed results, anticipate the likely consequences.

4. *The use of colorful language.* People tend to remember ideas that are either novel to them or potentially useful—those that have a high stimulation valence. We plant metaphorical phrases like time bombs, set to go off when clients slip back into mediocrity outside the group. We also like to model the intrinsic beauty of language, respect for the order of words. All clients leave our groups better able to communicate, more fluent in their expressive powers.

5. *Group leaders avoid the use, whenever possible, of depersonalizing jargon.* Too many experts are insensitive to their audience—physicians when they tell patients they have some tongue-twisting condition that could easily be described in five-letter words, or mechanics when they authoritatively diagnose a car as having some strange syndrome of engine disturbance.

6. *Sexist and class-discriminating terms are avoided.* In what has been the fastest growing cultural change in human history, dating a mere 20 years since the civil rights and women's rights movements began in earnest, our language already reflects the new order. Words like *mankind, manpower, freshman, coed,* and *housewife* are rapidly becoming obsolete. Stereotypic expressions, biased statements, insensitive verbal transgressions have no place in therapeutic groups.

7. *Group leaders should use language that is precise, direct, and behaviorally descriptive.* On the one hand, it is of paramount importance that misinterpretations resulting from muddled language be avoided. On the other hand, it may sometimes be expedient to speak ambiguously about an idea to permit multiple, personal interpretations among participants. Among therapists, a favorite riposte to a request for clarification is "What did you think I meant?"

WORDS TO AVOID IN THERAPEUTIC GROUPS

Words, in and of themselves, are neither good nor bad. Nevertheless, some words common to client usage act as symptoms of underlying illogical, distorted, or irrational thinking patterns. Most experienced group leaders have trained themselves to monitor client speech patterns and language usage, both to collect meaningful data about how they characteristically speak and to attend more closely to the subtleties of communications. Sometimes a little bell rings in our head, an alert that some principle of reality has been violated.

There are words, usually indicative of cognitive distortion, that make it much more difficult for group members to experience change. These words thrive on the force of externally controlled factors like fate, luck, "it," or "them." An attitude of resignation, despair, hopelessness sets in when one verbalizes statements that imply "I can't help it, it's not my fault."

Rudestam (1978) catalogued the semantic structure of language used in therapy. Studying the works of Perls, Korzybski, Bandler, and Grinder, he constructed a pathological vocabulary that clients use in their fuzzier thought processes. To these sources can be added the contributions of Albert Ellis, Milton Erickson, and several of my own ideas. The following dictionary calls to attention unproductive words and errors to be avoided in group therapy.

Fair

"Who says the world is fair?" echoes through the offices of therapists throughout the world. This confrontation was among the first attempts by professional helpers to challenge the erroneous assumptions of stated language. Obviously, if the world were a fair place, people would treat one another with respect. There would be no crime, poverty, or sickness. All people would get what they want; they would also get what they deserve.

Unfortunately, however, this is not the case. Neither an Eleventh Commandment, the Bill of Rights, nor the Magna Carta guarantees that people will get everything they want whenever they want it. To shout "foul!" is to complain unrealistically that the universe has not complied to one's special wishes.

"I guess this is one of those times when you didn't get what you want. Has that ever happened before? Is it likely to happen again? Are you so special that because you don't believe things are fair, they should therefore change, and the world should accommodate itself so that your life will be easier?"

Platitude

"These troubled times call for men of stature," said the therapist to the midget. By borrowing someone else's tired and trite formulation of language it is possible to conduct an entire group session without uttering a single original statement. Tyler and Thurston (1977) offer such classics for the platitudinal counselor as: "It takes two to tango" (for the schizophrenic), "Don't take life too seriously; after all, you'll never get out of it alive" (for the client with existential angst); "Take two aspirin and call me in the morning" (for the suicidal group member). Platitudinal comments spare us from having to *think* about what we really have to say. It also helps clients to feel like insignificant repositories for other people's trash.

Luck

Someday there may prove to be a reality base for ideas like "luck," "fate," "Karma," "coincidence," and "astrological signs." However comforting it might be to believe in such external forces, for the most part, these concepts only make inertia and procrastination a lot more likely. As empiricists and scientists, we model to our group members the qualities of logical analysis. "Where is the evidence that these concepts exist? And even if they do exist, how is it helpful for you to believe in them?"

Group members who habitually use these words often admit that they exercise little control over their lives—they are puppets, victims of some mysterious force. They renounce responsibility for their actions and defer their fate to something outside themselves. The swift and certain answer to a claim of luck or fate is to vigorously challenge its actual effect on outcomes. "Are you saying that the reason you run such a successful business today has nothing to do with your personable style, your instinct for taking advantage of ideal situations, your willingness to take risks, but only because you are lucky? I wonder how that belief comforts you?"

Need

To *need* something is to require it for continued physical survival. The only things we ever truly need are oxygen, nourishment, and shelter from the elements, although a case could also be made for sex and human touch. No one ever needs anyone or anything else. A great many things in life are desirable, wantable, preferable, or terrific, but none is actually needed. People whose *needs* go unfulfilled experience panic and fear; unsatisfied *wants* only produce discomfort or inconvenience.

Whenever group members use the word *need*—as in "I need this job" or "I need feedback from the rest of you"—they are helped to substitute the words *want, prefer,* or *desire.* It is no great catastrophe to do without a thing we might *prefer* to have in life; after all, we've been disappointed many times before. But the deprivation of a need implies torture or death.

Can't

"I *can't* come to the group today.
"You *can't* come today? I see. You mean you're either chained to your
    bed or in an advanced state of coma."

This little helping verb, so anonymous when buried in a sentence, is among the most abused of all words. *Can't* relinquishes one's power and control. It means that one is unable to do something. To say "I *can't* get a job" is very different from saying "I don't know how to get a job" or "So far, I've been unable to find a job." Similarly, "I *can't* confront him in this group" is different from "I *won't* confront him," "I *choose* not to confront him," or "I don't *want* to confront him." In reality, there is very little one *can't* do in this world if one is willing to suffer the consequences.

Never

First cousin to *always* and *forever, never* is an overgeneralization that exaggerates reality. The use of these words leads to a false sense of hopelessness. Who can say what might happen in the future? "Perhaps you may not feel happy very often in the future, but you would have a bitter task ahead if you were to *never* feel happy again, not even for an accidental instant, and were *always* to feel depressed."

Because these words reinforce a sense of helpless resignation (Why try since you will *always* be this way?), the client's motive to change becomes handicapped. By altering *never* or *always* to the more flexible *sometimes* or *occasionally*, people admit that they can function effectively in some situations: "Much of the time I feel slightly depressed, but sometimes I feel quite good."

Expect

Expect goes hand in hand with disappointment, for the latter is not possible without the former. The amount of time spent anticipating an event is directly related to subsequent disappointment if the event does not turn out as *expected.* To minimize expectations is to reduce or prevent disappointment in the future.

It is one thing to attempt to predict future occurrences but quite another to indulge in fantasies that only pre-empt what one hopes will occur. How bored one feels, how much one lives in the future and in fantasy, how much one tries to control and anticipate, will all contribute to the frequency of *expect* in one's vocabulary. The oracle on the mountain advises, "Expect nothing, and you will never be disappointed."

Must

The use of *must* implies a demand that things be a certain way; it is a command to the universe to pay attention and cooperate extra hard with one's wishes. Ellis (1977a) coined the memorable term *musterbation* to highlight the frenzied self-abuse people subject themselves to when they publicly or privately declare that they deserve some result. As children pout when they don't get their way, grown-ups unrealistically order the world to deliver on demand. Group members play variations on the linguistic theme: "I *must* do well." "Other people *must* treat me fairly." "I *must* get my way." The obvious retort is that time-tested strategy perfected in childhood: "Who says?"

Problem

Problems usually have solutions, and people who have problems spend their time trying to find them. They mount a mission in search of the Holy Grail, Truth, or some such answer that will disperse this storm cloud forever. Since problematic people, by implication, are inadequate, inept weaklings, it is highly unlikely that the search will lead to a satisfactory result.

Only in mathematics do problems have single solutions. Geometric theorems can be proved, algebraic equations may be factored, sums, dividends, and products can be calculated to find solutions to problems. In group work, the words *concern* or *trouble* can be substituted for *problem*. Concerns don't necessarily imply that something must be rectified or that there is a single answer that will fix things.

I'm

These two letters and apostrophe have kept more people from changing than all the excuses in the world. Short for "I am," "I'm" is a self-defining descriptor that irrevocably reduces the totality of a human being to a convenient label. "I'ms" are overgeneralizations, oversimplifications, and more: they offer a flawless excuse for running in place. When "I'm shy," I am blessed with a condition as certain as "I'm North American" or "I'm 30." "I'm shy" also brings with it "I'm always shy, I was born this way, I will always be shy, I can't help it." Statements can be rephrased in a way that implies control, temporary states, and situation-specific behavior: "I *act* shyly," "I *behave* shyly."

Maybe

"Maybe," "perhaps," "I think so," "I guess," "possibly," "I don't know" are all safe ways of avoiding a commitment. They are evasive words which group members use to back out of tight situations. When these ambiguous responses are used, the group leader has to work extra hard to get some clear declaration of opinion or intent. Shown here is a typical evasive dialogue which can sometimes be stopped through persistence.

Group Leader: "How do you feel right now?"
Client: "Kinda strange."
Group Leader: "Strange meaning nervous?"
Client: "I guess so."
Group Leader: "What is going through your head that is making you feel strange?"
Client: "Um—Ah—"
Group Leader: "That you aren't in control of this situation?"
Client: "Yeah, maybe."
Group Leader: "And that you don't like being in this vulnerable situation?"
Client: "You could say that, I guess."
Group Leader: "Well, what do you believe will happen next?"
Client: "I don't know."
Group Leader: "What do you imagine is in store for the future?"
Client: "I just can't say. How should I know?"
Group Leader: "Take a wild guess. What do you guess is going to happen next?"

Awful

When something is awful, nothing could ever be worse. *Awful* or *terrible* implies that some catastrophe has occurred that the person cannot survive. The use of these words usually involves an exaggeration or distorted perception in which the person feels both frustrated and helpless. Therapeutically, it is helpful to confront the client's ungrounded assumption that things are, in fact, awful.

"If it is awful that you flunked your class, what then would we call it if you had been permanently kicked out of school? And if you were kicked out of school, that would not be terrible either, since there is always something worse that could occur. Certainly, this is inconvenient, embarrassing, frustrating. But, *awful?* It is very difficult for you to prove that anything is ever totally bad."

Made

The misuse of verbs creates an unhealthy distortion of reality in which cause-effect relationships become confused. Since one's own neurons and synapses, the stuff from which feelings are constructed, are inaccessible to others in the world, it is difficult to believe that anyone can *make* another feel anything. Short of physical contact, feelings are self-manufactured states.

When language signals that cognitive distortions are going on inside a client's head, the group leader vigorously challenges the rational base for the distorted beliefs: "He *made* you cry. How exactly did he do that? Do you have a 'cry button' on your forehead that he can push at will? Did he reach inside your brain, perhaps through your mouth or ears, twist a few neurological connections, and thereby make you cry? In fact, you did it to yourself *after* you heard what he said."

It

The use of ambiguous pronouns like *it*, *they*, *we*, and *people* send incomplete messages to listeners. The full meaning of a thought, its depth, detail, and totality, is left unsaid. The deeper meaning, the significant parts of the communication, are the features of the statement that the group leader can work on.

"When you say that people in general don't like you, which people are those? Every one in the Western hemisphere? Everyone you know? Or just your younger brother?"

"You just used the pronoun *we*. Who, exactly, are you speaking for beside yourself?"

"*It* really got to you? How exactly did *it* do that, and which *it* are you referring to?"

Wrong

"Right," "wrong," "good," "bad," and other value judgments imply that there is some absolute standard of measurement by which all behavior in every culture may be assessed. Except for those who endow a book, like the Bible or the Koran, with such divine power that each word must be interpreted literally by a single preacher, there is no touchstone for determining whether anyone else's behavior is absolutely right or wrong.

One behavior might be better than another, more productive or effective relative to some other choice; but to label someone or something good, bad, right, or wrong is to live out Sartre's credo that all humans "desire to be God." Even if such a deity exists, it is unlikely that He sits in the sky with a blackboard keeping track of our good and bad thoughts. Only when the language of value judgments has been eliminated from group members' vocabularies can they hope to be accepting of one another.

"Who says that it is *wrong?*"
"How do you know that it is bad for him just because it is bad for
    you?"
"Who are you to judge everyone in the world, calling them immoral
    because they don't act as you would like?"

The preceding entries certainly do not constitute an exhaustive list, but they do provide a sampling of the kinds of destructive language that signal reality distortions and obstacles to change. They are vocal symptoms of underlying cognitive and affective processes. Language is, after all, about the only thing we have to work with. Group leaders help people to change by listening and talking, using language with scalpel-like precision.

The experienced group leader can always become a more expert communicator, a more fluent poet, and a creator of therapeutic images. Watzlawick (1978), however, emphasizes the greater need for therapists to speak their clients' language rather than forcing them to learn to speak ours. The reason why traditional therapies take so ridiculously long, he suggests, is because clients are expected to master a foreign language before they can be helped. The therapist can use language, as a chameleon changes color—to suit the environment.

> In other words, the therapist not only does his utmost to arrive at
> an understanding of the client's values, expectations, hopes, fears,
> prejudices—in short, his world image—as quickly and as com-
> pletely as possible, but he also pays attention to the *actual* lan-
> guage of his client and utilizes it in his own verbalizations
> (Watzlawick, 1978, p. 140).

People can be pragmatic in their choice of language and flexible in changing their speech. Their vocabularies, which give concrete labels to abstract ideas that are catalogued in the brain, change easily with the times. For these reasons, the group leader may concentrate on changing the behavior of group members by changing the language they use to describe their worlds.

CHAPTER 6

Macro- and Micro-Diagnostics

There is a story about a billion-dollar luxury liner, outfitted with every possible appointment, convenience, necessity, and designed to gratify every decadent demand that could possibly be of interest or use to its several thousand prominent passengers. This floating Taj Mahal, booked solid for months by wealthy citizens and cargo exporters, exhibited a phenomenally delicate profit margin in which time was equivalent to money. For this great ship to sit idle for even an hour, much less for a day or a week, would cost the company millions in delays, late penalties, and inconvenience for everyone concerned.

Every effort had been made to ensure that the ship would operate at peak efficiency. The engine room had as many backup systems and fail-safe mechanisms as an Apollo rocket. No quality had been overlooked in building the most reliable, durable mechanical equipment money could buy. The engine room was staffed by officers, experts, and mechanics from around the world. Each stood vigil in a gleaming white uniform looped with gold braid and brass buttons. Computer systems, draped in pastel plastics and steel, lined the walls. Nothing could possibly go wrong.

Except that the ship's engines somehow would not start. The crew had tried everything to remedy the situation as the passengers paced restlessly for an hour, then two. The captain frantically wired around the world for advice, getting nothing in return but sympathy. So the great ship stood idle in its berth. Experts and engineers were at a loss what to do next. Finally, an officer recalled hearing about a mechanic who could fix anything. For 60 years he had repaired broken-down engines of every sort, though his methods were alleged to be somewhat unorthodox.

After scouring the dockside streets, the crew finally located the weathered old man in a bar. Creaking slowly to his feet, he agreed to help solve their problem and shuffled to the scene, pushing a wheelbarrow full of greasy tools. He entered the engine room, surveyed the scene, and ordered everyone to give him room. Like a rat, he scurried from one end of the room to the other, feeling parts, smelling the air, nodding absently to himself.

After several tense minutes the observers grew restless. The old man's staccato grunts became more urgent as he settled into a corner of the room with hundreds of brightly color-coded pipes spread in every direction. Selecting an obscure pipe, he studied its shape and form for a moment, then returned to his wheelbarrow to search for the correct tool. Finding an immense monkey wrench, he strolled over to the pipes, reared back with his wrench, and, to the astonishment of everyone, gave one of the pipes a great whack. The shudder reverberated along the gleaming metal until, a minute later, the engines sputtered, hiccupped a few times, then settled into a gentle purr.

The old man was embraced by the other engineers, and the captain solemnly approached to offer his gratitude. As the ship finally began to get underway, the captain took out the company checkbook to pay the mechanic. "How much do we owe you?" he asked. "$50,000," replied the old mechanic. The captain sputtered: "You old crook, how dare you overcharge us for the little you did. For an expenditure this large I must clear the amount with the owners. You'll have to submit an itemized statement."

The mechanic nodded, found an old scrap of an envelope in his pocket, and scribbled his bill:

Mechanic's Bill for Fixing the Ship

Hitting the pipe $10.00
Knowing where to hit the pipe $49,990.00

Total $50,000.00

Philosophers, engineers, surgeons, mechanics, plumbers, and group leaders are all skilled diagnosticians who find out exactly what is wrong, how it broke down, and what needs to be done to put it back together. But all the skills of a mechanic or techniques of a group leader are useless without knowing precisely where and how to "hit the pipe." In the case of group leadership, diagnosis has a special value in identifying individual (microlevel) as well as collective behavior (macrolevel) patterns. Economists, too, think in terms of macro- and microlevel concepts—respectively, that which affects a whole system and that which affects any component of the universe.

Haley (1976) thinks of macrodiagnostic labels as the crystallization of a repeated sequence of behavior within a social organization, such as a family unit or group structure. He believes that the therapist must be included as part of the presenting problem since she or he formulates, and defines the issues in diagnostic terms. According to Haley, these professionally created problems make human dilemmas chronic by constructing a group system that encourages conformity to expected norms. A schizophrenic residing in a hospital, for example, will experience a lot of trouble by failing to live up to the staff and ward rules for appropriate schizophrenic behavior.

> The nurse just now picked up one of the sheets I have written. She read it—looked at me oddly—and asked what in the hell I thought I was doing. And because she expected an answer in keeping with my strange occupation—I did not have the heart to disappoint her. So I gave her an answer that fitted. I told her that I was Shakespeare, the reincarnation of Shakespeare trying to side-step a strait-jacket. (I'll admit that I feel queer enough to be the reincarnation of something but I doubt if Shakespeare would claim me.) But hurray! She came back down the aisle with a whole ream of paper and said to me: "Go to it, Shakespeare" (Jefferson, 1964, p. 13).

Group leaders use methods of reliable diagnosis much different from those operating from, say, a hospital staff approach. It is crucial for group leaders to be able to label client self-defeating behaviors, not for the sake of pigeonholing a person into a discrete category, but to get a handle on specific problem areas as a prerequisite for systematic change efforts. This process of microdiagnostics gives the group leader a much more comprehensive framework for understanding and practicing effective therapeutic observations.

While *microdiagnostics* deals with labeling individual client actions, *macrodiagnostics* is concerned with the larger processes that help the leader to assess what is going on in the group. What can the heavy silence mean? What effects are minicoalitions having on total group functioning? Why can't things seem to get started? These and similar critical questions permit the group leader to think macrodiagnostically while analyzing significant themes as they arise.

THE FUNCTIONS OF LABELING

The computer was designed by the human mind. It makes binary decisions by placing a single datum into a particular category based on some classification overlay. Things fit over here in this round hole or over there in that square hole. If we should come upon a thing that fits in neither one hole nor the other, we may create a third, triangular hole, or we may squeeze, mold, or reshape the mutant thing until it fits into one of the existing holes.

Humans are by nature schematic beings whose brain capacities function according to the limitations of the classification systems available. When the child creates a cognitive category indicating that big, brown four-legged animals with tails are called "cows" and is then confronted with a thing called a "horse," the mind is forced to broaden its classification scheme to include the new element of the class. "The division of the perceived universe into parts and wholes is convenient and may be necessary, but no necessity determines how it shall be done" (Bateson, 1979, p. 42).

There are many examples to support the human need to classify parts and wholes into convenient, orderly systems, even in the field of mental health. The first cave people were able to determine who among their citizens was strange enough to warrant drilling holes in their skulls to let the demons escape. The ancient Egyptians diagnosed mental dysfunctions on the basis of uterine positions; the patient would later be treated by having her vagina fumigated. The Babylonians relied on the goddess Ninkharsag and her eight assistant gods to recognize disease syndromes. The physician Empedocles of Sicily diagnosed imbalanced humors of yellow and black bile, phlegm, and blood. The Hippocratics and their methods of clinical medicine initated the first comprehensive mental disease classification system including personality and behavioral characteristics.

Throughout history, until Emil Kraepelin (1856–1926), practitioners had sought creative ways to identify patterns of mental sickness. A favorite clinical diagnosis process of the Dark Ages was to initiate "trial by water" (the "patient" who drowned was a witch) whenever a person exhibited deviant behavior sufficient to draw attention. In recent years, we have had Sheldon's ectomorphs, mesomorphs, endomorphs and other body types as diagnostic correlates. Before that, phrenology, palm reading, and astrology were all in vogue as diagnostic devices. A brief history of psychiatry, psychology, and education is, in fact, an account of the evolution of more accurate, consistent, and valid diagnostic schemes.

But diagnosis is not just used for convenience or because it is aesthetically pleasing to have people grouped in neat little places. Diagnosis is the process of understanding the client, "a system of classification that the therapist uses to establish goals and select the most advantageous base for promoting learning" (Robinson, 1978).

Shertzer and Stone (1980) summarize the further functions of diagnosis:

- to make predictions about client behavior so that a therapy plan can be formulated that will fit with anticipated outcomes
- to summarize client problems, their causes, and abnormal features based on observable characteristics
- to determine the unique personality dynamics of each case
- to identify skill deficiencies in client functioning
- to understand the significance of client behavior
- to create working hypotheses that aid this understanding of another individual

Diagnostic thinking is the culmination of deductive reasoning to reach pragmatic conclusions that will guide leader behavior. Therapeutic diagnosis is essentially a process of problem formation in which the client's concerns are simplified to manageable levels by reducing the significant variables to the lowest common denominator without sacrificing their essential qualities. For example, a group member could complain of the following behavioral symptoms:

1. compulsive drive to achieve straight As in school
2. perfectionistic standards and expectations for friends and lovers
3. bouts of depression after events that should have been exciting (exams, dates, new experiences)
4. reluctance to cooperate with early therapeutic efforts although verbalizes a great desire for help
5. has very few friends and, although lonely, does not approach interesting strangers
6. feels trapped living at home, quarrels with family but can't find affordable housing
7. is almost always in control of social conversation, leading the discussion and introducing the topics
8. is extremely skilled at communication and extraordinarily perceptive regarding others' feelings
9. engages in a lot of approval seeking with group leader, showing off superior mind
10. acts condescendingly toward a group member of the opposite sex
11. is the only group member who preferred not to receive feedback in the introduction exercise

12. acts moody in the group whenever another person reports substantial progress
13. is fantastically insightful in understanding the origins and payoffs of the presenting concerns but balks at the prospect of talking in terms of goals
14. refuses to do any psychological homework between sessions
15. is extremely supportive, caring, and helpful to group members perceived as less intelligent and capable
16. withdraws when faced by confrontation; will not fight back

This is only a sampling of possible cues indicative of the client's characteristic behavior. We could also mention a variety of other data, which may or may not be relevant, such as how other group members react to the client or what the client has done previously to cope with difficulties. But let us assume that these 16 behavioral symptoms are those most important to the situation (an invalid assumption in reality, when we *never* know whether we have accumulated enough background). The group leader must now decide which symptoms are the most significant. Based on the available evidence, what may we logically conclude is the most reasonable diagnosis of this client's principal problem? We don't care to categorize or classify; we only wish to label specifically the main concern in need of resolution.

Themes of approval seeking, psychological dependence, and externally controlled thinking are all prevalent here, as are attitudes of perfectionism and a fear of failure. Following intensive, in-depth scrutiny, the diagnostic arrow eventually pointed toward the client's reluctance to take risks of any kind. She had programmed her life and relationships to maximize security and predictability, preferring to remain alone rather than to risk feeling vulnerable. She worked methodically in school, not because she enjoyed learning or wanted good grades, but because she needed the structure and routine of compulsive studying. She avoided parties or any social setting where she had to relinquish total control. Within the group, she resented anyone who was willing to take risks because risk taking reminded her of her own inadequacies.

The clinician is in the unenviable position of playing detective to determine which pieces of evidence are important, which symptoms need further investigation, what variables are confounding the picture or masking actual circumstances, and what causal relationships are involved in the situation. In this problem-formation, the therapist can as easily complicate the existing difficulties by misjudgment, oversimplification, and illogical thinking as reconcile the conflicts. In the words of Lord Berkeley: "We first raise the dust and then claim we cannot see" (Watzlawick, Weakland, & Fisch, 1974).

DISLABELING EFFECTS OF DIAGNOSIS

Bakker (1975) claims that the main reasons clients don't change have less to do with clients than with our "dislabeling" conceptions and interventions. If a chronic patient makes remarkable progress just after entering psychotherapy, we sometimes tell ourselves that the changes weren't real—just a temporary symptom alleviation to avoid confronting deeper issues. We contribute to the myth that change is difficult and unlikely when we focus on stable personality factors that may no more be altered than one's physical appearance. When medical model concepts are applied that emphasize disease processes, change to counteract the supposed degenerative effects is quite difficult.

The standard psychiatric labeling process involves considerations that are designed not only for the patients' benefit but also for the convenience of insurance companies, hospitals, research directors, and the practitioner. The game is to invent a 5-digit number from the *Diagnostic and Statistical Manual of Mental Disorders* (DSM-III) that can be plugged into the appropriate blank spaces on the Blue Cross forms. No treatment begins, no help is offered, no therapeutic wheels are set in motion, until the medical establishment is first satisfied in its craving for a diagnostic number.

Hopefully, this microdiagnostic process involves a detailed examination of mental status, a series of structured interviews, psychological testing, a developmental case history, medical and neurological examinations, and finally a differential diagnosis that covers the diagnostician in case the best guessed judgment is wrong. The clinician collects all the available symptoms and then attempts to arrive at a label that best summarizes most of them. That no three diagnosticians can reliably agree on the same diagnosis, or even on the same observable symptoms, for the same patient supposedly speaks more for clinical inadequacies than of any deficiency in the system. A client's bestowed label depends very much on the biases of the diagnostician, the prestige of the patient, how other people have reacted to the patient's behavior, and the societal norms that vary across race and culture. In diagnosing diagnosis, Small (1978) concludes that it suffers from the same maladies that afflict disadvantaged clients— malnutrition, prejudice, identity confusion, and lack of dignity.

Kogan (1959) found that a diagnosis may be expressed in terms of the equation:

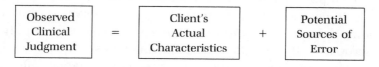

$$\boxed{\begin{array}{c}\text{Observed}\\\text{Clinical}\\\text{Judgment}\end{array}} \quad = \quad \boxed{\begin{array}{c}\text{Client's}\\\text{Actual}\\\text{Characteristics}\end{array}} \quad + \quad \boxed{\begin{array}{c}\text{Potential}\\\text{Sources of}\\\text{Error}\end{array}}$$

where "potential sources of error" could be influenced by any of the following variables (Stuart, 1970):

- the clinician's expectations
- the clinician's theoretical orientation
- the clinician's personal biases
- the clinician's inaccurate observations
- the clinician's illogical reasoning
- the client's inconsistent behavior
- the client's socioeconomic background
- the client's personality style
- the client's perceived similarity to the clinician
- the client's attitudes toward treatment

There is one additional problem in the use of traditional diagnosis: the proliferation of "psychoese" language. Rosen (1977) coined the word *psychobabble* to describe the overuse of nonsensical words for classifying feelings and thoughts. Now, Rosen laments, people no longer feel depressed, they are "bummed out"; they aren't tense but "uptight"; not inhibited but "hung-up"; not fearful but "paranoid"; not strange but "schizzed-out."

Unfortunately, therapists in general and group leaders in particular are responsible for spreading this disease. Benshoff (1978) offers a whole glossary of confusing terms that we model to our clients. When we say "meeting your own needs," what we really mean is: "You are not acting as we want you to." When we say "share," what we really mean is "spill your guts." When we ask for a feeling, what we really want to see is an emotional reaction. "Shaking with terror or sobbing with disappointment are two good responses, and throwing up is always acceptable" (Benshoff, 1978, p. 165). It's not that we so much enjoy speaking in the riddles of verbal fashion, nor do we consciously create a vocabulary full of clichés, simple typologies, and phrases. It is rather that it is easier to borrow other people's language than to create our own.

Della Corte (1980) believes that the labeling craze is more than just a current fad. Like slang, psychological jargon is deliberately ambiguous, permitting its use in any situation with satisfying results. It allows the communicator to sound knowledgeable and up-to-date, yet makes it possible to alter the meaning of words after the fact. But Della Corte contends that the terminology also serves several useful functions. It provides an important illusion of diagnostic validity, but, more crucially, it promotes a feeling of cohesiveness among the people who speak in common tongue. For instance, after John Denver graduated from EST, he was interviewed by *Rolling Stone* to the following effect.

> How far out it is to be a bird and fly around the trees. I am what I've always wanted to be and that is the truth. And I think—in fact, it's not what I think, but I observe that if people were to really take a good look at themselves, they are exactly the way that they have always wanted to be.... My experience is that if I can tell you the truth, just lay it out there, then I have totally opened up a space for you to be who you are and that it really opens up all the room in the world for us to do whatever we want to do in regard to each other. If I don't like you, I'll tell you. And that's great (Rosen, 1977, p. 28).

So much for the power of group settings to indoctrinate participants into their language systems. Group members feel belonging; they are part of a special club with its own fraternal codes and communication. It feels good to be able to recognize predictable behavior patterns, match them with a memorized label, and play amateur psychosleuth when the diagnosis is yelled aloud:

"You're 'parenting' again."
"Quit being a Manipulative Monopolizer."
"Your 'Hostile Child' is showing."
"If you weren't so 'passive-dependent,' you wouldn't have this
    problem."

Somewhere in the back of the group member's head a little ball chinks into place, the diagnosis is confirmed: "So *that's* the name for what you were doing" (as if by giving a name to a thing we unravel its mysteries).

DIAGNOSTIC ALTERNATIVES

Stuart (1970) claims that the principal problem of current diagnostic practices is that they are based on "Aristotelian rather than Galilean logic, which results in the postulation of entities which cannot be shown to exist" [p. 75]. He further specifies intrinsic weaknesses in the system where (a) the diagnosis is made in the context of a threatening situation; (b) the discrete categories are not mutually exclusive; and (c) the categories are so complex as to defy reliable application.

One of the most startling shortcomings of the "new, improved" DSM-III is its almost total disregard for interpersonal behavior and social-psychological variables (McLemore & Benjamin, 1979). Since group leaders are largely concerned with interpersonal behavior, the psychiatric nosological system is virtually useless as a functional tool. All the interpersonal approaches to diagnosis that we have inherited from Horney (1945), Berne (1966), Sullivan (1947), Adams (1964), Bales (1970), Ohlsen and Pearson (1965), and Hill (1971) have been ignored in the current system, leaving group leaders to fend for themselves.

Begelman (1976) has compiled an exhaustive list of criticisms against traditional psychiatric diagnoses which yield, in the opinion of Adams, Doster, and Calhoun (1977), surprisingly little useful information about the client's behavior. The reliability of the system has been questioned by a number of researchers (Zigler and Phillips, 1961, 1965; Zubin, 1967; Rosenhan, 1973; Temerlin, 1975). It fosters a disease concept of emotional concerns, giving the client an excuse for remaining helpless: "It's not my fault. I've got an anxiety neurosis. No wonder I can't relax." It presumes that everyone with the same label has the same problem, a misconception that sabotages any effort to individualize therapy. The labels become stereotypical and stigmatizing. They dehumanize the patient and have a strong bias toward searching for pathology. Finally, Begelman (1976) and McLemore and Benjamin (1979) point out that psychiatric labels have little value for establishing prognoses, constructing treatment plans, or even predicting behavior.

To counter the limitations of traditional diagnostic practices, McLemore and Benjamin (1979) recommend using an interpersonal model that takes into account the client's functioning within a social context. This has obvious advantages for practitioners working in group settings in allowing the interpersonal diagnosis to include: (a) a focus on social behavior rather than on disease, (b) a relatively stigma-free description of behavior, (c) more reliable and consistent applications, and, (d) implications for prescriptive therapy within an interpersonal context. The authors then formulate the beginnings of a working model in which a group member's behavior is labeled in terms of its effects on self and others.

They illustrate with the example of a parent who routinely uses power tactics on a child *(hostile blame – interpersonal)*. The child internalizes the hostility, creating guilt. The guilt, now interpersonally diagnosed in the context from which it developed, can be effectively countered by the group leader who uses *empathy* and interjects intrapsychic healing forces such as *support*. This interpersonal diagnostic system can therefore be reliably applied to predicting consequences as well as to understanding etiology.

Virginia Satir (1972) has developed a diagnostic system that also lends itself well to interpersonal group situations, particularly in family therapy and in analyzing macroconcepts and interdynamics. Satir's patterns of group communication include those who are *placaters*, who avoid conflict at the cost of their integrity; *blamers*, who attempt to show strength by placing the focus on others; *computers*, who rely on intellectual, ultrarational ploys to hide vulnerability; and *distractors*, who make us dizzy with irrelevancies. Ineffectivey run groups would therefore exhibit these incongruent communication styles in conjunction with closed-system rules and restrictions.

Other interpersonal classifications, such as those mentioned by Kottler, Vriend, and Dyer (1975), Ohlsen (1977), and Corey (1981), focus more specifically on group member behavior rather than on style or personality. Such a distinction is crucial to avoiding the *dis*labeling process of typecasting people rather than what they do. The therapeutic implications are, of course, that once self-defeating behaviors are productively labeled, they may be changed. Personalities, style, nature, disorders imply a degree of stability and permanence that would therefore resist alteration.

The following list of behavioral labels represents a meaningful selection of common self-defeating behaviors found among group members. Only after these difficulties are clearly and specifically identified, *with the client involved in the self-diagnostic process*, can the group leader hope to go to work on them. This summary of dysfunctional behaviors is therefore converted into the labels to which clients can most easily relate. They include microdiagnostic (intrapersonal) as well as macrodiagnostic (interpersonal) behavioral indices.

Intrapersonal Behaviors
Procrastination: Acting as if by waiting long enough a concern will go away by itself.
Behavioral example: a group member repeatedly declares that she

she wishes to make certain life-changes but never seems to have the time to act.

External Control: Demonstrating a lack of control over emotions, behavior, or oral habits.

Behavioral example: "I just can't help it. The depression just came over me."

Living in the Past: Hiding from the present by using the past as an excuse for the way one is.

Behavioral example: "But I've always been this way. I've never been good at speaking up in groups."

Self-Pity: Feeling sorry for oneself and helpless to do anything about it.

Behavioral example: "I wish, just once, I could get a girl to go out with me again."

Guilt: Punishing oneself for some regretted misdeed in the past.

Behavioral example: "If only I could have known, maybe she'd be all right today."

Worry: Spending time thinking about future things that could happen but over which one has no control.

Behavioral example: "What if it rains during the picnic? I don't know what I would do."

Psychological Dependence: Demanding that the world be a certain way in order to be happy; having life ruled by external schedules; having attachment to another person that involves needs rather than wants.

Behavioral example: "I can't just go out and get a job unless my husband gives his permission."

Rigid Thinking: reluctance to give up untenable positions with a vested interest in certain ideas; getting into hopeless verbal battles.

Behavioral example: a group member who has a difficult time changing views or admitting that she or he is wrong.

Ethnocentricity: Judging the world and other people's actions according to a narrow, personal value system.

Behavioral example: a group member who criticizes another for acting differently than she or he would act.

The methodology for diagnosing any of these phenomenological patterns is usually done within the context of an exploratory behavioral assessment in which the group leader attempts to get a handle on the nature of the presenting concerns. Both Lazarus (1973) and Kanfer and Phillips (1970) developed a 7-component assessment paradigm based on the client's behavior, affect, sensation, imagery, cognition, and interpersonal relationships. The diagnostic framework incorporates an analysis and clarification of the client's problem, an assessment of motivation and reinforcement levels in the client's life, a reading of biological and social-cultural experiences, as well as an analysis of the client's self-control, social relationships, and physical environment. All these factors together form a meaningful diagnostic pattern that not only summarizes the exact nature of client difficulties but implies the best therapeutic alternatives for treatment.

Gottman and Lieblum's (1974) problem-assessment strategy involves treating client symptoms, not as important in themselves, but as warning flares that therapeutic efforts are necessary. "A good assessment should suggest hypotheses for intervention and not merely result in categorization or labeling" (Gottman & Leiblum, 1974, p. 25). They therefore contend that client diagnosis ought to include the following questions:

- How and why did the client decide to seek help?
- What has the client already attempted to do to resolve the problem?
- What are the client's expectations for treatment, including leader and group member roles?
- What is the client doing that she or he should not be doing because it is disturbing to others?
- What is the client doing that is disturbing to self?
- What are the client's operating assumptions and cognitive structures?
- Is the presenting concern interactive in nature? Who else is involved?
- How often, when, and where does the presenting concern arise?
- What reinforcers and maintenance variables are perpetuating the client's self-defeating behaviors?
- What events and experiences in the client's past are relevant to the current problem?
- What are the client's characteristic functioning levels in life skills (sleeping, eating, loving, sex, integration skills, appearance, moods, energy level, walking)?
- What are the client's behavioral assets, deficiencies, and abilities?

Either of these diagnostic systems, or even a traditional mental status examination, requires that the clinician think analytically to isolate significant variables for further investigation. The intrapersonal behaviors also form a backdrop for understanding the broader macrodiagnostic concepts found in interpersonal behaviors.

Interpersonal Behaviors

Approval Seeking: Deliberately or unconsciously speaking or acting to win the leader's or other members' good opinion, even at the expense of one's personal convictions.

Behavioral example: whenever a client speaks, he makes eye contact only with the leader.

Mothering: Acting as a rescuer and nurturing figure to reduce one's personal level of discomfort over conflict.

Behavioral example: "I wish you'd stay off Michael's back. Can't you see he's had enough?"

Politicking: Speaking for others in the group without their consent.

Behavioral example: "We don't like the way things have been going."

Boring: Speaks in a monotone with little animation; prone to rambling about inappropriate irrelevancies.

Behavioral example: "I guess—I don't—have—much—to say."

Jesting: Inappropriately making jokes and clowning to win attention, disrupt group focus, or shrug off a painful confrontation.

Behavioral example: a client starts laughing hysterically, making funny faces of rejection right after receiving direct confrontation.

Withdrawal: Passive behavior characterized by silence, blank expression, and escape defenses.

Behavioral example: throughout a session, one client scoots back chair, stares out window, and doodles on paper.

Martyrizing: Taking on the image of a sufferer who has no choice but to shoulder the burdens of the world.

Behavioral example: repeatedly complaining about how miserable life is but doing nothing to change the situation.

Interrogating: Excessive aggressive questioning with an implied demand for the "right" answers.

Behavioral example: "Why are you so weak you can't face up to me?"

Monopolizing: Self-centered rambling, storytelling, and talking to the point where it is difficult for others to have group time when they want it.

Behavioral example: "Did I ever tell you about the time—?"

Shrinking: Playing pseudoleader by dispensing advice or over-intellectualizing.

Behavioral example: "I think my problem is just a manifestation of the unresolved hostility I feel toward my father."

Evasiveness: Watering down the truth out of a fear of hurting others' feelings or from vulnerability.

Behavioral example: "You want feedback? I think you're a pretty nice guy."

Broader Patterns

In addition to the interpersonal dimensions of macrodiagnosis, the group leader is also concerned with the broader patterns of group dynamics that predict future outcomes. The practitioner will want to identify aspects of collective behavior in order to prepare appropriate interventions for circumventing problems, to protect individual rights against pressure toward conformity, and to orient oneself, as a sailor would read the stars to make certain the voyage is on course.

The first signpost to assess is the *group synergy* (Cattell, 1948). What is the accelerated collective energy that is available in the session? Are participants focused on what is happening? **Synergy** is the productive cooperation among clients that maintains a harmonious atmosphere sufficient to meet individual therapeutic goals. Based on the attitudes, motivation, and behavior of all members at any given time, the total synergy of a group may be dynamic or in need of recharging. There is a contagious transmission of excitement which the group leader carefully monitors, occasionally intervening to keep productive energy flowing smoothly.

Interchange compatibility is a term coined by Schutz (1958) to describe the mutual expressions of inclusion, control, and affection among group members. To what extent are clients reciprocating interpersonal needs from one another? Who is giving and who is taking? Are exchanges roughly balanced as to which clients are offering support, taking risks, using group time, or giving feedback? If only a few members are receiving most of the help, doing most of the talking, or taking most of the time, the interchange compatibility factor is unbalanced. The group leader would then be signaled to spend more time drawing out other clients while keeping dominant members more in control.

All groups have subgroup coalition formations which must be identified for the purpose of determining their effects on total group member functioning. These interpersonal attraction/repulsion patterns could conceivably inhibit natural drives toward cohesion and mutual intimacy by setting up competitive factions. Who rescues whom? Who attacks whom? Which members are most similar/ dissimilar? Who defers to whom? Who knows whom outside the group? What alliances affect group outcomes in what ways? What payoffs do participants accrue as the result of their joint actions?

The level of trust and cohesion must also be accurately read at frequent intervals. A high frequency of "we" statements, equal contributions, cooperative statements, expressed liking of group experience, unprompted participation, and mutually supportive comments would indicate a group of individuals functioning at high levels in these dimensions (Krumboltz & Potter, 1973).

Any of these few macrodiagnostic targets or some of the predictable problems and critical incidents discussed in Chapter 7 require the group leader to be a special breed of diagnostician. There is a pragmatic motive to the labeling process. The therapist hopes to identify common themes and provoke client self-diagnosis so that a clear vision is provided of exactly where the therapeutic effects are headed.

CHAPTER 7

Critical Incidents and Predictable Problems

During the span of a human life, there occur critical periods in which specific biological, cultural, and psychological factors make their influences known. As these developmental factors arise, individuals must master a set of skills to resolve novel conflicts and adapt to crucial growth spurts or all future progress will become retarded (Havighurst, 1972). The infant who fails to develop emotional attachments to a parent, the child who does not learn socially acceptable ways to seek adult attention, or the adolescent who never masters abstract reasoning are all doomed to spend their lives in a state of compromised functioning (Piaget, 1956; Erikson, 1963; Gazda, 1978).

Throughout the duration of a group there are also a series of predictable stages. In therapeutic groups, as in human evolution, progressive development leads to potential problems. Every experienced group leader comes to recognize these critical incidents that can so easily sabotage therapeutic effectiveness. Within a single instant, all our training and preparation must come into play; a split-second decision must be made as to the best way to handle the situation; and we must live with the consequences forever.

The instantaneous decisions that group leaders must make when confronted with critical situations in the field are not unlike those required of jet pilots. According to Tom Wolfe (1980), successful flyers all have an elusive but necessary quality called "The Right Stuff," which they must unhesitatingly exercise during a crisis.

> Being a fighter pilot ... presented a man, on a perfectly sunny day, with more ways to get himself killed than his wife and children could imagine in their wildest fears. If he was barreling down the runway at two hundred miles an hour, completing the takeoff run, and the board started lighting up red, should he (a) abort the takeoff (and try to wrestle with the monster which was gorged with jet fuel, out in the sand beyond the runway) or (b) eject (and hope that the goddamned human cannonball trick works at zero altitude and he doesn't shatter an elbow or a kneecap on the way

out), or (c) continue the takeoff and deal with the problem aloft (knowing full well that the ship may be on fire and therefore seconds away from exploding)? He would have one second to sort out the options and act, and this kind of workaday decision came up all the time [p. 26].[1]

Similarly, being a group leader presents a professional with more ways to mess up other people's lives than our spouses, children, or clients could possibly imagine in *their* wildest fears. With reported casualties reaching as high as 80% (Lieberman, Yalom, & Miles, 1973) or even 47% of participants (Gottschalk, 1966), Hartley, Roback, and Abramowitz (1976) urge practitioners to become more aware of the variables that produce deterioration effects. Certainly, groups run by experienced and well-trained therapists will do a lot less potential damage than encounter groups led by lay people. However, it is the critical incidents that short-circuit progress in groups—the problem clients, crisis stages, and pivotal moments—that will ultimately determine positive experiences in members, if their leaders handle them smoothly.

Just as jet pilots have less than a second to make a critical decision that will affect their immediate well-being, group leaders are regularly faced with conflicts in which their chosen course of action, selected within an instant, will ultimately affect the safety of a dozen persons in their charge. If a belligerent and absusive group member "comes barreling down the runway" determined to wreak havoc on unsuspecting peers, the leader must make one of three choices: (a) confront the client with the inappropriate behavior (and risk alienating/embarrassing/ridiculing/damaging him); (b) ignore the behavior and attempt to extinguish the actions (and allow potential abuse to ripple throughout the group, destroying intimacy, cohesion, and perhaps the defenses of a vulnerable member); or (c) try to use the outburst as a stimulus for openly working through the issue (allowing the client to manipulate group time and draw attention to himself, inadvertently rewarding his deviance). There are perhaps a thousand other legitimate courses of action which lead, however, to no single, "correct" solution to the problem.

The purpose of this chapter is to reintroduce pragmatic group leaders to a catalogue of the most common critical incidents that occur in groups so that they may better prepare themselves to handle anticipated problems as they arise.

COMMON CRITICAL INCIDENTS

A number of writers have constructed lists of critical themes requir-ing leader intervention, among them Grieger and Boyd (1977), Yalom (1975), and Cohen and Smith (1976). Most noteworthy among the critical incidents are several significant nominations that must be handled with particular skill, sensitivity, and diplomacy. For in-stance, in every group there are a number of "firsts" that command the attention of every participant until they can be integrated into the existing scheme of things. Every novel stimulus requires that an or-ganism adapt to the altered physical/psychological environment. The first time the therapist says "I don't know," shock waves ripple among the clients until they figure out the implications of having a leader who is less than perfect. Other firsts can be just as traumatic.

Some of the most important firsts and critical incidents have here been described as they would arise chronologically.

First Impressions

As group members first enter the room and begin to make them-selves comfortable (and uncomfortable), they will check out the competition. On the basis of their perceptions and biases, they will form limited, narrow first impressions of one another.

"Am I in the right place? Look at some of these people. Big Ears over there looks like he stepped out of a *Gentleman's Quarterly.* I bet he carries his blow dryer in the car. This girl with the horn-rims is going to be trouble. She looks like she's sitting on a broom, pissed off at the world. I like that guy she's sitting next to, though he seems even more nervous than I do. I *know* I'm not going to like these older guys with their pinstripe suits and snotty attitudes. I wonder what these people think of me?"

In the initial encounter, group members will tend to write off those whom they perceive as different or strange and will attach them-selves to a few persons who may hold values similar to their own. Coalitions are established which must eventually be expanded to reflect more open acceptance of all persons, regardless of their life-style preferences and personal traits. Clients will need to be quickly helped to move beyond superficial encounters and predictable small talk to deeper levels of honest communication.

Opening exercises designed to start the group with structured introductions often help to dispel negative reactions because all people become more attractive after they have made disclosures. Residual limiting impressions, those that were reinforced during the introductions, will dissipate further if participants are given an opportunity to express them aloud. In one such exercise, clients are instructed (on the pretext of remembering one another's names) to select the animal that a given person most reminds them of. After clients creatively introduce themselves, they are offered the chance to hear how they initially come across to others in the group.

"Arthur, you remind me of a turtle. You seem quiet, lazy, unassuming. You are content to bask in the sun. Yet you love to swim and explore beneath the water where no one can see."

"Nicole, my first impression of you is of a basset hound. You appear loyal, protective, cuddly. You're a good tracker with your nose to the ground. But you feel awkward, ungainly, and powerless, or at least you sit that way."

This exercise or one like it will get first impressions out in the open. It provides feedback to people in a relatively structured, non-threatening manner. It helps clients (a) to hear nondefensively how they come across to others, (b) to become more accurate in interpreting others' behaviors, (c) to get practice in giving constructive feedback, (d) to become more congruent between the images they believe are projected and the ones that people actually see, (e) to collect significant data about one another, and (f) to be more accepting and flexible in their perceptions of others, more willing to appreciate individual differences (Brown, 1978).

Unequal Participation
Within minutes of the first group session, it becomes evident that the willingness of clients to participate is uneven. Some persons enthusiastically contribute all that is available to their consciousness while others pout, sulk, or cautiously wait to see whether disaster befalls those who leaped before they looked. Resentment builds in those who have given much but who don't see their partners reciprocate. Cautious and reserved members may resent those who "hogged" most of the group time, feeling that they'd have spoken up if they had been given more time. Frustration levels increase as feelings of inadequacy become evident during introductions.

Often the leader will deliberately use a well-tested structured exercise that is designed specifically for ensuring equal input among members. A leveling effect can be programmed into the introductory activity by providing specific instruction on appropriate behavior and by allowing all clients the same amount of time. A three-minute timer can be used to encourage conciseness and meaningful introductions that include such basics as expectations for the experience, present feelings, stated goals, characteristic functioning patterns, troublesome behaviors, apprehensions, and predictions of what will occur.

In later stages of the group, unequal participation is confronted more directly by drawing out the passive members (while also protecting their rights to privacy) and encouraging overactive members to be more discriminating in their decisions to speak up. Generally, additional feedback is invaluable in this situation because passive members will receive support that their opinions are valued while overactive members will learn of specific instances when they ramble and focus on themselves. It is only when participation becomes equally distributed that feelings of belonging, identification, cohesion, and intimacy will develop.

Statement of Superficial Concerns

The inherent ambiguity of the group situation, together with diversified client expectations, lead to much confusion and uncertainty. Members may argue about the "real" purpose of the group, stalling progress until some unifying themes and common goals come into focus. Early attempts to resolve differences in interests, background, style, needs, and goals will be unsuccessful until a common language has been developed. The group leader works to restate and clarify client messages in a way that creates greater cohesion and mutual identification.

"When you describe your problems arising from being overweight all your life, I think that all of us could relate to the experience of being an outsider. I noticed Kevin averted his eyes, Samantha looked embarrassed as if she were self-conscious about her physical appearance, and everyone else sort of looked inward. When you mentioned that you were in this group, not because you're weird like everyone else in here, but only because you want to drop 40 pounds, I was again reminded of the concerns that most of you share in common. Your problem is not so much a matter of losing 40 pounds—I'm sure you've found a dozen diets that will help you shed the weight for a few months until you gain it all back—but rather a lack of self-control.

"You are a constant victim of the external world. You see a billboard and start humming the McDonald's jingle until you fill your face. You look at your watch and decide it's time to eat, whether you're hungry or not. I bet that this problem of being externally controlled is not limited to your overeating behavior nor is it unique to you in this group. You've already said how easily you are hurt by others, a symptom of externally controlled emotions. Tabby and Nadine share that difficulty when they lose their tempers so willingly. And all the rest of you mention in some context how you aren't in control of your lives. To say that the only way you intend to use this group is as a diet support system is to grossly underestimate your own potential for change and the collective resources available here to offer assistance."

After clients initially state their reasons for joining the group, their goals, and how they intend to use their time, it will become evident that there are varied interpretations of what is expected. After the first go-around, some clients will have bravely volunteered deeply serious concerns—about their marriage, their sanity, or their sexuality. Others will decide to play it safe (or perhaps they just aren't skilled at self-diagnosis), declaring such goals as "I want to get my parents off my back," "I'd like to get a promotion in my work," or "I want to understand myself better."

It is the job of the group leader to universalize these concerns, translating each from a superficial, narrow orientation into one to which everyone can relate: "When you say you want to get your parents off your back, what you really mean is that you let others get to you. You're also not good at confronting people who abuse you. Does anyone else have a similar problem?"

Small Talk

Until group members learn the rules about appropriate topics for discussion, there is much rambling, small talk, and digression that is unrelated to therapeutic growth. Most people attempt to generalize their behavior from other group encounters, such as parties and meetings, to their actions in therapeutic groups. They have learned to wear plastic smiles, engage in trivial conversation, hide their true feelings, and play games of deception that are patently unacceptable in a counseling setting. If the group leader allows such chitchat to continue, clients assume they are acting as they are expected to act;

but if the chatter is cut off and their usual defenses are stripped away, they begin to feel even more vulnerable. The group leader's task is to model appropriate socializing behavior that is sensitive, direct, and concise while encouraging members to avoid small talk. Silence is preferred over an incessant outflow of trivia.

Some clients will persistently bring discussion back to small talk about politics, baseball, soap operas, or the weather. It is only by educating them that therapeutic groups become different from social groups, that clients will begin to realize how and why they waste valuable group time. After a while, participants will begin to monitor themselves with regard to trivial, distracting discussions.

Collective Silence

A beginner usually makes the mistake of assuming that all group members are part of an uncooperative conspiracy to resist treatment. Their lack of dramatic, *observable* behavior is interpreted as a sign of reluctance to participate. But since only one member can speak at a time, there is *always* group silence except for the voice of a single person.

Some members wait patiently, knowing they are not yet ready to contribute anything meaningful. Others clam up because they don't understand what is expected of them. At least one client will deliberately keep quiet just to see what the leader will do. Another might be working on a self-defeating behavior of talking too much and so refrains from making input. A few will be using the silent time productively to gather their thoughts, integrate new ideas, or formulate a plan. Someone else may be relaxing, resting, regrouping energy after a period of intensity. The point is that all choose silence for their own personal reasons.

The leader who approaches this critical incident with the goal of reducing his or her own discomfort is likely to find trouble along the way. Such an attitude might be expressed as: "I don't know what's wrong with everyone today. I thought we were making some headway, but I guess I was wrong. But that's O.K. If you want to sit there and waste our time, I can wait as long as you can" (folds arms, pushes back chair, pouts, and scowls until someone feels guilty enough to speak).

It is almost always helpful to select one person (usually the client who seems most responsive at that moment) and to address an inquiry in a more personal fashion.

Leader: Fred, I notice that you have been very quiet for the past few minutes. What would you imagine Tony and Louise are thinking about over there in the corner?

Fred: Uh—Gee, I don't know. I was just thinking about whether I wanted to use group time tonight. I think Louise looks kind of bored because she keeps yawning and looking at you to *do* something. Tony just looks like he's daydreaming.

Leader: Well Fred, what do you think *we* should do now?

With a co-leader around, it is more fun to drop the problem in his lap. Whoever is the fastest draw can say: "Jack, what do you make of this silence? I'm a little confused because a number of people look like they want to speak but seem to be holding themselves back."

However the problem is managed, it is the style of execution that is most important. The group leader wants to state that silent periods are acceptable, even desirable and necessary, but also encourage risk taking by members who are too intimidated to speak their minds. By keeping our fingers on the pulse of each participant we can readily interpret the meanings behind "silent action" and so gear our strategies to meet the requirement of each situation.

Functional Deafness

When few meaningful communications can be induced in the early sessions of a group, self-centered monologues become the norm. Clients unskilled at attending to one another will fail to give others their full concentration. Human relations specialists have always been fond of structuring exercises to enhance the quality of inter-communication. Participants may be paired off and requested to repeat verbatim everything that has just been said to them before they are allowed to respond. Advanced group leaders are usually able to intervene without seriously disrupting the flow of things: "Beth, before you continue with your anecdote could you repeat what José just said to you?" Or in another situation: "As you were receiving feedback from the others, you acknowledged their messages before they were even warmed up. It is as if you were only pretending to appreciate their comments when actually you had no intention of giving their ideas consideration."

Often the problem must be brought out in the open by discussing how difficult it is to concentrate on other people's talk while you are at the same time rehearsing your own speech. The behavior can then be interpreted as a fear of saying the wrong thing, a case of performance anxiety that cripples one's attending powers.

First Angry Outburst

Even though we can predict that at some point during the early group sessions someone will have an angry outburst, the foreknowledge doesn't much reduce the startled response when the event occurs. We tell ourselves and our clients that spontaneous emotional expression is good, that it is an example of what we are here for—to work through negative feelings. Still, the first uncontrolled tantrum is almost always traumatic.

The angry person starts turning colors, the neck muscles stand out, and the energy builds to a very loud crescendo. The anger may be self-directed, resulting from frustration; it may be a hostile action to agitate or disrupt proceedings; it may be a definitive last-ditch defense against perceived attack; or it may be an honest acknowledgment that sore toes have been stepped on.

In whatever form and manner the first anger arises, the leader must deftly intervene to prevent casualties among other group members who are not prepared to handle the confrontation constructively. An explanation is in order in which the therapist simultaneously acknowledges the validity of the anger, gives permission for it to continue (unless it is grossly abusive), and reassures group members that the steaming client is indeed playing by the rules.

Once the anger has been labeled, the catharsis is directed toward some resolution of the problem. The most important point is for the therapist to treat this spontaneous conflict in the same calm, accepting, controlled manner with which any other conflict would be resolved. After analyzing the reasons and motives behind the anger, working through destructive attitudes that were responsible for the outburst, as well as through any interaction variables with other members who were involved, the therapist can lead the client to express the anger more effectively.

Schuerger (1979) recommends controlling therapeutic anger by four means: 1) encouraging directness, honesty, and precision of expression; 2) making certain that complaints are specific and complete; 3) following through the anger with involvement in the conflict or with the target person(s); and, 4) teaching more socially acceptable alternatives for working through hostility.

A hard lesson that every schoolteacher must learn is that there is a fundamental difference between *being* angry and *acting* angry. In situations where negotiation, pleading, and logical reasoning fall on deaf ears, an angry outburst is the only way to get people's attention enough to communicate that you are serious. However, when an angry display is called for—to stop a fight in the classroom or to get an insensitive group member to quit infringing on the personal rights of others—it is possible to do so without *feeling* out of control on the inside even though you *look* out of control on the outside.

The group leader may choose to cap the erupting volcano with instruction on controlled anger—how group members can dissipate anger when they feel it rising, how to express anger nondefensively, and how to use angry experiences for future growth.

Giving Advice

From movies and television, clients often acquire distorted expectations of what will happen in therapeutic groups. Since most people operate from a problem-solution orientation anyway, there is a strong drive to solicit and give advice as soon as the presenting concern is expressed. Group members feel pity, empathy for their friend in trouble. They want to help the person to solve his difficulties in the quickest way possible—by dispensing advice.

Even before the concerns have been sufficiently explored, group members will be jumping in with "Have you tried—," "If I were you —," or "My advice to you is—." The advice givers feel great because they feel that they are *doing* something to resolve the ambiguity of the situation and make the pain go away. They breathe a sigh of relief; "Well, we fixed that problem. Who's next?" The client-in-focus, of course, loves the advice and soaks up as much of it as possible. One doesn't have to take responsibility for the advice's outcome when someone else gives the advice.

The group leader must step in during these early home-remedy swap-sessions, explain how and why they are going on, and describe the reasons why they are destructive in the long run, although they temporarily help everyone to feel relieved. "Mickey, how is it helpful for you to hear these suggestions before you are done sharing what is wrong? And even if this advice is followed to the letter—you go home and say what they told you to—what will you have learned to do next time? You will have learned that when you have problems in the future, you find someone else who will tell you what to do."

Power Struggles

Power struggles begin in earnest once group norms have become reasonably stabilized. Those who have initiated discussions fight for control, believing that they have contributed the most and so deserve recognition. Actually, the early initiators are smooth talkers, usually with experience in other groups. They are overly prone to giving advice to others based on the delusion that problems are easily solvable if only they can find the "right" solution.

Some members try to ace the leader out of the authority role, challenging actions and blaming mistakes, while others align themselves in a protective posture to defend the leader against all criticism. Clients try all their best tricks to win leader approval, some by demonstrating compliance and flexibility, others by being rebellious and independent. When they speak, all client eyes will be intently focused on the leader, looking for the slightest sign of displeasure.

Dependency issues come to the forefront, producing simultaneous resentment and relief. Clients expect the leader to take full responsibility for providing entertainment and so tend to hang back. The leader tries to extinguish such dependence by slightly withdrawing, allowing leadership spaces to be filled by those who want the responsibility. By voluntarily yielding power, the leader is automatically seen as less threatening. The power struggle takes a back seat once the aura of Godliness is stripped from a leader who is perceived as perfect in all ways. When limitations and weaknesses are willingly displayed, the leader is a less attractive target for hostile acts.

Disruptive Clients

In almost every group there is someone who is a bit unusual, different from the rest. There appears to be an unwritten law of the universe that states: for every conglomeration of persons, numbering more than a few, who are gathered together for a common purpose under a set of rules, there will always be one person who, though well-meaning and good natured, will be completely "off-the-wall." This person, heretofore referred to as slightly "out-of-it," lacks basic skills for attending to group happenings and so marches to the beat of a different drummer.

The Diagnostic and Statistical Manual—*DSM III* (1980)—of the American Psychiatric Association is full of terms to label such "unusual" persons in groups: antisocial personality disorder, conduct disorder, oppositional disorder, adjustment disorder, narcissistic personality disorder, histrionic personality disorder, or even that grand old favorite—schizophrenia. Regardless of the classification scheme, such persons sometimes slip through the screen we use to filter out deviants.

In preliminary interviews they may appear friendly, helpful, and motivated. Even in initial group sessions they can be cooperative or at least controlled. Then we begin to notice little indications that things aren't quite right. Their comments tend toward irrelevancy with few transitions between thoughts. They are oblivious to the focus of group interaction. When they feel left out they attempt to add their input on another matter of importance to them. More often than demonstrating psychotic features, they simply lack the sensitivity to tune into the group channel, so caught up in their own static that their perceptual systems are distorted. Or they may merely enjoy drawing attention to themselves.

In most cases, off-the-wall group members are only a bit distracting with their digressions, but they can be downright lethal if their frustration levels reach a melt-down. They can waste valuable group time, create hostilities in other participants who resent the intrusions, and prove very trying for the most patient of group leaders. It takes great restraint to not blurt: "Will you please shut up and wait your turn? Can't you see we're in the middle of something very important which you keep interrupting with your blithering idiocies?" As it is, we feel guilty even thinking such thoughts since the distracter usually tries so hard to be helpful.

The other group members look to us for direction. All forward movement ceases until the immediate distraction is put to rest. And generally, the main problem is that off-the-wall clients are oblivious to how they come across. Sometimes it takes (a) maximally direct confrontation (b) by unanimous consensus of all present (c) with very specific supporting examples of inappropriate behavior (d) preferably acted out in the past 3 minutes (e) described in a nonthreatening manner that enables the person to save face.

Candidly, I am not particularly adept at handling the off-the-wall client, even when I follow my own guidelines. My own frustrations, feelings of inadequacy, and self-condemnation for not detecting the problem earlier get in the way. Furthermore, this client doesn't play by my rules but by a unique form of logic that permits verbal abuse, selective memory, and a thinking process that resembles a Jackson

Pollack canvas. When all else fails, I usually resort to an individual conference to weed the client out of the group and into a different therapeutic setting. It is at such times that I begin only half-kiddingly to joke about whether I have made the right career decision.

Acute Anxiety

When a person is matched to a challenge that is perceived as either too difficult or that requires the use of unavailable skills, anxiety results. The overwhelming, panicky realization that you might be in over your head, that things might get out of control and ultimately destroy your existence, is the subjectively experienced state of anxiety. It is not just a matter of *having* anxiety; but *being* anxiety (May, 1958).

The anxious person might start shivering with cold and sweat simultaneously. Breathing pace will increase, as will hand tremors, body shakes, and feelings of unsteadiness. Nausea, vomiting, dizziness, and choking sensations might also accompany the attack. A spectacle unfolds before the group. The anxious person, attempting to control the symptoms, finds that panic becomes even more pronounced as a breaking point is approached. It is frightening enough to brave anxiety within the privacy of one's own home or in a therapist's office, but to do so before a group of persons whose approval has become important is too much to bear!

Freud (1926) was among the first to suggest that anxiety serves a useful function by acting as a danger signal that prepares the organism for combating threat. Like an athlete or a gladiator, the anxious person's body chemistry clicks into "fight or flight" gear, rushing blood to the muscles, stopping digestive processes, constricting blood vessels in the skin to minimize bleeding from injury, releasing epinephrine to open breathing tubes, increasing heart rate and oxygen flow, and dilating pupils to better perceive danger (Bockar, 1976).

Spontaneous anxiety, such as might occur in a group, can be triggered by a number of factors, the most common of which involves helping efforts getting too close to the mark before the client feels fully prepared to change. The instinctual alarm signal that is supposed to warn the occupant of potential danger instead burns down the house (Hoch, 1950).

Beck (1976) describes the anxious client as someone with an "overactive alarm system," one who responds to the slightest hint of perceived danger by psychologically fleeing in panic, thus actually creating harm—a constant state of anxiety that prevents any possible change. He further conceptualizes anxiety as a thinking disorder that involves exaggerating or distorting reality, involuntary overvigilance, and "catastrophizing" about possible outcomes. When a group member with a low tolerance for frustration and impoverished interpersonal skills attempts to express ambiguous feelings or to integrate confronting feedback from other participants, anxiety can arise.

Beck's assumption that the alarm is worse than the fire does little to appease the other group members, who don't know that World War III hasn't really started in their colleague's body. Wracking sobs, tears, moans of anguish can be traumatic for untrained spectators to watch. One client's anxiety becomes contagious and spreads throughout the group unless the leader can swiftly and confidently intervene to offer relief.

The use of meditation, relaxation, or hypnosis to dispel acute anxiety in groups is often helpful. Before any further action can take place, the client's fears must be pacified and the observers must be convinced that things are under control. Using a firm, commanding voice, the leader distracts the anxious client from panic feelings by directing attention to rhythmic breathing, a focal point to stare at, and/or the systematic relaxation of muscle groups.

One of the first groups I led contained a young woman who was devastated because her husband had run away with her best friend. She couldn't talk about the episode without crying. I was successful enough at calming her down so that I was able to use some imagery rehearsal. She visualized herself walking down the street, confronting her husband unexpectedly, and, before we had the chance to have her practice staying relaxed, she lost all semblance of composure. Her behavior became so dramatically tense and out of control that *we* started to panic. The other group members looked to me for reassurance and all I could offer was a sickly, apologetic smile.

Finally, I *pretended* to know what was going on and proceeded to administer psychological first aid until she was calm enough to continue the therapy at a *much* slower pace. Her message, however, was clear, and I remembered thereafter to follow the client's lead instead of moving at a speed that felt comfortable for me. Unfortunately, I can't give this anecdote a happy ending. The woman dropped out of the group the following week, explaining that the anxiety *in* the group was much worse than any of the fears within her own head.

Prejudicial Incidents

Now that the ice has been broken and an atmosphere of honesty prevails, people are more willing to reveal their prejudices and biases toward those with a different lifestyle. Group members will choose sides: blacks versus whites, feminists versus male chauvinist pigs, atheists versus believers, old versus young, rich versus poor, middle class versus outlaws. Since they feel that permission has been granted to say whatever is on their minds, participants open an attic of stored judgments about every conceivable ethnic, socioeconomic, racial, or religious life style represented in the group. The magic words "You people" will then preface any number of creative combinations of abuse.

"You people are just looking for charity."
"You people are all a bunch of lesbians."
"You people don't care about anything except your damn possessions."

Sexist stereotyping, racial tensions, and other critical incidents that result from overgeneralized thinking are best handled by making the confrontations personally based rather than on a cognitive plane. All the ignorance and rigidity that stems from a lack of personal involvement with the scorned population, the "Archie Bunker Syndrome," are dissipated after people are given the opportunity to confront one another on a personal level.

In one group, in which sexist and prejudicial comments were creating further gaps in understanding and greater hostility, time was taken out to confront the problem directly. Everyone was instructed to change sex and race simultaneously. White females became black males. White males became black females, and so on. Discussion was then directed to a topic controversial enough to ensure that members would play their roles to the hilt and identify strongly with the experiences they least understood.

White males pretending to be black women complained that they felt exploited. Black women playing the roles of white men shared their frustration in not being able to find jobs because of reverse discrimination. Black males acting as white females disclosed their fears of being successful; they felt they were scaring away men. And white females, assuming the minds of black males, exaggerated all the ridiculous stereotypes—bragging about how large their penises were, calling out derogatory names, and expressing much anger at having been discriminated against. The result of this psychodramatic structure will certainly lead to greater sensitivity and understanding of one another's unique positions.

Resistance

Bandler and Grinder (1979) facetiously admonish therapists for attributing all unsuccessful therapeutic efforts to client resistance. Whenever group leaders try something that doesn't work, instead of trying something else, they are inclined to blame clients for being uncooperative.

Vriend and Dyer (1973d) mention the different forms that client resistance can take, including open hostility, defensiveness, noncooperative silence, avoidance, and strained civility. Resistance can also take the form of being overly cooperative and compliant (Redl, 1966; Haley, 1973). The group member who continuously sports a congealed smile and who says thank you sweetly to every confrontation is a *lot* more difficult to manage than the client who is more honest about perceived threat.

Gottman and Leiblum (1974) structure a flow chart for analyzing resistance by formulating a series of sequential questions.

- Is resistance due to the client's behavioral repertoire or to interactional variables in the environment?
- Is resistance due to some internal conflict in the client?
- Is resistance due to a skill deficiency in the client?
- Is resistance being maintained by positive consequences?
- Is resistance due to problems in the therapeutic relationship?

To these systematic queries we might add another: is resistance the result of interpersonal circumstances occurring in the group? The particular variety of resistant behavior, how and why it is maintained, and what specifically the client is attempting to avoid will determine the choice of intervention strategy to handle this incident.

After the appropriate source of resistance has been identified, Gottman and Lieblum recommend using situation-specific interventions. The group leader may choose to simply label and interpret the suspected resistant behaviors or may look inward first to make certain that the problem is not due to impatience or unrealistic expectations on the therapist's part. If the client is apprehensive about taking *any* risks, steps might be taken to ease him or her into situations in a progressive fashion. Perhaps trust levels in the group need to be adjusted to reduce the fear of failure, or maybe the leader needs to alter the therapeutic style to be more facilitative.

An alternative interpretation of resistant client behaviors views the process of change as an inherently stressful adaptation. When a group member refuses to cooperate, it may be a sign that intervention effects are on target. It is when a client enthusiastically embraces suggestions for change that we become most suspicious about the accuracy of our treatment.

Once it has been acknowledged that resistance is taking place, it is essentially a matter of discovering which of a thousand leadership behaviors will best move progress forward. Just as in the martial arts where an opponent's own force is used to block aggressive actions, psychological resistance can be used constructively. Watzlawick, Weakland, and Fisch (1974) counter nonsense, not with common sense, but with a move that destroys a client's game plan: "You've got a good point. Why should you change?" Instead of offering further encouragement and motivation (the logical move), the therapist may (irrationally) prescribe a relapse. One of Milton Erickson's favorite ploys was to command an overtly cooperative patient to resist treatment, thereby stripping any satisfaction from the rebellious activities: "The only way the patient can resist is by not relapsing but continuing to improve" (Haley, 1973, p. 31).

In the case of a female patient resistant to losing weight, Erickson (1982) instructed her to follow his therapeutic regimen exactly as prescribed. After eliciting her solemn promise that she would do so, he told her:

> "Let both your unconscious mind and your conscious mind listen. Here's the way you go about it. Your present weight is 180 pounds. I want you to gain 20 pounds and when you weigh 200 pounds, on my scale, you may start reducing. . . .
>
> When she reached 200 pounds she was very happy that she could begin to reduce. And when she got to 130 she said, "I'm never going to gain again."
>
> Her pattern had been to reduce and gain. I reversed the pattern and made her gain and reduce. And she was very happy with the final result and maintained that weight. She didn't want to ever again go through that horrible agony of gaining 20 pounds (Erickson, 1982, p. 40).

Hopper (1978) prescribes working through group member resistance by providing sufficient structure and comfort in early sessions, liberal leader modeling of cooperative group behavior, and by realistic expectations on the therapist's part for predicting when, how, and why such behavior occurs. A great many explanations are viable for a variety of motives behind resistant activities, which is why they are so difficult to handle. They are probably the most critical of all incidents that will occur in any group under many disguised forms and different labels. A group member may exhibit resistant behavior for any of the following 15 reasons.

1. The client doesn't want to be in the group in the first place but is only attending to satisfy the demands of someone else, such as a spouse, teacher, friend, or supervisor. Surprisingly, this is one of the easiest types of resistance to handle because the client is usually outspoken and honest about resentments. When external incentives for participation are hidden, however, the reluctance will take a more subtle and sneaky form.

2. Resistance is frequently an adjustment reaction to a novel situation. Therapeutic groups are strange places to the uninitiated. Only a fool would take the apparent concern, empathy, and safety at face value until phenomenological confirmations are experienced.

3. Under pressures to conform to group norms, all but the very meek feel the need to flex their individuality. Resistance can thus be an expression of rebelliousness, an unwillingness to be grouped as a part of the whole.

4. Much client anxiety may be centered on negative expectations of what the group experience might offer. The person who anticipates "mind games," hostility, "touchy-feely" exercises, and a dogmatic, rigid leader will be more likely to erect protective barriers. Even if projected negative outcomes don't materialize, the client will still resist to be on the safe side.

5. The unusual and flexible leadership style of most group therapists presents a confusing image to clients at first. Authoritarian, democratic, and laissez-faire behaviors might all be in evidence within a single hour. The leader is definitely an authority figure to group members, but a very unconventional authority nevertheless. However warm and caring, the therapist's actions still represent "the powers that be" to anyone who doesn't have power. Resistance can therefore be a testing of limits to carve out pecking-order roles. If there was ever a place to challenge authority by resisting compliance to expectations, a therapeutic group is the ideal.

6. Considering how few moments there are during the day in which a person is not an active participant of some group at work, home, church, school, or play, it is amazing that so many people

have social fears of groups. Teachers, who spend their professional lives performing in front of groups, can reach a moderate state of panic when trying to speak up in graduate classes. Lawyers, physicians, and other human-service professionals who communicate with people all day long often clam up in a group situation. This fear of being judged by others and of interacting in groups sparks a lot of resistance in those who want to speak up but feel they can't perform adequately in front of their peers.

7. A corollary of the social-fear motive is resistance due to a fear of failure. Persons who are used to feeling totally successful in their chosen profession and peer groups feel out of their element in a therapeutic group. They expend every ounce of energy trying to make themselves look good and logically spurn any opportunity that involves the spontaneous or unpredictable, where perfect competence isn't guaranteed on the first trial.

8. The Great Unknown makes people think twice before they leap. Some group members become very slippery to avoid having to take risks. They will work like crazy on self-awareness or insight, but when the time comes to apply new knowledge in the real world, they find their courage has left town without them.

9. Resistance can be a sign of someone who enjoys manipulating others. It is, after all, an attention-getting ploy that evokes emotional responses in other members and even in the leader. It is like a 2-year-old kid drunk with power from the realization that simply by uttering the word *no* he can send grown-ups into fits of desperation. The resistant client can stop leader actions dead in their tracks, collect laurels of pity from others, and at the same time feel like a poor victim who can't help the situation.

10. Every group member has formulated preferences for how she/he prefers all other participants to be and to act. When they don't cooperate according to the plan, resistance can be used as a way to punish offenders: "I'll show you all for not treating *me* right, acting as *I* would. I'll make you suffer. You know how excited you've been getting over the progress I've made? Watch this—I'll go back to the way I was."

11. Resistance can also be an act of jealousy to sabotage forward motion. Every time a group member makes significant life changes, it helps other clients to feel more dissatisfied with their inertia. A client can then refuse to cooperate with group proceedings knowing that by resisting she/he no longer has to feel threatened by the rules the productive members are following.

12. The expression of ambivalence is not only evident in sabotaging other clients' progress in the group but is strongly reflected in one's own attitudes toward changing: "I want to be different from what I am, but I don't really want to handle the consequences of this growth—having to be responsible for my life."

13. A group member experimenting with new behaviors experiences frustration similar to that of an infant trying to practice turning over. Like the infant, who will pout and fight after a desperate effort, the client will resist "handling" when his or her patience is worn thin. What looks so easy for the leader to do is impossible for the client to feel comfortable imitating. Resistance in this case acts as a warning to the therapist to back off until the client's energy supplies are replenished for a counterattack.

14. Resistance is also used as a pacing mechanism to stall for time. In the language of physics, resistance is the drag that slows down the force of movement. When change accelerates too quickly, the human mind will attempt to decelerate progress to more comfortable levels that allow breathing space.

15. Finally, resistance can be a strategy of personality style. Some folks take pleasure in resisting *anything* because it is intrinsically satisfying for them to participate in conflict. They love the challenge of argument and controversy and will switch sides fluently, depending on which point of view offers the best opportunity for antagonism. Such persons resist because they are strong-willed enough to appreciate the stimulation that comes from locking horns with a powerful adversary.

Setbacks

After significant progress has been made, clients often regress to previous self-defeating behaviors when they are under duress. Group members' worst fears are confirmed—that any changes made are only temporary reprieves. Once a client backslides, all the other group members vicariously experience the setback, wondering when it will happen to them.

Sufficiently preparing participants for the realities of change—two steps forward, one step back—minimizes panic reactions. Confidence grows with the knowledge that even if a return to previously ineffective functioning should occur, the client can readily fight back to the new line of scrimmage just as before.

Somewhere during the middle of a group's life, once members have had a taste of personal mastery, the leader can deliberately provoke situations that require the use of newly learned skills. The clients can then practice recovery strategies within the safety and support of the group. Certain themes—for instance, the subject of death—become critical incidents by their highly emotionally charged nature.

Yalom (1980) sometimes introduces a dying cancer patient to a group of reasonably healthy individuals, hoping to provoke a confrontation with the inevitability of death. Instead of eliciting an atmosphere of morbid fatalism, however, the content spans the usual assortment of presenting concerns. In addition, at one time or another, each group member is given a bonus by facing his or her own death anxiety as a participant in the struggle as well as a spectator in the dying process of a peer. The concept of setback is reframed within a positive context, providing opportunities for flexing one's new-found strength rather than highlighting weaknesses.

"I Won't Be Me"

Grieger and Boyd (1977) have investigated common themes that clients use to dispute rational thinking in order to preserve their irrational ideas. Frequently, group members will "cop a plea" to keep the heat off when a session gets too intense. Unless a leader is prepared to challenge vigorously the validity of statements such as the following, a critical incident will emerge that is very difficult to handle.

"This group is turning me into a phony."
"All this problem-solving stuff is making me into a talking computer."
"I don't recognize myself any more—I'm losing my identity."

As a last-ditch effort at holding on to "good old me," however pained, anxious, or depressed such a person was, the client will resort to uncompromising measures. It is as if the "new me," with all its competence and control, is too frightening to face: "At least when I looked into the mirror I knew what to expect—those comfortable blotches, those bags under the eyes, that sour disposition. Now when I shave in the morning a happy face that I don't recognize smiles back. I'm not sure I like it either."

This cognitive dissonance can be dispelled by using the typically confrontive, logical responses of the cognitive-emotive therapist. Grieger and Boyd (1977) suggest responses like "How can you possibly be anyone else but you?"

We ask the client whether he would lose his identity if he were required to change from being right-handed to left-handed. Then we show him that, although he would find it awkward for a period of time to switch handedness, he would with persistent effort use his left hand more often, more comfortably, and perhaps with more facility until it became "natural" for him [p. 254].

Boredom

After working patterns have become established and group members can reasonably predict the outcome of each session, the following will typically occur. The leader will get reports from members, all saying how much they enjoy the group. People will fight over who gets group time. They will all do a little exercise to get their heads primed. Someone will cry; someone will laugh. A few people will get most of the attention. They will summarize what they learned, get feedback from others about how wonderful they are. Then an atmosphere of boredom may take over.

Unless there is a liberal dosage of spontaneity, humor, varied formats, unpredictable agendas, and a free-flowing, flexible structure to the group, clients will grow restless and lethargic. Boredom is the supreme enemy, the state of existence in which time moves intolerably slowly. When clients become bored, their perceptions of time in the group alter dramatically. Clients require a constant bombardment of stimulation to keep them occupied. They cannot stand being alone in a room unless the television or stereo is blaring. They can't eat without reading the paper. They can't sit still for more than a few minutes. Their counterparts, who are relatively immune to boredom, have a never-ending fascination for involving themselves in any activity. In the dentist's chair, they will count the hygienist's nose hairs. In a faltering group, they will have a list of favorite activities to keep themselves happy until things pick up. They might make odds on who will speak first or reflect on what is holding them back. However they choose to handle the situation, they obviously have skills that bored clients lack.

The beauty of group work is that the heterogeneity of participants encourages people to teach from strengths. "Kathryn, while you sit there restless, sulking, and yawning, staring out the window, wishing you were somewhere else, hoping that I'll do something to rescue you from this fate worse than death, Becky sits over there happy as a clam. I wonder why she is so content to enjoy her thoughts, why she gets herself involved when she is restless, when you are powerless to do anything but suffer boredom?"

STRATEGIES FOR HANDLING CRITICAL INCIDENTS

There are other critical incidents and predictable problems that frequently occur: termination and re-entry problems, conflicting goals between leader and participants, turning the group into a gripe session, or difficulties with oversolidarity in which the pervasive closeness that has developed only confirms the suspicion that people outside the group cannot be trusted. All these incidents may be dealt with in a systematic fashion that involves several sequential steps.

First, the group leader must be able to recognize critical incidents when they are occurring. This macrodiagnostic process involves some fairly clear notions regarding what exactly constitutes a critical incident. The operational definition will probably be consistent with one's theoretical framework. For example, one fairly pragmatic definition describes a critical incident as any observable, sufficiently complete client action that permits inferences about that person or group process and requires some leader intervention (Flanagan, 1954; Cohen & Smith, 1976).

Second, the group leader must be able microdiagnostically to identify the specific variety of critical incident that is occurring by noting its effects on individual members and their reactions. Cohen and Smith (1976) suggest examining the context in which the event occurred, including precipitating factors that led up to the incident, relevant background, group climate, timing, and the intensity of member responses. The specific diagnostic decision may then include figuring out what happened, why and how it occurred, and whether a leader intervention is called for to resolve the therapeutic issue.

Once the critical incident has been clearly dissected, the leader formulates an optimal plan for creating therapeutic insight from the wayward ingredients that are prevalent. Enter a client who is chronically late for sessions. Add a colleague who, while using group time that is interrupted, is experiencing much frustration over prolonged inertia. Throw in for good measure a few miscellaneous yawns, impatient squirms, and resentments from the gallery. Voices and blood pressures rise. Acceptance, tolerance, and politeness decline. The leader takes a deep breath, mumbles reassuring words to the effect that "We seem to have gotten carried away," then attempts to use the outburst as a constructive lesson for understanding effective confrontation.

In resolving interpersonal conflicts such as these, the practitioner will want to clarify communication, structure specific goals satisfactory to all parties, filter out distracting variables, and use compromise and consensus strategies to avoid win-lose situations (Frey, 1979). Critical incidents *are* critical because they can be used for better or for worse. Rather than dreading and avoiding them, the pragmatic group leader should calmly face such predictable problems and sometimes even encourage their development, secure in the knowledge that they can be transformed into stimuli for accelerated growth.

The critical incidents of therapeutic groups are very similar to the developmental tasks of individual human growth. Both natural processes arise during certain predictable, invariant, suquential periods in the life of a group or individual, "successful achievement of which leads to happiness and to success with later tasks, while failure leads to unhappiness in the individual [or group], disapproval by the society, and difficulty with later tasks" (Havighurst, 1972, p. 2). As the child must form meaningful human attachments in the first months of life, master basic survival skills in the first few years, build an identity during puberty, establish autonomy, responsibility, and involvement in adulthood, so, too, will clients go through a series of progressive crises which, on mastering the skills necessary to resolve the conflicts, will lead to greater personal mastery both as a group participant and as a human being.

CHAPTER 8

Compatible
Co-Leader Functioning

ADVANTAGES OF CO-LEADERSHIP

There has always been resistance to the idea of using two leaders in a group. Critics warn that the partnership is more for the benefit of therapists than of clients (Haley, 1976), that it can set up destructive competition (Balgopal & Hull, 1970) and toxic relationships (Corey, Corey, Callanan, & Russell, 1982), that it is economically wasteful (Russell & Russell, 1979), that it establishes a special high-status subgroup of two that can lead to other cliques (Bowers & Gauron, 1981), and that it raises erotic issues between male and female partners (Dickes & Dunn, 1977). Bowers and Gauron (1981) feel that because there is no specific provision in our ethical codes that outlaws sexual behavior between co-therapists, such conduct will inevitably occur because of the close relationship. Russell and Russell (1979) note that co-therapy formats have been frequently abused in marriage counseling cases where one leader has "pranced, shown-off, pontificated, competed" or "may collude with the couple, engage in oblique interpretation, and exhibit narcissistic or bizarre behavior" [p. 42].

Pragmatic group workers have co-led and will continue to do so because they recognize certain therapeutic advantages to working in a partnership that are not possible in soloing, even though research has not conclusively demonstrated this superiority (Gurman & Kniskern, 1978). Many experienced leaders attribute their high morale, continuing growth, and avoidance of burn-out to their willingness to work in tandem with compatible colleagues. Other distinct advantages of co-led groups are evident.

1. Group work has been criticized for affording individual members less opportunity for therapeutic time. When a 1:1 ratio between helper and helpee is increased to a 10:1 ratio, there are bound to be people lost in the shuffle. Whereas a client in individual counseling has the luxury of being an "only child" with the therapist's total

attention, the client in a group setting is only one of a dozen siblings competing for attention. In a 2-hour group of 12 participants, each member is entitled to an equitable share of only 10 minutes. Two group leaders, however, can ensure better coverage and more efficient use of therapeutic time. One leader can choose as a primary responsibility making certain that each person has an opportunity to speak.

2. The more leaders there are in a group, the more resources are available for clients. Co-leaders can cover each other's blind spots and tunnel vision. If one therapist has an aversion to interacting with rebellious "smart asses," the other leader may be less skilled in communicating with conventional, obedient clients: "What my co-leader means when he says that you have the typical 'middle-class housewife syndrome' is that because you feel restless and bored sitting at home all day you have lots of idle time available to manufacture new problems."

With mutually vigilant partners, the biases, prejudices, weaknesses, and shortcomings of each therapist can be minimized. Co-leaders become responsible to each other for their actions, in addition to their societal, institutional, group member, and self responsibilities. This added safety feature may reduce even more the frequency of casualties.

3. Shapiro (1978, p. 157) believes that "every group can be conducted best by more than one therapist" because the co-leader becomes a "reality-based sounding board for the other partner." Group work can be a lonely business. The constant pressure, repeated conflict, and highly charged atmosphere can wear down even the most hardened professional. The use of co-therapists minimizes omissions, subjective distortions, and mismanagement of tricky situations (Russell & Russell, 1979). Diagnoses can be better targeted, interventions can be better timed, and group time can be better spent.

4. Rosenbaum (1971) has noted that having two leaders is more convenient for clients, giving them better value for their money. If one therapist is sick, on vacation, late, or tied up, the other can take over. Or if one leader is having a tough day, feels run-down or temporarily lethargic, the partner can keep things hopping until enthusiasm becomes contagious. Far from encouraging a therapist to "slide," lazily deferring decisions and actions to a peer, co-leadership involves shared responsibility for more territory. There are fewer excuses for making mistakes or overlooking valuable content when double the resources are available.

5. Many novel ideas expressed in a group are initially rejected because they seem so foreign. Two leaders can endorse each other's verbalizations, reinforcing and supporting the attempts of each at motivating client change. After one leader introduces a concept, confronts a client, or initiates a process intervention, the second leader may choose to offer supportive examples and substantiating data. Each intervention becomes more powerful when implemented with forceful consensus.

"I noticed that you had a smirk on your face while my partner was explaining the ways you deliberately seek attention in the group. I, too, have observed you in action. Earlier today, for instance, whenever you spoke, you would only make eye contact with me and ignore everyone else. Even when I averted my gaze, you would stare at my forehead rather than talk to anyone else. It is as if my opinion is the only one that counts."

6. Many counselors and therapists shy away from running groups because of the strain on their attention span. It is virtually impossible for a solo leader to fully attend to every subtlety requiring individual focus. In addition to possessing the skills and knowledge necessary to counsel an individual in the group, the therapist must also continuously take the pulse of every other member in the group. The single leader's brain cells are thus overloaded with busy signals.

"I've got to press Sandra harder. She's slipping away with her typical game-playing manners. Perhaps I could—. Oops. Why is Rob squirming over in the corner? Did I hit one of his nerves? There go those giggling guys again. I better interrupt them before they begin their distracting jokes. Where was I? Oh, yeah, I was formulating a plan to motivate Sandra. But she keeps looking to Jody and Melanie for approval. I must break that destructive bond between them, they keep protecting one another from any growth. And there's Cary acting bored again, dying for attention. I've got to ignore him and get back to the problem at hand. But what *is* the problem at hand?"

Two leaders working in tandem can systematically divide the duties that require a leader's attention. While one therapist is leading an exercise, the other can help to moderate. While one is talking, the other can be scanning member faces for reactions. While one is preoccupied with counseling a client, the other can divide his or her energy between cueing other members to respond, making sure they stay involved, and objectively assessing the progress of interventions.

7. With co-leaders, clients can experience support and confrontation simultaneously. There is a greater willingness to accept con-

structive feedback when it is offered nonthreateningly. It is therefore possible for one therapist to circumvent a client's defenses and resistances by playing a nurturing, soft role at the same time the partner is pointing out inconsistencies in that client's behavior.

Co-leader A: I can really feel for you. I know it hurts. I can see by your tears how much pain you are in. It is so overwhelming to be in the single world again, forced to fend for yourself. You wonder if you'll ever find a lover again.

Co-leader B: Yet feeling sorry for yourself won't make things any better. Wishing and hoping for deliverance won't make it happen. You keep blaming yourself for everything you might have done differently if you had had another chance. But there is not another chance for your wife to come back. That's over forever. And I am sitting here wondering why week after week you play these same dumb games. The tears, the dejected, pitiful looks, the same old stories. We've heard them over and over again. What does it take to get you to work and create a new and better life for yourself?

Co-leader A: I know that was difficult for you to hear, but perhaps she is right. You know that we care for you, that we hate to see you suffer like this. How do you feel now? What are you thinking?

8. There are special advantages in applying the co-leader model to marital and family therapy, which is, after all, just a form of group work in which all participants are related. The therapeutic coalitions that inevitably form within family therapy structures can be brought out more flexibly by two therapists. Lantz (1978b) recommends establishing affiliations with particular family members to facilitate interpersonal structural changes. He suggests that one therapist can deliberately flirt with a spouse of the opposite sex as a way to get the other, more reserved spouse more involved. In another situation, the other therapist may act as a scapegoat by deliberately mimicking a family member who is being picked on, thereby taking the heat off the badgered person and redirecting it toward himself or herself.

9. The likelihood of group member identification and compatibility with the leader is increased if there are two options available. When co-leaders are of different sexes and represent different ethnic and socioeconomic backgrounds or personality styles, group members can gravitate toward the person they perceive as being most similar to themselves. It is generally agreed, for instance, that sex therapy with opposite-sex therapists is effective because the leaders

can model a positive couple relationship at the same time they make it easier for the husband and wife to relate to their own sex (Masters & Johnson, 1970; Wolman, 1976).

In a study demonstrating the effects of a dual therapy team on improving marital relationships, Epstein, Jayne-Lazarus, and De Giovanni (1979) found that couples learn more adaptive communication roles and constructive conflict resolution by observing the modeled behavior of male-female co-therapists, particularly when the relationship they demonstrate is compatible with client expectations. Other writers recommend that healthy relationships be systematically modeled by co-therapists to encourage complementary sex roles, flexible attitudes, and appropriate dominance patterns in couples (Sonne & Lincoln, 1966; Rice & Rice, 1975). Finally, co-led groups can be designed advantageously for specialized client populations, such as children from broken homes, who have never seen authority figures interact in a free and open manner (Zimpfer, 1971).

10. The dilution of authority between two group leaders can make it easier for members to feel less rebellious and threatened. The team provides a model of healthy, ideal relationships between powerful, respecting persons. Other advantages of using two leaders include spreading out dependency effects in clients and mutually sharing the burden of working with depressed, lonely people.

In summary, co-led groups have the potential to be more dynamic, safe, exciting, and interesting for clients and therapists alike. Most of the disadvantages of co-led groups arise from the unproductive relationship between therapists (Gans, 1962; David & Lohr, 1971; Galloghy & Levine, 1979). Unless the partners can work as a complementary team, much group time can be wasted in power plays, bickering, and mutual sabotage.

"Two heads are better than one as long as both are working" (Galloghy & Levine, 1979, p. 296). When there are inequalities of roles in dominant-submissive patterns or when relationships become confounded with personal conflicts, there is bound to be trouble. Fortunately, most of the disadvantages and dangers of co-leadership can be minimized, if not eliminated, by taking precautions in the selection and preparation of an effective partner.

RECRUITING AND TRAINING A CO-LEADER

Choosing a co-leader, like selecting a spouse, is too often a random process. Therapists are more often matched according to convenient considerations, such as the proximity of their last names in the alphabet, than by any systematic rationale. In a doctoral-level group practicum, co-leaders were paired in just this manner. Because Joelle and Jay happened to be sitting across from one another one day they ended up as a team to lead a group of sophisticated students. With 5 minutes during the break to plan their strategy, the co-leaders naively believed they were ready to take on the world. "After all," they reasoned, "we're intelligent, sensitive people. We're doctoral students in counseling. We know our stuff and what to do."

The group began smoothly enough with Joelle and Jay returning to a member who had received help during the previous session. After the report was completed, they began to search for another candidate who wished to use group time. As frequently occurs, a great silence fell as members checked out one another to determine who would volunteer next. Growing nervous, Jay resorted to a strategy that he had relied on many times before; he picked a person who he thought might want to use the group time: "Gerry, I notice you're getting fidgety, as if you want to speak up but are a little apprehensive. I remember a few weeks ago you were complaining about how powerless you felt at home. Is there anything I can do to make it easier for you to talk?"

But before Gerry could respond, Joelle interrupted with *her* agenda: "Perhaps it would be better to wait for someone to *volunteer* to use the group rather than one of us doing the selecting. People should take responsibility for their own behavior in here."

More silence. Jay leans back, crosses his arms, and waits.

"Well then," Joelle interjects, "perhaps we should try an exercise designed to get things moving. Why don't we go around the group—."

"Excuse me, Joelle," Jay interrupts exasperatedly, "but I thought that we'd already selected a client who might like to go to work. Gerry looked as if he was just ready to jump in when you interrupted him. Judy and Geoffrey also act like they'll be ready with a little prodding. Why waste time with an exercise?"

Joelle angers visibly. "*We* didn't select a client, *you* did. Furthermore, it isn't our job to pressure people to perform. They must go at their own pace. If you weren't so authoritarian—," and so forth.

To quote Napier and Whitaker (1972, p. 498), "you need to get married before you have children." Particularly in marriages of convenience, or when co-leaders have been involuntarily assigned by supervisors, there will be much strife until partners work out their differences. In spite of their problems, Joelle and Jay probably could have functioned effectively as a team had they sufficiently prepared each other, communicated at length about their preferences, and compromised on certain basic assumptions.

A number of researchers and practitioners suspect that most of the potential dangers inherent in group work are determined by how irresponsible, aggressive, and incompetent the assigned leader is. Most of the potential abuses of co-leader functioning are likewise determined by the quality of therapist matching (Roman & Meltzer, 1977). Weinstein (1971) therefore recommends that certain guidelines be followed to ensure a productive relationship. This relationship includes mutual trust, acknowledgment of inherent personality differences in operating style, and roughly equivalent ability so that leaders view each other as partners. Balgopal and Hull (1974) also assert that co-leaders should be flexible, verbally free to express concerns to each other, know their personal limitations, and be able to address issues of conflict and dependence.

From Lennon-McCartney and Rogers-Hammerstein to Woodward-Bernstein and Masters-Johnson, all successful teams have had essentially identical qualities. World-class doubles tennis partners can anticipate each other's moves with uncanny accuracy; they know exactly where each partner will be positioned on the court at any moment. Tag-team wrestling partners well understand their limitations and physical endurance; they know when to rest and let the other partner take over. Master bridge players can read the subtlest signals in a partner's face so that they can expertly play into each other's hand. Co-authors tend to choose their partners on the basis of complementary experience, style, temperament, and skills. Selecting a compatible co-leader for group work should not be a random process any more than choosing a partner in any other important endeavor.

As to specific requirements in co-leader matching, Corey and Corey (1977) warn that the decision should be based on a lot more than personal attraction. Trust is an essential element. The partnership should be an open relationship, a model of constructive compromise. There should be a great willingness to learn from each other. Co-leaders should be extremely flexible in their style and orientation so as to maximize the advantages of matching complementary personality styles—perhaps pairing a spontaneous person with one who is more reflective and deliberate.

Mutual respect is important so that co-leaders feel safe in disclosing their fears, limitations, and weaknesses to each other. Only by being aware of mutual strengths and limitations can co-leaders know how to best utilize them (Gans, 1957). Once relevant variables are matched according to these established criteria, co-leaders can then form a meaningful division of labor.

ISSUES FOR PREPLANNING

Co-led groups can be potentially frustrating experiences for all parties concerned, even when the leaders genuinely like and respect each other. While one therapist is heading in one direction, attempting to facilitate a group member's insight, the other therapist may be pursuing a different goal, thereby short-circuiting both helping efforts. Clients can be caught in the middle of a psychological tug-of-war that determines who will win a senseless power struggle.

Group Leader A: And so it is very important that you practice being more assertive when—

Group Leader B: Even more important than the practice, you absolutely *must* stay in touch with your feelings. Do you know what I mean?

Client: Yes, but—

Group Leader A: Let's give you an opportunity to practice being assertive right here in group. Pick out someone—

Group Leader B: —whom you have strong feelings for and share them with that person.

Group Leader A: Actually, I was about to ask her to confront her boss in a role-play situation.

Client: I'm confused.

Group Leader B: Yes, that's apparent. That's why I want you to work through the confusion before you confront anyone.

Group Leader A: But first shouldn't we help her to—

   (Fade as leaders come to blows.)

In addition to struggles of competition between leaders, most conflicts and inefficient functioning are due to inadequate preparation on the leaders' part. Just as a vocal duet must rehearse endlessly or as racquetball partners must devote hours of practice to learn each other's moves, so must co-leaders negotiate their roles ahead of time.

During preliminary planning sessions, co-leaders can decide who will open the group and who will close it, who will take responsibility for time-keeping and other practical functions. At this time co-leaders should negotiate their roles, deciding who will specialize in particular strategies or conflicts. Specific precedures should be standardized and instructions for implementing psychodramatic structures talked through.

There can also be considerable discussion of a philosophically compatible format that is flexible enough to allow for individual differences in leader style and background. While working only with identical theoretical affiliates is unnecessary, it is probably counterproductive to pair an orthodox psychoanalyst with a radical behaviorist. Mixed marriages work quite well if both co-leaders are open, flexible, and motivated enough to learn from each other. Actually, the greatest benefit for therapists in the co-leader structure is that it not only allows for, but maximally facilitates, an open exchange of ideas. A therapist cannot help but increase his/her repertoire of group skills as the result of observing and working with a respected colleague.

A part of initial planning sessions can be devoted to learning how each other's minds characteristically function: "What do you do when a group member refuses to participate?" "How do you handle silence?" "What goes on inside your head when you are waiting for responses?" "How do you anticipate dealing with conflicts between us that arise in the group?"

At this time one therapist may cue the other to observe leadership behaviors, paying particular attention to a skill that is being refined: "After the group I'd appreciate your assessment of my ability to stay neutral and not inadvertently let my biases slip. Please watch me carefully in this regard since I have been told before that I tend to shape clients to answer questions the way I have in mind."

In pregroup briefings, co-leaders may create a set of signals between them as an abbreviated private language system. Standard cues can be developed for pacing time, switching counseling focus, or indicating future direction; specific signals can be selected for temporary communication channels. If one leader, for instance, wants to be monitored on a tendency toward rambling, the co-leader can unobtrusively signal during appropriate instances to bring this behavior to attention. Another prearranged hand movement might indicate the beginning of a planned sequence to focus on a particular group member or group exercise. Other nonverbal signals can be developed to communicate other messages:

- "I don't understand where you're going."
- "Help me, I'm stuck."

- "Keep it up; you're doing fine."
- "Start to wrap things up."
- "Lighten up; you're pushing too hard."
- "Let's try something else."

Prearranged signals can be augmented through prerehearsed strategies in which co-leaders discuss how they will handle predictable critical incidents. At this point, leaders should also discuss the structure of sessions as well as screen prospective clients together. Favorable, cooperative expectations can be set up in clients ahead of time by arranging conferences with co-leaders. The therapists can then compare notes on each participant as a means of understanding how each one thinks, conceptualizes behavior, and would proceed with the case. They can share initial impressions of clients, discuss anticipated special problems, rehearse how they might work with them and create compromise strategies with which both partners would feel comfortable.

An egalitarian co-therapy relationship is established by formal and informal channels of communication, mutual acceptance, and shared mutual responsibility. This alliance simultaneously permits both individuality and the opportunity for each to help the other grow (Getty & Shannon, 1969).

TANDEM TECHNIQUES

Together with the increased popularity of co-therapist structures comes the advent of new helping technologies specifically designed for this medium. Just as violin concertos are composed differently from piano sonatas, co-led groups require specialized structures if they are to function effectively and capitalize on their intrinsic advantages. Though some minor style adaptations are necessary when therapists work with partners, equally important is the mastery of adjunct leadership techniques that are ideally suited for co-led groups.

Across-the-Group Communication

The first of these tandem strategies evolves from the open relationship common among co-therapists. There comes a time when one partner doesn't understand where the other is going or when one leader becomes confused by events that have developed or experiences frustration over intense resistance. In such instances the leaders may decide to communicate to each other across the group. The dialogue may be initiated for a number of reasons, most notably to share thinking aloud.

"Miriam, we've been working with Gail for the better part of a hour and I've yet to see much progress. Every time we get close to the root of things, she backs down. I can't decide whether we should move on to someone else while she rests, or whether she is actually inviting us to push harder."

"I agree, Ronnie. This is getting us nowhere. Personally, I think Gail is having a great time playing games with us, though she's probably unaware that they are games. Let's confront her directly and force her to make a decision."

Gail, of course, attends carefully to this interaction, gleaning insight into her behavior, and then has sufficient time to prepare herself for the next phase. The other group members, who are participating as co-leaders-in-training, listen to the interchange sensitively. They learn a lot about how the therapist's mind functions, how it analyzes problems and comes to a resolution. As they become more fascinated with the process of group work, with the skills of promoting insight and action, they also grow more proficient at applying the concepts to themselves.

Communicating across the group also allows leaders to synchronize their actions. It often happens that one therapist will begin a series of interventions on the basis of a hunch. When the direction is not readily apparent, the other therapist is left behind, impatiently twiddling thumbs. This problem can be overcome by sharing the agenda aloud.

"Ronnie, follow me for a moment. I have an idea I want to try. While I work with Laura, Phyllis, and Jeff, I want you to note their reactions throughout the encounter. I think you'll catch on soon enough, as will the rest of the group."

Intragroup leader communications can also be initiated for pacing reasons or to confront behavior in an indirect, nonthreatening manner:

"I notice that this side of the group is getting bored. Shall we liven things up a bit?"

For whatever reasons across-the-group talking is used, the result is usually desirable as long as leaders have a specific, defensible rationale for doing so. Certainly co-leaders can operate more efficiently as a team when they keep each other informed. And clients most definitely appreciate the opportunity to watch their leaders demonstrating their most open, genuine, and honest style.

Psychodramatic Duets

J. L. Moreno was fond of employing co-leaders in psychodramatic routines. One therapist would work as a director, structuring the role-play situation; the other would act as an "auxiliary ego" to the principal protagonist. Since the time of Moreno's original work, practitioners have become quite inventive in using multiple group leaders in psychodramatic strategies. A co-leader may reflect different aspects of a client's personality—acting as a hostile double, as the "rational" or "feeling" self, or may choose to mirror the client's true intentions by means of exaggeration.

Group Leader: What then, Isaac, would you really like to do?
Isaac: I just don't know.
Auxiliary Ego: (standing behind shoulders) I really do know, but I'm afraid to say.
Isaac: Well, maybe I'd like to try something different for a change.
Auxiliary Ego: I'm sick of my life the way it is but I feel trapped—like I don't have a choice.
Group Leader: What would you like to do differently?
Isaac: I just don't know!
Auxiliary Ego: (makes sounds of chicken clucking with arms flapping)
Isaac: I *do* know exactly what I want, but if I say it out loud you'll throw it back in my face if I back down.

A strategy suggested by Getty and Shannon (1969) utilizes "participating ego" and "observing ego" roles to allow the temporarily less active leader to assist all other group members in becoming more aware of how proceedings are affecting them. While one therapist becomes totally immersed in helping a client work through a concern, the "observing ego" works in a supporting manner to keep others involved. Each person's nonverbal behavior can be closely and continuously scrutinized for responses to stimuli. When appropriate, they can be cued to share their personal reactions as feedback or empathy to the client-in-focus.

Dyer and Vriend (1973b) describe "role working" psychodramatic structures in which co-leaders take on the parts of guardians of Heaven and Hell. Group members are required to explain why they deserve entry, thereby evaluating the meaning of their lives. Other imaginary scripts can be enacted in a courtroom where co-leaders become prosecuting and defense attorneys while group members play jury and witnesses to the hypothetical crime, usually some irrationally guilt-inducing incident. Scenarios could similarly be played out in other creative settings where co-leaders take complementary therapeutic roles. Sacks (1973) describes an additional 80 possible strategies in which co-leaders can capitalize on auxiliary ego techniques.

Subdivided Groups

Lantz (1978) describes a group technique that was created specifically for co-leader functioning. Using one-way mirrors that allow unobtrusive observation, a co-therapy team can facilitate better understanding among family members by allowing them to analytically watch one another in action. While one therapist directs communication among family members as they bicker and fight, the other can sit with the rest of the family behind a one-way mirror so that they may gain insight into interaction patterns. The observing therapist can thus help family members to make sense of what they witness, interpreting incomprehensible actions, answering questions, and leading discussions about inner reactions felt during the sequences.

In one family therapy group composed of divorcing couples and their children, the parents stayed with one group leader while their children went with the other into the observation booth to watch the proceedings. Most of the parents felt inhibited by the children's presence though they knew it was important to openly discuss the impact of the upcoming divorces. This compromise arrangement was structured to allow the parents to verbalize concerns for their children's welfare as well as for the forthcoming drastic changes in their own lives.

During one heated discussion, the parents were sharing their misgivings about being single parents. How would the kids react to dates being brought home? How would they adjust to the absence of their other parent? Meanwhile, just a few feet away, on the other side of the mirrored wall, the children had questions of their own. Why did Mommy and Daddy stop loving each other? How come they were yelling at each other? The patient and understanding co-leader can help to appease the children's fears by addressing their apprehensions. The dialogues that were initially stimulated by this twin-group structure can be continued when they meet again in the whole group. Each co-leader brings a unique perception of the experience, and each group member has an honest appraisal of the conflicts involved.

The same principle can be applied to any group where there is an apparent crack in cohesion. For example, if age factors, gender conflicts, racial tensions, or attitudinal variables enter the picture as decisive forces, the group could be temporarily split with each co-leader running a smaller unit to deal with the issues. Inhibitions would thereby be reduced, and participants might feel more comfortable getting themselves started in a smaller, more homogeneous group. Once stated goals are met, co-leaders can once again merge their efforts to heal the deepening gulf among participants.

Fishbowl structures can also be employed in which an inner group takes turns with an outer group in actively pursuing intense interactions. While members of group A explore their feelings of frustration at being misunderstood, members of group B observe the session as their leader programs them to watch for certain things or whispers to them. Afterward, group B members can take center stage to talk about their observations while group A members become active spectators.

Dual Sex Structures

The co-leader format has become standard operating procedure for helping couples with sexual dysfunctions. Masters and Johnson (1970) pioneered the dual-sex therapist approach as a way to ensure that both husband and wife would have a confidante to relate to in the discussion of sensitive and embarrassing issues. It is generally easier for a woman to relate to another woman when discussing her inability to reach orgasm, just as most men feel more comfortable talking to a male therapist about a problem in maintaining an erection. Although there have been no well-controlled studies to date clearly demonstrating the superiority of either dual-sex therapist teams or co-led groups over single-therapist formats, group leaders find much intuitive appeal in pursuing the team approach.

In a couples group where clients complain of male-oriented sexual dysfunctions such as impotence and premature ejaculation, the problems of wives as well as of the husbands can receive balanced attention from male-female co-leaders.

Male client chorus: This is so humiliating to talk about. Our masculinity is compromised, our feelings of human competence are com-

pletely demoralized. We can't even satisfy our wives, take care of
them in bed, much less satisfy ourselves. We wish they weren't
so demanding all the time. We're so afraid of failing that we're
bound to fail every time we try.

Female client chorus: It's so frustrating to get all worked up and
then be left hanging because they can't perform. They never had
this problem before, why now? Is it something that we're doing?
We thought we were attractive enough women, but now we even
question our abilities. They make us so angry that it's not even
worth trying any more.

Male co-leader response to male chorus: Your sense of masculinity
is totally tied up in your sexual performance? Are you competing
on a football field? Have you never make mistakes before, performed less than your expectations? How can you possibly expect to relax in bed and enjoy sex when every thought revolves
around: "My God, what if I can't do it. She'll make fun of me. That
would be terrible. Boy oh boy, do I hope this works *this* time. I
wonder if this means I'm gay? A *real* man could take care of
business. I've got to do it this time, I've just got to."

Female co-leader response to female chorus: I never realized you all
were so powerful that you take responsibility for your husbands'
actions as well as for your own. Of course you take this personally. And, yes, you *do* feel guilty. You wonder if there's something
wrong with you because your husbands want to forget that the
problems exist while you say that sex is important.

Male-female leadership partnerships also work well with adolescents who are experiencing identity confusion. Boys and girls should
all have significant role models to emulate. At the same time, they
could learn to relate better to the opposite sex under the tutelage of
their therapists.

In one group of 15-year-olds, the theme had been centered on the
frustrations of being dishonest. The girls complained that when they
found boys they liked, they were forced to play passive, eye-batting
games until the boys finally got the message to approach them. The
female leader asked why they didn't take more initiative in self-
disclosing ways. When the girls complained that the boys would only
panic and run if the girls were to take the lead, the male group leader
used self-disclosure to show how enjoyable it is to be approached
once in a while instead of always having to take responsibility for the
way things go.

Guest Co-Leaders

The possibility exists, for a group with the right sort of composition, of introducing an occasional guest co-leader who has expertise in some needed area. Presumably this guest would not be resented or destroy cohesion if a fairly well-developed, secure atmosphere already existed and if all persons involved were adequately prepared.

A co-leader might be recruited who has specialized knowledge of human sexuality or of career decision making, depending on stated needs. Theme sessions could be structured around topics such as logical thinking processes or the spirit of Zen. In every case, the regular group leader(s) provide continuity while the guest co-leader(s) add diversity and excitement.

Guest co-leaders add a unique dimension to the group process. Clients often find that it is worth sacrificing a little intimacy by bringing in an outsider if the person is sensitive to their needs, low-key in approach, and a compatibly functioning partner with the principal therapist(s).

Co-Leader Interviews

Self-disclosures can be even more potent therapeutic devices in tandem structures. When two therapists know each other intimately, are familiar with each other's background and experience, their mutual awareness can be put to work in illustrative ways. Co-leaders can cue each other or conduct mini-interviews to elicit significant material and model openness.

In the example that opened the book—of the therapist whose daughter slit her throat with an electric knife—the gruesome story can be shared for therapeutic purposes by one co-leader interviewing the other: "Ivan, when you hear Cheryl talking about her guilt in not being a perfect parent, what comes to mind? I recall that you lived through the ultimate parental guilt trip when your daughter tried to kill herself. How did you handle yourself?"

Another example demonstrates the manner in which group leaders can effectively and indirectly self-disclose helpful anecdotes.

Co-leader A: I notice that Bruce keeps coming back to the kids as his main excuse for staying in the marriage. He seems to believe that by being a martyr and living with a woman he doesn't love he's somehow doing the best thing for the kids. Your parents were divorced when you were quite young. Did the experience traumatize your life?

Co-leader B: No, quite the opposite. It was only *after* my parents split up that things got better. I saw my father more often because he didn't have to escape from the house any longer. When my parents started dating other people, for the first time I saw grown-ups kissing and hugging each other. Until that point I had assumed that all husbands and wives show their love by slamming doors in each other's faces.

Interviewing techniques can also be used as a method of clarification. One leader may ask the other to elaborate by drawing out comments, asking for supporting examples or even embellishment of the original ideas. Leader communication will be more clearly understood when co-therapists monitor each other's language, asking for further interpretation or clarification when necessary.

Playing Doubles

Napier and Whitaker (1972) compare co-led groups to the bilateral partnership involved in doubles tennis. While one player falls back to take the long shots, the other rushes to the net to take most of the short interaction. It is rare for both to work simultaneously on the same shot. Generally, turns are alternated according to one's preferences and present position on the court.

Most interrogation teams well understand this idea. Often, one group leader will deliberately specialize in a complimentary, nurturing style while the other will choose to be more engaging. After one partner works aggressively to jar information loose, the softer, consoling partner will then offer comfort. Once the persons on the other side of the net alter their style, defense, or attack, the group leaders can flexibly change their team functioning to throw a lob, ground stroke, or volley.

Rice, Fey, and Kepecs (1972) identify six co-leader style options. The "blank screen" leader is passive, anonymous, and safe, rarely taking any risks or being provocative. The "paternal" therapist is objective and businesslike, inclined to analyze the past. The "transactional" leader is much more casual, spontaneous, and present-moment oriented while the "authoritarian" leader is goal oriented and structuring. "Maternal" therapists are highly verbal, supportive, and interpretative. "Idiosyncratic" therapists are critical, conforming, and programmed.

Each of these co-leader styles is, of course, interchangeable depending on circumstance and mood. Some therapists prefer partners to be similar in style, thereby ensuring compatibility but sacrificing variety; others enjoy partners with different but complementary styles. In tennis or in group work, a doubles team works well together when both players can flexibly change their styles to fit the needs of the situation.

DEBRIEFING

In addition to the sizable advantages to clients, the co-therapy model offers many educational benefits for group leaders. Indeed, the most prevalent use of co-led groups is in counselor/therapist training programs in which clinicians can receive hands-on experience while under close supervision. Even for group leaders with roughly equal status and experience, there are ample opportunities for mutual growth. Regular debriefings should therefore be scheduled to process the happenings of the previous session. This is most often done on an informal basis. As the last client leaves, the co-leaders inevitably pivot on their heels and ask "So what did you think?"

In the debriefings, co-leaders will first want to critique each other's performance as honestly as possible, giving specific, constructive feedback about interventions that appeared helpful, wasteful, or harmful. They will next check each other out as to behaviors that were not understood. Certain "lessons for beginners" will predictably crop up if one of the leaders is a student, intern, or less experienced clinician. The supervising leader might point out the following common mistakes:

- not sufficiently scanning client nonverbal behaviors to interpret reactions
- being too passive, safe, and timid in getting involved
- acting self-indulgent by rambling excessively or using self-disclosure inappropriately
- following own agenda so closely that actions were in conflict with co-leader
- staying on a superficial level by not sufficiently exploring the individual or group dynamics
- speaking in a monotone, showing little enthusiasm or excitement
- wasting valuable group time by letting clients engage in intellectual small talk
- not using co-leader enough in supportive ways

- using too limited variety of interventions, mostly restricted to reflections of feeling and summarizing responses
- trying to solve problems too quickly because of own discomfort with ambiguity
- becoming too interrogative, bombarding clients with inappropriate questions
- allowing clients to use general pronouns like "we" and permitted some clients to talk for others without their consent
- permitting clients to use the group for griping about things and people that can't possibly be controlled
- never helping clients to focus on concrete goals that they could commit themselves to work toward
- becoming too intolerant of silent periods, forcing people to talk before they felt ready
- not attempting to generalize the stated concern by drawing in other participants and looking at common themes
- asking clients "why?" when they didn't yet understand what the problem was, much less have an answer
- not managing time properly, allowing a few people to dominate and then focusing disproportionately on one idea
- reinforcing precisely the behavior that needed to be eliminated

For experienced group leaders, who make fewer mistakes of this sort, debriefing sessions might be devoted to analyzing group dynamics and identifying possible therapeutic goals for each client. As the pathologist conducts an autopsy to figure out what caused a body's death, co-leaders can use their debriefing sessions to identify cause-effect occurrences from the "dead session." With each hour that they work together, co-leaders can become even more growth-committed, questioning their actions, noting their effects, and pragmatically filing for later use those techniques and skills most likely to produce positive results and calculated therapeutic risks.

PART 3

Pragmatic Group Leadership Strategies

As group members learn from us, we learn from them. Each group session pushes us to become more knowledgeable, more skilled, more effective. Our continual state of self-training helps us to make our own personal and professional lives more satisfying. As our expertise grows so do the standards we have for our actions.

After mastering the basic group leadership skills there are many advanced strategies that flexibly allow intervention on more complex and creative levels. The pragmatic group leader will borrow any and all useful techniques from a variety of approaches, adapt them to specific situations and clients, and refine them until they are thoroughly integrated into his or her personal structure.

CHAPTER 9

Productive Risk Taking

Freedom and anxiety are intertwined. With freedom comes choice, and with choice comes the realization that there are no right answers, no guaranteed solutions, only viable options. The more options available to a person, the more freedom that person has. And freedom posits taking absolute responsibility for one's life. According to Sartre (1957), humans are condemned to freedom because, once thrown into the world without a choice, they become responsible for everything they do. "It is therefore senseless to think of complaining since nothing foreign has decided what we feel, what we live, or what we are" (Sartre, 1957, p. 53).

Only later does it occur to us that freedom begets responsibility, which begets risk, which in turn begets anguish. This angst can be combated only by exercising one's freedom, by taking risks and choosing actions even though they may be wrong. "The first act of freedom," William James (1890/1950) wrote, "is to choose it."

Even suffering can be deliberately chosen. The ultimate freedom is to exercise one's will in the face of logic and reasoning, to fight determinism to the last breath, even if it means choosing suffering. In Dostoyevsky's *Notes From the Underground* (1864/1960) the protagonist does just that—stubbornly risks his sanity to choose emotional pain:

> Twice two makes four seems to me simply a piece of insolence. Twice two makes four is a pert coxcomb who stands with arms akimbo barring your path and spitting. I admit that twice two makes four is an excellent thing, but if we are to give everything its due, twice two makes five is sometimes a very charming thing too.
>
> And why are you so firmly, so triumphantly, convinced that only the normal and the positive—in other words, only what is conducive to welfare—is for the advantage of man? Is not reason in error as regards advantage? Does not man, perhaps, love something besides well-being? Perhaps he is just as fond of suffering? Perhaps suffering is just as great a benefit to him as well-being? Man is sometimes extraordinarily, passionately, in love with suffering, and that is a fact [p. 209].

The anxiety that results from the choice—no, the responsibility—to take risks is the principal focus of therapeutic groups. Helping clients involves bringing together intention, will, and risk (May, 1969). A client's wishes and desires are transposed into a higher level of consciousness, the motive to act, which is then converted from the decision and will to change into the actual risk of changing.

Risk taking is central to all that changing involves. Unless one is prepared to take chances, to experiment, to try out new strategies, to look into the unknown and pursue what lies ahead even though one is hesitant and afraid, then all the talk is meaningless. Since risking necessarily involves the possibility of loss or injury, there is justifiable hesitation on the part of the client to minimize adverse consequences such as heightened vulnerability, rejection, reputation damage, or loss of self-esteem. "Nonetheless, client risk taking is basic to group therapy, for it generates the here-and-now material that is a prerequisite for meaningful interpersonal transactions" (Bednar, Melnick, & Kaul, 1974, p. 34).

Groups are natural places for therapeutic experimentation because group members are more likely to make riskier decisions here than they would alone, both to increase their status and to diffuse responsibility (Brown, 1965; Stoner, 1968; Shaw, 1981). The group is an ideal environment with built-in dynamic support systems to encourage risky behavior. These inherent pressures can be naturally fermented by the leader without artificially introducing any foreign ingredients. People are more willing to share self-revealing information to others who have taken similar risks (Jourard & Jaffee, 1970; Worthy, Gary, & Kahn, 1969) and are much more willing to do so after an introductory group discussion focusing on a sample of risky problems (Clark, 1971; Pruitt, 1971).

The desire to win peer approval plus the competitive nature of most people helps to encourage a contagious risk-taking effect in groups. Furthermore, when individuals are given feedback indicating that their level of risk taking is not up to par, they become more revealing. This "risky shift" phenomenon has helped to explain why group decisions are generally less cautious and conservative than individual decisions (Stoner, 1968; Runyan, 1974; Spector, Cohen, & Penner, 1976). Whether because responsibility is more diffused, because riskiness is a cultural value, or because adventurous group norms force compliance, there is much evidence to suggest that group settings are ideal for promoting risk-taking behaviors (Shaw, 1981).

Our society generally places a highly favorable and prized value on risk taking (especially if the results are profitable). Our most glorified heroes tend to be explorers (Columbus, Magellan, Neil Armstrong); radical writers and artists who risked peer disapproval and ridicule to make their statements (Freud, Van Gogh); scientists and philosophers who were ahead of their time (Einstein, Russell, Galileo, Socrates); and daring military geniuses (Napoleon, Alexander, Eisenhower). We admire risk taking in others even if we are afraid of it in ourselves.

When group members discover that they are far from the risk-taking norm, the value most prized in a therapeutic group, dissonance is heightened until they change in a direction more consistent with the adventurous status quo. To create a favorable impression in others, clients must become more risky in order to demonstrate that they are part of the "in-group."

Much of what group work accomplishes is to provide a safe structure for participants to practice taking risks. Whether a decision needs to be made, a confrontation must take place, or a new skill is to be learned—whenever change occurs—an element of risk is involved. The Great Unknown beckons: I dare you. To the rear lies all that is secure and predictable, safe and comfortable, however self-destructive such inertia might be; ahead, somewhere in the darkness, lies truth. Maybe.

INHIBITING INFLUENCES

Even the most reluctant of group members will readily agree that risk taking is absolutely necessary for any change to occur. A dreaded confrontation will have to take place. A new job is just beyond the horizon. Loneliness can be countered only by socially approaching attractive strangers. There is no shortcut to eliminate the inevitable risk that accompanies an exploration into the Great Unknown.

One primary goal of the group leader is to promote an atmosphere of low extrinsic risk so as to minimize subjectively experienced intrinsic risks (Niles & De Voe, 1978). Initial sessions do not provide a natural environment for relaxing and the spilling of guts. Members are uncertain what will happen and how they should respond. They are threatened by the faceless strangers, intimidated by the imposing leader, repulsed by certain peers, and fearful of what they might have to do. Altogether, initial group sessions can be hell for clients very eager to experiment with new behaviors but desperately afraid that others will disapprove of them.

Several inhibiting influences sabotage risk-taking efforts in groups and in group members' minds. People avoid taking risks, for example, because of the neurotic payoffs they receive. They don't have to work hard at changing. They can feel sorry for themselves. Their psychological maintenance system ensures that they can remain safe. Once these factors are identified, specific strategies can be used to neutralize their negative effects. In the Japanese martial art Aikido, an opponent's aggressive energy is countered with balanced movements that turn the force against him. Likewise, the oppositional dynamics in groups that make risk taking appear so ominous can be harnessed for constructive purposes to make the work more fluent.

A client's readiness to take risks can therefore be encouraged by the natural pressures in groups conducive to creating more dissonance in self-satisfaction levels. The more internal conflict that is intensified by group interaction, honest feedback, and other factors, the more willing, even desperate, the client becomes to change the status quo. It is only when one looks in the mirror with total disgust that one is sufficiently motivated to do something about the false image. The following variables are additional inhibiting influences common to group settings. Only after each has been identified can group leaders take steps to neutralize their effects.

Fear of Consequences
The most readily apparent inhibitor to taking risks is that of the perceived consequences. Before taking any action, especially one that involves unknown factors (such as how others might react), considerable time is spent estimating probable and possible outcomes. Group members tend to exaggerate what could conceivably occur and to magnify the potential dangers. They often inflate their sense of self-importance, believing that everyone else has nothing better to do than constantly to scrutinize their behavior.

If clients would let us into their heads during their hesitation to speak out, if we could watch a videotape of what is going on inside, we would probably see a bizarre spectacle. As the person admits aloud that she has frequently fantasized having sex with two men simultaneously, the videotape rolls along showing some members vomiting, others laughing hysterically, and a few openly astonished. In actuality, the worst possible reaction would be that members don't do or say *anything*.

There are also realistically projected consequences the likely outcomes of which make an action a bad risk. Backgammon, for instance, requires that a player calculate all possible outcomes from an opponent's throw of the dice and then make the most aggressive move on the board that has the fewest *acceptable* risks. Essentially a symbolic form of interpersonal risk taking, backgammon trains the mind to consider what you have to gain versus what you have to lose. The aggressive player who takes frequent *calculated* risks will always win over the more cautious player. The key, of course, is to help group members assess probable outcomes realistically and to encourage them to operate on those assumptions.

The fear of consequences can be minimized by keeping the fear within acceptable parameters. Byrd (1974) developed certain rules of risk taking for middle-management executives, a professional group that tends to play it safe even though personal promotions and company profits are based on taking frequent calculated risks.

The first rule is never risk more than you can afford to lose. When a client asks: "What is the worst possible thing that could realistically happen?" the disasters enumerated are much less horrendous than what had been anticipated. A client reluctant to take a new job fantasizes about all the possible catastrophes that could occur as the result of the career change; but when pressed to specifically verbalize what could happen, she finally admits the worst outcome: if the job doesn't work out, she might have to search for another. Realistic potential losses can be predicted fairly accurately from available data. Once decisions are made as to what a person is willing to sacrifice, behavior can be planned to stay within those acceptable limits.

The second rule is not to risk a lot for a little. If potential gains don't far exceed anticipated losses, it hardly seems worth the effort to take the risk (although "high-rollers" will opt in favor of the unknown whenever there is a tie, just because it is fun for them to confront the unknown). A moderately satisfied group member who has earned the respect of peers by speaking with care and deliberation is unlikely to throw her respected style out the window in favor of a more spontaneous, impulsive manner (at least until she understands that it is better to have more choices than fewer choices).

The final rule of risk taking is an integrative application of logic and emotion, of Western and Eastern thought, of physics and Tao, of right and left cerebral hemispheres: put your trust in the odds *and* your intuition.

All-or-None Law

An individual's willingness to take risks is also stifled by distorted views about what risk taking involves. The human propensity to think in dichotomies has no basis in reality except perhaps in physical laws, such as the absolute minimal threshold necessary for a nerve impulse to be conducted. This all-or-none law may apply to a circumstance such as being pregnant (as one cannot be "somewhat" or "partially" pregnant), but it has no place in the conception of risk taking. When a group member reasons that the only two options available are either to clam up or to spill one's guts unreservedly, the likely course of action is clear. For this reason, clients must be helped to dispel their absolute notions in favor of seeing behavior along a gradual continuum.

Bednar, Melnick, and Kaul (1974) identify levels of client risk along a developmental scheme, beginning with self-disclosure, the least threatening variety; then moving to interpersonal feedback, which requires considerably more skill yet involves less predictability of outcome; and finally group confrontation, the highest possible level of risking. Group confrontation in which a member shares dissatisfaction with a current activity can virtually explode with negative consequences considering the limitless choice of possible disasters. Everyone could unanimously boycott the outspoken member, ridicule his or her opinions, and use the outburst as an excuse for devious psychological torture. Worse, the person could be totally ignored.

These different levels of risking can be ordered on a gradient so that the therapist may progressively encourage low-level toward high-level risking, slowly inoculating participants' exposure to perceived danger. In this way absolutism is replaced by relativism, allowing more possible choices for client action.

In one introductory group exercise used to establish cohesion and intimacy swiftly, participants are requested to share a meaningful secret about themselves that no one else knows. This can be done anonymously on paper, thereby minimizing the level of risk, or it can be done aloud in which clients "own" their secrets. In either case, the group begins on an intense note because the content involves deep issues and all participants are given the opportunity to "get their feet wet." This exercise was put to work by Norton, Feldman, and Tafoya (1974) in an attempt to determine the riskiest themes prevalent in group members' shared secrets.

By far the riskiest secrets were those concerning sex; secrets about expressing violence or fears of being insane were also considered difficult to share. In their study, the researchers asked college-age group members to write anonymously the one thing they would be most afraid to reveal aloud. They collected 359 secrets on a staggering array of subjects that people consider risky to disclose, a conclusion not altogether surprising. Experienced group leaders continuously observe clients sweating and stammering for five minutes before they finally reveal the "terrible secret": "I once fantasized that I was the opposite sex." Other supposedly risky secrets included: "I'm on the pill," "I'm lost and lonely," and "I'm bored with my social life."

The ten secrets that were considered to be the riskiest (as judged by four independent reviewers with an inter-rater reliability of 88%) were ordered as follows:

1. I have had an incestuous relationship with a member of my family.
2. I have been in a mental institution.
3. I have V.D.
4. I masturbate almost every night.
5. I have homosexual tendencies.
6. I sometimes feel I have to kill someone.
7. I once jacked-off in the grad reading room of the library.
8. I deal and take speed.
9. I am constantly toying with the idea of killing myself.
10. I stole half of my books from the bookstore.

Knowing what most people regard as risky disclosures is helpful to group leaders so that we may gently ease them into the content of sessions without frightening them too early. When we model examples of risky disclosures, we can select topics that we know are very difficult to share to lay the groundwork for others to respond on intense levels.

Fear of Failure
Throw a frisbee and a dog will leap into the air, stretch its mouth open, and try to catch the spinning disc. If the dog should miss and land sprawled on the ground with the frisbee bouncing atop its head, what would happen next? The dog would probably not whine, cry, pout, and feel sorry for itself. It would not develop performance anxiety and become so hypersensitive that it could never again go after a frisbee without crippling self-doubt. The dog would probably wag its tail, pick up the frisbee, and return enraptured to the human for another toss. But when humans don't live up to their expectations, when they make mistakes or miss an opportunity or act less than perfect, they think of themselves as failures (Dyer, 1976).

Individuals naturally differ in their propensities to take risks; also, great variation exists in the degree to which people will make rational choices. Persons who are preoccupied with winning approval and who have a high fear of failure are less able to adjust their risk-taking strategies to fit situational requirements; they will consistently act inappropriately conservative or reckless. Those who are less concerned with group members' opinions will make more intelligent decisions about when and how to take a risk (Kogan & Wallach, 1967; Bern, 1971).

The alternative to a failure-avoidance orientation is to behave without accompanying self-judgments. The group leader must work with clients to wipe out anticipatory regret that inhibits experimentation. A group atmosphere conducive to risk taking is one in which the possibility of failure does not exist. People do or they don't do. Period. In one exercise, adolescents were given practice at handling rejection and eradicating the word *failure* from their vocabularies. They were instructed to ask one another for things they knew they would never get and then to remain calm in the face of disappointment. If, when they took interpersonal risks, the worst thing that could occur was not that they could fail but that the other would not respond, then they felt more free to take risks.

Inhibiting Stress

It is well-known that a little anxiety improves performance of a well-rehearsed task while too much anxiety can result in stage fright. Unfortunately, the situational factors prevalent in therapeutic groups may produce toxic levels of stress that curtail risk-taking actions. The pressures to conform, performance anxiety, comparisons to peers, approval seeking, and other group norms are all anxiety-provoking stimuli. Hypervigilance is also evident in group situations in which a person enters a state of helpless panic in the face of an oncoming threat with insufficient time to prepare evasive action. For the same reason that people may freeze during a fire escape or other group crisis, group members may allow the prospect of an impending risk to cripple thought processes and constrict effective strategies for countering the threat.

A favorite method for teaching reading to first graders used to be to arrange the children in a circle (the teachers must have heard from psychologists that circles, like pyramids, have healing properties) and then to have them take turns reading a story aloud. However benign the intention, the result of this exercise (as I recall it) was that each kid would wait in panic, counting the number of places until his or her turn, and then fall apart from stress when the cue finally arrived. Another effect was that as soon as your turn was over, you could daydream for the rest of the period while your friends suffered the wait.

Novice group leaders often make the same mistake in their efforts to expose clients to take risks. When an introductory exercise requires people to tell something about themselves each in turn around a circle, clients usually spend the time rehearsing their introductions instead of attending to others. After their turn is taken, they will spend the rest of the hour patting themselves on the back with relief.

The inhibiting stress can be intensified or diminished through the use of structure, depending on when and how it is introduced. Early group structure in which expectations, goals, and roles are clarified helps to make risk taking easier (Bednar, Melnick, & Kaul, 1974). When clients understand what is appropriate behavior, how the group process will emerge, and what is likely to happen, they are a lot more willing to take therapeutic risks (Goldstein, Heller, & Sechrest, 1966).

We can soften the impact of anxiety-provoking stress by preparing participants for the experience. For instance, giving constructive feedback to one another reduces stress by providing certain guidelines to diminish the ambiguity of the situation. Risks can be structured according to spontaneous circumstances where rehearsal anxiety won't get in the way: "Just now you gave me that look where you stare down at me as if I were a bug you want to squash." Structure can involve specific declarations of risk: "When I get home tonight my husband will be dozing in front of the television. I'll explain to him that I'm uncomfortable and dissatisfied with the amount of work he does around the house and then negotiate a more equitable arrangement."

Providing minimum structure works to reduce inhibiting stress; so does encouraging familiarity and intimacy. If people can be helped to feel more comfortable, they will be much more willing to try out new behaviors.

Degree of Comfort

At the other extreme, feeling *too* comfortable with oneself may also diminish a person's motive to take risks. As noted earlier, people don't change as long as they are minimally comfortable with the way they are. Often group leaders must intensify the dissonance in people so that they will work to reconcile their inner conflict between the status quo and the desired future. Group members are not likely to take risks until they feel externally, or preferably internally, pressed to do so.

Many group techniques are designed to make clients feel uncomfortable with their ineffective selves. Once the ball is rolling and a few courageous clients jump in with both head and heart, the others begin to notice how attractive the risk takers are. They may at first be resentful and later jealous, but eventually they are respectful of their more venturesome colleagues. "If they can do it, so can I" is the hoped-for conclusion they will reach.

In one group, a middle-aged man listened restlessly to the tearful complaints of a college student who had just broken up with her boyfriend. Apparently, they had been dating since high school and had settled into a fairly comfortable routine. Eventually bored with the relationship, the girl decided to break it off even though she was giving up some great times. "What has this to do with me?" wondered the older gentleman, suddenly aware that he was feeling hot and sweaty. "After all, my marriage has been good for the past 24 years. We've raised two pretty nice kids. We have a nice house, kind friends, and we're very considerate of each other's needs. But this girl blows away her boyfriend just because she doesn't love him intensely. What the hell *is* love, anyway? That's the stuff you see in movies!"

Another group member supported the girl by disclosing that he had wanted to do the same thing with his lover. He had lived with his first and only gay lover for some years until he, too, had settled into a comfortable but dependent routine. It had taken him almost six months to work up the courage to leave. "I really admire your spirit for not letting things drag on. There was a great temptation for me to wait until I could find another lover before I left my old one. What you're doing takes a lot of strength, especially when what you're leaving is so convenient."

The older man now begins to sweat profusely. His heart pounds. Finally he speaks out: "Is it really so terrible to have a comfortable marriage? I mean, sure, some things are boring and predictable. We have sex every Wednesday and go out for dinner every other Friday. We go to sleep every night after the late news, though on Mondays we sometimes watch Johnny Carson. Sure, it's gotten to be a drag. I don't believe I've loved my wife for 10 years. But is it really worth giving up a 24-year investment just because it isn't all that exciting? Well, maybe it is. What should I do?"

This person's discomfort is multiplied in direct proportion to the risk taking going on in the rest of the group. As others shared their apprehensions, it became more acceptable to admit his own fears. Finally, he was motivated to risk opening up because his discomfort had become intolerable. Keeping his secret safe did not seem all that attractive compared to the great relief he could feel on unburdening his soul. The more honestly he spoke, the more quickly his temporary comfort level reached a point of equilibrium, at least until he decided to retreat once again to his delusional safety.

Illusion of Safety

Like the ostrich that buries its head in the sand believing that because it cannot see danger, danger will not see it, people deceive themselves into believing they have invulnerable protection against the outside world. By having convinced themselves that they are safe, they need take no risky action that could jeopardize the present, temporary tranquility.

One such victim of the safety illusion was Doug, who had worked as a top executive for a major corporation for almost a decade. During his ascent, pushing for innovative changes, he had of course made enemies. Now Doug was unhappy in his work: his actions were constantly countermanded, his opinions were ignored, and he was rendered powerless by people both above and below him. But Doug was reasonably comfortable. He had a pension plan. He liked his neighborhood. His office was attractive, and over the years he had made some fine friends. If his job wasn't the best, at least it was secure (or so he would tell himself on declining every job offer that came along). Finally, everything collapsed around him. He was aced out of his position, blackmailed into resigning, and at 55 years of age he was too old to start over. The illusion of total safety crumbled. Doug had waited too long, deceiving himself that taking risks was not necessary because his position was unassailable. So much for *that* illusion.

So many group members list and total their blessings, then spread them around as reminders of how good things really are. In reality, however, the only thing that one can logically expect is the unexpected. The only true safety is in the knowledge that one is fully prepared to give something up if a productive risk becomes necessary. But believing this and selling the idea of risk taking to clients are quite different matters.

SELLING PRODUCTIVE RISK TAKING

Jerri was extremely resistant to taking risks of any kind, finding it much easier to comply with her parents' and friends' expectations than to search for meaningful goals on her own. Whenever she "accidentally" took a risk, such as confronting another group member or approaching a stranger at a party, she would deny that the action was a risk because it wasn't all that difficult to do. She eventually verbalized a risk that she wanted to take badly enough to place herself willingly in a vulnerable position. Although she desperately feared rejection, she was panting at the prospect of initiating a romantic relationship with a man with whom she had long been smitten.

When queried by group members as to what exactly she had to lose by approaching the man, it took her at least two minutes of silence before she finally admitted that she was stumped. She felt frightened that he might ridicule her brutally, although she knew that he was a sensitive man who liked and respected her. At worst, he might express a willingness to keep the relationship on a friendship basis, thereby reassuring her that he was truly in love with her mind rather than with her body. If he should respond with romantic overtures, her wish would be fulfilled. Either way she couldn't lose.

Jerri was now able to think of risk-taking experiences as opportunities to enhance, rather than to destroy, existing security. By holding back, she was cheating herself of growth experiences and depriving her loved ones of seeing in her an independent spirit that had lain dormant for so long. In retrospect, Jerri laughs at her former reluctance to initiate risks.

In the group session that had made the difference, all action had been suspended. Not only was her progress stopped dead, but all forward movement in the group had halted. Everyone had started playing it safe, engaging in polite conversation, dutifully saying the right thing when called on to speak. Typical of most groups, a period of temporary cowardice had developed. Clients had mentally counted their chips and decided that mediocrity isn't so bad after all, at least considering the alternative.

It was quickly determined that the fear of risking was the pervasive theme. All the symptoms were evident: a high frequency of artificial flattery, warning looks of "don't tread on me," evasiveness, reluctance to declare goals, contentment with the status quo, increased fear of leader interventions, and much protective defensiveness. Though individual members commonly exhibit these behaviors, rarely does this coward's plague strike all who are present at once.

A radical procedure was needed. Members were once again beginning to enjoy the false sense of security that comes from the "hiding phase" of Hide-and-Seek. The group leader decided to try a scolding approach, a minilecture intended to remotivate clients toward action, reminding them why they had joined the group in the first place. The purpose of such an impassioned speech is to highlight all the crucial elements of the change process that are involved in attacking the path of most resistance—taking productive risks.

Perhaps the most difficult task for group leaders is to sell productive risk taking to clients. To gear up for a dramatic pitch seems eventually to be necessary in every group. Usually there has been some impasse and people have begun more skillful dodging. Conversation has become safe and predictable, involving low-risk topics or those that have been previously brought up. Sometimes clients will revert to their old standard defenses: "I just don't have anything to work on right now. My life is going pretty well."

Particularly in the early sessions, members will exhibit much reluctance as they cautiously test the water. Stubbornly they cross their arms and demand: "Prove to me that any of this will make a difference. Why should I go out on a limb when it can so easily break off?" At this point the ball is in our court. It is up to us to recruit potential risk takers to take the plunge.

A Hard-Sell Speech

Sometimes it becomes necessary to give a hard-sell speech, one of the few times we resort to lecture tactics as a matter of choice. If pep talks work well when coaches give them to athletes as a motivating force, why shouldn't they also work for us? Occasionally I catch myself checking whether the time is right and the players are ripe for the big pitch. I take a deep breath, bore holes in their heads with the intensity of my gaze, and then deliver one of my favorite therapeutic speeches, usually intended to shake group members out of their inertia.

This speech always contains certain elements, although its form may change. (a) It must be entertaining. (b) If long-winded, it is for the purpose of repeating important themes. (c) It makes things seem easy. (d) It is educational and informative. (e) It is self-disclosing. I admit that I have the same concerns but (f) that I did something about them. (g) It is not *too* scolding in its tone. (h) It gets clients jumping in their seats to get started on their productive risks. The following is a sampling of the marketing strategy I employ to sell risk-taking to group members:

How many times have you found yourself trapped in a boring, entirely predictable conversation? When is the last time a friend asked your opinion and, instead of giving it to him honestly, you told him only what he wanted to hear? How long ago did you last approach an attractive stranger? When was the last time you did something completely new, something that you had never tried before? How many times have you stifled yourself from speaking your mind in here? When is the last time you took a risk?

There are different kinds of risk taking, some of them productive and others potentially harmful. Jumping out of an airplane without a parachute, getting into fights, and ridiculing others are examples of the latter. Productive risk taking, on the other hand, usually takes the form of expanding or broadening one's experience for self-growth. Although taking the risk itself is often not pleasurable, the satisfaction of trying something new is. Taking risks is exhilarating. It is no accident that so many people like to gamble, drive fast, or play dangerous sports, though even more people experience the dangerous unknown vicariously through books, TV, and movies.

Productive risk taking helps you to overcome fears, develop self-confidence, and enlarge your life experiences. Examples include risking the disapproval of others by doing what you want; risking honesty and sincerity when you reveal yourself to others; risking discomfort, inconvenience, or rejection by becoming intensely involved with another; risking failure by trying something new; or risking change by ridding yourself of self-defeating behaviors.

What is risky for one person is not necessarily so for another. To some people, ending a long relationship, a marriage, or a friendship is the most difficult task imaginable. Others fear quitting a job or starting a new life. Still others avoid failure at all costs. Think about what *you* are most afraid of risking. Is it meeting new people? Becoming intimate with someone in or out of this group? Ridding yourself of your dependencies? Trying something new? Exploring the unknown? There is a surefire sign that you can use as a reliable guidepost as to what is risky for you. When your stomach feels queasy or your legs feel jittery because you're trying to avoid doing something that you really want to, that's an indication a risk is in sight.

It's easy for me to recall those painful images of the past when I struggled to pursue the unknown—times when all thought and activity seemed suspended waiting for me to make a decision. The same process occurs in everyone. I would think of something that I really wanted to do; but before I had a chance to carry out my plan, I would scare myself senseless with all the things that could go wrong, all the disastrous results that could occur as a consequence of my bumbling ineptitude. Of course, the disaster that I imagined, even if it did arise, could never be worse than all my self-inflicted misery, lamenting what a spineless jellyfish and gutless wonder I was for giving in to my fears. One incident that recurred throughout my college years is still a source of inspiration to me. You will all be able to see a little of yourselves in me.

The setting is a small midwestern university. I am in my dormitory room, the lights dimmed, seductive music in the background. Although my roommate conveniently left the room an hour earlier, I am not alone. An attractive female companion is sitting next to me, discussing the cafeteria food, her art history course, and plans for the future. I'm not listening. Instead, I'm thinking how much I want to kiss her. At least four times my mind orders me to make a move, but my body fails to obey. I am crippled by my thoughts. "What if she hates me and slaps me in the face?" "What if she doesn't like it and thinks I'm inept?" Or the worst thought of my adolescent naivete: "What if she *does* like it? Then what do I do?"

Inevitably my self-debate would end in an ultimatum to myself. I would begin a countdown from ten as I prepared—nine, eight, seven—to kiss her gently on the lips—six—and hold her in—five—my arms. I always—three, two—chickened out before I got to one. Then the real self-abuse would start. Eventually I became so frustrated and angry with my behavior that I decided no rejection from anyone else could possibly hurt more than my own self-condemnation.

After years of practice at taking risks, I am now better equipped to deal with others' disapproval of me as well as with breaking down my own resistances. Today, if I were to encounter a potentially risky situation, such as wanting to try or say something I've never attempted before, and I feel myself hedging and backing away, that would be a signal for me to go forward and conquer my fears. I remind myself of all my past hesitations and what they cost me. Then I convince myself that the only way I will ever become more effective in my life is by mastering new behaviors instead of mindlessly reworking old ones.

Right now, think about the risky things you've wanted to do for a long time but continuously put off because of fears. Is it making a career switch? Telling someone what you really think? Speaking up more honestly in this group? Sharing something personal for which you are afraid others will condemn you? Whatever it is, you are probably giving yourself a lot of excuses for not taking action.

You like your security, safety, and predictability no matter how miserable or ineffective you are. Taking risks means changing in some ways, having to learn something new, and that's hard work. Sure, it would be nice to be a fully functioning, happy individual who is in control, but not if you have to work for it. You'd prefer to sit back and wait for some magical transformation to take place in your mind, making you into the person you'd really like to be. After all, you've believed for a long time that you'll always be as you are, and there's very little you can do about it.

Forget that nonsense that you are controlled by your past. So what if you were toilet trained too early or saw your aunt naked in the shower. You have many good excuses for the way you are and the reasons you got that way; but your past will continue to shackle your present moments and future efforts as long as you believe that you are powerless to change. Avoid taking risks, experimenting with new behaviors, really working on yourself to grow and you will remain the same old, inert, predictable, listless self. The choices available to you are only as limited as your imagination. If you choose to alter dissatisfying aspects of your behavior, this commitment will help to motivate your journey.

Think again about the things you don't like about yourself, behaviors you would like to change, anything from nose picking or overweight to feelings of excessive guilt. Whatever the undesired behavior, you've learned to live with it. It brings comfort because it resembles a stable character trait. After all, you've always smoked, worried, been dependent, fat, unhappy, or nervous. Why change now?

Why, indeed? Because you lead basically a boring existence. Your life routine runs like clockwork. Why should you risk what you have for something unknown? I could give you many reasons, but they are all my own motivations for structuring new experiences in my life, discovering novel solutions to problems that confront me. I cannot do your work for you, nor can I convince you to make your life more exciting and meaningful.

It is totally up to you. The next time you catch yourself censoring risky thoughts or hesitating to speak up in the group, ask yourself what you really have to lose. Question your motives for playing it safe. Take a deep breath and then plunge. It is *only* by taking risks that you can ever expect to make changes in your life. If you don't venture forth in this group, exploring new territory, encountering people more intimately, you will be condemned to a life of stale mediocrity. The choice is yours. Now does anyone have anything to say?"

If the minilecture has had its effect, group members start to get fired up. They also feel a little guilty for hanging back, but the momentum has begun. Since risk taking involves a response inhibition behavioral model rather than a response deficit model, a great part of the group leader's work involves coaching clients to do what they have already learned to do selectively since birth. Promoting risk taking is among the most difficult challenges for group leaders. Clients fight back every inch of the way, forcing us occasionally to wonder why we must sell an idea that is so obviously beneficial. At this point, it might be helpful to observe the example of a group wrestling with the issue of risking as its theme.

CHAPTER 10

Risk Taking in Action

To illustrate some of the principles, concepts, and techniques discussed thus far in relation to risk taking and change, I have included in Chapter 10 a verbatim transcript of a group session in action. This sequence is not designed to show the flawless effectiveness of any one particular approach. Rather, it reflects honestly many of the flaws, mistakes, and ineffective intervention attempts that group leaders inadvertently make.

Immediately after the session, the group leader played back the tape, recording his own reactions and feelings as he recalled them occurring. Another therapist, who had recorded her observations of the session behind a one-way mirror, helped to cue the group leader as to possible reactions. The session's verbal transactions are here set in roman type; the therapist's internal thoughts and feelings, in italics. In addition to providing an opportunity for experiencing the risk-taking process in action, this format permits the reader to understand the rationale behind each intervention.

The client-in-focus was Chris, a 24-year-old woman who had been attending the group irregularly, whenever she had a concern that troubled her. It had been three weeks since her last visit, which had been her sixth in three months. Part of the difficulty in dealing with this client was the therapist's previous inability to get her to commit herself to continuing the sessions on a regular and systematic basis.

Notice that the group leader operated under the assumption that the client might never return. Consequently, minimal effort was expended toward making her feel comfortable by means of small talk. Also, the pacing of the session was rushed, and the group leader was a little impatient. Whenever possible, however, interventions were intended to help the client leave the session with something specific and concrete, with the feeling that something definite had been accomplished which could be further worked on, practiced, and developed between sessions. It was assumed that any substantial progress made in the session would be sufficient to motivate the client to return.

In addition to the group leader and Chris, participants include Danny, Beth, Carol, Nathan, Nancy, Myron, Ethel, and Michael, all of whom were group members.

TRANSCRIPT OF A GROUP SESSION

Group Leader: *(Chris looks good today. Tentative smile. She's prepared for something. I'm a little nervous. I hope we talk in an area I know something about. O.K. Block out the world. Focus within the room.)* Well Chris, you indicated that you wished to use group time today.

Chris: I would like to work on my relationship with my boyfriend. Uh. I'm at a point where I want to terminate it and I'm terrified to do that. Let me tell you a little bit about it. *(Whew! Another get-the-hell-out-and-run-but-I-wish-I-didn't-feel-so-guilty concern.)* I've known him for maybe four years. I've had a serious relationship with him going on our third year. Two years and a couple of months.

Group Leader: Uh huh. *(It sounds like she's reciting a speech.)*

Chris: About a year, a year and a half of that, I've been living with him. It is a really good relationship—*(You mean "it was")*—in terms of meeting both of our needs. Um. When I talk about that I mean that he's a really nice person. He's really thoughtful. He's constantly telling me good things about myself. *(She's into approval seeking. Says "really" a lot, too.)*

Danny: You need him to tell you good things about yourself?

Chris: Yeah, I like that. *(Must remember to come back to that.)* He's tremendous for my ego. He's always saying "You're so cute," "You're fun." *(She is cute. It irritates me that I notice that.)*

Group Leader: You started out by saying that you wanted to get out of your relationship—*(If she wants to get out why is she talking so much about how nice it is?)*—with your boyfriend, yet you've spent the past few minutes talking about all the great things about that relationship.

Chris: Why don't I get out? Is that what you want to know?

Group Leader: *(You know it is.)* Uh huh.

Chris: O.K. I want to get out because I feel like I want to play. I want to meet a lot more people. I feel like the relationship is too confining.

Group Leader: *(Beating around the bush. Might as well get down to the basics right away.)* When you say that you want to meet more people, do you perhaps really mean that you want to meet other men and have more varied sexual relationships?

Chris: Yeah. I guess you could put it that way.

Group Leader: (She talks in terms of being controlled rather than her controlling herself.) You're feeling that the relationship is confining you rather than you confining yourself within the relationship?

Chris: Uh. I have confined myself in the relationship. This weekend I didn't do that. I was away from home for the weekend, so I had a great time, And I really enjoyed it. I met a lot of guys. And I talked with guys. *(You had a good time in spite of yourself and all the limits you place on yourself.)* I realized once again how restless I am in my own relationship with my boyfriend. I just want to get out. I want to meet people again. *(I don't think she's ready yet to lay some stuff on her. Maybe I should wait a little longer. It's so hard to stifle myself.)* Have relationships with lots of people as opposed to one. *(Have several admirers tell you how cute you are rather than just one.)* He's talking in terms of marriage. He really wants to settle down. And I feel I just want to go. You know? I want to be free from him, and I want to be free from a lot of things. *(Like yourself for instance.)*

Group Leader: Your expectations are much different from his for what the relationship should be? *(What a dumb question to ask. Obviously they must be.)*

Chris: Right. He knows my expectations. He knows that I don't want to get married. He's known that all along. Um. I just told him that I was getting restless and that I wanted to leave recently. And that's when we started talking about marriage again. And when he talks about marriage I start feeling really guilty. *(A cause-effect relationship. He can get to her any time he wants.)*

Group Leader: Feeling guilty because why?

Chris: Feeling guilty because he really loves me a lot and I can't return that love. I do love him but I can't love him completely and say you're it for the rest of my life.

Group Leader: So because you can't love him the way he'd like you to, feeling guilty makes up for that? Like that's paying your retribution to him because you can't love him? Spend X amount of minutes feeling really shitty about it to pay him off.

Chris: Yeah. That's my payment. *(Why don't you pay him in green stamps instead?)*

Group Leader: Do you like that? *(I forgot to ask her what "feeling guilty" means to her.)*

Chris: No, I don't like it. When you're bad, you feel guilty. That's something that has been with me a long time. *(She's using the past, or the way she was, as an excuse for staying the same.)*

Group Leader: Because it's been with you a long time, does that mean it's going to continue to be with you?

Chris: No, I don't have to keep it. *(You don't believe that.)* But I can't feel good about treating him shitty. *(But how does your feeling bad help him feel better?)* Like this weekend I went out with guys, and I've had a good time. I actually found a guy that I really like. And I could say—fell in love with, quote, unquote. *(You mean you liked him enough to justify sleeping with him.)* Not that I would start a whole relationship with him, but I really fell in love.

Group Leader: Uh huh. *(I'm confused. I lost track. Where do I go now? Maybe check out some background data about her functioning.)*

Beth: You fell in love in just one day? *(Whew! Saved by the bell.)* Gee, I wish that could happen to me. *(Oops, she's digressing.)*

Chris: I enjoyed that. You know, I felt alive. And I felt, uh, excited again. I felt really high. And in my relationship—it's just so solid and stable. Never changes.

Danny: What is your boyfriend's name?

Chris: Mike.

Danny: Mike? Have you talked to Mike about this at any great length?

Chris: Ummmm. Yeah. We spent three hours talking about it one night. And I didn't tell him that I wanted to leave him because—I told him that I wanted to leave him because I wanted to move on. And I wanted to visit lots of places and meet a lot of people. And he didn't fit into those plans. *(Must support her.)*

Group Leader: That must have been really, really difficult for you.

Chris: That's an understatement.

Group Leader: So you are telling him what you want, and that's not fitting in with Mike's plans. But Mike knows how to get to you. If he can't get your love, he knows he can keep you there by helping you to feel guilty about leaving. Letting you know he can't survive without you and that you're responsible for him. *(Hey, that was good. How come she's not responding?)* Would you say that's accurate?

Chris: Yeah, that's accurate. He does provoke guilt feelings. *(There she goes with external control again.)*

Group Leader: He promotes them in you, or you promote them in yourself? *(I'm asking too many close-ended questions.)*

Chris: He helps them along. He knows how to manipulate me to feel bad. *(You've been a good teacher.)* He just knows how to do that.

Carol: And you make it real easy for him by playing along.

Chris: Oh yeah. I make it tremendously easy for him. [*Laughs*] Um. I just want to go about life and fall in love when I want to fall in love. Make love with whomever I want to make love with. Not just with one man. And I don't want to feel bad just because I want to make love with other men.

Carol: And none of these needs or wants are being met within your relationship as it is now? *(Nice phrasing. Neutral. Didn't imply she's taking a side, although she really is.)*

Chris: No, but it's really tough. Because our relationship is, in a way, kind of like a marriage. There just isn't the paper. *(I want to ask her some things about the past; I'm not sure if they're relevant to the present.)* You know, all of our stuff is pooled together. Whatever I imagine—O.K., I fantasize about the move. I know I want to do it. I know I'm going to do it. *(Now you're thinking from strength. Positively. But I thought her original concern was making a decision whether to get out or not. It sounds like she already knew. Maybe she just used that as an opener.)* In order to get out of the relationship, I really have to move out of the house. I couldn't invite guys into the house with him there. So, uh, when I fantasize about the move it's awful. It's terrible. *(Disasterizing. Using up her present moments so she doesn't have to think about them.)* Because three-quarters of the shit in that house is mine.

Group Leader: *(Help her to see that the worst isn't so bad. She's so afraid of taking risks.)* What are you disasterizing about that could go wrong?

Chris: Well, the flashes I have are me carrying boxes out and Mike looks forlorn. *(Sounds like a soap opera.)* You know. That's one. And that drives me nuts. Uh, another one is going back to the house after I've emptied out my stuff and seeing how empty the house is. There would be no towels, no dishes, no sheets. *(No you.)* He'd have to start all over again. Besides the fact he just signed the lease for another year and I don't think he could pay that rent money alone. *(She has a whole lot of reasons worked out.)*

Group Leader: So you're spending a whole lot of your time worrying about how—*(I forgot his name.)*—he's going to get along. He's going to be messed up. And it's all your fault. If he goes out and kills himself, it will be all your fault, and you'll probably have to spend the rest of your life feeling guilty about it.

Chris: Nooo. *(You don't believe that.)* There are two things. One is: what if I'm making a mistake? *(So, that's it. Fear of the unknown.)*

What if he is the best person for me. He's really a great person. What's going to happen if two years from now I discover I really do love him and I really did want to marry him? *(She expects an answer from me? Better jump in quick before Nathan takes over and distracts things.)*

Group Leader: Then you'll have realized that you probably made a mistake and will wonder what it would have been like. *(Am I pushing too hard?)* But there is no way, in fact, that you could prove it one way or another. In spite of the fact that the relationship isn't all that you'd like it to be, you are in a kind of certainty now. Everything is predictable. Sure, it's scary to venture out into the unknown, but that is sometimes the price you have to pay for moving out of mediocrity. In talking about getting out of that relationship, there's a certain amount of risk involved. Sure, it sounds beautiful to be free again, and be independent, and go out with as many men as you want, but you don't know for sure whether you will find loneliness or pleasurable privacy. *(She doesn't understand yet.)* So one of the things you may be telling—

Nathan: Chris, I really think your problem is that you don't appreciate what you've already got. If my girlfriend ever thought like you did—. *(Here we go again. Better cut him off before he does any real damage.)*

Group Leader: Nathan, excuse me. How is what you are telling Chris helpful for her to hear?

Nathan: Um. Well. I guess I thought she was being too hasty. I mean she—*(I've got to pin him down and then get back on track.)*

Group Leader: Talk directly to Chris instead of about her.

Nathan: Oh, yeah. I mean you might be jumping into something without thinking it through. *(Oh, no. He's reinforcing her fear.)* What you have isn't heaven, but at least you're never lonely. *(Now Nathan is talking about himself.)*

Chris: That's true—I'm not lonely. When I get out there I might be really lonely. I don't know if I can handle it. *(She wants me to tell her that she can.)* Going home to an empty house. I don't know if I'd want that. Because when he's in the house it's a really warm thing. You know when you walk in—*(Keep her on course. But should I reflect her ambivalence more or keep going?)*

Group Leader: Will you ever know if you like it unless you try? *(Maybe Nathan is right. I'm pushing too hard.)*

Chris: No. I've never lived alone. *(That frightens her.)* I don't know if—well, I imagine liking it. Cause I have this image of the career woman being really busy and having a good time. I know that's not going to happen all the time. But I know a lot of people. If it is lonely, I can do something about it. *(That's the spirit! But I sense fear in getting along without others.)* In terms of girls at least. I don't know a whole lot of guys around here, and that would take time probably. Besides I don't want that kind of relationship again for awhile.

Group Leader: What kind of relationship is that?

Chris: I want to avoid getting serious with anyone for awhile. I want to be able to experience a lot of people.

Carol: But at the same time you're not getting serious with someone else you still don't want to feel lonely. You want your privacy, and your privacy is important to you, and your independence is important to you, but you're still afraid of that loneliness.

Chris: Right. *(Dig some more.)*

Group Leader: Chris, how long have you been thinking about moving out?

Chris: A few months. *(Pin her down. Show her the time she wastes.)*

Group Leader: A few months. Two months?

Chris: Yeah. It happened one weekend I had these dreams about a couple of old boyfriends, and, uh, they're boyfriends that I would like to see again. And after a weekend of dreams I realized how restless I was in our relationship, and that happened two months ago. *(The unconscious at work in her dreams. Confronting time. Show her what she's doing.)*

Group Leader: You've spent 60 days and 60 nights into wishing behaviors, into wanting to be somewhere else than you are now?

Chris: Uh huh.

Group Leader: For 60 days you've been thinking about it but haven't worked yourself up to whatever courage or motivation that it takes to get out? *(Am I being too harsh?)*

Chris: Right.

Group Leader: How long do you intend to wait before you stop wallowing around in your crap and get that magical feeling you seem to be anticipating before—

Chris: Well, I know I can't move right now because I don't have enough money saved. *(What horseshit!)*

Group Leader: You can't move out? If you wanted to move out, you couldn't? *(Provoke alternatives.)*

Chris: Well, I could live with someone else. Conceivably I could

move out after next paycheck and give somebody $50 to let me
stay with them for two weeks. But what I should do is wait till I
save up $400. *(Is this what she wants to do?)*

Group Leader: What you *should* do?

Chris: I mean the right move to me would be to just take my stuff in
the house where it's at and move it to the place where I want to
be. O.K.?

Group Leader: O.K. *(I don't understand what I just said O.K. to.)*

Chris: Which is another house. That way I can keep my dog. *(Dog?
Where'd the dog come from?)* In an apartment I couldn't keep my
dog. Um. And I don't have money to move into a house right now.
In order to do that right, I should save up that money and then
do it. *(And procrastinate for another 60 days.)*

Group Leader: And then maybe things will resolve themselves without you having to do anything and take any risks.

Chris: Yeah, I guess so.

Group Leader: The only thing I question is whether money is the
real issue or just an excuse for further procrastination. *(I think it's
about time to do some summarizing.)* I think it's appropriate to
clarify exactly what it was that you started out wanting to work
on. It seems to be a dicision-making process, that you're in a
situation now that has certain positive aspects, which you've
been able to express—*(Substantiate with her data to make it
more personally meaningful.)*—the security, the belonging, the
lack of loneliness, having a bed to sleep in with a warm body next
to you, and there are also some negative factors which we have
identified: loss of your independence, loss of privacy, lack of
growth, and cutting in on a lot of things that you'd like to be able
to do but don't feel free enough with the shackles that you've
imposed upon yourself. Although you started out wanting help
in making your decision, it is now apparent that you have
already made it, and you now feel bad about it and are immobi-
lizing yourself. The guilt you feel for Mike is an example of this.
(I'm out of breath. I should have had her do the summarizing.)

Chris: Well, I feel guilty also because he is the first giver I have ever
experienced. *(Oh, can I relate to that! I remember—Stop it!)*

Beth: So, you owe him something because of that?

Chris: Yeah. [*Laughs*] I feel that way. In past relationships I was the
giver and, uh, guys were the takers.

Beth: So now the shoe is on the other foot, and you feel the power to
hurt him just like you were hurt in the past.

Chris: Wow, yes.

Group Leader: Mike taught you something. He was the first guy who gave to you and—

Chris: —and I've been taking and taking and taking. And now what I'm going to do is just take myself out of there and totally blow him away.

Group Leader: And you feel like a total witch. Further, you spend another large bulk of your time worrying about what might happen in the future. And goddam Mike, why isn't he making it easy for you? You are expecting it to be easy.

Chris: Well, I know it's not going to be easy. *(Liar.)* It's going to be tough. That's why I spend all my time procrastinating. *(She hit that one before I did.)*

Group Leader: It is going to be tough. You know that. You may even believe it. You've invested a lot of time, energy, and emotion into this relationship with someone who I presume you once felt very strongly for. *(Maybe I should have checked that out some more.)* There are a lot of memories, a lot of experiences that you have vested in this relationship. And it is difficult to cut them off.

Chris: Yeah. [*Long silence*] *(I'm at a loss as to where to go from here. Perhaps move into self-understanding.)*

Group Leader: Chris, we've been able to identify some behaviors that you aren't particularly effective in, or at least as effective as you would like to be, such as guilt, worry, approval seeking, and the whole notion of external control, feeling that other people control you rather than you controlling yourself, and also believing that other people are that way. Mike is controlled by you rather than him controlling himself. I think it's very important, before we move on to establishing some goals and alternatives, that you understand exactly what you get out of acting in these dumb-ass ways and why they continue to persist. It is obvious—*(I hope.)*—that you wouldn't be acting in these ways unless you were getting some payoffs. Both positive and negative payoffs that reinforce your behaviors. Can you think of what these payoffs might be? All the really great things you get out of feeling guilty about hurting Mike.

Chris: It keeps me where I am. *(It's incredible how quickly and perceptively she is following.)*

Group Leader: O.K. You stay the same and you don't move.

Chris: Um.

Group Leader: And that's safe.

Chris: That's very safe. That's instead of taking a big move and dealing with all the shit involved. I know I can deal with all the shit that happens in the relationship, like the guilt, or the feeling bad, or the restlessness.

Group Leader: So in the short run it's easier to stay where you are: immobilized, procrastinating, feeling guilty, worrying, into approval seeking and external control, using up your present moments.

Chris: Right. Um. *(She's starting to run out of steam. Should I rescue her?)*

Group Leader: What are some other great payoffs you get out of feeling guilty?

Chris: I don't know. *(Quick. Someone bail me out.)*

Nancy: Well [*Long pause*], I wonder. Is it really easier to feel guilty than it is to be a self-actualized person?

Group Leader: Well, certainly in the short run it's easier to keep feeling guilty. After all, you've had a lot of practice. You don't even have to work at it any more, you're so good at it. You've been doing it your whole life.

Chris: [*Laughs*] You should see. I've been doing it since I can remember. *(She's struggling. Time to move in.)*

Group Leader: But in the long run the payoffs you get from feeling guilty aren't anything compared to what you could be getting.

Chris: You see, that's just it. I can't find that many payoffs about it. I would really like to know.

Group Leader: All right. So you'd like to come up with some payoffs in feeling guilty besides just sitting back and waiting—*(Keep stalling until I can think of something.)*

Myron: You know, it's a secure way. You don't have to take any major risks. *(Rescued in the nick of time.)*

Group Leader: O.K. *(Must relax. My impatience is tying me up.)*

Ethyl: It's a lazy way, too. You don't have to use up any energy. You just get to sit back and complain.

Group Leader: *(Now I've got it!)* Another thing related to guilt that we alluded to before was that because you can't love Mike the way he loves you, you're feeling like you can make up for it by paying the equivalent price in guilt.

Chris: Yeah. That's a definite payoff I get.

Group Leader: And this moves us to why you continue to feel guilty even though you know it's destructive. *(Does she follow the reasoning?)*

Chris: [*Long silence*] Maybe that goes back to the payoffs. I continue to feel guilty because that's the easiest thing to do, at least right now.

Group Leader: Right. But in the long run it's the action, the taking of risks, that really makes life exciting. You decide to act, feel, and think in these ways instead of more productive ways because of the benefits we've identified. To act differently you need to make a conscious choice. [*Long silence*] (*Is she following me? Check her out.*) Where is it that you'd like to go from here?

Chris: Well, I've made a decision in my head. (*Good for you.*) I would like to move on. I'm going to do it. The problem I have is with my heart, with my emotions. It's going to be a terrible experience to live through. There's another factor too. (*She's found another loophole.*) And that is a lot of our friends are mutual and I'm wondering what will happen to the relationships.

Michael: That happened to me with my divorce. My ex-wife and I had to practically divide up our friends. One for me, one for her. It was a pain, but it wasn't all that difficult.

Chris: Does that mean that by terminating my relationship with him that I have to terminate my relationships with our friends? (*Put the ball back in her court.*)

Group Leader: Is that going to make a difference?

Chris: Well, maybe. No, I guess not. (*She doesn't believe that. I'll call her on it.*)

Group Leader: You sound like you're giving me the answer that you think I want. (*Maybe I'm being too directive.*)

Chris: Well, I couldn't give up those friends right now.

Group Leader: You couldn't or you choose not to? (*We're starting to get off track.*)

Chris: I choose not to. I really enjoy those people right now. I wouldn't want to give up those relationships.

Group Leader: And who says you have to?

Chris: I guess I'm expressing that fear. (*Get her back on track.*)

Group Leader: The real issue is how you're going to move out and not feel like a complete idiot. (*Maybe that's not the real issue.*) Not feel that you've hurt anyone and not feel that you have to use guilt as a payment.

Chris: Right. That's the answer.

Group Leader: And feel really good about this decision that you've made.

Chris: Yeah, that's going to be really tough to do.

Group Leader: (Now my motivation rap.) I agree. It's tough. So what? Are you going to let that stop you?

Chris: No, I'm not going to let anything stop me from doing it. [*Group members applaud*] I just don't want to walk away feeling totally messed up. That's going to be the tough part. [*Pause*] I don't know how to do that. How to walk away from the situation still liking myself. I want to figure out the magic pill I have to take. *(She's asking for help.)*

Group Leader: So you're asking us how to transcend you—

Chris: No, I'm not asking that from you. I think that's something I can come up with. *(Good girl.)* I've thought about a lot of different things I can do. I can go to people who I get the warmest vibrations from. I can go to people who can make me feel good. *(Her external control is showing again.)*

Beth: But you're using other people as reference points. You are saying that you don't have enough strength to make yourself feel good. You need other people to help you feel good, because you aren't in control.

Chris: At that time, yes.

Beth: Isn't that moving from one crutch to another? *(Good point.)* You get out of your unhealthy relationships by locking yourself into dependent ones. Using others' approval to make you feel good instead of saying: "I don't care what others think of me. If my friends do really care for me, they will support me in anything that I think is right."

Chris: Yeah. Yeah.

Group Leader: Chris, you talked before of your healing and adjustment process taking months, and I don't know how accurate that really is. *(What I really mean is—not very accurate.)* I think that right now, right this minute, you can make a decision that you don't want to feel shitty about yourself anymore. *(Get her commitment to change.)* You can say: "I know it's going to be hard work, and I know I will sometimes slip into my old style."

Chris: Uh huh.

Group Leader: But I'm going to make this decision right this minute. I'm not going to wait another 60 days. Right this minute I choose to be different. It is risky and does entail some hard work and unknown elements—you may lose people's approval of you, but what you will gain is the feeling of doing exactly what you want to do. You must realize that your feeling bad doesn't help Mike any, and it certainly doesn't help you.

Chris: Right. I know it doesn't help me any.

Group Leader: *(Now move in and nail her.)* Are you prepared to make such a commitment?

Chris: [*Long silence*] *(How long should I let this silence go?)* I feel like I can, but I'm not totally positive I can handle it. *(I should back off.)* I suppose if I can handle this, I can handle anything I run into in the future. The other half of me resists like hell. The money. The friends. The guilt. And where do I go for strokes? *(We need to get some role playing into the session to give her practice confronting Mike. I'll juggle it for a while.)*

Group Leader: You can get to the point where you no longer need strokes from anyone. It feels good to get them. It's nice when people approve of what you do but not necessary. You don't need it to continue living.

Chris: I know I have the strength for my own self-approval. I've gotten through tons of stuff before. I think I'm going to need all of it in this move [*laughs*]. It's like a bucket. The self-approval bucket. *(What's that mean?)*

Group Leader: What is the first crucial point in your action program? You've made your decision to move out. What's next?

Chris: O.K. the two crucial things are: one, telling Mike of my decision. I've told him before I'm restless. I did not tell him it had anything to do with him.

Danny: What was it like when you told Mike before?

Chris: Oh Jesus! It turned into three hours of him asking me questions and me having to justify myself.

Group Leader: So it was a really tough experience to live through. *(And she's disasterizing there will be a repeat performance.)* You were really ineffective—

Chris: And the next day I was bummed out and I was depressed all day. So the second step is saying "I want to move away from you" and knowing that he's going to fire a barrage of questions and accusations at me and try to manipulate me into feeling bad so I'll change my mind.

Group Leader: Have you been thinking about when you're going to take this risk? *(Pin her down to specifics.)*

Chris: Real soon.

Group Leader: Like when? *(She's starting to balk. Definitely needs practice. We can phase in some role playing.)*

Chris: Oh, I was too tired last night. And, uh—

Group Leader: Would you like to practice and role play what it would be like right now? *(I'm jumping around a lot. There's so much to cover.)*

Chris: All right.

Group Leader: *(Better check out what Mike is like first.)* Who in this group most reminds you of Mike and how he acts?

Chris: I guess Myron does a little. [*Everyone laughs*]

Group Leader: Can you handle it, Myron? O.K. Since Myron doesn't know Mike, show us what he is like. Myron will play you. You play Mike at his absolute guilt-inducing best. Make it as difficult as you can.

Chris: I'll do that. *(Here we go.)*

Myron: [*Playing Chris*] Mike, can we talk for a few minutes?

Chris: [*Playing Mike*] Sure, Crispy. *(Crispy?)*

Myron: Mike, I've made a decision to move out. My decision is completely unnegotiable. I just want to tell you.

Chris: Move out?

Myron: Yeah. Our relationship is going nowhere. I'm being stifled. I'm not doing all the things I want to do.

Chris: I haven't stifled you. I've let you be free. I never put any demands on you.

Myron: Please hear me out. There is nothing to argue or talk about I've made a decision. I'm going to act on it. I care for you, Mike, but I must leave and there's nothing you can do to change my mind.

Group Leader: O.K., that was fantastic. Now switch roles, and let's practice a dress rehearsal for the big debut of the new you. You be yourself, and Myron will play Mike.

Chris: Mike, I have to talk to you. I've been thinking about something for a long time and I've been—I mean, I've decided that I want to move out. *(She's really nervous.)*

Myron: [*Playing Mike*] Chris! What do you mean move out? Do you know what you mean to me. *(She's already starting to melt.)* I can't live without you here.

Chris: This is something I've been thinking about. I don't feel terrific about it, but it's a decision that I think would be best for me.

Myron: But what about me?

Chris: You want things from me that I can't give, or won't give.

Myron: Chris, I just want to stay in this relationship with you. I'll do anything. I'll change. *(She's folding. Myron is too convincing.)*

Chris: It isn't a matter of you changing. That wouldn't work. My

decision may seem selfish to you. I don't expect you to understand. It doesn't really matter that you do. *(That's a lie.)*

Myron: You're so harsh, so cruel. *(Hold back Myron.)*

Chris: That may be true, but I'm standing by my decision. *(Good
girl.)* I want to experience new things and new men.

Myron: You mean I'm not enough for you?

Chris: You're plenty. You're a great person. I'm not talking about
that, though. *(Should I break in and help her?)*

Myron: You say I'm a great person and then you're moving out on
me.

Chris: Ohhhh. *(She needs help. Is it time to rescue yet?)*

Myron: I was the first one to give you anything. And now you're
stabbing me in the back.

Chris: Shut up and listen to me. I'm trying to tell you something, and
you aren't listening. *(Great recovery.)* If you want to feel stabbed,
then that's fine. I can't help how you feel. *(I'll whisper in Myron's
ear to reinforce her effectiveness in standing up to him.)* I want to
get out.

Myron: Well, I guess you couldn't put it more plainly. *(She's looking
like a victor.)*

Chris: [Laughs] I did it. I did it!

Group Leader: You seemed to fluctuate between moments of real
strength to points where you were starting to let him get to you.
(Identify some nonverbal cues.) Your face was getting all bent out
of shape. Your eyes were getting watery. Your hands were shaking. It was really difficult for you, but you did it. *(Time to pin her
down.)* You said you were going to confront Mike. When is this
going to happen?

Chris: I thought you might have forgotten about that. *(There goes
that resistance flag again.)* Well, I don't know. I feel really vulnerable. Like if I tell him tomorrow, or tonight, or the next day, then
where do I go? *(She's wiggling away from taking a risk.)*

Group Leader: So you're now coming up with more procrastinating
behaviors about why you should postpone telling him for the
next few days.

Chris: Right.

Group Leader: Because you have these fears—

Chris: It's not so much where I'm going to go. You know, I have to
find a place, and I know this girl who is just moving into an
apartment. Or maybe—

Group Leader: Taking this one step at a time, the first step—

Chris: —is telling him.

Group Leader: That seems to be what is bothering you the most. The actual moving itself is physical labor. The hard thing is telling him and then dealing with yourself afterwards.

Chris: O.K. I want to walk in and tell him, and I want to be strong throughout the whole thing, but I also have these bad feelings.

Group Leader: But that's all in the past. *(I hope I'm not being too optimistic.)* And although periodically you may slip back into the way "the old Chris" used to be, now you're going to do something about changing it. *(We could teach her some imagery now to help her relax.)* There are even some ways that you can practice cutting that stuff out of your thinking.

Chris: What do you mean? *(I wish had more time to get into this. I could have budgeted better.)*

Group Leader: By imagining and vividly visualizing the crucial situation, feeling your anticipated negative reactions, cutting them out by choice, and substituting more appropriate responses. *(There's not enough time.)* Maybe we can get back to this at another time.

Chris: All right. *(She doesn't know what she agreed to.)*

Group Leader: To go back a little way, you've been resisting the idea of confronting Mike because of some fears that you have. Now it's getting down near the wire, and we're asking you when you're going to lay this stuff on him.

Chris: Uh. [*Long silence*] Probably within the next couple of days. *(There she goes again like a yoyo.)*

Group Leader: Within the next few days? When?

Chris: I think tonight would be a good time.

Group Leader: Tonight? *(That is soon.)*

Chris: Tonight we're going to sit down, and I'm going to let him know what is going on. I'm going to let him know that I'm not tired of him but of the relationship. And I've made a decision to act.

Group Leader: What about your negative feelings?

Chris: They aren't getting me anywhere. I'm letting them get me down. I don't want to feel down. So I won't.

Group Leader: Fantastic! Next week you will be able to report on what you did and how you were effective.

Chris: Right. *(Now is the time to lock her into coming back.)*

Group Leader: Chris, you've been coming to the group sporadically.

No matter what happens this week, can we expect to see you next time?

Chris: Sure. And thanks, guys, for giving me all this time.

Group Leader: O.K. Who else would like to work on something—?

ON RISKING

In varying qualities and quantities, risking is part of every human endeavor. Taking a risk requires choosing among several possible courses of action, any of which may bring about consequences that leave the individual worse off than before. All living is uncertain, unpredictable, uncontrollable, hazardous. The only risk we never have to choose is our own mortality.

To live a life without risks, without deciding or choosing, is to live a life unfulfilled, an empty existence with neither responsibility nor freedom. Therefore, the most meaningful of activities that a group leader can perform is to train clients to become more willing participants in the risk-taking process (but without unduly pressuring them, as was evident in the vignette). Once inhibiting influences are removed and clients are prepared to make intelligent choices, motivated to act on their honest intentions, encouraged to experiment with unknown factors, immunized against crippling disappointments, only then will they truly come alive.

The avoidance of risking can be equated with spiritual, if not with physical, death. After all, we are alive but a few instants in the relative time of the universe. When we practice for death while we sleep, when we feel boredom and inertia, when we waste our time hesitating to take action, that much faster do we wither away. Death is a frightening metaphor for the avoidance of risks, as Thornton Wilder observed in his play *Our Town:* "It is an attempt to find a value above all price for the smallest events in our daily life" (Wilder, 1938/ 1958, p. xi).

> All the dead inhabitants of "our town" lie buried atop a hill. They watch the stars. They cry out in regret and anguish to a new resident among them: "Do any human beings ever realize life while they live it?" And the bitter reply: "That's what it was to be alive. To move about in a cloud of ignorance; to go up and down trampling on the feelings of those about you. To spend and waste time as though you had a million years" (Wilder, 1938/1958, p. 62).

CHAPTER 11

Creative Metaphors

Most of the service professions rely on an impressive armory of technological gadgetry for helping their patients. Dentists have their little mirrors, X-ray machines, cavitrons, nitrous oxide, and miniature picks and shovels to mine tooth decay. Neurologists rely on brain scans to aid their diagnostic decisions; cardiologists use electroencephalograms; and internists know just the right questions to ask and places to feel to determine what ails their patients. Once the problems are identified, they may be quickly dispersed with a few injections, pills, or slashes by a surgeon's scalpel. Voila! The appendix is removed, and, with it, all the accompanying discomfort.

Group leaders have no stethoscopes or tongue depressors with which to probe client problems. Oh sure, perhaps we have a few psychological tests to play with, but M.M.P.I. profiles or Kuder scales are nothing compared to the cold, calculating efficiency of a radiologist's analysis. With a few notable exceptions, we have no pharmaceutical weapons to combat our clients' problems of loneliness, boredom, shyness, poor grades, existential angst, or nosy in-laws. Group leaders have no surgical procedures to remove psychological malignancies. We cannot dissolve psychic pain with any proven laboratory strategies, nor can we reliably produce similar outcomes using any application of technology. To serve our clients, we have only our minds and our skill at communicating what is in them. The use of language, the ordering of words into meaningful sequences, is virtually the only means available for therapists to help people change in groups.

Human beings most often think in terms of images and stories. Robert Frost believed that "all thinking is metaphorical." H. Parkhurst claimed that "any supreme insight is a metaphor." Kenneth Burke agreed: "Whole works of scientific research, even entire schools, are hardly more than the patient repetition, in all its ramifications, of a fertile metaphor." C. S. Lewis repeated the theme "All our truth, or all but a few fragments, is won by metaphor" originally proposed by Nietzsche: "To know is merely to work with one's favorite metaphors.... And what therefore is truth? A mobile army of metaphors.... Truths are illusions of which one has forgotten that they are illusions" (Shibles, 1972). Haley (1968) believed that all client concerns are stated metaphorically: the phobia, the depression, the confusion are symptomatic analogies of a deeper coping struggle.

We dream of intricate plots while asleep and construct elaborate fantasies during idle waking moments. The ability to reason in abstract images appears to be a uniquely human trait. Bateson (1979) related the anecdote of a computer that was asked by its programmer whether it could ever think like a person. The computer printed out "That reminds me of a story."

The informal, free-flowing tale told by a guru, the formally constructed image used by a minister, the bedtime story with a moral told by a parent, the symbolic image created by the psychoanalyst—all are examples of therapeutic stories in action. Such images, whether in the form of metaphor or anecdote, are among the most powerful tools that group leaders can use.

THERAPEUTIC METAPHORS

Water—the ace of elements. Water dives from the clouds without parachute, wings, or safety net. Water runs over the steepest precipice and blinks not a lash. Water walks on fire and fire gets blisters. Stylishly composed in any situation—solid, gas, or liquid— speaking in penetrating dialects understood by all things—animal, vegetable or mineral—water travels intrepidly through four dimensions, *sustaining* (Kick a lettuce in the field and it will yell "Water!"), *destroying* (The Dutch boy's finger remembered the view from Ararat), and *creating* (It has even been said that human beings were invented by water as a device for transporting itself from one place to another, but that's another story). Always in motion, everflowing (whether at steam rate or glacier speed), rhythmic, dynamic, ubiquitous, changing and working its changes, a mathematics turned wrong side out, a philosophy in reverse, the ongoing odyssey of water is virtually irresistible (Robbins, 1976, pp. 1–2).

The ever-present, everlasting, ever-adapting nature of water. Water is part of the composition of all living things. It is a silent witness in all human acts. It cares nothing about money, who is president, whether you live or die. Water endures; it will flee your body after it has outlived its usefulness. Water feels no guilt or anger. It shrugs its indifferent shoulders to war and famine. It knows no pain; it expresses no sympathy.

The 80 years or so that we temporarily inhabit this planet as living beings are but an infinitesimal speck in what Carl Sagan (1977) terms the "Cosmic Calender." When you consider that the water molecule has been around for several billion years, what difference can it make what you do with your ridiculously short life of several decades? If you think it is a long time until your next birthday, consider how long you will be dead. One hundred years from now, who will care whether you were divorced, lost your job, or even existed? Will water care when your heart stops beating?

Put your hand on your heart. Feel it beating, pumping blood throughout your body. It's a living organ that is destined to wear out after beating about three billion times in your lifetime. Seems like a lot, but you've already used up a billion of your allotment. Even now, while you've been daydreaming, another few thousand slipped by, gone forever. How long did you sleep last night? That's about 30,000 heartbeats. And how many moments have you thrown away feeling sorry for yourself, steeped in depression? Each time your heart beats, you lose another second of your life, forever.

The monk, the guru, the master, the shaman, the healer, the teacher, the therapist and group leader all instruct by metaphor. By spinning tales of what other people do, the therapist introduces his clients to the realities of hope. "His metaphors and parables make it necessary for the pilgrims who would be disciples to turn to their own imaginations in the search for meaning in their lives" (Kopp, 1972, p. 13).

Images of water and of heartbeats create powerfully influential and enduring thought patterns. Each time group members become aware of their hearts beating they are reminded of how they waste their present moments in needless suffering. Every time they think of water cascading down a waterfall or feel it massaging their bodies in the shower, they are reminded of nature's indifference. Whenever they inflate things out of proportion to reality, disasterize or worry, or take anything too seriously, they can think humbly of water and heartbeats. These enduring metaphors act like time-release medication, flowing through the bloodstream long after the group sessions have ended.

Stories need not even make sense to be effective in facilitating change. Sometimes, the most ambiguous, obscure metaphors can have the greatest effect.

The last time I went to see Milton Erickson, he said something to me. And as I was sitting there in front of him, it didn't make sense. Most of his covert metaphors have made ... eons of sense to me. But he said something to me which would have taken me awhile to figure out. Milton said to me "You don't consider yourself a therapist, but you are a therapist." And I said "Well, not really." He said "Well, let's pretend ... that you're a therapist who works with people. The most important thing ... when you're pretending this ... is to understand ... that you are *really* not ... you are just pretending ... and if you pretend really well, the people that you work with will pretend to make changes. And they will forget that they are pretending ... for the rest of their lives. But don't you be fooled by it" (Bandler & Grinder, 1979, p. 136).

The Sufi Master, a spiritual and religious group leader of the East, relies almost exclusively on the use of parables to bring enlightenment to group members. According to Einhorn (1979), the instrumental functions of such therapeutic tales include promoting psychological shocks to group members by exposing their unconscious motives, invalidated feelings, and spiritual inertia. The Sufi stories contain themes that are purported to connect with the "essence" of the group. These "internal dimensions" help to promote self-awareness and insight on hidden levels. They stimulate discussion of significant themes and help group members to confront their foolish behavior:

> Nasrudin is sitting in his living room when an eagle alights on his windowsill. Having only seen pigeons before, he regards the bird as a misshapen pigeon. "What an unfortunate bird!" he exclaims, "Someone has neglected you!" Fetching his scissors, he trims its magnificent beak and talons. "There," he says with satisfaction, "Now you look more like a bird" (Williams, 1971).

The Chinese proverb that one picture is worth a thousand words is also true of metaphors, which are verbal pictures—concise, purposeful images that convey vivid messages. But metaphorical pictures are abstract, left open for many possible interpretations. They are powerful communicative devices for promoting insight, motivating action, or initiating group interaction precisely because they can be personally applicable to each individual.

The best stories have always been those with many different symbolic meanings. They not only transmit cultural information but have morals like Aesop's *Fables*, themes like Grimms's fairy tales, or lessons like Homer's parables. In our technological world, film has replaced the campfire as the most common storytelling medium. People leave theatres with tears or smiles. Through the process of identification, they conquer armies, slay dragons, win lovers, all the while munching popcorn in an air-conditioned room.

All stories, whether in the form of metaphor, parable, epic poem, fable, song, novel, or tale, have a protagonist who must resolve a conflict by overcoming obstacles (Gordon, 1978). For the audience, confronted by equivalent personal struggles, dramatic metaphors provide an illuminated path through the dark unknown. They offer hope, stimulate action, and sometimes even offer specific solutions which can be adapted for personal use.

Waldren, McElmurry, Bowens, and Israel (1980) note that the reading of children's stories to college-age students reduces their level of tension, facilitates discussion of sensitive issues, cements peer relationships, and helps them to relive the magic of being read bedtime stories. In the dormitories students gather together in their pajamas with cuddly stuffed animals while a guest group leader reads from a favorite children's book such as *The Cat in the Hat*, *The Little Prince*, *The Wind in the Willows*, *The Gnome from Nome*, or *The Giving Tree*. Hidden within the pictures and prose of children's stories are often found wonderfully powerful metaphors for grown-ups. *The Velveteen Rabbit* tells how toys become real:

> "What is REAL?" asked the Rabbit one day, when they were lying side by side near the nursery fender, before Nana came to tidy the room. "Does it mean having things that buzz inside you and a stick-out handle?"
>
> "Real isn't how you are made," said the Skin Horse. "It's a thing that happens to you. When a child loves you for a long, long time, not just to play with, but REALLY loves you, then you become Real."
>
> "Does it hurt?" asked the Rabbit.
>
> "Sometimes," said the Skin Horse, for he was always truthful. "When you are Real you don't mind being hurt."
>
> "Does it happen all at once, like being wound up," he asked, "or bit by bit?"
>
> "It doesn't happen all at once," said the Skin Horse. "You become. It takes a long time. That's why it doesn't often happen to people who break easily, or have sharp edges, or have to be carefully kept. Generally, by the time you are real, most of your hair has been loved off, and your eyes drop out and you get loose in the joints and very shabby. But these things don't matter at all, because

once you are real you can't be ugly, except to people who don't understand" (Williams, 1975, pp. 16–17).[1]

The astute group leader can do a lot with the metaphoric messages in the previous passage. In a group of college sophomores, the discussion rattled back and forth between several intense issues:

"My boyfriend treats me like a shabby old toy, but I don't think it's exactly because he loves me."

"That brought back such vivid memories of the freedom I had as a kid. It was so much fun to stay locked in my room and occupy myself all day long talking to my toys as if they were my best friends. Now my life is so damn complicated I don't even have the time to talk to myself."

"Sometimes I just don't know what is real anymore. Are all of you real or just figments of my imagination? You sure don't act real with all the games that are played in this group. Or, maybe I'm just like the rabbit who wants to be real. I'm just a wind-up toy with a busted spring."

"If you've got to be hurt to be real, I don't want any part of that nonsense. I've been dropped on my head so many times I can't feel my brain any longer. Oh, I've tried to be real with people before; but every time I act up front and honest, I end up vulnerable and rejected. I think it's better to stay away from reality; fantasy is a lot more fun."

"That was one heavy-duty little story. If I understand what it's all about, I think it's saying that to be real you have to take risks, you have to love without fear. There are those of us in this group who act fragile or have sharp edges, and until we stop being afraid of getting broken we will never learn to love ourselves, much less anyone else."

There are many specific ways in which therapeutic metaphors can be optimally beneficial in groups. Previous chapters mentioned the importance of having a defensible rationale for *every* intervention used, and the use of metaphors is no exception. To tell a story for its pure entertainment value, to play with language creatively just to feed a leader's self-indulgent need for strokes—both waste valuable time in a therapeutic group. While there are virtually unlimited instances in which metaphorical techniques might be used constructively, there are a few basic patterns in which they appear consistently useful.

[1]Excerpt from *The Velveteen Rabbit* by Margery Williams. Reprinted by permission of Doubleday & Company, Inc.

Metaphorical Techniques

Illustration and reinforcement. Certain themes predictably recur in groups. The question "whom can I trust?" always arises, as does the fear that any progress made will be short-lived. It is not uncommon, and perhaps not unrealistic, for clients to believe that they will eventually slip back to self-defeating behavior patterns in spite of the momentum that has been created. Again, some group members will inevitably express a concern related to approval seeking or psychological dependence. And does there exist a single group in which at least one person is not having difficulty cutting an overprotective parent's apron strings?

The issues of parental dominance and destructive dependence can be approached in several ways. We can give a minilecture on the subject or lead eventually into an opportunity for rehearsal confrontation in the group. Whichever strategy is preferred, therapists are always hungry for verbal images to illustrate major themes dramatically.

So much have we been talked to in our lives, so many lectures and so much advice have we been given that we remember very little of it all. While geometric proofs and algebraic formulas come and go in our memories, the image of our math teacher doing something strange remains indelible. To ensure that group members will forever remember crucial therapeutic messages, particular tales can be collected to illustrate themes. Dyer (1976) is fond of stimulating psychological independence by relating an anecdote that demonstrates the masterful behavior he is discussing.

> Walt Disney produced a superb film some years ago entitled *Bear Country*. It traced a mother bear and her two babies through the first few months of the cubs' lives. Mama-bear taught the cubs how to hunt, fish, and climb trees. She taught them how to protect themselves when they confronted danger. Then one day, Mama-bear, for her own instinctive reasons, decided that it was time to leave. She forced them to scamper up a tree, and without even looking back, she left. Forever! In her own bear mind, she had completed her parental responsibilities. She didn't try to manipulate them into visiting her on alternate Sundays. She did not accuse them of being ungrateful, or threaten to have a nervous breakdown if they disappointed her. She simply let them go [p. 191].

Promoting insight. Much of what is called client resistance is in fact the awkward attempt of a therapist to effect change. Insight and self-awareness often hurt; it is painful to confront discrepancies between what we have always believed to be truth and what we now learn is delusion. This revelation often forces a domino effect: to alter one part of a system changes the whole system.

When a group member declares that he has for years been stifling his wife by trying to make her fit into his mold, he also suggests that this is a condition he will have to change. If this man is to discover the destructive pattern of his behavior, he must do so in a way that will be palatable to him. Metaphorical anecdotes offer a way of confronting clients with their foibles diplomatically so that they will be more willing to listen with both ears. The man might not respond to being directly confronted with the destructive interdependence of his marriage, but he may be willing to listen to a story with a similar theme.

Dominance always creates victims. Threats and aggression provoke open or smoldering hostility. One human being who seeks to dominate and control another will eventually encounter rebellion. A point comes when a person will no longer accept being ordered about; a child, a spouse, a prisoner will eventually realize there is nothing left to lose. Alexander Solzhenitsyn skillfully relates the determined resistance of a person without power, freedom, or independence. The interrogator dominates by the threat of consequences until the prisoner refuses to play the game any longer:

> "Listen, don't go too far just because I choose to be polite to you. . . ."
>
> "If you were rude to me I wouldn't talk to you at all. You can shout at your colonels and your generals as much as you like because they've got plenty to lose."
>
> "We can deal with your sort too if we have to."
>
> "No you can't." Bobykin's piercing eyes flashed with hatred. "I've got nothing, see? Nothing! You can't touch my wife and child—they were killed by a bomb. My parents are dead. I own nothing in the world except a handkerchief. These denims and this underwear—which hasn't even got any buttons"—he bared his chest to show what he meant—"is government issue. You took my freedom away a long time ago and you can't give it back to me because you haven't got it yourself. I'm forty-two years old. You gave me twenty-five years. I've done hard labor, I know what it is to have a number instead of a name, to be handcuffed, to be guarded by dogs, to work in a punitive brigade—what more can you do to me? Take me off this special project? You'd be the loser. I need a smoke" (Solzhenitsyn, 1968, p. 106).[2]

[2]From *The First Circle*, by A. Solzhenitsyn. Copyright © 1968 by Harper & Row, Publishers. Reprinted by permission.

Suggesting a change in tactics. For many good reasons, therapists usually avoid giving advice or permitting group members to prescribe courses of action. Advice given in a group provokes one of two things, both destructive. First, the advice could be disastrous. Advising a man to stay in a floundering marriage gives him hypertension and ulcers. Recommending that a person confront her friend about perceived injustices only makes things worse. A group member urged to quit his job and find another only compounds his original dissatisfaction problems. Each of these clients would now have a perfect scapegoat: "You ruined my life. How could you tell me to do this?" Group members love advice for just this reason. They ask for it, beg for it, knowing that they will not have to think for themselves or take responsibility for the outcomes.

Second, the advice might work. The client who discovers that suggestions offered by the leader or group members helped to resolve the problem only learns to come back for more next time, to depend on others for solutions, to be less self-reliant. Whenever another or similar problem comes up, the client will come back to the group, or to anyone else willing to dispense wisdom, rather than attempting to find his or her own form of truth. By giving *helpful* advice, even when it saves the client time, we keep group members on the yellow brick road to Oz.

Group discussion on a focused issue. In quick succession, several group members disclose their dependency problems in various relationships, a theme of several recent sessions. Some persons complain about how little say they have in their lives; others wish that their spouses or lovers would take a more active role. One woman feels sexually helpless because she must wait for her husband to initiate sex. A meek gentleman whispers that he wishes he could spend more time alone without his wife ordering him about. Others describe how they are so melded to their spouses that they have lost their sense of personal identity. Everything is togetherness at the exclusion of separateness. Everything is "we," "if you want to, dear," and "O.K., I'll be right with you."

The group leader can initiate a theme-oriented group session related to dependent love relationships by introducing a metaphor borrowed from biology.

> The self-marking of invertebrate animals in the sea, who must have perfected the business long before evolution got around to us, was set up in order to permit creatures of one kind to locate

others, not for predation but to set up symbiotic households. The anemones who live on the shells of crabs are precisely finicky; so are the crabs. Only a single species of anemone will find its way to only a single species of crab. They sense each other exquisitely, and live together as though made for each other.

Sometimes there is such a mix-up about selfness that two creatures, each attracted by the molecular configuration of the other, incorporate the two selves to make a single organism.... And, more surprising, they cannot live in any other way; they depend for their survival on each other. They are not really selves; they are specific *others* (Thomas, 1979, pp. 4–5).

This account of collaboration between the nudibranch sea slug and the medusa jellyfish in the Bay of Naples is a wonderful metaphor for explaining interdependent relationships in marriages. If one partner becomes destructively parasitic, the collaboration abruptly ends to the dissatisfaction of both species. Yet by completely pooling their resources, they also lose their sense of identity. Likewise, when two human beings live together, each with separate bodies and individual needs, they, too, must reach a state of mutual compromise allowing both to flourish.

The tone has now been set to pursue the interdependency topic further. Participants can collectively brainstorm about the causes of the conflicts, how they may be handled, and which strategies may prove most successful in resolving the issues.

Countering self-defeating thinking. Many people demand that the world conform to their needs and expectations. They engage in chronically irrational thought patterns, deluding themselves that they occupy the center of the universe. Like spoiled 2-year-olds, they believe that Mommy, Daddy, Humpty Dumpty and all the King's Men were put on Earth to cater to their every whim. They surrender their intellect in the delusional pursuit of some abstraction known as Truth or Justice, at least for themselves. (This, of course, is but one of many possible thought distortions common in client behavior.)

But truth, according to Nietzsche (1864/1972), is a worn-out illusion which no longer has the power to affect the senses. All language, all thought, is metaphorical. We translate a sense perception into an image, then metaphorically name this thing, even give it a masculine or feminine gender. In the chaos around us we attempt to make order to justify our existence as if it needs an excuse. To the client who exaggerates self-importance and thus feels a need to inflate the significance of every act, Nietzsche offers a metaphorical challenge.

Although certainty of knowledge would be nice and absolute prediction would be convenient, the reality of daily life provides only ambiguity and frustration. And ambiguity is, after all, what metaphors are all about.

> In some remote corner of the universe, effused into innumerable solar-systems, there was once a star upon which clever animals invented cognition. It was the haughtiest, most mendacious moment in the history of this world, but yet only a moment. After Nature had taken breath awhile the star congealed and the clever animals had to die.—Someone might write a fable after this style, and yet he would not have illustrated sufficiently, how wretched, shadow-like, transitory, purposeless and fanciful the human intellect appears in Nature.... Nothing in Nature is so bad or so insignificant that it will not, at the smallest puff of that force cognition, immediately swell up like a balloon, and just as a mere porter wants to have his admirer, so the very proudest man, the philosopher, imagines he sees from all sides the eyes of the universe telescopically directed upon his actions and thoughts [p. 1].

Because metaphors are literary devices, their frequent use can excite clients to continue their renaissance education by exploring literature. Whereas there are specific instances when metaphors can be optimally beneficial, such as to enlighten or entertain, verbal images can also provoke change if they are carefully constructed.

THE STRUCTURE OF METAPHORS

Metaphors began to take on a therapeutic value under Freud and his fellow psychoanalysts who realized that the world's great literary classics offered symbolic allusions to the major themes of human conflict. During the decade following Freud's death, Milton Erickson began systematic clinical investigations of the role that metaphor could play in therapeutic communication. He devised hypnotic routines by which to promote unconscious changes in subjects, noting that the structure of language in metaphors, the precise choice of words and vocal intonation, were as important to the cure as the metaphor's theme. Thus, sharing an anecdote reached dizzying levels of complexity in the Erickson technique.

> The words, by their arrangement into phrases, clauses, and sentences, and even their introductory, transitional, and repetitive uses, could be made to serve special purposes: building up emphasis or cutting it short, establishing contrasts, similarities, paral-

lelisms, identifications, and equations of one idea to another, all of which would effect a building up of a series of associations and emotional responses stimulated, but not aroused directly, one idea to another, sequential relationships of various ideas, and objects, shifts of responsibility and action from one character to another; the use of words that threatened, challenged, distracted, or served only to delay the development of the narrative were all employed to formulate a story possessing a significance beyond its formal content (Erickson, 1944, p. 312).

Erickson might pronounce the word *you* to involve the client in the story gently; he might later use the command *you will* as part of the narrative when he is really offering the client a therapeutic suggestion. Enunciating the single word *you* in the metaphor takes on the significance of a double entendre, a directive, an invitation for identification, a distraction, and a reinforcer. Erickson used anecdotes and metaphors as a subtle way to promote change at preconscious levels. He planted cued images in clients' brains which would later help to make previously unacceptable ideas more palatable.

The use of complex constructions in therapeutic metaphors has been further refined by David Gordon (1978), who offers several grammatical rules for building effective stories. The effective metaphor should be well formed—that is, it should involve changes over which the client has potential control. It would do little good to narrate a story for a group in which the characters have the magical power to make people like them by wishing it were so.

Another necessary requisite is isomorphism, which involves logical equivalents between group member relationships and those of the characters in the story. If a bickering, competitive triangle exists in a group, the leader would wish to create a metaphor that exemplifies similar interrelationships among characters, such as a conflict among a prim and proper penguin too pompous to ever apologize, a self-centered centipede who is sick of sneak attacks, and an aggressive aardvark who is antieverything. The resolution of the real-life conflict would need to be carefully plotted so that the outcome of the story is compatible with group member goals. The aardvark, centipede, and penguin, in coming together to their mutual benefit, would have to do so in ways acceptable to the observing clients.

Not only must the content of the metaphor be logically constructed to contain therapeutic messages, indirect advice, modeled success, and acceptable problem resolution, but the syntax must follow certain rules of "therapeutic grammar." Erickson's attention to the detail of language was further formalized by Gordon, who also integrated the work of Bandler and Grinder (1975) and Satir (1972).

Metaphors are likely to be most influential if they are deliberately vague in the use of nominalizations, unspecified verbs, and referential indexes. Group members can personalize the themes to fit their unique situations if they are allowed to fill in the details. Gordon recommends that if the details of a description are insignificant to the major themes of the story, leave them ambiguous so that clients have the freedom to visualize the scene according to their perceptual preferences.

Effective metaphors are concise and efficient, using the fewest possible words to convey the most powerful image. They are an economical form of communication insofar as they say more than ordinary language but do so in a more memorable way. In *The Executioner's Song* (1979), for example, Norman Mailer succinctly describes the reactions of two friends listening to a story Gary Gilmore tells about his antics in prison: "Brenda and Johnny's smiles had become as congealed as the grease on a cold steak" [p. 68].

Good metaphors are both appropriate to the situation and tailored to the audience. They are designed to heighten certain aspects of a message in a manner that will be best received by the listeners. In a group of obese adults who have repeatedly complained about their problems in controlling oral behavior, blaming their fatness on genes, luck, fate, their mother-in-law's cooking, and other assorted external variables, the following excerpt from *Mouthing Off* might drive home the therapeutic point.

> Your mouth is completely obedient; it asks no questions and gives no lip. It meekly obeys orders from the brain which commands: "Swallow it!" Could you imagine what would happen as you enjoy a leisurely meal and are about to inject a forkful of hot food when your mouth snappily interrupts: "Are you kidding? You want *me* to swallow this nasty, slimy, green stuff? No way. I don't care if spinach does make you strong, this is where I draw the line. I've done a lot for you. When you get tired, I'm the one who has to drink that black, bitter, hot stuff. When you get the aches, I'm the one who's got to swallow those pills to cure them, even though my friends in your stomach drown in acid indigestion. Every time *you* get the munchies, I have to indulge your whims. You want it, brain? *You* eat it. I quit!" (Kottler, 1981).

Finally, a metaphor should continue to build the character, the image, the ethics of the group leader. If a leader wants to come across as a guru, the metaphorical language ought to reflect "guruesque" images of "oneness," "oracles," and mysterious parables that can only be answered in riddles. If the preferred style emphasizes playfulness, spontaneity, enthusiasm, appreciation of the absurd, and humor, the choice of metaphors ought to reflect dry wit. R. D. Laing (1965), for instance, shares the anecdote of the schizophrenic, who, when asked if he was Napoleon, replied no. A lie detector test indicated that he was lying.

With the advent of even more refinements in metaphor construction, including such techniques as intradimensional shifts, recalibration, Satir categories, synesthesia, submodality crossovers, anchors, triggers, and reality-stackings, the simple art of storytelling seems startingly complex. Whatever happened to lullabies and bedtime stories? In spite of technological breakthroughs and scientific methodologies, the creation of metaphors will forever be an artistic enterprise, a showpiece of human communication and therapeutic action.

CHAPTER 12

The Uses of Humor in Groups

Counseling and therapy are notoriously serious businesses. Tears. Anguish. Guilt. Conflict. Deceit. Suicide. Violence. Helplessness. Turmoil. Therapists add little comic relief to lighten the aura of despair. Those pipes, tweed jackets, white lab coats, omnipotent nods, framed diplomas, book-lined walls, and cliniclike odors aren't exactly conducive to a rollicking good time. But clients aren't paying to have a good time. They want to suffer and do penance, and we do keep them in line.

There are medications designed to balance mood alterations, straitjackets and wet sheets for discipline, shock treatments for the uncooperative, and verbal spankings for those with individual initiative. Mental institutions are particularly instructive examples of how the mental health profession frowns on laughter. Rachel, who passed her adolescence in a mental hospital, reports that humor was strictly forbidden. Although humor became an underground form of rebellion on the wards, inmates were repeatedly warned: "This is no laughing matter. You know where you are, don't you?" Yet humor was the only way to hold on to sanity in an insane place. By making fun of her predicament, ridiculing the staff, and laughing at herself, Rachel was able to exercise minimal control over her life, to pretend she had freedom in a completely powerless situation.

Ironically, though patients are not allowed to laugh at themselves or at us, it is socially acceptable for the public to laugh at them. We appear to find emotionally disturbed people amusing and entertaining. A partial list of terms that have been invented for referring to therapy clients is absolutely staggering.

crazy	bonzo
demented	zoo zoo

242

parboiled	spacey
out-to-lunch	playing without a full deck
2 brains—but one is lost and the other is looking for it	whacko
	veged out
nuclear	nurd
space cadet	goggle-eyed
been visited upstairs	freaked out
few pickles shy of a barrel	flipped out
	punchy

We are allowed to laugh at them, but they aren't allowed to laugh at us their zoo keepers? "Exactly," Rachel replies. "You see, on the wards, the only time we were given official permission to laugh was in our therapy group—when the shrink told a joke. If we slipped up at any other time we were tied in wet sheets or punished in some other devious ways for 'resisting treatment.'"

When humor is mentioned at all, the literature of psychotherapy claims that it impedes therapeutic progress. Unless carefully monitored and kept in control, humor can "mask hostility behind a false façade," block the client's stream of feeling, confuse a client who is unable to determine when the therapist is serious, interfere with free association, "restrict the range of the patient's responses," be used as a defense for handling anxiety, diminish the importance of a client's illness, bottle up repressed anger, and encourage the therapist to be self-indulgent, exhibitionistic, and hostile (Kubie, 1971). Might it also cause cancer?

True, there may be some danger in abusing humor within groups because it makes ridicule easier and may waste valuable time if things stay silly for too long. There are also a few leaders who use their groups as a stage for themselves to win appreciative applause. In his scathing criticism of humor in therapy, Kubie (1971) reluctantly admits that most abuses occur among beginning practitioners. Among more experienced therapists, humor can be an effective tool. The pragmatic group leader who is aware of the many potential abuses of humor may use it judiciously to accomplish various therapeutic functions.

THERAPEUTIC EFFECTS OF HUMOR

What is this strange behavioral display that involves, in Desmond Morris's (1977) observation, howling, hooting, barking, wrinkled nostrils, weeping, crinkled lips, closed eyes, and a stamping foot? Koestler (1964) adds to the description "the co-ordinated contraction of fifteen facial muscles in a stereotyped pattern and accompanied by altered breathing" [p. 29]. Bierce (1911/1940) further defines it as "An interior convulsion, producing a distortion of the features and accompanied by inarticulate noises. It is infectious and, though intermittent, incurable" [p. 75].

Laughter is a discharge of energy that results from sustained tension. It eases strains and shock. It is a means of handling the incongruous, unexpected, awkward, disorderly and nonsensical. As reviewed by Hertzler (1970), laughter also serves many useful social purposes. It is among the most expressive forms of communication. It may convey quiet appreciation or self-assurance. It may indicate shame or embarrassment, delight or exhilaration. It may signify shock, surprise, exuberance, incredulity, or nervousness. In group situations, laughter may communicate warmth and friendliness, collective amusement and exuberance. Laughter can send messages of approval and applause, insult and defiance, bitterness and sarcasm, rejection and ridicule. There are few expressive forms that can say so many varied things, and there are few communicative devices that can serve so many therapeutic uses.

Humor and Group Cohesion

Inoffensive, esteeming humor has been found consistently to increase the solidarity of group members (Martineau, 1972). It acts as a social lubricant, easing group cohesion into a unified experience (McGhee, 1979). Humor draws people closer together by relating to a common focus—the shared response to a single stimulus. In fact, the first signs of genuine laughter can sometimes be used as a yardstick to measure the progress of affiliative relationships. The creation of in-jokes that can be understood only by members of the group offers evidence that true cohesion has developed. And every group seems to create its own special jesting style, usually focusing on characteristics of individual participants or of the leader.

The therapist can take an active role in modeling the importance of humor by introducing concepts of self-parody. Ordinarily, the "them-against-me" attitude that is part of a group's beginning can be quickly dissipated by revealing the attitude in a humorous fashion. Even a self-conscious group leader finds subtle ways to draw people closer together by getting them to laugh at their predicaments, suggesting "We're all in this together." A social equalizer, humor cuts across status lines. It emphasizes commonality and invites intimacy. Group members feel closer to one another, more trusting and cohesive, when they can laugh together.

Humor and Therapeutic Parody

An experienced group leader can use humor to cut through layers of client inertia. Napier and Gershenfeld (1981) suggest that group leaders should deliberately make use of humor by taking advantage of spontaneous occurrences, absurd situations, discrepancies, inconsistencies, paradoxes, and irony. They believe that group members become more sensitive, less fearful of taking risks, and more open when they feel comfortable laughing at their mistakes and failures.

Group members prone to pathological self-pity are so skilled at feeling sorry for themselves, at making themselves miserable, that it takes a dramatic exaggeration to help them confront their concerns directly. Although sarcasm and parody may be interpreted as ridicule, they can also be used constructively: "If you're going to suffer, why do a half-baked job of it? Why not become an expert at self-torture?" Dan Greenberg (1966) offers advice on such important life skills as creating a first class anxiety, the power of negative thinking, selecting a 3-dimensional worry, optimum brooding conditions, basic worries about noises in the night, how to lose friends and alienate people, and—the most important misery-making ploy for a group session—how to get people to reject you.

He suggests adopting a "reject-me" image ("be apologetic, boring, critical, complaining, impatient, irritable, jealous, nervous, suspicious, and wishy-washy"), developing a whiny, nasal, reject-me tone of voice, and a reject-me posture ("Learn to enter a room as though you expected at any moment to be struck in the face") (Greenberg, 1966). The innovative group leader can even structure a rejection exercise along the Greenberg scheme in which participants practice rejecting one another in the most brutal ways possible.

Kathy: Could I get some feedback from the rest of you as to how I come across as a person?

Sharon: I think you're O.K.

Leader: Come on, you can do better than that.

Bobby: Well, sometimes you do act a little snobby.

Kathy: I act snobby? Thank you for being honest.

Leader: No, no, Kathy. If you really want to get rejected, defend yourself, be argumentative and obnoxious. Act hurt so the rejector will know that he or she is on target.

Kathy: I see. Gee, I didn't realize I was such a loser. I guess that means nobody in here would possibly want to be my friend. I mean, since I think I'm too good for you and everything, and because I'm—

Leader: Excellent, Kathy. Let your shoulders sag a bit and pout your lips. That's right. Now go in for the kill.

Kathy: I'm having a party tonight after the group, and my boyfriend thinks it would be real fun to invite the neurotic dingbats over from my group. I told him you probably had better things to do, and besides you wouldn't know how to handle yourselves in my house. But he insisted I go through the motions of asking you anyway. Would you like to come?

Humor and Boredom

Nothing is more conducive to retarded learning than boredom. Ask any hyperactive kid or class clown. It is unrealistic to expect anyone to pay attention to a group happening, however brilliant its message, if its delivery is without vigor. People are allergic to boredom; it makes existence intolerable. In *Catch 22*, Joseph Heller created a character who was so terrified of dying that he attempted to stretch every second to its peak by deliberately boring himself. He noticed that if he lay on his back staring at the ceiling for hours, time would seem to last much longer, thereby prolonging his subjective life. But group members are usually more interested in making time fly. Ambivalent about joining a group in the first place, they will seize any excuse to drop out. Boredom may be more responsible for creating dropouts (in schools or groups) than any other single variable.

The growing pains associated with group experiences are quite enough without the prolonged misery of drawn-out time. Just because therapy is serious does not mean that it can't be enjoyable for participants, filled with laughter as well as tears. Frankl (1978), Klein (1974), Greenwald (1975), and Ellis (1977b) all enthusiastically endorse the use of humor to enliven sessions and make them more interesting for clients. Ellis (1977b) even suggests that

> emotional disturbance largely consists of taking life too seriously;
> of exaggerating the significance of things; of what I have called,

with humor aforethought, catastrophizing, awfulizing, or horribliz-
ing—like the reading of papers at scientific meetings, for example,
an obvious disturbance in its own right [p. 262].

As we recall our significant educational experiences, all the boring
lectures, predictable discussions, and routine structures merge into
one big meaningless blob. We probably don't know the 14 symbolic
themes of a Shakespearean play, but we can certainly recite verbatim
a joke the teacher told. Significant learning is synonymous with
dramatic, interesting introductions to an issue. Humor, parody,
fun, and laughter are prime ways to make group experiences more
palatable.

Humor and Humanness

Viktor Frankl's method of "paradoxical intention" relies on exaggerating symptoms to create a more conscious awareness of a client's
self-defeating behaviors. We can conquer our fears by distorting
them to logical extremes. For a hysterical woman with chronic
trembling, for example, Frankl (1978) prescribes a massive dose of
humor to obliterate the undesired behavior.

Therapist: How would you like to compete with me in shaking, Mrs.
N.?
Patient: [*Shocked*] What?
Therapist: Let us see who can shake and tremble faster and for how
long?
Patient: Are you suffering from these shakes, too?
Therapist: No, I am not suffering from them, but I can tremble if I
want to. *(I began to shake)*
Patient: Gee. You are doing it faster. [*Trying to speed up and smiling*]
Therapist: Faster. Come on, Mrs. N., faster.
Patient: I can't. *(She was becoming tired)* Quit it. I can't do it any
more.
*(She got up, went in the day room, and brought herself a cup of coffee.
She drank the whole cup without spilling it once)* [p. 121].

Lantz (1978a) and Lamb (1980) also describe the systematic adoption
of humorous exaggeration to help clients separate themselves from
their neurotic symptoms. Laughter is substituted for anxiety in the
process of spontaneously stripping oneself of negative defense
mechanisms.

To isolate and even change problems, group members can exaggerate the unique humanness of clients. This strategy is often used in role-played situations, using mimicry to highlight blind spots in clients' perceptions of themselves. In a technique that Dyer and Vriend (1977) term "role shifting," group members randomly select the name of a fellow participant and enact that person throughout the duration of the session. There is no more entertaining method for confronting one's characteristic flaws and foibles than to observe someone else sitting, talking, and gesturing like oneself. The humor implicit in dramatic license allows people to see how others perceive them.

Humor and the Taboo

Most jokes are either sexual, prejudicial, or aggressive in character. They usually deal with taboo subjects that are not ordinarily allowed entry into conversation. They ridicule minority groups, express forbidden thoughts, poke fun at someone else's expense, nonthreateningly confront people with their disapproved behavior, and give people an excuse to act cruelly. In short, much of humor deals with the taboo and is the only acceptable social outlet for discussing sensitive topics.

In therapeutic groups, humor can be used safely and supportively to provide a bridge between client reluctance and client motivation to change. Initial attempts to explore sensitive issues often take a jesting form to test the water before the plunge. For example, one gentleman, who had been withholding a dark secret since childhood, spent the better part of an hour building up to his disclosure by joking about brother-sister jealousies. Like a court jester, he interrupted the group proceedings to interject humorous comments about how kids can inadvertently hurt one another when they are only fooling around. Instead of ignoring or extinguishing the inappropriate comments, the group leader chose to respond in kind.

When she was a child, she said, she had once short-sheeted her little brother's bed to revenge some earlier mischief, and he had sprained his ankle from the force of thrusting his legs into the sabotaged bedding. The joking gentleman laughed heartily, then abruptly began to sob. When he was 5 years old he had accidentally killed his little sister in her crib while playing Cowboys and Indians with a loaded pistol. The guilt had been locked within him for four decades until the dam had burst through the hole punched in his wall. Humor had set things in motion.

The celebrated humorists of our time—George Carlin, Richard Pryor, Woody Allen, and Erma Bombeck, to mention a few—make their living by sharing stories. They perform a necessary service for their audiences by making them laugh at subjects they would in other circumstances never think about. Lenny Bruce's infatuation with taboo language and Woody Allen's preoccupation with the taboo topic of death are typical:

> Once again I tried committing suicide—this time by wetting my nose and inserting it into the light socket. Unfortunately, there was a short in the wiring and I merely caromed off the icebox. Still obsessed by thoughts of death, I brood constantly. I keep wondering if there is an afterlife, and if there is will they be able to break a twenty? (Allen, 1976, p. 8).

Erma Bombeck's innocent portrayal of the sexual taboo provides still another example of how humor allows us to laugh at our inhibitions.

> My son was five years old when his teacher sent home a note informing me he was sexually immature.
> I confronted her the next day after school and said, "What is this supposed to mean, Mrs. Kravitz?"
> "It means we had a little quiz the other day on reproductive organs and he defined every one of them as an Askyourfather. You are sending a child into the world, Mrs. Bombeck, who thinks Masters and Johnson is a golf tournament and fertilization is something you do in the fall to make the lawns green!" (Bombeck, 1972, p. 60).

Finally, in J. P. Donleavy's *The Unexpurgated Code* (1975) he advises prospective social climbers on appropriate manners for handling sensitive problems. Once again the taboo subject of death is handled with humorous irreverence, poking fun at the subject voted as most devastating to talk about: "Upon Being Told the Fatal News That You Have Only So Long to Live and That It Is Not Long."

> Of course this news may enrage you so much that you start throwing things, blaming and accusing everyone and generally behaving in a hostile manner. Of course this kind of antic only shows you should have been dead long ago.
> If you are the nice kind of average person, moisture in the eyes is permissible but do not burst into floods of tears. This alarms others into acute apprehension concerning the moment when their turn comes. Unless death has whispered I am here, make a reasonable

effort to keep going. This is often a bleak period unless you have large assets and people around you who will benefit thereby and which prospect keeps them cheerful beyond belief. However, take strong objection to any dancing joy at your sinking. Your final will and a pen handy, plus a couple of witnesses hostile to your heirs, should make the merry take heed (Donleavy, 1975, p. 51).[1]

Humor and Ambiguity

As much as group members would like to have their conflicts wrapped in neat little bundles containing clear and definitive answers, they are instead confronted by the ambiguous. Words like "probably," "perhaps," "maybe," "how about," "try this," and "I don't know" preface most leader statements because there are no certainties in therapy, only probabilities. Group members are helped to think realistically when they are requested to try a new behavior or to wrestle with a novel thought and "see if it works for you."

Most adult humans seem cognitively retarded when it comes to Piaget's stages of development: though we have the ability to think abstractly after age 12, we still prefer to think concretely. We like tidy solutions to our problems, and, most of all, in the face of the eternal mysteries we like some semblance of order and predictability. This strong aversion to dealing with ambiguity can sometimes deter progress in therapeutic groups as reasoning and exploration powers become severely restricted.

Humor can be useful for encouraging group members to confront ambiguous issues in subtle ways. After all, jokes and jests rely on basic incongruity for their appeal, as Kant and Schopenhaur first observed (Keith-Spiegel, 1972). Humor simultaneously forces people to think on different planes, to resolve the paradox satisfactorily, to reason abstractly, to discover meanings, to create possible interpretations. And the best humor, like the best art and music, may be legitimately interpreted in a number of different ways according to one's perceptions and powers of observation.

Humor and Existential Angst

At the root of anxiety is angst, an old German word that describes the free-floating human condition in which the meaning of life becomes muddled and frighteningly elusive. This "existential disease" of

---

[1]Excerpted from the book *The Unexpurgated Code: A Complete Manual of Survival and Manners* by J. P. Donleavy. Copyright © 1975 by J. P. Donleavy. Reprinted by permission of Delacorte Press/Seymour Lawrence.

spiritual emptiness occurs during periods of adjustment and stress, when a person is confronted by questions of death, isolation, alienation, responsibility, freedom, will, and other issues that Jean-Paul Sartre, Martin Heidegger, and Paul Tillich have explored. While it has no exact English equivalent, *angst* is a first cousin to "anguish" but may also be more accurately related to "dread," a more powerful affective state (May, 1958). Angst is anguish of the soul and a mummified psyche, usually a temporary state that all persons experience at different levels of intensity when considering the meanings of life.

Angst can be as trying for the therapeutic practitioner to work with as it is for group members to handle. Essentially, life is taken too seriously. Every action is given inflated importance; every decision is seen as a crucial struggle. Listlessness and boredom alternate with manic efforts to reduce dissonance, to take some action, *any* action. And until some constructive plan is discovered for moving forward, angst holds on. It sinks in deeper and keeps people going around in a depressive cycle.

When attempts are made to tackle angst with the same serious intensity in which it thrives, the negative feelings are sometimes validated. While individual sessions are well suited to the necessary dialogues for giving life meaning, group atmospheres can be counterproductive. Angst is contagious. Some clients who are feeling fine allow themselves to be pulled down by the depressing stuff of others, and content of the group takes on a somber, monkish tone.

One way to combat angst is by following rules different from its own. When group members persist in wallowing in existential grief, humor can make a dramatic contrast between pain and pleasure. At worst, humor only temporarily distracts the client from self-torture. At best, however, its potential for therapeutic good is boundless.

Humor and Hostility

Peterson (1975) studied the management of humor in therapy groups by plotting the patterns of laughter that occurred throughout sessions. It was noted that a typical 90-minute group contains about 20 separate attempts at humor, usually initiated by three principal members. Pollio and Edgerly (1976) comment on the prevalence of laughter in groups: "It is as if everyone knows humor is important in group (and individual) psychotherapy; no one seems to know exactly how to teach would-be therapists what to do with it" [p. 222].

In their systematic analysis of comic style, they discovered hostility to be a universal theme. Both in Peterson's study of therapy groups, in which 75% of the jokes tended to be self-directed or other-directed aggression, and in professional comedians who rely on "butts" for their jokes, the hostility denominator accounted for most of the variance among eight different style factors. Don Rickles and Richard Pryor exhibit obvious aggression in their humor, but almost every other comedian demonstrates the characteristic in more subtle form. Thus, Johnny Carson and Dick Cavett are reasonably polite with their condescending witticisms; Woody Allen, Phyllis Diller, Tommy Smothers, the Three Stooges, and Laurel and Hardy are all self-deprecating.

The problem for the group therapist is to manage humor to minimize aggressive and hostile effects. Clients must be taught to discriminate between the kinds of jokes that are used for smoke screens or to belittle people and those that celebrate life and display self-enhancing creativity.

Humor as a Creative Enterprise

Freud (1960) regarded the practice of humor as one of the most creative activities in which a human being can engage. It is the highest expression of the pleasure principle, the most sophisticated of defense mechanisms, and a never-ending challenge to expand one's sense of play. Singer (1973), in fact, proposes that the earliest signs of human creativity are found in the 2-year-old's game of make-believe and fantasy, behaviors that are associated with creativity in later adulthood (Helson, 1965). In a review of the relationship between humor and creativity, McGhee (1979) also concludes that creative children tend to be those who better appreciate, initiate, and understand humor. They use fantasy as a playground for experimenting with novel ideas and creating the most stimulating and chuckling internal environment possible.

In perhaps the most ambitious treatise exploring humor and creativity, Arthur Koestler drew parallels between a sense of humor and other creative activities in literature, science, and the arts. According to Koestler (1964), the riddle, pun, satire, witticism, joke, or comic simile all share common elements with the works of a poet, composer, or artist.

> Humor depends primarily on its surprise effect: the bisociative shock. To cause surprise the humorist must have a modicum of originality—the ability to break away from the stereotyped routines of thought. Caricaturist, satirist, the writer of nonsense-humor, and even the expert tickler, each operates on more than one plane. Whether his purpose is to convey a special message, or

merely to entertain, he must provide mental jolts caused by the collision of incompatible matrices [pp. 91–92].

Humor is a spontaneous expression of joy and—the culmination of human cognitive evolution—the power to improvise in abstractions and create multilevel messages. Certainly, there ought to be reservations regarding its use in groups such as those cited by Kubie (1971). Like any intervention, however, the therapist's skill, motive, and rationale will determine whether it will be helpful or harmful.

Cole and Sarnoff (1980) call for a closer marriage between creativity and counseling, emphasizing that psychological helpers should more often rely on techniques that encourage spontaneous, playful expression.

Foster (1978) ranks the quality levels of humor on a "Carkhuff-type" scale to demonstrate that it is not a matter of humor being destructive or constructive but a matter of how it is implemented. This continuum might be used as a yardstick to judge the relative appropriateness of humor in various therapeutic situations.

Malamud (1980) invented "The Laughing Game" as a group exercise for increasing client self-responsibility. He uses structured experiences conducive to giggles that motivate passive group members by encouraging them to make one another laugh. Clients learn through the causality of humor that they need not feel victimized by external conditions beyond their control. Dyer (1980) sees humor as the antidote for most emotional suffering because it is very difficult to feel depressed or anxious while laughing. Admittedly, laughter is a *very* temporary cure, but its beneficial effects far exceed the few pleasurable moments it creates. With the social interaction advantages of therapeutic groups, humor affords the leader intervention choices not possible in other circumstances. Laughter, like yawning, is a contagious phenomenon, infecting all persons within hearing.

Comparing Renaissance comedic theater and contemporary therapeutic practice, Klein (1974) concludes "that the miniature world of the theatre and the phenomenological universe of the client both emerge from an arbitrary verbal syntax which circumscribes the number and nature of the possible alternative explanations of reality" [p. 233]. The jester, the fool, the Falstaffian character speak truth behind their antics. Kings accept their candor only because the delivery appears so innocent. As the play unfolds, assumptions are clarified, distortions and inaccuracies are corrected, gaps of knowledge are filled in. Finally, the protagonist's self-ignorance is revealed. The audience laughs. Our hero exits, stage left. Enlightened. *With* the girl.

A Continuum of Therapeutic Humor in Groups (Adapted from Foster, 1978).

DESTRUCTIVE HUMOR				CONSTRUCTIVE HUMOR
Level 1	*Level 2*	*Level 3*	*Level 4*	*Level 5*
Humor is hostile, tasteless, or derisive; puts a group member down or ridicules an ethnic, sex, or minority group; causes withdrawal and emotional damage	Detracts from client concerns; is irrelevant and ill-timed; wastes valuable group time; is self-indulgent; results in "polite," false laughter; masks true feelings	Mild sense of group member appreciation; alleviates boredom; group members acknowledge humor	Humor deeply appreciated by group members; much spontaneous laughter; cohesion develops; more relaxed atmosphere; strengthened relationships; greater willingness to explore relationships	Humor transcends laughter; provides major insight and self-awareness to group members; significantly moves a client toward action

CHAPTER 13

Expanding the Range of Leader Behaviors

Most group leaders can reliably demonstrate a core of basic interventions. One such skill, *multiple attending*, requires the leader to maintain continuous surveillance on all the subtleties of human communication within the group—facial expressions, bodily movements, vocal intonations, message content (Allan, 1982). Gill and Barry (1982) have integrated several existing classification schemes into a definitive catalogue of group-focused counseling skills that pragmatic practitioners frequently use.

The range of common leader behaviors would include many of the following: accurately labeling various cognitive, affective, and behavioral data as they are manifested within and among group members; task refocusing to maintain theme-related coordinated behavior; eliciting observations, reactions, and feedback in response to group happenings; implicit norming of characteristic group behavior; consensus seeking to reach agreement on a course of action; diverting inappropriate participant involvements, and other skills identified by Lieberman, Yalom, and Miles (1973); Dyer and Vriend (1973a); Ohlsen (1977); and Gill and Barry (1982).

Expanding this base of fundamental helping skills is necessary for survival in the field. The unique demands of group work require that practitioners continually augment their range of leadership behaviors in a given conflict situation. To hold clients' attention over the long haul, to encourage creative solution seeking, to facilitate spontaneous, productive interaction, and to help clients to take risks, the group leader must have the widest range of armaments available.

To expand their knowledge base as well as their skill competencies, group leaders should become at least minimally familiar with related fields that intersect our profession. Philosophy was mentioned earlier as desirable study for practitioners. A smattering of medicine would also be helpful so that group leaders can understand basic mind-body interactions—the effects of physical disease on psychological behavior and the effects of emotions on physical functioning. Moreover, therapists should know the potential uses and abuses of psychopharmacological agents which group members may be taking in conjunction with their treatment. It would be useful to know that constipation, lethargy, weight gain, and other side effects are common with tricyclic antidepressants or that diet restrictions limiting the intake of cheese, Chianti, and pickled herring are necessary with monamine oxidase inhibitors.

Certainly, nonmedical group leaders ought to know when it is appropriate to make referrals for medication reviews. For example, cyclical manic-depressive moodswings can be much more effectively treated with Lithium therapy than with group therapy (Fiève, 1975). With all possible personal resources mobilized for immediate action, including a broad range of skills and knowledge, there is a greater likelihood that the most appropriate intervention strategy will be chosen for the greatest good of group members.

PERSONAL AND PHYSICAL CONSIDERATIONS

Personal Control

First and foremost, group leaders are maximally in charge of their personal bodies and minds. As an athlete exercises rigorously to improve muscle tone, strength, agility, and endurance, the group leader, too, must be in superb physical shape. The mind is likewise finely tuned and trained; vocal tonality is extremely well developed, providing a range rivaling that of an operatic soprano. Facial expressions are constantly monitored, sometimes showing a poker face to hide inadvertent value judgments; other times, the face is openly expressive for the purpose of providing clear feedback or reinforcement. To demonstrate support or authority, the body, too, conveys subtle nonverbal messages on demand.

In short, group leaders are meticulously in charge of their personal space so that the fullest range of messages may be sent at will, and communications will not be misinterpreted. Hence, the more therapeutic skills and choices that they add to their repertoires, the more effectively they can accurately read and convey verbal messages.

Territoriality

The next consideration, after personal control, is that of understanding and readily employing therapeutic variables in the physical environment. In a sense, the group leader becomes a spatial engineer who can manipulate physical space with the assurance of a chiropractor rearranging spinal alignments.

The concept of *territorial privacy*, for instance, has important implications for therapists in their expanded knowledge and application of group dynamics and outcomes. In Robert Ardrey's (1966) careful observation of the Ugandan kob's arena behavior, he notes that these creatures respect territorial space and rights above their mating instincts. Once a male kob has secured a stamping ground, it may not be invaded except through rigid rules of challenge and combat. The strongest and most virile antelopes thus command the choicest real estate in the center, with invisible but nevertheless impenetrable boundaries warning all but the sexiest females to stay away.

The invisible boundaries that insulate a kob against invasion, the nervous compulsion of a dog to sprinkle every tree with the scent of its urine, and the human passion for building fences around our backyards or our bodies, all attest to the significance of territoriality in group behavior. The group leader must fully understand this behavior, both to interpret it and to facilitate other behaviors, such as cooperation or respect. Among nations or individuals, war occurs when one party feels that its legitimate territorial space (physical or psychological) has been invaded. All animals have a need for privacy:

> antelopes, golden and gleaming, spread across a swelling African veld; spaced cattle in an English field; birds resting on a telephone line that we pass in our cars, each separated from his neighbor by a distance so invariable that they resemble beads on a string or markers on a giant ruler (Ardrey, 1966, p. 159).

Human behavior in groups is not much different. Group members are very reluctant to give up their seats once they have claimed them; ownership is determined by squatters' rights. Invisible boundaries pervade group behavior. Characteristic interaction distances become established depending on factors such as age, gender, race, social status, or cultural differences (Shaw, 1981). In addition, many other physical factors affect group behavior, including lighting intensity (Carr & Dabbs, 1974), noise (Glass, Singer & Friedman, 1969), and physical proximity (Sommer, 1969)—all variables that the group leader can manipulate with a wide range of intervention strategies.

That group leaders are addicted to the use of circles, that we deliberately seat ourselves next to antagonistic clients or across from passive ones, typifies the attention we pay to physical interventions. Even an elementary school teacher attempts to break up destructive coalitions by rearranging seats as the first disciplinary strategy. We could, of course, carry this a step further in our work by creatively enlarging on the physical dynamics of groups. For example, we may attempt to centralize communication patterns by spreading the more garrulous clients around the group or hope to stifle approval seeking by deliberately seating ourselves outside the group for a time. Other strategies available to the group leader are described in the pages that follow.

Spatial Interventions

When the marital therapist arranges chairs about the room so that each of the three participants—husband, wife, and therapist—sits equidistant from one another, the physical environment acts in a therapeutic capacity. Husband and wife must face each other when they speak. Neither feels the therapist to be aligned more with one partner than with the other. Each participant has an equal contribution to make. In contrast, the therapist who sits enthroned behind a desk, expecting clients to pay homage when in the sanctuary, will get quite a different set of responses.

> It is important to remember that the client *is not your equal,* he has come to you for help and thus he should indicate this symbolically by some action, such as giving you a rose or three of his paychecks or groveling a bit. Some practitioners have settled for the expedient of letting the client sit in the less comfortable chair and being addressed by an old Greek title pronounced "doctor" and spelled G—O—D (Tyler and Thurston, 1977, p. 102).

Participants choose their seats with deliberation. Dominant individuals choose central positions; passive persons attempt to hide under the leader's wings. People jockey for position next to those for whom they feel an affinity or attraction. The leader, too, will play musical chairs each week, hoping to encourage participants to break social barriers. The leader may sit across from someone who needs drawing out or between two distracting participants.

My policy is to suggest that members make it a point to sit in a different seat, next to different people, each week. This strategy encourages people to take their security with them rather than feeling that it is mystically vested in their favorite chair. It also dramatically alters group interaction patterns as people have more opportunities to get to know more people as a function of geographic proximity. Also, when the leader changes location each week, members don't get in the bad habit of looking in one direction every time they speak.

Milton Erickson was particularly sensitive to the impact of spatial positions in groups. Erickson, who would go so far as to match his breathing rate to that of his clients, imitate their speech patterns to win greater rapport, or use his body to accentuate hypnotic suggestions, also strongly advocated using whatever physical manipulations were possible. When working with hostile family members, he was likely to use spatial compartmentalization techniques to prevent other group members from barging into the conversation. He might also control a session by frequently requesting clients to switch chairs, leaving their resistance behind in their previous place. Haley (1973) reports a typical Ericksonian intervention capitalizing on the potential of spatial manipulations.

> If I send someone out of the room—for example, the mother and the child—I carefully move father from his chair and put him into mother's chair. . . . Or if I send the child out, I might put mother in the child's chair, at least temporarily. Sometimes I comment on this by saying, "As you sit where your son was sitting, you can think more clearly about him" [p. 33].

Nonverbal and Physiological Variables

Certain Indian medicine men have so sensitized themselves to the most minute color changes in the flush of a person's cheek that they can distinguish a dozen different emotional states. The martial arts student of Shin-Shin-Toitsu Akido is trained to monitor the most infinitesimal shifting of weight in a sparring partner in order to mirror the movement with perfect grace. Stage magicians can appear to have telepathic powers by their ability to see things invisible to the untrained eye. During his apprenticeship to Don Juan, Carlos Castaneda taught himself to transcend looking into seeing to perceive the essence of things in the world.

Magician, wizard, and therapist all require an extraordinarily fine-tuned perceptual system to see a heightened reality that is invisible to the uninitiated. Group leaders command respect because of the training, experience, and hard work that has made them exquisite instruments for interpreting human behavior. We appear to read minds. We understand things that are incomprehensible to others. We can predict that certain behaviors will produce certain outcomes. All the same, we have a lot farther to go. We still tune into only a limited number of possible actions; we attend to perhaps a few hundred different variables; we collect data that is relevant only to our immediate concerns. Yet the number of possible data to monitor, to add to our conceptual vocabulary, is infinite.

Few non–medically trained professionals, for instance, pay attention to psychophysiological and autonomic responses in group members. Shallow breathing, pupil dilation, pallor, rashes, and other physical symptoms don't exist for those who are not trained to notice them. Similarly, blinking, tremors, and other nonverbal movements have meaning only when acuity notes their existence. We have, in short, an impossible mission: to notice everything in a client's behavior that might have meaning.

Subgrouping

Though we are fond of dyads and triads, many other combinations are possible depending on desired outcomes. For instance, after two group members have used group time to confront each other about long-standing conflicts, they may each be asked to take half the group to receive structured, private feedback before they re-encounter each other. In one subgroup, all six colleagues may agree that a client has overstepped her bounds by ignoring the other person's rights or that she should stop responding so defensively to every attempt at being helpful. In the other subgroup, the client may be cautioned that he is playing it too safe, being dishonest with himself, and trying to placate everyone's wishes. After the feedback, the group may be reunited to help the clients reach some resolution.

In another structure, triads can be used to reduce initial hesitance and mistrust in a risk-taking exercise. If one client was exploring his fear of having homosexual impulses and other members shared similar fears but were reluctant to disclose details, the leader might decide to subdivide the group for the purpose of their sharing feelings, values, and fears about being sexually attracted to the same sex.

In a subgrouping structure that is a common introduction to sexual attitude reassessment groups (SARs), participants are asked to explore their body images. First, group members are paired off to interview each other regarding their attitudes and feelings toward male and female bodies as well as their dislikes and joys about their own bodies. Questions may be asked about shame, inhibition, favorite body parts, or whatever is interesting. Next, the group members meet to introduce their partner's body, to share insights, and to discuss less threateningly sensitive issues related to sexuality.

Finally, group members may also be paired in fishbowl structures. Two members who rarely listen to each other may be asked to move their chairs to the middle of the group, tune out the audience, and practice listening and responding skills. The others will remember the same principles in their future encounters. As witnesses to the exercise, they can also help process what happened and offer valuable suggestions for improving communication.

Thinking on One's Seat

I was once running a group in which a member was working on her compulsive need for winning the approval of significant people in her life. She spent a disproportionate amount of energy figuring out what her sister-in-law, husband, and college professors wanted to hear and would then do her best to satisfy their expectations. It was deemed appropriate to solicit the reactions of other group members as to how they viewed her approval-seeking behaviors within the group itself. Did she defer to any specific people? Would she stifle her true feelings in favor of those that would be universally accepted? Did her bodily movements, posture, eye contact, vocal tones signal placating gestures? Was she deliberately engaging in bootlicking behaviors within the group?

One or two initial comments made it clear that the other clients were focusing on how incredibly, disgustingly nice this woman acted. She was always coming to people's rescue, defending them against injustices by confrontive co-leaders. She always had something wonderfully sweet to say about everything. Meanwhile, this sweet little old lady (as she liked to project herself) batted her eyes, smiled indulgently, and promptly thanked each member for his or her kind thoughts. Things were going nowhere. In fact, her approval-seeking behaviors were inadvertently being reinforced by polite peers who didn't wish to sully her self-image of a "proper" lady who always knew the "right thing to say."

It was time to abandon the agenda. The true sign of pragmatic group leaders is their willingness to try something new when they are confronted by inertia. Flexibility and creative improvisation are the keys to successful quarterbacking, to great jazz, and to effective group leadership as well. Plans are made to be altered, and no therapeutic strategy is going to be optimally beneficial unless it can be molded to fit the ever-changing circumstances within a group.

This constructive feedback strategy, which had always worked for me before, is supposed to help clients to assess the impact of their self-defeating actions realistically. It's not supposed to make things worse. But here was this woman rattling off the fantastic psychological benefits she was getting from approval seeking: avoidance of conflict and of risk taking, making other people happy, not having to think for herself, and a score of other payoffs.

Then it occurred to me that her physical presence made stark honesty impossible. No one could be so heartless as to tell this gentle cocker spaniel with the big brown eyes that she was a lazy, yellow-bellied chicken who was afraid of taking risks. There was no doubt that she had either to leave the room or become invisible for group inhibitions to be reduced. An inspiration came. By turning her chair so that her back would face the group, we could talk about her more openly. Bingo! The effect was fantastic. (Only later did I learn that others had used this technique before me.)

Once her back was turned, group members described her as a coward, an invisibility indistinguishable from the wallpaper, a well-meaning but meek person who enjoyed being stepped on, and a woman who acted as if she were to be thrashed at any moment. Her downcast eyes, stiff posture, nervous hand movements, and apologetic voice were all noted. Finally, group members described the ways in which they felt offended and cheated because they could never distinguish the woman's true feelings from those she worked so hard to manufacture.

In the hush that followed as group members awaited her reactions, the little old lady, wearing a grandmotherly smile, slowly turned her chair around and proceeded to articulate all the reactions that she'd stored up for each person during the past months. Gone was the self-deprecating manner. With both candor *and* diplomacy, she expressed her thoughts on every imaginable subject, responded to each person on an intense level, even deliberately said some controversial things to note how they were received. To her surprise, spontaneous applause broke out. Not only was no one offended by her outburst, but group members respected her all the more for her honesty.

And so a vicious approval-seeking cycle ended because the group leader was willing (a) to determine the specific outcomes he wished to reach; (b) to formulate a strategy and rationale for accomplishing that goal; and most important, (c) to alter his agenda to design spontaneously a new, improved version better suited to the therapeutic situation. In this case, the leader was able to reason through the dynamics that appeared to be restricting maximum effectiveness and then systematically to remove the obstructions that prevented change.

Using Time
Time is not an absolute that is measured by a clock. No two seconds weigh the same. Time expands during boredom and contracts during involvement. The experience of time is affected by a number of

factors that radically influence the behavior of different people. A younger person experiences a single minute as lasting much longer than does an older person. People of different cultures and ethnic backgrounds also relate differently to time. For example, an American businessman who equates time with money will act differently from an Indian who believes in reincarnation and that life therefore is timeless.

In this sense, we are not dealing with a standardized unit called a *second*, which is actually "1,192,731,700 cycles of the frequency associated with the transition between the two energy levels of isotope cesium 133" (Austin, 1968). In therapeutic groups, the concept of time becomes most significant in the *relative* value it has for clients. People who escape from the present by living in the past through nostalgia, guilt, or reminiscence; people who live in the future through fantasy, anticipation, and worry; people who use drugs or sleep to hide from their troubles obviously don't value their time very greatly.

Group leaders must think in terms of cost-effectiveness and be guardians of time to make certain that it is neither wasted nor abused. Rambling and small talk are rarely tolerated; on a pro-rated basis, minutes may cost up to $3 apiece (if 12 members are paying $25/session for a 100-minute group). In these terms, a long-winded story could cost $30! When the leader is extremely time-conscious and group members are extremely time-wasteful, either because they don't realize the value of each minute or because they are sabotaging time-utility as a form of resistance, we have a difficult situation.

Perhaps a primary motive of group leaders is to use the concept of time as an overriding factor: "Do we want to be using *our* time in this way?" "How have you maximized *your* time in the last three minutes of silence?" "In what ways are you not appreciating *your* time as much as you could?" Time is also important in the pacing of certain interventions. Like the trial lawyer, stand-up comic, or playwright, the group leader must time comments to coincide with the readiness of group members to hear them (McClure, 1978).

The Drama of Change

When the Austrian hypnotist Franz Mesmer set up his "animal magnetism" baths that were purported to produce startling behavioral changes among group participants, he gave great attention to the dramatic elements of the therapeutic milieu. Lighting, music, his own dress and demeanor all heightened the suggestive effect of his treatment and procedures. Today, we still play on clients' favorable expectations to change. The diplomas on the wall, the book-lined shelves, the plush furniture, the three-piece suits or white lab coats certainly lend an aura of authority to the setting.

Group therapists are also fantastically accomplished dramatists. We write scripts that rival the plays of Tennessee Williams in their realism and passion. We participate as players in dramatic productions so absurd as to make Eugene Ionesco or Edward Albee's plays look predictable. We are versatile in our performances—sometimes harsh, brittle, cynical; other times, soft, sincere, and responsive. We play heroes and heavies, character parts and supporting roles. Sometimes we produce, direct, or write the musical scores for the productions. In any case, we spend a good part of our time participating in the drama of change.

The tasks of a group therapist have expanded considerably since the days of Victorian Vienna when the leader was expected to play the part of a no-nonsense nursemaid to control the antics of participants. Yet, at about the same time that Freud was experimenting with his "talking cure," J. L. Moreno was playing with kids in a park, helping them to act out their fantasies. Moreno had hit upon great subjects for his "dramatic therapy" because children are spontaneous, uninhibited, creative, and enthusiastic about pretending. Moreno learned from the children as much as they learned from him; indeed, all group therapists could profit by expanding their repertoire of child skills.

From these attempts to act out real-life experiences for catharsis, for insight, and to resolve conflicts, psychodrama was born. Though psychodramatic structures and role playing have now become standard operating procedures for most group leaders, the underlying principles of these techniques have not. The drama of group interaction is often relegated only to appropriate instances: "Now it is time to do a role play." The visible variables clearly indicate this procedure. A confrontation is necessary. The subjects are willing. Tension and inhibition are high. Structured practice and rehearsal are indicated.

Yet the role of drama in group leadership can be considerably expanded by the pragmatist. Drama *is* a unity of themes with heightened interest. The function of dramatic literature is first to entertain and, once audience attention has been secured, to instruct. Dramatic movements are exaggerated. They alleviate boredom and capture interest. They spread enthusiasm and excitement contagiously.

A drama student trains the vocal cords, musculature, and facial expressions to convey even the subtlest gestures. Similarly, group leaders have trained themselves as mimes when they parody client actions; as improvisationists when they forcefully create dramatic metaphors; as comedians when they attempt to relieve tension; as poets when they construct memorable verbal images; as playwrights, directors, producers, and, above all, as actors in everything they do. Rather than merely walking through a role, however, they exhibit genuineness and sincerity in their performances.

Whether the therapeutic situation calls for an affectionate friend or Merlin the Magician, the therapist must deliver an award-level performance. With little time for rehearsal, the group leader is *always* before a critical audience. Frowns are misinterpreted as rejection. A vacant stare may be read as boredom. It is difficult to scratch an itch without the gesure being noticed, interpreted, and personalized by attentive participants.

Once the seats are occupied, the curtain rises, lights dim, and an air of expectancy settles around the circle: "What surprises are in store for us today? I hope it's a good show. The critics liked it last week. But you know how inconsistent these temperamental shrinks are." And during the next two hours, usually without intermission, the group leader will run through a complicated series of dramatic performances.

- Karen reports that she forgot to complete her self-imposed assignments in risk taking and then searches the group leader's eyes for a glint of disapproval. The group leader feigns casual indifference.
- Samuel hedges his bet by demonstrating reluctance to make a decision. While he claims contentment as a spectator, the group leader leaps out of a chair and assumes a scarecrow pose, humorously illustrating the consequences of total inertia.
- Jalaine expresses a strong desire to confront her nagging, insensitive boss. The group leader spontaneously assumes the boss' role, imitating his habits and the chronically irritating whine that she finds so offensive.
- Bernard speaks in a soft, melodic whisper. His words, however insightful, are seldom heard. Yet his face is constantly lighted with feeling. The group leader delivers a sensitive monologue on what Bernard's face is expressing while his voice is silent.
- Following an initial surge of progress, group sessions begin to lose intensity after the fifth week. The group leader recites a carefully worded, impassioned soliloquy to encourage further involvement.

These examples fail to mention the subtle changes in voice modulation, body expression, and facial communication that are part of *every* leader intervention. The group therapist is a veteran of first-run dramatic performances that make soap operas pale in comparison.

Uses of Imagery

Previous chapters have discussed the expanded roles of metaphoric language in group leadership. Therapeutic imagery is only one example that has been selected as a technological outgrowth of the attention directed toward linguistic/cognitive leadership strategies for promoting change. Pragmatic group leaders have the awesome task of keeping up with the latest innovative techniques so that they may be altered to fit the unique requirements of group situations.

Clients use imagery to overcome fears, phobias, or anxieties by imagining pleasant scenes when confronted by stressful situations. Panic responses can be blocked by using enjoyable fantasies as distractions to overcome problems such as school phobias (Lazarus & Abramovitz, 1962) or the pains of childbirth. Since therapeutic groups are usually highly stressful situations during the early stages, scenes of positive imagery can be constructed to help anxious and shy group members relax sufficiently to be able to verbalize their concerns.

One particularly high-strung group of clients, whose collection of symptoms included high blood pressure, ulcers, stuttering, hand tremors, and other physical signs of destructive stress, was given a dose of positive imagery as part of their orientation to group proceedings. They were instructed that on noticing the telltale signs of tension that make them feel reluctant to speak up, they should instead visualize themselves sitting around an open campfire with trusted good friends.

The open sky would be dotted with stars. In the background they could hear the steady drone of the ocean (the air-conditioner hum). They could smell the fire and feel its soothing warmth. Everyone would be preoccupied with his/her own thoughts, paying little attention to the others. "And all of a sudden you begin to feel safe and comfortable, completely relaxed. You find that you really want to speak up. You know that no one else is judging you; they are focused on their own concerns. And the more you feel the warmth of the fire, the great expanse of the sky, the vigilance of the stars, and the camaraderie of the people you trust, the more you want to open up to them."

One creative and very controversial application of therapeutic imagery has been in the treatment of cancer. In their holistic approach to health, Simonton and Simonton (1975) view cancerous symptoms as excessive strain on the mind/body system. An unsynchronized body expresses negative emotions on a cellular level by creating malignancies. It is hypothesized that the same diseases that result from destructive attitudes and emotional despair can be wiped out by "healing visualizations" of quite a different sort. After patients are taught to relax, they are asked to use therapeutic imagery to supplement the administration of any medications.

> The scenario runs like this: The drug transforms her leukocytes into voracious sharks and the cancer cells into "frightened, grayish little fish." The shark/leukocytes pursue the grayish fish/cancer cells, which are envisioned as disorganized and disoriented, and then pounce upon them, rending them to bits with their long, jagged teeth, and destroying them. At last, when the cancerous areas have been cleared out completely, the sharks are transformed into ordinary white blood cells once again and continue to course through her bloodstream. The chemotherapeutic agents, together with any "fish/cancer" refuse that remains, are visualized as being flushed out with her body fluids. All is peaceful; all is clean and healthy within (Scarf, 1980, p. 40).

In the perhaps not too distant future, group leaders will be recruited to use such imagery techniques on a regular basis in hospital settings. As the following section demonstrates, each year for the past several decades, since group leadership began its dramatic rise, practitioners' helping technologies have multiplied.

PERSPECTIVE ON GROUP WORK

Although most historians trace group work's beginnings from the early 1900s, it has been around since Classical Greece. In the following dialogue written by Aristophanes (Alexander & Selesnick, 1966), Socrates is shown working in very much the same manner as analysts do today.

Socrates: Come, lie down here.
Strepsiades: What for?
Socrates: Ponder awhile over matters that interest you.
Strepsiades: Oh, I pray not there.
Socrates: Come, on the couch!

Strepaisades: What a cruel fate.

Socrates: Ponder and examine closely, gather your thoughts together, let your mind turn to every side of things. If you meet
with difficulty, spring quickly to some other idea, keep away from
sleep [p. xiii].

The group leader's repertoire of therapeutic skills remained unre-
markable until the Victorian Era, when many "patients" found
symptom relief in Mesmer's "animal magnetism groups" due solely
to the "therapist's" persuasiveness. At the turn of the present century, however, group leadership behaviors began to expand. The
trend began with self-help groups, later to be improved by "tuberculosis classes" offered on hospital wards by inspirational group
leaders. Next, psychoanalytic methods were applied to group settings, then "activity therapy" in which patients worked on projects
together for psychological benefits.

The group leader's healing capacities multiplied again with the
advent of psychodrama. Then recreational therapy with children and
group guidance techniques entered the scene, finally culminating in
a separate helping system known as group therapy. Family therapy
techniques first became popular in the 1940s, group counseling in
the 1950s, and human potential groups in the 1960s. The 1970s
brought to the group practitioner behavioral treatments as well as
innovations from varying theoretical systems—the transactional
analysis, Gestalt, and human relations approaches among others. It
is a safe prediction that group leadership behaviors will continue to
expand throughout the 20th century, at least until we are replaced by
computers.

Reaching a Larger Audience

Mental health centers, social service centers, schools, and other
human service agencies across the country are always short of funds,
staff, and time to serve client populations adequately. So immense
are caseloads that active therapy groups don't even make a dent in
the backlog of people wanting help. Further, only a small portion of
the community is willing to overcome the stigma of seeing a "shrink."
Not only are many people with personal problems reluctant to seek
help, but people who would like to grow in new dimensions would
never choose to recruit a professional for assistance either.

Group leaders can reach considerably more clients by offering in
the community personal growth courses which bypass the stigma

and space limitations of traditional therapeutic groups. One such workshop, entitled "Principles of Effective Living" (PEL), consists of lectures, practical demonstrations, structured small-group exercises, and discussions to personalize relevant concepts. While structure, format, and content can be flexible and situation-specific, it is usually best to meet in weekly two-hour sessions. Continuity is thus maximized over a period of six to ten weeks, and participants have the opportunity to apply new skills to their life situations.

Generally, each session has a minilecture on such topics as "Controlling Negative Emotions," "The Dynamics of How People Change," "Learning to Diagnose Your Self-Defeating Behaviors," "Recruiting More Dynamite People into Your World," "Living in the Present Moment," "What Causes Approval Seeking," and "Understanding Love." The number of participants can range from 10 to 300, and these people are subdivided into smaller permanent groups of 6 to 10 to work on specific theme-centered tasks related to lecture topics. If staff is available, a skilled leader should be assigned to each group, though leaderless groups can be used with roving consultants. Exercises are implemented for building trust, cohesiveness, and specific skills; topics may include systematic problem solving, taking productive risks, meaningful introductions, effective confrontation strategies, and promoting spontaneity.

All PEL activities are centered on the idea of personal mastery; that is, all persons, regardless of their present level of functioning, can learn to be more effective human beings. The "educational" mental health counselor, though necessarily more of a teacher than a remedial therapist, is concerned with producing the same sequential process of change that occurs in the counseling process. Workshop participants are helped to identify their self-defeating behaviors, understand the payoffs that accrue to such actions, determine which behaviors they wish to change, set constructive goals, and practice new skills aimed at reaching those goals.

The group leader can focus on more than helping people who are already hurt. Future emotional problems can be reduced by equipping relatively normal people with self-help skills that aid them in working through their concerns before they reach crisis proportions. The educational format of PEL courses makes it less threatening to the consumer, allowing the therapist to reach into the community for people who would like help but are afraid to ask for it.

The potential leader should also be aware of a few problems associated with these workshops. Unless some screening is done, a few

persons may enter the workshop with radically different expectations from those of the leader. A severely neurotic individual who
needs intensive long-term therapy would, for example, not be an
optimal candidate. There are also some unique ethical problems in
running self-help workshops. In a large group, for example, it is
difficult to protect the individual rights of participants, to ensure that
people don't have negative experiences. There is also a danger of
promising prospective participants sensational goals that cannot be
delivered.

Most of these problems can be minimized by using competent and
trained small-group leaders who can keep their fingers on the pulse
of participants' thoughts, feelings, and behaviors. Any advertising of
the courses should understate what they can do, making it clear
from the outset that they are *not* therapy.

Group leaders should expand their already formidable repertoires
to include lecture skills, fielding questions, organizational structures,
and working with large audiences because the potential benefits of
these minicourses far outstrip the dangers. If nothing else, workshops like PEL can be a means of ensuring that people can get help
before they desperately need it.

Television is playing an important role as psychologists, psychiatrists, counselors, and social workers have greater access to greater
numbers of "group members" sitting in their homes. Talk-show
guests, authors, lecturers, and group leaders who publicly demonstrate their craft function, in a way, as therapists who help people in
millions of small living room groups.

Another expanded set of skills that group leaders will probably
master is related to mind-body issues. Medicine and mental health
are moving in an integrative direction so that the pragmatic practitioner can help the client from both a physiological and psychological perspective. Diet, exercise, supplemental vitamins, and body
manipulations will be combined with psychological intervention to
treat the "whole patient," body and mind alike.

Finally, group leaders are becoming more sensitive to issues related to temporary versus permanent cures. Follow-up evaluations
will become more important as practitioners search for ways to help
group members faster and to ensure that therapeutic efforts are
maintained over a long period of time. Energies will also be expanded to select adjunct methods (Chapter 14) that will work effectively when the therapist is not around.

CHAPTER 14

Adjunct Structures

The goal of any therapeutic adjunct is to intensify any work done within the more traditional latitudes of group work practice. Since the average client spends more than 100 waking hours each week outside the therapeutic encounter, the time logged in the group represents less than 2% of the thoughts and feelings that clients experience. A client may enter the hallowed chamber each session, itching to get started on two intensive hours of hard work—introspection, confrontation, integration. But then the group disbands until next week, and the client re-enters the real world, perhaps acting just as ineffectively as before.

Within the safety of the group, the client is a superstar at risk taking because the atmosphere is conducive to trust, respect, acceptance, and human kindness. One's comrades praise every intelligent comment. Confronting a conflict head-on wins enthusiastic support. The client is continually reinforced for growing, at least until the following week. Once outside, however, smiles fade and it can be total bananas behavior for a week. Tempers are lost. Self-pity returns. All is forgotten, or temporarily suspended, until the next group meeting.

This doesn't happen all the time, perhaps not even frequently; but group members report often enough that the glowing effects of the group experience don't even outlast the weekend. Unless they are given opportunities to think about their insights every hour—while they eat or drift off to sleep, when they are anxious and depressed, during television commercials or rides in the car—the memories quickly fade. If people do not practice new skills regularly, they will never become part of natural functioning.

It is to permanently set the cure that group leaders invent adjunct structures for maintaining therapeutic changes. Unlike our colleagues in medicine who have the use of high-technology tools for assistance, we *create* tools to remind our clients to continue working on themselves between sessions. We use all the help we can get to ensure that changes are individually personalized by each client and

271

that these desired changes are perpetuated long after the last group session.

Chapter 14 reviews some of the more functional adjuncts currently in use by group leaders who seek innovative ways to supplement their "talking cures." By combining the technology from pharmacology, electronics, cultural geography, the biological and social sciences, as well as artistic contributions from literature and the humanities, we can more powerfully promote long-term client changes.

We now have access to various hardware from the communication field, such as audio and video recording equipment, computer systems, and absentee-cueing systems. From such writers as Anaïs Nin and Albert Camus we have inherited the literary legacy of journal keeping. Many novelists, as well, have provided psychologically sophisticated literature for self-reflective study, spawning the discipline of bibliotherapy. We can use behavioral technology, such as environmental programming, contingency reinforcements, psychological homework, and people monitoring. Field excursions are ways of augmenting group experiences creatively, and pyschodramatic structures provide clients with systematic behavioral practice and insight. The medical profession has taught us to use psychopharmacology, regimented exercise programs, and even vitamin supplements to help group members to stabilize emotional reactions. In each case, sister disciplines have contributed valuable tools which innovative group leaders may incorporate into their repertoires.

JOURNAL KEEPING

Anaïs Nin's 150,000 pages of diary entries comprise one of the outstanding literary-autobiographical works of this century. Apart from its other uses to an aspiring writer, Nin and her colleagues saw the intensive journal primarily as a tool for self-exploration.

> We taught the diary as an exercise in creative will; as an exercise in synthesis; as a means to create a world according to our wishes, not those of others; as a means of creating the self, of giving birth to ourselves. We taught diary writing as a way of reintegrating ourselves when experience shatters us, to help us out of the desperate loneliness of silence and the anxieties of alienation (Nin, 1978).

Progoff (1975) describes journal keeping as a "transpsychological" approach to growth because it capitalizes on techniques active

Intensified Therapeutic Influence through Adjunct Structures

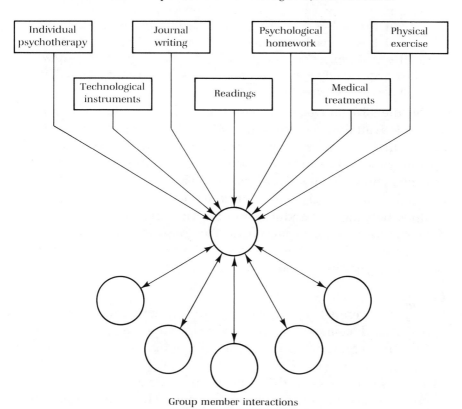

Group member interactions

within an individual that are not available to group therapy sessions. It counterbalances the *we*ness of groups or the helper's role in individual therapy by encouraging the creative and spiritual enrichment of one's inner life.

Although inclined toward mysticism, Zen, and spiritual enlightenment processes, Progoff nevertheless offers sound counsel to scientifically trained professionals. In his view, the journal teaches self-reliance; it provides an inner sanctum in which a person may practically and safely experience greater personal mastery. He suggests that it is possible to see the "Tao of growth" by guiding his group members in their personal journeys through the Period Log, Time-Stretching, Inner Wisdom, Steppingstones, Twilight Imagery, Internal Dialogues, Dream Enlargements, and other journal techniques that plan for self-exploration combined with group interaction and feedback.

The *Intensive Journal* workbook is specifically designed to provide an instrument and techniques by which persons can discover
within themselves the resources they did not know they pos-
sessed. It is to enable them to draw the power of deep contact out
of the actual experiences of their lives so that they can recognize
their own identity and harmonize it with the larger identity of the
universe as they experience it (Progoff, 1975, p. 10).

The intensive journal is perhaps the single most useful therapeutic
adjunct available to group members for deepening work accomplished during sessions. Journal keeping has become standard
operating procedure among group leaders of various theoretical per-
suasions and for many sound reasons. The advantages may be sum-
marized from several sources (Kottler, 1978c; Rainer, 1978; Kaiser,
1981), which can be used as part of a "marketing strategy" to introduce the idea to group members. The following potential uses are
from the journals of a group member who wrote diligently during the
course of a year-long group.

Catharsis

First and foremost, a journal is a convenient repository for all
thoughts and feelings swelling inside and bursting to express themselves. Since Freud had originally intended therapy to be a vehicle for
releasing stored psychic energy, the journal is a more appropriate
place for self-expression than the group sessions themselves. All too
often clients waste valuable group time complaining about their lives
beyond the point where complaint is helpful; but the journal offers
an eternally vigilant ear, always ready to accept unconditionally any
and all cathartic entries:

"I despise this sonofabitching place. I'm so damn tired of all these
idiots telling me what to do with my life, how I should think, what I
should wear, how I should speak. It would be different (maybe) if
they could get their own acts together first before they try and direct
my life. I hate nothing worse than a bunch of loud-mouthed hypo-
crites who get off on the power of making other people feel miserable. I would so much like to stand up to these assholes and tell them
what I really think—that they are self-centered, rigid-thinking, insensitive, irresponsible peasants who delude themselves into believing
they are royalty."

Introspection

The journal is a place to talk to oneself, to reflect on significant
happenings both in the group and in the real world. Systematic
writing trains one to think more analytically and introspectively

about one's actions, to ponder inconsistencies and underlying motives, to reconcile other perceptions with self-image. "The feedback from the other group members as to their first impressions of me is very incongruent with how I think I come across. I appeared shy and studious, which is certainly a new image for someone like me who pretends so much to be a "man of action."

Self-Intimacy

While group sessions usually focus on people as social beings, journal writing complementarily concentrates on the private self. By exploring their own intimate thoughts in conjunction with the interactive group work, clients are better ensured of making independent decisions as well as of preserving personal identity. A particular group meeting can often act as an impetus for clients to turn inward, exploring the implications of an issue for themselves, then further exploring the most relevant dimensions in their journals.

"I left the group with a boring, wasted feeling in the pit of my stomach. Like I hadn't grown any. And I wasted my time watching one of my cohorts grilled at the stake. It was only until now, after becoming more aware of my own dependencies on people I love, that I realize I had, in fact, been pounded on the head. I, too, feel guilt, obligation toward my grandparents who love me so devotedly and live their lives through mine. Must I repay this debt?"

Processing Insights

Even an exceptional human mind cannot keep pace with the kaleidoscope of new ideas presented in a typical group meeting. Concepts are often introduced on an abstract or general plane requiring systematic personalization of the material. Each participant must be continually asking questions: "What are they *really* saying?" "What does this mean?" "What has this to do with me?" "How might I apply this to my life?"

Each novel concept, every lesson worthy of recall, must be fully understood, interpreted, generalized, applied, coded, and stored in memory for retrieval on demand. To accomplish these tasks, it is not only desirable but necessary for clients to process insights gleaned from group sessions into bite-sized pieces that can be swallowed without indigestion. "One of the main points of last session is that a person is ultimately responsible only to himself. Problems that arise as the result of another person's actions must be seen only within the context of how I allow it to affect me. The implications of this are awesome: I need never feel helpless again."

Dialogue with Group Leader

One of the principal disadvantages of therapeutic groups is the premium placed on leader accessibility. The therapist is simply not readily available to clients in this time-shared structure in which each participant may command only one-sixth, or even one-fifteenth share. When many people vie simultaneously for leader attention, some will inevitably be shortchanged. Moreover, even a socially skilled and assertive client who is able to maximize leader expertise during sessions will be left in the cold between meetings. Questions and comments that come to mind during the week must often be shrugged off.

A possible solution to this problem lies in using the journal as a place in which clients can create dialogues with the leader. The leader's ear is thus always on call, at any time of the week, whenever the client has need for a confidential conference. If clients later decide to share their journals with the therapist, responses, reactions, and feedback can be inserted throughout the pages:

"I don't much like the idea of not being in control of what goes on in this group. These leaders act like they know it all, but I don't really trust them. Or I should say *you*, since you're both reading this journal. That's another thing I resent. How the hell am I supposed to privately explore my thoughts when I know that you two will be giving this the once-over?"

Self-Discipline

People experimenting with journal writing often complain that it is hard work. Sometimes you're too busy or feel that you have nothing to say; other times it's too painful to get into personal matters. In either case, it takes resolve and effort to carry through with the task. Like the change efforts attempted in therapy, journal keeping requires considerable self-discipline.

"I find myself, day by day, growing stronger. The reinforcement mechanisms for change are operating at an extremely effective level. I can't even put my finger on how I've changed. I just think differently. I'm much more positively critical, demanding of myself. Just by nature of the fact that it is 8:00 A.M. on a Saturday and I'm sitting here writing instead of sleeping is indicative of my new self."

Creative Expression

The unique communication style of group work lends itself to an emphasis on scientific inquiry, inquisitive exploration, and a playful experimentation with novel ideas. It is hoped that these qualities will become part of the content of the journal, making it a forum for creative expression.

"Organization is the hardest part of writing, deciding what to put where. With the greatest fluidity I can sit down almost anywhere and write acceptable, if not interesting, prose. But my writing style does not include a sequential flow of pages from beginning to end. Like the free association of a slot machine, a spark clicks, triggered by a memory, a sight, a sound. From there, the idea writes itself from the nucleus outward. A string of jumbled beads is thus left around my neck, in need of sorting. And *that* is the most confusing, challenging task of all. I get frightened by the power of a writer to alter pieces, no—first to create them from nothing, then to put them *anywhere*."

Goal setting. "I notice that I keep trying to win my father's approval for the things that I do. Alternative: to keep my own counsel and quit running to him each time I accomplish some task. Goal: to stifle the urge for others' approval. In the group I must restrain myself from saying things that I don't necessarily believe in—just to win *your* approval and strokes."

Structured self-counseling. "I have a desperate, neurotic need for recognition by an impartial audience. I am not at all concerned about the approval of my parents or friends or anyone else close to me. That is the confusing part: I don't feel I have to prove my wonderfulness to anyone I know. It is the people I don't know whom I make so important. I must make extraordinary efforts to remind myself that (a) I don't become a more worthy human being just because I convince strangers that I am important; (b) it is a losing proposition anyway since I cannot convince *everyone*; and (c) I must tell myself that I am important to myself and those who love me—what difference do other opinions make?"

Systematic practice of new thinking. "What an interesting idea we learned today—that other people can't reject me unless I permit them. So often I let myself be put in vulnerable positions where other people can control my life. This evening I tried something new. I walked up to a girl, as usual; but *this* time when she didn't respond to me—instead of feeling dejected I told myself: 'Big deal. So she didn't like you. That doesn't mean you are ugly or stupid. Maybe next time things will work out differently. And if they don't . . . I can live with *that* too.'"

Dream analysis. "Only since my baby was born have I had these incredibly vivid dreams. Naturally, I am being pursued by some suitably grotesque creature, who instead goes after the baby. I struggle.

I fight. Just as the baby is devoured I wake up screaming, in tears. Never have I felt so damn vulnerable. It is bad enough to have to protect myself, much less this little one who cannot fend for himself."

Remembrances, memory. "In this book I've been reading by John Nichols a little boy asks his mother if raindrops are alive. His mother nonchalantly replies: 'I think so, isn't everything alive and infused with the spirit of God?' The boy, not to be put off, asks again: 'Then does the rain have dreams, too, like us?' While his mother stammers, searching her memory for the correct response, the boy inwardly smiles, points toward the sunlit mountains in the distance, and answers his own question: 'Rainbows are the rain's dreams.' If rain dreams, can it also cry?"

Progress and growth. "Last night I stumbled into an opportunity to use the confrontation skills that I have unknowingly acquired in the past few weeks from this group experience. I found myself using phrases that I heard in the group. To be quite honest I thought that last week wasn't that useful. Apparently I learned more than I thought."

A celebration of life. "Today I have fulfilled my greatest dreams. Perched atop an overhanging cliff at 10,000 feet (higher than eagles dare fly) overlooking the valley below, my skis swinging in a rhythmic pattern to the wind and snow, I lived. It was then that I realized that I had been thinking about absolutely nothing—my mind a complete blank. How precious are these moments devoid of thought and feeling. I never once thought to myself 'This is beautiful.' My unconscious had already accepted this fact; felt no inclination to bother the rest of me with a lapse in concentration."

BUG-IN-THE-EAR

In training fighter pilots during World War II, it was discovered that students needed real-life experiences in the cockpit, with opportunities for independent judgment while at the same time they could receive immediate feedback on their performances from their flight instructors. An apparatus was thus constructed to allow trainees to receive continual, unobtrusive supervision during their mastering of new skills.

This electronic system, consisting of a headphone and a microphone, was later adapted by Korner and Brown (1952) into a "mechanical third ear." By converting a hearing aid into a private receiver or by using an inexpensive pocket radio with an earphone, an individual can receive unobtrusive feedback through a wireless microphone. This absentee cueing system has been used to teach projective testing to clinical psychology interns (Korner & Brown, 1952); to instruct student teachers (Herold, Ramirez, & Newkirk, 1971); to train group counselors (Cohn, 1973); and to provide immediate feedback supervision to therapy clients (Patterson, Jones, Whittier, & Wright, 1965; Stumphauzer, 1971).

According to Haney, Sewell, Edelstein, and Sartin (1975), a Bug-in-the-Ear can be created using a pocket-size transistor radio as a receiver by setting it on an open FM frequency and using an inexpensive wireless FM microphone as a transmitter. Requiring a capital investment of about $30, this instrument opens limitless therapeutic possibilities that may be integrated into group situations. Since the Bug-in-the-Ear provides instant support and feedback to the client *with no one else able to hear,* target behaviors may be reinforced, altered, or extinguished systematically and immediately at the same time that anxiety is reduced (Kottler, 1977).

Investigators who have experimented with this therapeutic instrument have noted several important points (Cohn, 1973; McClure, 1973; Kottler, 1977).

1. Client and therapist/coach should agree in advance on specific instances when intervention is indicated. Example: "Whenever you see me backing down from a confrontation, let me know."

2. Practice sessions with the instrument are necessary to familiarize the client with its operation and help him or her adjust to the difficulties in tuning into simultaneous conversations (i.e., the one going on in the group and the voice coming in from the "third ear").

3. Comments made on the device should be concise, clear, and abbreviated to minimize confusion. Example: Instead of the coach saying "You're kidding yourself when you believe that the client will do what you say," the comment could be more briefly worded "Follow through!"

4. Cues should be restricted, whenever possible, to timely pauses in discussion so that clients don't lose their place.

5. Clients preferred consulting rather than authoritarian roles on the part of the coach.

6. Dependency on the device can be minimized if cues are phrased so as to allow clients freedom on how to act.

7. Cues can be of different varieties:
Reinforcement cues: "Well done!"
Support cues: "You're doing fine."
Cues on manner: "Slow down."
Cues on timing: "Confront him now."
Insight cues: "What are your payoffs from being silent?"
Action cues: "Notice what you are doing with your hands."
Content cues: "You completely ignored her feedback to you."
Interpretation cues: "He's trying to test you."

8. The client, too, should have created a signal system for communicating to the coach:
Scratch eyebrow: "Repeat and explain, I don't understand."
Touch ear: "Please be quiet. Not now. I want to hear what's going on."
Look at coach: "Help me!"

Applications to Group Work

1. Clients can receive immediate feedback during the group sessions on their self-defeating or fully functioning behaviors. A group member may, for instance, request opportunities to become more assertive in the group, and the cueing system may be used to aid her with timing or phrasing. More important, within seconds after an assertive attempt the coach can come in with a response: "Great effort! But you backed down at the end with your ingratiating smile."

2. Clients who act inappropriately or impulsively, as well as those who are attention seekers or poor reality testers, can be restrained without the embarrassment of public censure. "Now is not the time to speak about yourself. You're taking the focus off Marilyn."

3. Resistance and withdrawal in passive group members can be overcome by encouraging participation. The coach can supportively stay on the client's heels: "What are you afraid of? Tell them what *you* think."

4. Tension and anxiety can be reduced in group members afraid of taking risks: "Calm down a little. Just relax—Take a few breaths—And *then* talk—That's it—You're doing just fine."

PRINTED HANDOUTS

Fiction and nonfiction bibliotherapy has been relied on as a therapeutic adjunct for decades (Schrank & Engels, 1981). Short stories, novels, plays, even self-help books are routinely prescribed by group leaders to augment themes that arise in the course of treatment. A client experiencing career confusion may be directed to Studs Terkel's *Working*. An adolescent with difficulties may be guided to *The Diary of Anne Frank* or *Catcher in the Rye*. Creative practitioners may write original material.

Every group leader has a series of standard minilectures that are routinely delivered to groups or to specific group members when the need arises. They are sometimes introduced as teaching aids in skill training; more often they are selected from one's repertoire when required. A group member who exhibits confusion between appropriate and inappropriate emotional responses could profit from a minilecture on the anatomy of emotions—how they are caused and how they may be altered to fit a situation's natural requirements. A group member who repeatedly speaks of catastrophic failures when expectations are not fulfilled might be exposed to an educational module on the distinction between wants and needs. Many other frequently repeated subjects require the therapist to deliver sermons from time to time.

To save time, to minimize repetition, to avoid turning a therapeutic group into a classroom, and to ensure efficient quality control of crucial educational materials, the minilectures can be standardized as handouts for clients to read between sessions. Not only are group members gratified to leave each session with something tangible in their hands, but the handouts ensure that they will think in structured ways about new ideas to which they are exposed. Moreover, in many instances the written word carries more weight than the same message spoken aloud. Clients can digest written material at their own speed, mulling over stimulating areas, internalizing new ideas, re-reading confusing or novel passages.

The handouts also help to solve the recurring problem of educating loved ones about the nature of the group experience. Most group members feel some frustration in dealing with friends and lovers who have a vested interest in the changes they have initiated. Some spouses feel threatened by the increased effectiveness their partners demonstrate as a result of the group. Others may show plain curiosity and interest in progress that can be readily observed. They don't want to be left behind; some may genuinely wish to upgrade the quality of their lives as well, once they see how masterful the client has become.

Handouts brought home can give everyone in the household a clear idea of what kinds of things the group covers. Loved ones can thus grow along with the group member as they are instructed in new learnings they find intriguing. A common language develops so that seeds planted in the group can begin to sprout within the interaction patterns at home. When the group member laughs at the "approval-seeking behavior" evident in a TV character, for example, family members will "understand where he is coming from."

The content of handouts can be tailored to fit the individual requirements of any group leader's philosophy and goals. Instead of always recommending readings from whomever *your* favorite theoreticians may be, personally created fare can be prescribed. Even those who regard writing as a chore will find that producing a series of handouts for captive audiences will not only improve their communication capacities but raise their esteem among their clients as well. While specific titles will be determined by individual preference and the unique demands of group members, I find the following to be particularly useful with most groups.

- "How You Make Yourself Miserable." An overview of the most common psychological self-torture techniques. Profiles such self-defeating behaviors as worry, guilt, and fear of failure, emphasizing that most internal suffering is self-inflicted.
- "How to Get the Most from Group Experiences." Detailed instructions for capitalizing on the learning opportunities available in therapeutic groups.
- "Developing Communication Skills to Help Others." A rationale for learning to be a more effective communicator. Specific guidelines help readers to improve their interpersonal skills.
- "Art of Confrontation." Applying knowledge of how groups function and of communication techniques to two very important situations. (a) A discussion of effective and ineffective confrontative styles shows the value of constructive feedback. (b) Readers are also shown how to assert themselves without threatening others and how to accept criticism without feeling attacked.
- "Take a Productive Risk." Motivates the reader to try new things enthusiastically, to experiment with creative behaviors, and to become more socially expressive.
- "How to Get Closer to People You Love." Motivates the reader to take risks in relationships by becoming more open and sincere. The reader is helped to initiate more intensity in existing love relationships as well as to find new relationships.
- "Are You Still Alive?" An explanation of how people "kill" their valuable present moments by avoiding living intensely. Sleep is

viewed as an example of practicing for death. Suggestions are offered for sleeping less and living more.

• "What to Do When You Feel Depressed, Frustrated, Anxious, or Angry." Examines the most common negative emotions that upset internal tranquility—how these emotions arise, why they occur, how they can be controlled or virtually eliminated.

There is no limit to other titles that could be reserved for use as needed: "Becoming More Assertive," "Disciplining Children by Teaching Self-Discipline," "Why There is More than Your Symptoms," "Moving into Another Career," "A List of Books to Help You Grow," "Being More Creative," "How You Make Yourself Sick," and "What to Do after the Group is Over."

FIELD TRIPS

Elementary school counselors and child therapists have long known that the most important work they do is outside their offices, on the playgrounds, in the sandboxes, on basketball courts, or on walks through the park.

Group leaders, too, are beginning to discover the practical advantages of taking field trips with their clients in order to help them apply newly learned skills to real-life situations. Under the therapist's supervision and support, group members can receive structured practice, constructive feedback, and encounter experiences similar to those they wish to master.

As a graduation exercise in a weight-loss group, all participants met for supper in an ice cream parlor. There they practiced self-restraint while ordering from the menu, slowed the pace of their eating, and still had a leisurely, delicious, healthful meal. The group leader was present to oversee the "therapeutic experience," reminding members of concepts they had learned and the weight-loss techniques they had internalized.

A group of young adults working on debilitating shyness were escorted to a dance by their group leader. As she waited behind the scenes, gently prodding her charges to take social risks, the adolescents began to feel a bit more comfortable and less conspicuous. One young lady, rejected by a potential suitor, was quickly surrounded by assigned partners who helped her talk through her feelings and encouraged her to try again. The group leader offered valuable suggestions regarding approach techniques.

Twenty senior citizens, growing increasingly dependent in their lives, consistently relied on staff members to do their bidding and complained of feeling increasingly useless. Group sessions focused on dependency issues, confidence building, and expanding their resources. Finally, they were set loose in the city's downtown area with only $3.50 each in their pockets. Each senior had 6 hours for independent entertainment. Bus routes had to be interpreted and the money carefully budgeted so that they could find meals and keep themselves productively occupied.

In a large southwestern city racial problems within the group had aligned blacks against Hispanics against whites. Group leaders assigned four persons from each minority group to a rubber raft that would ride the rapids of the Colorado River. Unless group members learned to cooperate, put aside their differences, and function as a team, they would find their outing very uncomfortable, dangerous, wet, and cold. Each night by the campfire the group leaders ran informal discussions to help participants respect and appreciate one another's cultural differences.

A nursery school had had an outbreak of gouges and scrapes as the result of fighting between 3-year-olds. The group leader spent a day in the playground demonstrating principles of sharing and asking permission for favors. When three kids wrestled for the privilege of riding the one available tricycle, the group leader was on the scene to break things up and to initiate a session on taking turns.

A group of unemployed adults can be taken on a tour of various industries; folks with drinking problems might be taken to a bar to practice self-restraint. In all these field trips participants are offered opportunities to move realistically and to apply the insights they have gleaned from their group sessions.

INDIVIDUAL AND GROUP TREATMENT

Wender and Stein (1949) were among the first to suggest combined individual and group therapy for clients. This adjunct delivers several advantages that would not be available through the exclusive use of either modality. Individual sessions may be scheduled to supplement group work:

- as a way to monitor clients' progress and more intensely to evaluate effects
- to build courage and confidence by supportively encouraging clients to take more risks

- to keep in line clients who act inappropriately
- to reinforce and individually apply concepts from the group sessions
- to generate possible content for the group
- to vigorously work through resistances
- to allay fears and anxieties related to trust
- to offer further reality testing of ideas
- to provide more in-depth analyses of behavior and motives and psychodynamically to interpret them more comprehensively
- to hold postgroup follow-up interviews to cement cures

More common is the practice of initiating individual therapy first, later adding clients to the group. The main advantages are that pregroup preparation may help the client to clarify expectations and set goals, train him or her to extract the most from the experience, discuss ground rules, provide guidance and structure, or create a "core contract" of skills to be mastered, as Egan (1976) suggests. Occasionally, however, clients choose to begin individual therapy after the group has been in progress—perhaps to have more therapist time, to work further on a specific concern, or to work with other family members in a supplemental way.

MEDICAL INTERVENTIONS

The overlap between psychological and physiological mechanisms that account for client behaviors is often muddled. Anxiety, for example, as expressed in a group session, may take the form of tightness, tension, inhibition, jitters, or similar symptoms. Accompanying physical factors may include stomachaches, dizziness, diarrhea, sleep disorders, or increased heart rate. Further, group members who report that they are feeling anxious might also be experiencing symptoms of hyperthyroidism, hypoglycemia, tuberculosis, pheochromocytoma, or a head injury (Bockar, 1976). Likewise with depression, the causal relationships may be unclear. Is the depression resulting from a psychological problem or might there be indications of Addison's Disease or premenstrual tension?

When depression or anxiety is physically based, psychological treatments like group work are likely to be ineffective and medical adjuncts more appropriate. For example, antianxiety psychotropic drugs such as Librium, Valium, Dalmane, and other benzodiazepines can be used to alter chemically a client's limbic system and subsequent behavior (Hare & Levis, 1981). Recently, vitamin therapy has used diet supplements to help clients stabilize certain mood states.

Though we have no way of knowing at this time whether vitamin therapy or diet alterations will make any significant difference in clients' lives, group leaders are turning more toward regular exercise programs as therapeutic adjuncts. In addition to the aerobic benefits of increasing circulation, reducing cholesterol levels and the risk of arteriosclerosis, exercises such as running are believed to provide a soothing balm for the soul. Group members often report a heightened sense of well-being, greater self-confidence, and increased vigor. They claim they feel better about themselves when their bodies are in shape. They sleep better and feel more relaxed during the working day. Group leaders are therefore likely to continue prescribing exercise routines and healthful eating habits as a way of life.

Each of the adjunct techniques described in this chapter offers clients productive means to continue their growth between group sessions. In fact, the more time that can be therapeutically programmed, the faster desired changes are likely to occur.

CHAPTER 15

Common Unethical Behaviors*

It is common for a book of this sort to close with a chapter on ethics. Practitioners are usually admonished to watch their p's and q's, stay out of trouble, and follow the described guidelines (see Van Hoose &. Kottler, 1977; Gazda, 1978; and Corey, Corey, &. Callanan, 1979, for examples). Clinicians are urged to study their ethical codes, familiarize themselves with relevant law, debate issues with colleagues, and closely monitor their behavior as well as the actions of peers, since ethics are virtually unenforceable from external sources (Kottler, 1978b). After all the hoopla and threats are over, professional organizations, licensing boards, and courts can do very little to scrutinize what goes on within the privacy of a therapist's office— unless, of course, a complaint is filed. Even then, it is quite difficult to do anything to halt the destructive behavior.

The advanced group leader is, on the basis of greater experience, expected to demonstrate a far more acute sense of ethics than those with less experience. No longer can we claim to be acting responsibly just because we aren't breaking any laws or professional codes. Ethics are not all-or-none phenomena, no matter what the judges and Moral Majority would like us to believe. Most of the field, and most attention, is directed toward the grosser forms of misconduct—sexual impropriety, breach of confidentiality, incompetence, negligence, and malpractice.

Professionals are indignant when a colleague is caught doing something inappropriate. An attitude prevails that ethics apply to "them," not "us." Yet we *all* act unethically at times. All of us in the field of group leadership are human beings prone to biases and weaknesses, vulnerable to deception and deceit on a small scale. Occasionally we make mistakes. To bring ethics into greater focus for

*This chapter is an expanded version from *Journal for Specialists in Groupwork.* Vol. 7, No. 3 Reprinted by permission of the American Personnel and Guidance Association.

group leaders, this chapter closes the book with a discussion of common unethical behaviors that usually go unchecked.

Ethics are of particular importance to group leaders because of the special problems that group work presents. As noted throughout the book, these problems make the practitioner vulnerable to error.

1. Verbal abuse and subsequent casualties are more likely to occur in groups than in individual treatment.
2. The therapist has less control over proceedings and client behavior. Potentially more things can go wrong before the leader can intervene.
3. The therapist has more control in influencing capabilities, a power that can be used for better or for worse.
4. Confidentiality can neither be guaranteed nor enforced because other group members don't necessarily live by the same moral code that we do.
5. Many group leaders practice without benefit of training, education, or supervision. There are no standardized criteria for acceptable qualifications. In the same city, a psychiatrist, psychologist, astrologer, palm reader, and prostitute can all label their professional activities as "group therapy."
6. Because groups are such intense environments, the risks for each member are greater. Change *and* damage are accelerated.
7. The screening of clients is frequently haphazard. Clients are often required to participate in the experience involuntarily.
8. Group work presents special re-entry problems for participants when the sessions have ended.
9. Dependency effects are more pronounced in groups.
10. There is no licensure, certification, or regulation that can effectively enforce the practice of responsible group leadership.

ONE ISSUE IN DEPTH

One ethical issue that has disturbed social philosophers for centuries has great relevance for contemporary group leaders—the innate conflict between the coercive force of groups and the individual autonomy of each member. Once people decide to pool their resources and work toward a common purpose, individual needs are necessarily shelved in favor of what is good for the majority. This compromise ensures that none of us gets exactly what we want, although most people get a little bit of what they are willing to accept. Our children are taught early in their education the values of cooperation, compromise, and sharing. Independent spirit, personal freedom, individual identity are diminished for the sake of serving the common good. Indeed, we would have chaos and anarchy without subjugating selfish interests for the benefit of human welfare.

Unfortunately, the indoctrination of The One by The Many has been only too successful. Human beings now live totally in a world of groups, alone only when in the bathroom. Marriages are often interpreted as a melding of lives. The family unit, the PTA, the bowling team, the nation, neighborhood, country club, professional organization, school, employer, religion, all provide a group identity—a "we" that we can believe in.

The structure of the universe easily diminishes egocentricity. To look up at the stars is to confront our insignificance. Even on this tiny planet, biologists, zoologists, and ethnologists tell us of the ultimate irrelevance of a single life. We are like ants, part of a total human society that makes us expendable at the whim of a crushing footstep.

> Ants are so much like human beings as to be an embarrassment. They farm fungi, raise aphids as livestock, launch armies into wars, use chemical sprays to alarm and confuse enemies, capture slaves. The families of weaver ants engage in child labor, holding their larvae like shuttles to spin out the thread that sews the leaves together for their fungus gardens. They exchange information ceaselessly. They do everything but watch television (Thomas, 1974, p. 12).

Lecturing to philosophy students at Columbia University, William James noted that *unity* has always been considered more important than *variety*. Mathematicians are constantly looking for common denominators, scientists for parsimonious principles, physicists for the reduction of matter into unifying laws, and philosophers for a vision of the world's unity. This preoccupation with oneness to the exclusion of manyness pervades all circles of intellectual achievement. Yet, as James asked, even though we pretend there is unity to the world, a cherished camaraderie of abstractions, "What is the practical value of the oneness for *us?* (James, 1907, p. 29).

Always the empiricist, the pragmatist concerned with logical consequences, James investigated the meaning of unity. Does it really exist? Is it possible? Is it desirable? If there is a Oneness, it would have the following characteristics.

1. Nothing is omitted. Everyone and everything is included, with no exception.

2. There is a total union of parts. Everything is connected, hung together, continuous.
3. The lines of influence among parts of the whole can be identified. The conductors form an unbreakable chain.
4. There is a single, absolute causal unity responsible for the actions of many.
5. There is unity of purpose and a set of common goals.

In sum, if unity were possible, the history of the world could be told as one story. But such is obviously not the case; no two objects, much less persons, are identical. Monozygotic twins and precision die-cut instruments may appear alike but actually have minute individual differences. Such concepts as *the average* and *differences* describe general behavior rather than the actions of any single person. There is *similarity* of purpose, even cooperation, among living human beings with regard to collective intentions, yet individual goals are perpetually at war with one another.

There is no group of people, no matter how homogeneous in values, religious beliefs, background, or presenting problems, that satisfies the monistic conditions enumerated earlier. The ethical issue for group leaders, then, is to capitalize on the therapeutic advantages of group settings while simultaneously protecting individual rights and values, a difficult proposition for even the most clear-headed philosopher/scientist.

SLIGHTLY UNETHICAL BEHAVIORS

Sheldon Kopp solicited testimony from a number of prominent therapists concerning their most embarrassing mistakes. The contributions collectively portrayed the clinician as a fallible being, a wise fool, a person who acts "just plain silly from time to time" (Kopp, 1976, p. 222). The ethical transgressions (admittedly minor) they reported included developing inappropriate social relationships with clients, deliberately lying to save face (and getting caught), acting seductively, and accepting clients who cannot really be helped. But there are many other "slightly unethical" behaviors that we commonly engage in without a moment's hesitation.

Little White Lies
"No pressure will be put on you to participate unless you want to."

Like "the check is in the mail," this is one of the great lies of our time. Though I never begin a group without making that claim, I must later admit honestly that no matter how earnestly I attempt to protect each member's rights, incredible pressure—subtle, unconscious, sneaky, and overt—will be imposed on those reluctant to get involved. Occasionally we will jump on the bandwagon, temporarily ignoring our previous promise, and use all our skills to manipulate reluctant clients to join in, even against their will. Are we excused from such transgressions? Certainly. We're only human. But copping a plea doesn't diminish the nature of an essentially unethical act.

There are constant tugs on every member to conform, to contribute, to be a regular guy or gal, and there are good reasons why we underplay these forces, attempting to reassure clients that their privacy will be respected. Realistically, we couldn't even begin a group without convincing participants that their freedom of choice will be encouraged. Nevertheless, is lying for the clients' own good strictly a moral act?

"Nothing you say will leave this room."

Another distortion that is necessary if any work is to be done, confidentiality cannot be enforced in a group (Davis & Meara, 1982). No matter what safeguards are taken, no matter how carefully we button our lips, no matter how much we emphasize the importance of privileged communication, someone will slip up. Some clients will inadvertently disclose confidential information during a mindless moment while others will deliberately run home with a bucket full of juicy details to spill. To be truly honest and aboveboard, we would have to report to our groups: "There is every reason to believe that any secret you share in here, any private thought you disclose, will be privy only to the people you see here. And oh yes, perhaps a few of their spouses and friends. And perhaps a few others who overhear—"

"I neither like nor dislike you; you're a client."

Inevitably some group members will ask directly how we feel about them. Recognizing the dangers of saying what we really think (whether positive or negative), we pretend that we don't feel at all. And most of the time, during sessions, we do guard against allowing our personal feelings to get in the way of therapeutic actions. Again, however, the therapeutic options are limited.

First, if we respond honestly, we risk being seductive if the feelings are positive or being perceived as hostile if the feelings are negative. Second, we could employ therapeutic maneuvers #4208 ("How would that be helpful for me to tell you?"), #4209 ("What difference would it make to you?"), or #4210 ("I'm sorry. I didn't hear you. Does anyone else have something to say?"). Third, we could share our problem: "I feel uncomfortable telling you my feelings because then I compromise my neutrality." But members might wonder why they should be honest when their leader is so evasive. Each of these responses creates potential problems we would prefer to leave alone. So, instead, we resort to little white lies—"but it's for their own good"—though not altogether certain that the excuse is valid.

"I bet your mother was a meticulous housekeeper."

How often we make interpretations, not to help the client, but to check out the accuracy of our predictions at the expense of wasting valuable group time. We formulate a hunch about why people act as they do, and, though this hypothesis may be completely unrelated to what the group members are currently working through, we broadcast the interpretation and smugly await confirmation. We feel good because our investigative skills have once again proved accurate, but the whole episode is merely an exercise in self-indulgence.

"I remember a time when—"

Inappropriate self-disclosure is another way in which group leaders focus on themselves at the cost of valuable time. Unless a therapist has a specific, defensible rationale, sharing personal stories is likely to be digressive. Each time a group leader engages in a long-winded anecdote which is not specifically intended to deliver an important message or to help a group member work through the presenting concern, the action is unethical in that it negates the clients' importance and wastes time (Van Hoose & Kottler, 1977).

Facilitative self-disclosure that is well timed and appropriately implemented satisfies certain criteria mentioned by Corey, Corey, and Callanan (1979): How crucial is it that group members perceive you as being human? What specific intentions do you have for revealing your personal life? How might clients' progress be hindered as the result of your self-disclosure? Only after these questions are addressed may the group leader be reasonably certain that self-disclosing interventions are indicated.

"I know I can help you."

In an effort to implant favorable expectations for success, we sometimes exaggerate what we can deliver. Although uncertain that we can keep our promises, we believe that such claims are necessary to keep up morale. Group members enjoy hearing this little lie. They desperately want optimistic assessments. In the same way that a physician prescribes a placebo, saying "I believe this will make you feel better," we justify our own little deceits.

"I wonder what would happen if I tried—"

Another ethical conflict centers on using clients as guinea pigs to practice an experimental treatment procedure. Are we justified in trying out new technologies before we are sure they are safe and before we've had sufficient supervision in their execution? After returning from a workshop or course or following the end of a book such as this, many new therapeutic ideas float in our heads, itching to be applied. After all, we cannot determine what an idea is worth until we try it out for ourselves. But where do we experiment? Can we counsel a group of white rats and then observe their behavior before trying out a procedure on human subjects? Do we wear warning stickers on our foreheads reading "Caution. The surgeon general has determined that these procedures may be hazardous to your health."?

The only viable alternative to stagnation is to experiment with new group strategies cautiously and critically, fully aware that they may not work out as intended. "Group work is a risky business anyway" we reason. "If the technique doesn't do the job, we won't use it again in similar circumstances. Let's just hope that no one is hurt too badly."

"If you work hard enough, you can be like me when you grow up."

Are we justified in creating miniature disciples, surrogate selves? So much of what constitutes group work involves great potential for clients to become dependent on the leader or on the group process. Many "groupies" do become addicted to group work, unable to function without a support system. Alcoholics Anonymous, for instance, operates on just that premise—that members must become as addicted to A.A. meetings as they used to be on their liquor.

If we are honest, we admit that some of us deliberately create dependencies in clients by sending out clear messages: "You *need* me to function. You can't get along without this group. This will take years of intensive treatment. By the way, do you have Blue Cross Insurance?" On a smaller scale, most of us sometimes see clients longer than is absolutely necessary, particularly professionals whose livelihood depends on client fees. It may be rationalized that *anyone* can profit from a group experience, no matter how long he or she attends the sessions. But there is usually a point of diminishing returns when a group member's cash investment results in nothing but greater dependency on the leader.

"Everybody in this group will be treated equally."

The U.S. Constitution guarantees that all people, regardless of age, sex, race, religion, appearance, and hair style, will have equal status. In reality, however, human beings have definite preferences as to the sort of people they would like to be around, and group leaders are no different. We like group members who are sexually attractive, who think as we do, and who come from similar backgrounds. In spite of our restraint, we may give more attention to those who smile and laugh more often at our jokes. Although we attempt to hide our biases, there are some in the group to whom we give less of our time and patience. In short, it is no more possible to treat all clients alike than it is for parents to love all their children equally.

Inevitably, we all act unethically because we are all imperfect beings, inconsistent, hypocritical. We muddle in the dark doing our best to be genuinely helpful but knowing that we can't possibly please everyone all the time. This confession can only be admitted by pragmatic group leaders who need no longer prove their competence.

> How does a doctor recognize the point in time when he is finally a "surgeon"? As my years as chief resident drew to a close I asked myself the question on more than one occasion.
>
> The answer, I concluded, was self-confidence. When you can say to yourself, "There is no surgical patient I cannot treat competently, treat just as well or better than any other surgeon"—then, and not until then, you are indeed a surgeon (Nolan, 1968, p. 278).

The experienced and pragmatic group leader understands that naked confidence, a well-integrated ego, a few primitive helping skills, and a strong sense of ethical conviction are about all that is necessary to practice this craft. Legislating more stringent laws to enforce competence, more specific ethical codes to regulate behavior, peer monitoring, review boards, licensing exams, and other external watchdogs—such efforts are sometimes used as a smoke screen to convince the public that we are trying to police our own ranks rather than actually deterring unethical behavior.

Ethical codes and laws are all very fine for publishing in professional journals, hanging on walls, or presenting to graduate students. There is understandably great confusion about to whom the group leader is primarily responsible when there are conflicting demands. Professional codes, institutional policies, legislative mandates, state and federal laws, peer practices, societal expectations, institutional policies, client needs and their parent's wishes all have legitimate claims. The awesome reality of group leadership is that, ultimately, practitioners must answer to themselves for their actions.

REFERENCES

Adams, H. B. "Mental illness" or interpersonal behavior? *American Psychologist,* 1964, *19,* 191–197.

Adams, H. E., Doster, J. A., & Calhoun, D. S. A psychologically based system of response classification. In A. R. Ciminero, K. S. Calhoun, & H. E. Adams (Eds.), *Handbook of behavioral assessment.* New York: John Wiley & Sons, 1977.

Alexander, F. G., & Selesnick, S. T. *The history of psychiatry.* New York: Mentor, 1966.

Allan, E. E. Multiple attending in therapy groups. *Personnel and Guidance Journal,* January 1982, 318–320.

Allen, W. *Without feathers.* New York: Warner Books, 1976.

American Psychiatric Association. *Diagnostic and statistical manual of mental disorders* (3rd ed.). Washington, D.C.: American Psychiatric Association, 1980.

Andolfi, M. Prescribing the families' own dysfunctional rules as a therapeutic strategy. *Journal of Marital and Family Therapy,* 1980, *6*(1), 29–36.

Anthony, C. P., & Thibodeau, G. A. *Textbook of anatomy and physiology* (10th ed.). St. Louis: C. V. Mosby, 1979.

Ardrey, R. *The territorial imperative.* New York: Delta, 1966.

Argyris, C. Theories of action that inhibit individual learning. *American Psychologist,* 1976, 638–654.

Argyris, C., & Schon, D. *Theory in practice: Increasing professional effectiveness.* San Francisco: Jossey-Bass, 1974.

Asch, S. E. Effects of group pressure upon the modification and distortion of judgements. In H. Guetzkow (Ed.), *Groups, leadership, and men.* Pittsburgh: Carnegie Press, 1951.

Austin, A. V. Standards of measurement. *Scientific American,* March 1968, 50–63.

Ayer, A. J. *Language, truth, and logic.* New York: Dover Publications, 1952.

Bach, G. R. *Intensive group therapy.* New York: Ronald Press, 1954.

Back, K. W. *Beyond words: The story of sensitivity training and the encounter movement.* New York: Russell Sage Foundation, 1972.

Bakker, C. B. Why people don't change. *Psychotherapy: Theory, Research, and Practice,* 1975, *12*(2), 164–172.

Bales, R. *Personality and interpersonal behavior.* New York: Holt, Rinehart & Winston, 1970.

Balgopal, P. R., & Hull, R. F. Keeping secrets: Group resistance for patients and therapists. *Psychotherapy: Theory, Research, and Practice,* 1970, *11*(4), 559–606.

Bandler, R., & Grinder, J. *The structure of magic* (Vol. 1). Palo Alto, Calif.: Science & Behavior Books, 1975.

Bandler, R., & Grinder, J. *Frogs into princes.* Moab, Utah: Real People Press, 1979.

Bandura, A. *Principles of behavior modification.* New York: Holt, Rinehart & Winston, 1969.

Bandura, A.   Psychotherapy based upon modeling principles. In A. Bergin & S. Garfield (Eds.), *Handbook of psychotherapy and behavior change*. New York: John Wiley & Sons, 1971.

Bandura, A.   *Social learning theory*. Englewood Cliffs, N.J.: Prentice-Hall, 1977.

Bandura, A., Jeffrey, R. W., & Gajdos, E.   Generalizing change through participant modeling with self-directed mastery. *Behavior Research and Therapy*, 1975, *13*, 141−152.

Baron, R. S., Moore, D., & Sanders, G. S.   Distraction as a source of drive in social facilitation research. *Journal of Personality and Social Psychology*, 1978, *36*, 816−824.

Bateson, G., Jackson, D. D., Haley, J., and Weakland, J.   Toward a theory of schizophrenia. *Behavioral Science*, 1956, *1*(4), 251−264.

Bateson, G.   *Mind and Nature*, New York: Bantam Books, 1977.

Bateson, G., & Jackson D. D.   Some varieties of pathogenic organization. In D. D. Jackson (Ed.), *Communication, family and marriage*. Palo Alto, Calif.: Science & Behavior Books, 1968.

Bayless, O. L.   An alternative pattern for problem-solving discussion. *Journal of Communication*, 1967, *17*, 188−197.

Beck, A. T.   *Cognitive therapy and the emotional disorders*. New York: International Universities Press, 1976.

Bednar, R. L., Melnick, J., & Kaul, T. J.   Risk, responsibility, and structure: A conceptual framework for initiating group counseling and psychotherapy. *Journal of Counseling Psychology*, 1974, *21*(1), 31−37.

Begelman, D. A.   Behavioral classification. In M. Herson & A. E. Bellack (Eds.), *Behavioral assessment: A practical handbook*. New York: Pergamon Press, 1976.

Bem, D. J., Wallach, M. A., & Kogan, N.   Group decision making under risk of adversive consequences. *Journal of Personality and Social Psychology*, 1965, *1*, 453−460.

Benjamin, A.   *Behavior in small groups*. Boston: Houghton Mifflin, 1978.

Benshoff, D. L.   A lesson "Psycholese" or how to "get a feel for" where your "helper" is "coming from." *Personnel and Guidance Journal*, November 1978, 164−166.

Bern, D. J.   The concept of risk in the study of human behavior. In R. E. Carney (Ed.), *Risk-Taking Behavior*. Springfield, Ill.: C. C. Thomas, 1971.

Berne, E.   *Principles of group treatment*. New York: Oxford University Press, 1966.

Bettelheim, B.   *The informed heart*. New York: Avon Books, 1960.

Betz, R. L., Wilbur, M. P., & Roberts-Wilbur, J.   A structural blueprint for group facilitators: Three group modalities. *Personnel and Guidance Journal*, September 1981, 31−37

Bierce, A.   *The devil's dictionary*. New York: Dover Publications, 1940. (Originally published, 1911.)

Blake, R. R., & Mouton, J. S.   The fifth achievement. *Journal of Applied Behavioral Science*, 1970, *6*, 413−426.

Bockar, J. A.   *Primer for the nonmedical psychotherapist*. New York: Spectrum Publications, 1976.

Bolan, R. S.   The practitioner as theorist: The phenomenology of the professional episode. *Journal of the American Planning Association*, 1980, *46*(3), 261−274.

Bombeck, E.   *The grass is always greener over the septic tank*. Greenwich, Conn.: Fawcett Publications, 1972.

Bowers, W. A., & Gauron, E. F.   Potential hazards of the co-therapy relationship. *Psychotherapy: Theory, Research and Practice,* 1981, *18*(2), 225−228.

Bradford, L., Gibb, J. R., & Benne, K. D.   *T-group theory and laboratory method: Innovation in re-education.* New York: John Wiley & Sons, 1964.

Bronowski, J.   *The ascent of man.* Boston: Little, Brown & Co., 1973.

Brown, R.   *Social Psychology.* New York: Free Press, 1965.

Brown, R. W.   Choosing and evaluating group techniques: A systematic framework. *Journal for Specialists in Group Work,* 1978, *3*(3), 146−153.

Bruner, J. S.   *The Process of Education,* New York: Vintage, 1963.

Byrd, R. E.   *A guide to personal risk taking.* New York: AMACOM, 1974.

Cantela, J. R.   The present status of covert modeling. *Journal of Behavior Therapy and Experimental Psychiatry,* 1976, *6,* 323; 326.

Caputo, P.   *Horn of Africa.* New York: Dell Publishing Co., 1980.

Carr, S. J., & Dabbs, J. J., Jr.   The effects of lighting, distance, and intimacy of topic on verbal and visual behavior. *Sociometry,* 1974, *37,* 592−600.

Cartwright, D.   Achieving change in people: Some applications of group dynamics theory. *Human Relations,* 1951, *4,* 381−392.

Cartwright, D., & Zanders, A.   *Group dynamics: Research and theory.* New York: Harper & Row, 1968.

Cattell, R. B.   Concepts and methods in the measurement of group syntality. *Psychological Review,* 1948, *55,* 48−63.

Cattell, R. B.   Psychological theory and scientific method. In R. B. Cattell (Ed.), *Handbook of multivariate experimental psychology.* Chicago: Rand McNally, 1966.

Charney, I. W.   Why are so many (if not really all) people and families disturbed? *Journal of Marital and Family Therapy,* 1980, *6*(1), 37−48.

Chessick, R. D.   *Great ideas in psychotherapy.* New York: Jason Aronson, 1977.

Clark, C. H.   *Brainstorming.* New York: Doubleday, 1958.

Clark, R. D., III.   Group-induced shift toward risk: A critical appraisal. *Psychological Bulletin,* 1971. *76,* 251−270.

Cohen, A. M., & Smith, R. D.   *The critical incident in growth groups: Theory and technique.* La Jolla, Calif.: University Associates, 1976.

Cohn, B.   Absentee-cuing: A technical innovation in the training of group counselors. *Educational Technology,* 1973, *13*(2), 61−62.

Cole, H. P., & Sarnoff, D.   Creativity and counseling. *Personnel and Guidance Journal,* November 1980, 140−146.

Cooper, C. L., & Mangham, I. L. (Eds.).   *T-groups: A survey of research.* London: Wiley-Interscience, 1971.

Cooper, I. S.   *The Vital Probe.* New York: W. W. Norton, 1981.

Corey, G.   *I never knew I had a choice* (2nd ed.). Monterey, Calif.: Brooks/Cole, 1982.

Corey, G.   *The theory and practice of group counseling.* Monterey, Calif.: Brooks/Cole, 1981.

Corey, G., & Corey, M. S.   *Groups: Process and practice.* Monterey, Calif.: Brooks/Cole, 1977.

Corey, G., Corey, M. S., & Callanan, P.   *Professional and ethical issues in counseling and psychotherapy.* Monterey, Calif.: Brooks/Cole, 1979.

Corey, G., Corey, M. S., Callanan, P. J., & Russell, J. M.   *Group techniques.* Monterey, Calif.: Brooks/Cole, 1982.

Cormier, W. H., & Cormier, L. S. *Interviewing strategies for helpers.* Monterey, Calif.: Brooks/Cole, 1979.

Corsini, R. *Methods of group Psychotherapy.* New York: McGraw-Hill, 1957.

Cozby, P. C. Self-disclosure: A literature review. *Psychological Bulletin,* 1973, *79,* 73—91.

Csikszentmihalyi, M. *Beyond boredom and anxiety.* San Francisco: Jossey-Bass, 1975.

Davis, F., & Lohr, N. Special problems with the use of co-therapists in group psychotherapy. *International Journal of Group Psychotherapy,* 1971, *2,* 143—157.

Davis, K. L., & Meara, D. M. So you think it's a secret. *Journal for Specialists in Group Work,* 1982, *1,* 3.

Della Corte, M. Psychobabble: Why we do it. *Psychotherapy: Theory, Research, and Practice,* 1980, *17*(3), 281—284.

Dewey, J. The bearings of pragmatism on education. *Progressive Journal of Education,* January 1909, 5—8.

Dewey, J. *Logic: The theory of Inquiry.* New York: Holt, Rinehart, & Winston, 1938.

Diedrich, R. C., & Dye, H. A. (Eds.). *Group procedures: Purposes, processes, and outcomes.* Boston: Houghton Mifflin, 1972.

DiLoreto, A. O. *Comparative psychotherapy.* Chicago: Aldine-Atherton, 1971.

Dimond, R. E., Havens, R. A., & Jones, A. C. A conceptual framework for the practice of prescriptive eclecticism in psychotherapy. *American Psychologist,* 1978, *33*(3), 239—248.

Donleavy, J. P. *The unexpurgated code.* New York: Delta, 1975.

Dostoyevsky, F. *Notes from the underground.* In *Three short novels of Dostoyevsky.* Garden City, N.Y.: Anchor Books, 1960. (Originally published, 1864.)

Dreikurs, R. *Group psychotherapy and group approaches: The collected papers of Rudolf Dreikurs.* Chicago: Alfred Adler Institute, 1960.

Dunn, Marian E., & Dickes, R. Erotic issues in co-therapy. *Journal of Sex and Marital Therapy,* 1977, *3*(3), 205—211.

Durkin, H. E. *The group in depth.* New York: International Universities Press, 1964.

Dyer, W. W. *Your erroneous zones.* New York: Funk & Wagnalls, 1976.

Dyer, W. W., & Vriend, J. Effective group counseling process interventions. *Educational Technology,* 1973, *13*(1), 61—67. (a)

Dyer, W. W., & Vriend, J. Role-working in group counseling. *Educational Technology,* 1973, *13*(2), 32—36. (b)

Dyer, W. W., & Vriend, J. *Counseling techniques that work.* New York: Funk & Wagnalls, 1977.

Dyer, W. W., & Vriend, J. *Group counseling for personal mastery.* New York: Sovereign Books, 1980.

Edwards, W. The theory of decision making. *Psychological Bulletin,* 1954, *51,* 380—417.

Egan, G. *Interpersonal living: A skills/contract approach to human-relations training in groups.* Monterey, Calif.: Brooks/Cole, 1976.

Einhorn, J. On sufism, sufi group study, and group leadership, *Journal for Specialists in Group Work,* 1979, *4*(3), 140—147.

Ellerbroek, W. C. Language, thought, and disease. *Co-Evolution Quarterly,* Spring 1978, 30—38.

Ellis, A.   *Humanistic psychotherapy: The rational-emotive approach.* New York: McGraw-Hill, 1974.

Ellis, A.   The basic clinical theory of rational-emotive therapy. In A. Ellis & R. Grieger (Eds.), *Handbook of rational-emotive therapy.* New York: Springer, 1977. (a)

Ellis, A.   Fun as psychotherapy. In A. Ellis & R. Grieger (Eds.), *Handbook of rational-emotive therapy.* New York: Springer, 1977. (b)

Ellis, A., & Harper, R.   *A new guide to rational living.* Englewood Cliffs, N.J.: Prentice-Hall, 1975.

Epstein, N., Jayne-Lazarus, C., & De Giovanni, I. S.   Co-trainers as models of relationships: Effects of the outcome of couples therapy. *Journal of Marital and Family Therapy,* 1979, 53—60.

Erickson, M. H.   Further techniques of hypnosis: Utilization techniques. In Jay Haley (ed.). *Advanced techniques of hypnosis and therapy.* New York: Grune & Stratton, 1967. (a)

Erickson, M. H.   The method employed to formulate a complex story for the induction of the experimental neurosis. In J. Haley (ed), *Advanced techniques of Hypnosis and Therapy.* New York: Grune & Stratton, 1967. (b)

Erickson, M. H.   Spellbinders: Entrancing tales of a master hypnotist. *Psychology Today,* February 1982, 39—45.

Erikson, E.   *Childhood and society* (2nd ed.). New York: W.W. Norton, 1963.

Eysenck, H. J.   The effects of psychotherapy: An evaluation. *Journal of Consulting Psychology,* 1952, *16,* 319—324.

Eysenck, H. J.   The effects psychotherapy. *Journal of Psychology,* 1965, *1,* 97—118.

Eysenck, H. J.   The logical basis of factor analysis. In D. N. Jackson & S. Messick (Eds.), *Problems in human assessment.* New York: McGraw-Hill, 1967.

Farb, P.   *Word play: What happens when people talk.* New York: Alfred A. Knopf, 1974.

Feder, B., & Ronall, R. (Eds.).   *Beyond the hot seat: Gestalt approaches to group work.* New York: Brunner/Mazel, 1980.

Festinger, L., Pepitone, A., & Newcomb, T.   Some consequences of deindividualization in a group. *Journal of Abnormal and Social Psychology,* 1952, *47,* 382—389.

Fiè
ve, R. R.   *Moodswing: The third revolution in psychiatry.* New York: Bantam Books, 1975.

Fish, J.   *Placebo therapy.* San Francisco: Jossey-Bass, 1973.

Flanagan, J. C.   The critical incident technique. *Psychological Bulletin,* 1954, *51*(4), 327—358.

Flowers, J. V., Booraem, C. D., & Hartman, K. A.   Client improvement on higher and lower intensity problems as a function of group cohesiveness. *Psychotherapy: Theory, Research, and Practice,* 1981, *18*(2), 246—258.

Foley, W. J., & Bonney, W. C.   A developmental model for counseling groups. *Personnel and Guidance Journal,* 1966, 576—580.

Foot, H. C., & Chapman, A. J.   The social responsiveness of young children in humorous situations. In A. J. Chapman & H. C. Foot (Eds.), *Humor and laughter: Theory, research, and applications.* London: John Wiley & Sons, 1976.

Ford, D. H., & Urban, H. B.   *Systems of psychotherapy.* New York: John Wiley & Sons, 1976.

Forer, B. R.   Therapeutic relationships in groups. In A. Burton (Ed.), *Encounter.* San Francisco: Jossey-Bass, 1970.

Foster, J. A.   Humor and counseling: Close encounters of another kind. *Personnel and Guidance Journal*, September 1980, 46—49.

Foulkes, S. H., & Anthony, E. J.   *Group psychotherapy: The psychoanalytic approach* (2nd ed.). Baltimore: Penguin Books, 1965.

Frank, J.   *Persuasion and healing.* Baltimore: Johns Hopkins University Press, 1961.

Frankl, V.   *The unheard cry for meaning.* New York: Simon & Schuster, 1978.

Freud, S.   Inhibitions, symptoms, and anxiety. *Standard Edition*, 20:77—175. London: Hogarth Press, 1926.

Freud, S.   *Group psychology and the analysis of the ego.* New York: Liveright, 1959.

Freud, S.   *Jokes and their relation to the unconscious.* New York: W. W. Norton, 1960.

Frey, D. E.   Understanding and managing conflict. In S. Eisenberg & L. E. Patterson (Eds.), *Helping clients with special concerns.* Chicago: Rand McNally, 1979.

Frey, D. H.   Conceptualizing counseling theories: A content analysis of process and goal statements. *Counseling Education and Supervision*, 1972, *11*, 143—150.

Frey, D. H.   Science and the single case in counseling research. *Personnel and Guidance Journal*, 1978, 263—268.

Galloghy, V., & Levine, B.   Co-therapy. In B. Levine (Ed.), *Group psychotherapy: Practice and development.* Englewood Cliffs, N.J.: Prentice-Hall, 1979.

Gans, R.   The use of group co-therapists in the teaching of psychotherapy. *American Journal of Psychotherapy*, 1957, *11*, 618—625.

Gans, R.   Group co-therapists and the therapeutic situation: A critical evaluation. *International Journal of Group Pscyhotherapy*, 1962, *12*, 82—88.

Garfield, S. L., & Kurtz, R.   Clinical psychologists in the 1970s. *American Psychologist*, 1976, *31*, 1—9.

Garfield, S. L., & Kurtz, R.   A study of eclectic views. *Journal of Consulting and Clinical Psychology*, 1977, *45*, 78—83.

Gazda, G. M. (Ed.).   *Basic approaches to group psychotherapy and counseling* (2nd ed.). Springfield, Ill.: C.C. Thomas, 1975.

Gazda, G. M.   *Group counseling: A developmental approach* (2nd ed.). Boston: Allyn & Bacon, 1978.

Geis, H. J.   Effectively leading a group in the present moment: A highly artistic, probabilistic, and professional task if one would by-pass traditional myths about group work. *Educational Technology*, 1973, *13*(2), 10—20.

Getty, C., & Shannon, A. M.   Co-therapy as an egalitarian relationship. *American Journal of Nursing*, 1969, *69*(4), 767—771.

Giedt, F. H.   Predicting suitability for group psychotherapy. *American Journal of Psychotherapy*, 1961, *16*, 582—591.

Gill, S. J., & Barry, R. A.   Group-focused counseling: Classifying the essential skills. *Personnel and Guidance Journal*, January 1982, 302—305.

Glass, D. C., Singer, J. E., & Friedman, L. N.   Psychic cost of adaptation to an environmental stressor. *Journal of Personality and Social Psychology*, 1969, *12* 200—210.

Glasser, W., & Iverson, N.   *Reality therapy in large group counseling.* Los Angeles: Reality Press, 1966.

Glossop, R. J.   *Philosophy: An Introduction to its Problems and Vocabulary.* New York: Dell Publishing Co., 1974.

Goldberg, C., & Goldberg, M. C.   *The human circle: An existential approach to the new group therapies.* Chicago: Nelson-Hall, 1973.

Goldberg, M. L., Passow, A. H., & Justman, J.   *The effects of ability grouping.* New York: Teachers College Press, 1966.

Goldfried, M. R.   Toward the delineation of therapeutic change principles. *American Psychologist,* 1980, *35*(11), 991—999.

Goldfried, M. R., & Goldfried, A. P.   Cognitive change methods. In F. H. Kanfer & A. P. Goldstein (Eds.), *Helping people change.* New York: Pergamon Press, 1980.

Goldman, M.   A comparison of individual and group performance for varying combinations of initial ability. *Journal of Personality and Social Psychology,* 1965, *1,* 210—216.

Goertzel, V., & Goertzel, M. G.   *Cradles of Eminence.* Boston: Little, Brown, 1962.

Goertzel, M. G., Goertzel, V., & Goertzel, T. G.   *300 Eminent Personalities.* San Francisco: Jossey-Bass, 1978.

Goldstein, A. P., Heller, K., & Sechrest, L. B.   *Psychotherapy and the psychology of behavior change.* New York: John Wiley & Sons, 1966.

Goodchilds, J. D.   On being witty: Causes, correlates, and consequences. In J. H. Goldstein and P. E. McGhee (Eds.), *The psychology of humor.* New York: Academic Press, 1972.

Gordon, D.   *Therapeutic Metaphor.* Cupertino, Calif., Meta Publications, 1978.

Gorsuch, R. L.   *Factor analysis.* Philadelphia: W. B. Saunders, 1974.

Gottman, J. and Leiblum, S.,   *How to do psychotherapy and how to evaluate it.* New York: Holt, Rinehart, and Winston, 1974.

Gottschalk, L. A.   Psychoanalytic notes on T-groups at the Human Relations Laboratory, Bethel, Maine. *Comprehensive Psychiatry,* 1966, *7,* 472—487.

Greenberg, D.   *How to make yourself miserable.* New York: Random House, 1966.

Greenwald, H.   *Direct decision therapy.* San Diego: Edits, 1973.

Greenwald, H.   Humor in psychotherapy. *Journal of Contemporary Psychotherapy,* 1975, *7*(2), 113—116.

Grieger, R., & Boyd, J.   Psychotherapeutic responses to some critical incidents in RET. In A. Ellis & R. Grieger (Eds.), *Handbook of rational-emotive therapy.* New York: Springer, 1977.

Gurman, A. S., & Kniskern, D. P.   Research on marital and family therapy. In S. L. Garfield & A. E. Bergin (Eds.), *Handbook of psychotherapy and behavior change.* New York: John Wiley & Sons, 1978.

Guttmacher, J. A., & Birk, L.   Group therapy: What specific advantages? *Comprehensive Psychiatry,* 1971, *12,* 546—556.

Haley, J.   *Uncommon therapy.* New York: Grune & Stratton, 1968.

Haley, J.   *Problem-solving therapy.* San Francisco: Jossey-Bass, 1976.

Haley, J.   How to be a marriage therapist without knowing practically anything. *Journal of Marital and Family Therapy,* 1980, *6*(4), 385—392.

Halpern, T. O.   Degree of client disclosure as a function of past disclosure, counselor disclosure, and counselor facilitativeness. *Journal of Counseling Psychology,* 1977, *24,* 41—47.

Haney, J. N., Sewell, W. R., Edelstein, B. A., & Sartin, H. H.   A portable inexpensive walkie-talkie-type "Bug-in-the-ear." *Behavior Research Methods and Instrumentation,* 1975, *7*(1), 19—20.

Hansen, J. C. (Ed.).   *Counseling process and procedures.* New York: Macmillan, 1978.

Hansen, J. C., Warner, R. W., & Smith, E. J.   *Group counseling: Theory and process* (2nd ed.). Chicago: Rand McNally, 1980.

Hardy, R. (Ed.). *Group counseling and therapy techniques in special settings.* Springfield, Ill.: C.C. Thomas, 1973.

Hare, N., & Levis, D. J. Pervasive anxiety: A search for a cause and treatment approach. In S. M. Turner, K. S. Calhoun, & H. E. Adams (Eds.), *Handbook of clinical behavior therapy.* New York: John Wiley & Sons, 1981.

Harmon, H. *Modern factor analysis.* Chicago: University of Chicago Press, 1967.

Hartley, D., Roback, H. B., & Abramowitz, S. I. Deterioration effects in encounter groups. *American Psychologist,* 1976, 247–255.

Havighurst, R. J. *Developmental tasks and education.* New York: David McKay, 1972.

Hayakawa, S. I. *Language in thought and action* (2nd ed.). New York: Harcourt, Brace & World, 1964.

Heckel, R. V., & Salzberg, H. C. *Group psychotherapy: A behavioral approach.* Columbia, S. C.: University of South Carolina Press, 1976.

Heller, J. *Catch 22.* New York: Dell Publishing Co., 1955.

Hellwig, K., & Memmott, R. J. Co-therapy: The balancing act. *Small Group Behavior,* 1974, 5(2), 175–181.

Helson, R. Childhood interest clusters related to creativity in women. *Journal of Consulting Psychology,* 1965, 29, 353–361.

Herold, P. L., Ramirez, J., & Newkirk, J. A portable radio communications system for teacher education. *Educational Technology,* 1971.

Hertzler, J. O. *Laughter: A socio-scientific analysis.* New York: Exposition Press, 1970.

Heslin, R. Predicting group task effectiveness from member characteristics. *Psychological Bulletin,* 1964, 62, 248–256.

Hesse, H. *Siddhartha.* New York: New Directions, 1951.

Higbee, K. L. Group influence on self-disclosure. *Psychological Reports,* 1973, 32, 903–909.

Hill, W. The Hill Interaction Matrix. *Personnel and Guidance Journal,* 1971, 619–622.

Hill, W. F. Further consideration of therapeutic mechanism in group therapy. *Small Group Behavior,* 1975.

Hoch, P. Bisocial aspects of anxiety. In P. Hoch & J. Zubin (Eds.), *Anxiety.* New York: Grune & Stratton, 1950.

Hopper, G. Resistance in counseling groups. *Journal for Specialists in Group Work,* 1978, 3(1), 37–48.

Horan, J. J. *Counseling for effective decision making.* Belmont, Calif.: Wadsworth, 1979.

Horney, K. *Our inner conflicts.* New York: W. W. Norton, 1945.

Hosford, R., & De Visser, L. *Behavioral approaches to counseling: An introduction.* Washington, D.C.: American Personnel & Guidance Association Press, 1974.

Huppe, B. F., & Kaminsky, J. *Logic and language.* New York: Alfred A. Knopf, 1962.

Jacobs, A. The use of feedback in groups. In A. Jacobs & W. W. Sprandlin (Eds.), *Group as agent of change.* New York: Behavioral Publications, 1974.

Jacobs, A., Jacobs, M., Feldman, G., & Cavior, N. Feedback II—the credibility gap: Delivery of positive and negative emotional and behavioral feedback in groups. *Journal of Consulting and Clinical Psychology,* 1973, 41, 215–223.

James, W. *Principles of psychology* (Vol. 2). New York: Dover Publications, 1950. (Originally published, 1908.)

James, W. *Varieties of religious experience.* New York: Random House, 1902.

James, W.   *Pragmatism*. New York: New American Library, 1907.

Janis, I. L.   *Victims of Groupthink*. Boston: Houghton Mifflin, 1972.

Janis, I. L., & Mann, L.   *Decision making: A psychological analysis of conflict, choice, and commitment*. New York: Free Press, 1977.

Jefferson, L.   These are my sisters. In B. Kaplan (Ed.), *The inner world of mental illness*. New York: Harper & Row, 1964.

Jeffries, D.   Should we continue to deradicalize children through the use of counseling groups? *Educational Technology*, 1973, *13*(1), 45—49.

Johnson, N.   Must the rational-emotive therapist be like Albert Ellis? *Personnel and Guidance Journal*, September 1980, 49—51.

Jourard, S. M., & Jaffee, P. E.   Influence of an interviewer's disclosure on the self-disclosing behavior of interviewees. *Journal of Counseling Psychology*, 1970, *17*, 252—257.

Kafka, F.   *The penal colony: Stories and short pieces*. New York: Schocken Books, 1948.

Kaiser, R. B.   The way of the journal. *Psychology Today*, March 1981, 64—76.

Kane, T R., Suls, J., & Tedeschi, J. T.   Humour as a tool of social interaction. In A. J. Chapman & H. C. Foot (Eds.), *It's a funny thing, humour*. Oxford, England: Pergamon Press, 1977.

Kanfer, F. H., & Phillips, J. S.   *Learning foundations of behavior therapy*. New York: John Wiley & Sons, 1970.

Kaplan, H. S., Kohl, R. N., Pomeroy, W. B., Offit, A. K., & Hogan, R.   Group treatment of premature ejaculation. In J. Lo Piccolo & L. Lo Piccolo (Eds.), *Handbook of sex therapy*. New York: Plenum Press, 1978.

Kazdin, A. E.   Covert modeling, model similarity, and reduction of avoidance behavior. *Behavior Therapy*, 1974, *5*, 325—340.

Keith-Spiegel, P.   Early conceptions of humor: Varieties and issues. In J. H. Goldstein & P. E. McGhee (Eds.), *The psychology of humor: Theoretical perspectives and empirical issues*. New York: Academic Press, 1972.

Kellerman, H.   *Group psychotherapy and personality: Intersecting structures*. New York: Grune & Stratton, 1979.

Kelly, E. L., Goldberg, L. R., Fiske, D. W., & Kilkowski, J. M.   Twenty-five years later: A follow-up study of the graduate students in clinical psychology assessed in the V.A. Selection Research Project. *American Psychologist*, 1978, *33*, 746 —755.

Klein, J. P.   On the use of humor in counseling. *Canadian Counsellor*, 1974, *8*, 233—237.

Koestler, A.   *The act of creation*. New York: Dell Publishing Co., 1964.

Kogan, L. S.   Validity, reliability, and the related considerations. In A. W. Shyne (Ed.), *Use of judgement as data in social work research*. New York: American Association of Social Work, 1959.

Kogan, N., & Wallach, M. A.   Risk taking as a function of the situation, the person, and the group. In *New directions in psychology III*. New York: Holt, Rinehart & Winston, 1967.

Kopp, S.   *The naked therapist*. San Diego: Edits, 1972.

Korner, I. M., & Brown, W. H. The mechanical third ear. *Journal of Counseling Psychology*, 1952.

Kottler, J. A.   *The effects of immediate feedback supervision on counselor anxiety and performance in a laboratory practicum*. Unpublished doctoral dissertation, University of Virginia, 1977.

Kottler, J. A.   How the effective group counselor functions. *Journal for Specialists in Group Work*, 1978, 3(3), 113–121. (a)

Kottler, J. A.   A question of ethics. *Journal for Specialists in Group Work*, 1978, 3(1), 21–24. (b)

Kottler, J. A.   The use of a journal in counseling. *Guidance Clinic*, November 1978, 6–7. (c)

Kottler, J. A.   Promoting self-understanding in counseling: A compromise between the insight and action-oriented approaches. *Journal of Psychiatric Nursing and Mental Health Services*, 1979, 17(12), 18–23.

Kottler, J. A.   The development of guidelines for training group leaders: A synergistic model. *Journal for Specialists in Group Work*, 1981, 6(3), 125–129. (a)

Kottler, J. A.   *Mouthing off: A study of oral behavior, its causes and treatments.* New York: Libra, 1981. (b)

Kottler, J. A., Dyer, W. W., & Vriend, J.   Group counseling scale for the self-analysis of fully functioning and self-defeating behavior. In W. W. Dyer & J. Vriend (Eds.), *Counseling techniques that work.* Washington, D.C.: American Personnel and Guidance Association Press, 1975.

Kottler, J. A., Vriend, J., & Dyer, W. W.   An evaluation scale for client use in individual and group counseling. *Michigan Personnel and Guidance Journal*, 1974, 6(1), 6–19.

Krumboltz, J. D., & Potter, B.   Behavioral techniques for developing trust, cohesiveness, and goal accomplishment. *Educational Technology*, 1973, 13(1), 26–30.

Kubie, L. S.   The destructive potential of humor in psychotherapy. *American Journal of Psychiatry*, 1971, 127(7), 37–42.

Lacan, J.   *Ecrits.* New York: W. W. Norton, 1968.

Laing, R. D.   *The divided self.* Baltimore: Penguin Books, 1965.

Lamb, C. S.   The use of paradoxical intention: Self-management through laughter. *Personnel and Guidance Journal*, December 1980, 217–219.

Lancaster, A.   Personal communication, 1981.

Lantz, J. E.   *Family and marital therapy: A transactional approach.* New York: Appleton-Century-Crofts, 1978. (a)

Lantz, J. E.   Co-therapy approach in family therapy. *Social Work*, 1978, 23(2), 156–158. (b)

Larry, T.   *Interpersonal diagnosis of personality: A functional theory and methodology for personality evaluation.* New York: Ronald Press, 1957.

Laughlin, P. R., Branch, L. G., & Johnson, H. H.   Individual versus triadic performance on a unidimensional complementary task as a function of initial ability level. *Journal of Personality and Social Psychology*, 1969, 12, 144–150.

Lazarus, A. A.   Multimodal behavior therapy: Treating the "basic id." *Journal of Nervous and Mental Disease*, 1973, 156, 404–411.

Lazarus, A. A.   *The Practice of Multi-Model Therapy*, New York: McGraw Hill, 1981.

Lazarus, A A., & Abramovitz, A.   The use of "emotive imagery" in the treatment of children's phobias. *Journal of Mental Science*, 1962, 108, 191–195.

Lee, J. L., & Pulvino, C. S. (Eds.).   *Group counseling: Theory, research, and practice.* Washington, D.C.: American Personnel and Guidance Association Press, 1973.

Levin, J.   *Learning differences: Diagnosis and prescription.* New York: Holt, Rinehart & Winston, 1977.

Levinson, D. J.   *The seasons of a man's life.* New York: Ballantine Books, 1978.

Lieberman, M. A., Yalom, I. D., & Miles, M. *Encounter groups: First facts.* New York: Basic Books, 1973.

Locke, N. *Group psychoanalysis: Theory and technique.* New York: New York University Press, 1961.

Lorenz, K. *On aggression.* New York: Bantam Books, 1966.

MacLennan, B. W. Co-therapy. *International Journal of Group Psychotherapy,* 1965, *15*(2), 154—166.

Mahlor, C. A. *Group counseling in the schools.* Boston: Houghton Mifflin, 1969.

Mailer, N. *The executioner's song.* Boston: Little, Brown & Co., 1979.

Malamud, D. I. The laughing game: An exercise for sharpening awareness of self-responsibility. *Psychotherapy: Theory, Research, and Practice,* 1980, *17*(1), 69—73.

Mann, B., & Murphy, K. C. Timing of self-disclosure, reciprocity of self-disclosure, and reaction to an initial interview. *Journal of Counseling Psychology,* 1975, *22,* 304—308.

Marcuse, H. *Eros and civilization.* New York: Vintage Books, 1962.

Markus, H. The effect of mere presence on social facilitation: An unobtrusive test. *Journal of Experimental Social Psychology,* 1978, *14,* 389—397.

Marmor, J., & Woods, S. M. *The interface between the psychodynamic and behavioral therapies.* New York: Plenum Press, 1980.

Martineau, W. H. A model of the social functions of humor. In J. H. Goldstein & P. E. McGhee (Eds.), *The psychology of humor.* New York: Academic Press, 1972.

Maslow, A. *Motivation and personality.* New York: Harper & Row, 1954.

Masters, W. H., & Johnson, V. E. *Human sexual inadequacy.* Boston: Little, Brown & Co., 1970.

May, R. Contributions of existential psychotherapy. In R. May, E. Angel, & H. F. Ellenberger (Eds.), *Existence.* New York: Simon & Schuster, 1958.

May, R. *Love and will.* New York: W. W. Norton, 1969.

McClure, W. J. Increasing group counseling effectiveness through appropriate pacing skills. *Journal for Specialists in Group Work,* 1978, *3*(3), 139—145.

McGhee, P. E. *Humor: Its origin and development.* San Francisco: W. H. Freeman & Co., 1979.

McGrath, J. C., & Altman, I. *Small group research.* New York: Holt, Rinehart & Winston, 1966.

McLemore, C. W., & Benjamin, L. S. Whatever happened to interpersonal diagnosis? *American Psychologist,* 1979, *34*(1), 17—34.

Meichenbaum, D. H. Examination of model characteristics in reducing avoidance behavior. *Journal of Personality and Social Psychology,* 1971, *17,* 298—307.

Meichenbaum, D., & Goodman, J. Training impulsive children to talk to themselves: A means of developing self-control. *Journal of Abnormal Psychology,* 1971, *77,* 115—126.

Milgram, S. Liberating effects of group pressure. *Journal of Personality and Social Psychology,* 1965, *1,* 127 — 134.

Mintz, E. E. Transference in co-therapy groups. *Journal of Consulting Psychology,* 1963, *27*(1), 34—39.

Moreno, J. L. *Psychodrama* (Rev. ed.). Beacon, N.Y.: Beacon House, 1964.

Moreno, J. L., & Elefthery, D. G. An introduction to group psychodrama. In G. Gazda (Ed.), *Basic approaches to group psychotherapy and group counseling* (2nd ed.). Springfield, Ill.: C. C. Thomas, 1975.

Morris, D. *Manwatching: A field guide to human behavior.* New York: Harry Abrams, 1977.

Mullen, H. Art therapy and the psychoanalytic group. In H. Mullen & M. Rosenbaum (Eds.), *Group psychotherapy: Theory and practice* (2nd ed.). New York: Free Press, 1978.

Muro, J. J., & Freeman, S. L. (Eds.). *Readings in group counseling.* Scranton, Pa.: International Textbook, 1968.

Myers, G. E., & Myers, M. T. *The dynamics of human communication.* New York: McGraw-Hill, 1973.

Napier, A., & Whitaker, C. A conversation about co-therapy. In A. Ferber, M. Mendelsohn, and A. Napier (Eds.), *The book of family therapy.* Boston: Houghton Mifflin, 1972.

Napier, R. W., & Gershenfeld, M. K. *Groups: Theory and experience* (2nd ed.). Boston: Houghton Mifflin, 1981.

Nietzsche, F. On truth and falsity in their extramoral sense. In W. Shibles (Ed.), *Essays on metaphor.* Whitewater, Wis.: Language Press, 1972. (Originally published, 1864.)

Niles, J., & De Voe, M. Counseling, risk taking, and the learning process. *Personnel and Guidance Journal,* October 1978, 99—102.

Nin, A. Preface. In T. Rainer (Ed.), *The new diary.* Los Angeles: J. P. Tarcher, 1978.

Nolan, W. A. *The making of a surgeon.* New York: Dell, 1968.

Ohlsen, M. *Group counseling* (2nd ed.). New York: Holt, Rinehart & Winston, 1977.

Ohlsen, M. M., & Pearson, R. E. A method for the classification of group interaction and its use to explore the influence on individual role factors in group counseling. *Journal of Clinical Psychology,* 1965, *21*, 436—441.

Okun, B. F., & Rappaport, L. J. *Working with families: An introduction to family therapy.* North Scituate, Mass.: Duxbury Press, 1980.

Osborn, A. F. *Applied imagination: Principles and procedures of creative problem solving.* New York: Scribner's, 1963.

Palazzoli, M. S., Boscolo, L., Cecchin, G., & Prata, G. The problem of the referring person. *Journal of Marital and Family Therapy,* 1980, 6(1), 3—10.

Palmer, J. O. *A primer of eclectic psychotherapy.* Monterey, Calif.: Brooks/Cole, 1980.

Palomares, U. *A curriculum on conflict management.* La Mesa, Calif.: Human Development Training Institute, 1975.

Parnes, S. J. *Creative behavior guidebook.* New York: Scribner's, 1967.

Patterson, G. T., Jones, R., Whittier, J., & Wright, M. A. The hyperactive child. *Behavior, Research, and Therapy,* 1965, 2, 217—226.

Payne, R., and Cooper, C. L. *Groups at work.* New York: John Wiley & Sons, 1982.

Perls, F. *Gestalt therapy verbatim.* Lafayette, Calif.: Real People Press, 1969.

Peterson, P. *Laughter in a therapy group.* Unpublished doctoral dissertation, University of Tennessee, 1975.

Piaget, J. *The origins of intelligence.* New York: International Universities Press, 1956.

Pollio, H. R., & Edgerly, J. W. Comedians and comic style. In A. J. Chapman & H. C. Foot (Eds.), *Humor and laughter: Theory, research, and applications.* London: John Wiley & Sons, 1976.

Powdermaker, F. B., & Frank, J. D.   *Group psychotherapy.* Cambridge, Mass.: Harvard University Press, 1953.

Pruitt, D. G. (Ed.).   Special issue on the risky shift. *Journal of Personality and Social Psychology,* 1971, *20,* 339—510.

Rainer, T.   *The new diary.* Los Angeles: J. P. Tarcher, 1978.

Redl, F.   *When we deal with children.* New York: Free Press, 1966.

Reeder, C., & Kunce, J.   Modeling technique, drug abstinence behavior, and heroin addicts: A pilot study. *Journal of Counseling Psychology,* 1976, *23,* 560—562.

Rice, D. G., Fey, W. F., & Kepecs, J. G.   Therapist experience and "style" as factors in co-therapy. *Family Process,* 1972, *11,* 227—241.

Rice, J. K., & Rice, D. G.   Status and sex role issues in co-therapy. In *Couples in conflict: New directions in marital therapy.* New York: Jason Aronson, 1975.

Ritter, B.   The group treatment of children's snake phobias using vicarious and contact desensitization procedures. *Behavior Research and Therapy,* 1968, *6,* 1—6.

Robbins, T.   *Even cowgirls get the blues.* New York: Bantam Books, 1976.

Robinson, F. P.   Counseling orientation and labels. *Journal of Counseling Psychology,* 1965, *12,* 338.

Robinson, F. P.   Modern approaches to counseling diagnosis. In J. C. Hansen (Ed.), *Counseling process and procedures.* New York: Macmillan, 1978, p. 313—322.

Rogers, C.   *Carl Rogers on encounter groups.* New York: Harper & Row, 1970.

Roman, M., & Meltzer, B.   Co-therapy: A review of current literature (with special reference to therapeutic outcome). *Journal of Sex and Marital Therapy,* 1977, *3*(1), 63—77.

Rose, S. D.   *Group therapy: A behavioral approach.* Englewood Cliffs, N.J.: Prentice-Hall, 1977.

Rosen, R. D.   *Psychobabble.* New York: Avon Books, 1977.

Rosenbaum, M.   Co-therapy. In H. I. Kaplan & B. J. Sadock (Eds.), *Comprehensive group psychotherapy.* Baltimore: Williams & Wilkins, 1971.

Rosenbaum, M., & Berger, M. (Eds.).   *Group psychotherapy and group function.* New York: Basic Books, 1963.

Rosenhan, D. L.   On being sane in insane places. *Science,* 1973, *179,* 250—258.

Rowe, W., & Winborn, B. B.   What people fear about group work: An analysis of 36 selected critical articles. *Educational Technology,* 1973, *13*(1), 53—57.

Royce, J. R.   The development of factor analysis. *Journal of General Psychology,* 1958, *58,* 139.

Royce, J. R.   Factors as theoretical constructs. In D. N. Jackson & S. Messick (Eds.), *Problems in human assessment.* New York: McGraw-Hill, 1967.

Royce, J. R.   Psychology is multi-: Methodological, variate, epistemic, world view, systemic, paradigmatic, theoretic, and disciplinary. *Nebraska Symposium on Motivation,* Lincoln: University of Nebraska Press, 1975. 1—63.

Rudestam, K. E.   Semantics and psychotherapy. *Psychotherapy: Theory, Research, and Practice,* 1978, *15*(2), 190—192.

Runyan, D. L.   The group risky-shift effect as a function of emotional bonds, actual consequences, and extent of responsibility. *Journal of Personality and Social Psychology,* 1974, *29,* 670—676.

Russell, A., & Russell, L.   The uses and abuses of co-therapy. *Journal of Marital and Family Therapy,* 1979, 39—46.

Russell, B.   *The basic writings of Bertrand Russell* (R. E. Egner & L. E. Denown, Eds.). New York: Simon & Schuster, 1961.

Ryan, T. A.   Goal setting in group counseling. In J. Vriend and W. W. Dyer (Eds.), *Counseling effectively in groups*. Englewood Cliffs, N.J.: Educational Technology, 1973.

Sacks, J. M.   Psychodrama: An underdeveloped group resource. *Educational Technology*, 1973, *13*(2), 37—39.

Sagan, C.   *The dragons of Eden*. New York: Ballantine Books, 1977.

Saretsky, T.   *Active techniques and group psychotherapy*. New York: Jason Aronson, 1977.

Sartre, J-P.   *Existentialism and human emotions*. New York: Wisdom Library, 1957.

Satir, V.   *Conjoint family therapy*. Palo Alto, Calif.: Science & Behavior Books, 1964.

Satir, V.   *Peoplemaking*. Palo Alto, Calif.: Science & Behavior Books, 1972.

Saunders, L.   *Cultural differences and medical care*. New York: Russell Sage Foundation, 1954.

Scarf, Maggie.   Images that heal, *Psychology Today*, Sept., 1980, 32—46.

Schanck, R. L.   A study of a community and its groups and institutions conceived of as behaviors of individuals. *Psychological Monographs*, 1932, *43*.

Scheidlinger, S., & Porter, K.   Group therapy combined with individual therapy. In T. Karasu & L. Bellak (Eds.), *Specialized techniques in individual psychotherapy*. New York: Brunner/Mazel, 1980.

Schneidman, B., & McGuire, L.   Group therapy for nonorgasmic women: Two age levels. In J. Lo Piccolo & L. Lo Piccolo (Eds.), *Handbook of sex therapy*. New York: Plenum Press, 1978.

Schrank, F. A., & Engels, A. W.   Bibliotherapy as a counseling adjunct: Research findings. *Personnel and Guidance Journal*, November 1981, 143—147.

Schuerger, J. M.   Understanding and controlling anger. In S. Eisenberg & L. E. Patterson, *Helping clients with special concerns*. Chicago: Rand McNally, 1979.

Schutz, W. C.   *FIRO: A three-dimensional theory of interpersonal behavior*. New York: Rinehart, 1958.

Seligman, M.   *Group psychotherapy and counseling with special populations*. Baltimore: University Park Press, 1981.

Shaffer, J. B., & Galinsky, M. D.   *Models of group therapy & sensitivity training*, Englewood Cliffs, N.J.: Prentice-Hall, 1974.

Shands, H.   *Semiotic approaches to psychiatry*. The Hague: Mouton, 1970.

Shapiro, J. L.   *Methods of group psychotherapy and encounter*. Itasca, Ill.: F. E. Peacock, 1978.

Shaw, M. E.   *Group dynamics: The pscyhology of small group behavior* (3rd ed.). New York: McGraw-Hill, 1981.

Shelton, J. L., & Ackerman, J. M.   *Homework in counseling and psychotherapy*. Springfield, Ill.: C. C. Thomas, 1974.

Shepard, M.   *Inside a psychiatrist's head*. New York: Dell, 1972.

Shertzer, B., & Stone, S. C.   *Fundamentals of counseling* (3rd ed.). Boston: Houghton Mifflin, 1980.

Shibles, W. (Ed.) *Essays on metaphor*. Whitewater, Wis.: Language Press, 1972.

Simonson, N.   The impact of therapist disclosure on patient disclosure. *Journal of Counseling Psychology*, 1976, *23*.

Simonton, O. C., & Simonton, S. S.   Belief systems and management of the emotional aspects of malignancy. *Journal of Transpersonal Psychology*, 1975, 7, 29—47.

Singer, J. L.   *The child's world of make-believe: Experimental studies of imaginative play*, N.Y.: Academic Press, 1973.

Slavson, S. R.   *A textbook in analytic group psychotherapy*. New York: International Universities Press, 1964.

Small, L.   The uncommon importance of psychodiagnosis. In J. C. Hansen (Ed.), *Counseling process and procedures*. New York: Macmillan, 1978.

Smith, D.   *Integrative counseling and psychotherapy*. Boston: Houghton Mifflin, 1975.

Smith, M. J., & Glass, G. V.   Meta-analysis of psychotherapy outcome studies. *American Psychologist*, 1977, 32(9), 752—760.

Solzhenitsyn, A.   *The first circle*. New York: Harper & Row, 1968.

Sommer, R.   *Personal space: The behavioral basis of design*. Englewood Cliffs, N.J.: Prentice-Hall, 1969.

Sonne, J. S., & Lincoln, G.   Importance of heterosexual co-therapy relationship in the construction of a family image. In J. Cohen (Ed.), *Family structure dynamics and therapy. American Psychiatric Association*, 1966, 20, 196—205.

Spector, P. E. Cohen, S. L., & Penner, L. A.   The effects of real versus hypothetical risk on group choice-shifts. *Personality and Social Psychology Bulletin*, 1976, 2, 290—293.

Spier, L.   *Language, culture, and personality: Essays in memory of Edward Sapir*. Menasha, Wis.: Sapir Memorial Publication Fund, 1941.

Stein, M. J. (Ed.).   *Contemporary psychotherapies*. New York: Free Press, 1961.

Stern, J. A., Bremer, D. A., & McClure, J.   Analysis of eye movements and blinks during reading: Effects of Valium. *Psychopharmacologia*, 1974, 40(2), 171—175.

Stern, P. J.   *The abnormal person and his world*. Princeton, N. J.: D. Van Nostrand, 1964.

Stockton, R., & Movran, D. K.   The use of verbal feedback in counseling groups: Toward an effective system. *Journal for Specialists in Group Work*, 1980, 5(1), 10—14.

Stogdill, R. M.   *Handbook of leadership*. New York: Free Press, 1974.

Stoner, J. A. F.   Risky and cautious shifts in group decisions: The influence of widely held values. *Journal of Experimental Social Psychology*, 1968, 4, 442—459.

Stuart, R. B.   *Trick or treatment: How and when psychotherapy fails*. Champaign, Ill.: Research Press, 1970.

Stumphauzer, J. S.   Low-cost Bug-in-the-Ear sound system for the modification of therapist and patient behavior. *Behavior Therapy*, 1970, 8, 124—129.

Sullivan, H. S.   *Conceptions of modern psychiatry*. New York: W. W. Norton, 1947.

Temerlin, R. K.   Suggestion effects in psychiatric diagnosis. In T. J. Scheff (Ed.), *Labeling madness*. Englewood Cliffs, N. J.: Prentice-Hall, 1975.

Thase, M., & Page, R. A.   Modeling of self-disclosure in laboratory and nonlaboratory interview settings. *Journal of Counseling Psychology*, 1977, 24, 35—40.

Thomas, L.   *The medusa and the snail*. New York: The Viking Press, 1979.

Thorne, F. C.   Eclectic psychotherapy. In R. Corsini (Ed.), *Current psychotherapies*. Itasca, Ill.: F. E. Peacock, 1973.

Tomkins, S. S.   A theory of risk-taking behavior. In R. E. Carney (Ed.), *Risk-taking behavior*. Springfield, Ill.: C. C. Thomas, 1971.

Trotzer, J. P. *The counselor and the group: Integrating theory, training, and practice.* Monterey, Calif.: Brooks/Cole, 1977.

Turgenev, I. *Fathers and sons.* Baltimore: Penguin Books, 1965.

Tyler, A. J., & Thurston, N. Platitudinal counseling. *Worm Runner's Digest,* 1977, *19*(1), 102−103.

Van Hoose, W. H. & Kottler, J. A., *Ethical & legal issues in counseling and psychotherapy,* San Francisco: Jossey-Bass, 1977.

Viscott, D. S. *The making of a psychiatrist.* Greenwich, Conn.: Fawcett Publications, 1972.

Vriend, J. *Variables I look for in any person I want to recruit in my world.* Unpublished manuscript, 1981.

Vriend, J., & Dyer, W. W. Behavioral characteristics of personal mastery (Tape 2), *Counseling for personal mastery: A casette tape series for building counselor competencies.* Washington, D.C.: American Personnel and Guidance Association Press, 1973. (a)

Vriend, J., & Dyer, W. W. A case for a technology of group counseling and a delineation of major group categories. *Educational Technology,* 1973, *13*(1), 12−18. (b)

Vriend, J., & Dyer, W. W. (Eds.). *Counseling effectively in groups.* Englewood Cliffs, N.J.: Educational Technology, 1973. (c)

Vriend, J., & Dyer, W. W. Counseling the reluctant client. *Journal of Counseling Psychology,* 1973, *20*(3), 240−246. (d)

Wachtel, P. L. What should we say to our patients? On the wording of therapists' comments. *Psychotherapy: Theory, Research, and Practice,* 1980, *17*(2), 183−188.

Wachtel, P. L. *Resistance: Psychodynamic and behavioral approaches.* New York: Plenum Press, 1981.

Waldren, T., McElmurry, T., Bowens, L., & Israel, D. The story of story hour. *Personnel and Guidance Journal,* October 1980, 108−109.

Watts, A., *The Book,* New York: Vintage Books, 1966.

Watzlawick, P. *How real is real?* New York: Vintage Books, 1976.

Watzlawick, P. *The language of change.* New York: Basic Books, 1978.

Watzlawick, P., Weakland, J., & Fisch, R. *Change: Principles of problem formation and problem resolution.* New York: W. W. Norton, 1974.

Weil, A. *The marriage of the sun and the moon.* Boston: Houghton Mifflin, 1980.

Weinstein, I. Guidelines of a choice of a co-therapist. *Psychotherapy: Theory, Research, and Practice,* 1971, *8*, 301−303.

Wender, L., & Stein, A. Group psychotherapy as an aid to out-patient treatment in a psychiatric clinic. *Psychiatric Quarterly,* 1949, *23*, 415−424.

Whorf, B. Grammatical categories. In J. E. Carrol (Ed.), *Language, Thought, and Reality.* New York: John Wiley & Sons, 1956.

Wiener, P. P. *Evolution and the founders of pragmatism.* Gloucester, Mass.: Peter Smith, 1949.

Wilder, T. *Our Town: Three plays by Thornton Wilder.* New York: Bantam Books, 1958.

Williams, M. *The velveteen rabbit.* New York, Doubleday, 1975.

Williams, R. J. *You are extraordinary.* New York: Pyramid Books, 1971.

Winter, S. K. Developmental stages in the roles and concerns of group co-leaders. *Small Group Behavior,* 1976, *7*(3), 349−362.

Wolberg, L. R.   *The technique of psychotherapy.* New York: Grune & Stratton, 1954.

Wold, C. N., & Fagundes, J. O.   Resolution of co-therapist's conflicts mirrored in brief family therapy. *Family Therapy,* 1977, *4*(1), 31—41.

Wolf, A. et al.   *Beyond the couch: Dialogues in teaching and learning psychoanalysis in groups.* New York: Science House, 1970.

Wolf, A., & Schwartz, E. K.   *Psychoanalysis in groups.* New York: Grune & Stratton, 1962.

Wolfe, T.   *The right stuff.* New York: Bantam Books, 1980.

Wolman, R. N.   Women's issues in couples treatment: The view of the male therapist. *Psychiatric Opinion,* 1976, *13*(1), 13—17.

Worthy, M., Gary, A. L., & Kahn, G. M.   Self-disclosure as an exchange process. *Journal of Personality and Social Psychology,* 1969, *13*, 59—63.

Yalom, I.   *Existential psychotherapy.* New York: Basic Books, 1980.

Yalom, I. D.   *The theory and practice of group psychotherapy.* New York: Basic Books, 1975.

Zigler, E., & Phillips, L.   Psychiatric diagnosis: A critique. *Journal of Abnormal and Social Psychology,* 1961, *63*, 607—618.

Zigler, E., & Phillips L.   Psychiatric diagnosis and symptomatology. In O. Milton (Ed.), *Behavior disorders.* New York: Lippincott, 1965.

Zimpfer, D. G.   Multi-leader approaches to groups in counseling and therapy. In J. C. Hansen & S. H. Cramer (Eds.), *Group guidance and counseling in the schools: Selected readings.* New York: Appleton-Century-Crofts, 1971.

Zubin, J.   Classification of the behavior disorders. In P. R. Farnsworth (Ed.), *Annual review of psychology* (Vol. 18). Palo Alto, Calif.: Annual Reviews, 1967.

Name Index

Abramowitz, S. I., 151
Adams, H. B., 143
Adams, H. E., 143
Adler, Alfred, 91
Allen, Woody, 249
Andolfi, M., 114
Ardrey, Robert, 257
Argyris, C., 25
Aristophanes, 267–268
Aristotle, 34, 68
Asch, S. E., 13
Ayer, A. J., 118

Bakker, C. B., 140
Bales, R., 143
Balgopal, P. R., 180
Bandler, R., 60, 101, 102, 112, 126, 165, 231, 240
Bandura, A., 89, 104, 105, 106
Barry, R. A., 255
Bateson, G., 78, 112, 123, 137, 229
Beck, A. T., 162–163
Bednar, R. L., 195, 199
Begelman, D. A., 143
Benjamin, L. S., 143
Benshoff, D. L., 141
Berkeley, Lord George, 140
Berne, Eric, 38, 143
Betz, R. L., 9
Bierce, Ambrose, 27, 92, 244
Bombeck, Erma, 249
Bonney, W. C., 21
Bowers, W. A., 174
Boyd, J., 152, 170–171
Brown, W. H., 278–279
Bruner, J. S., 59
Burke, Kenneth, 228
Byrd, R. E., 198

Calhoun, D. S., 143
Charney, I. W., 114
Clark, C. H., 76
Cohen, A. M., 152, 172
Cole, H. P., 253
Cooper, I. S., 40
Corey, G., 20, 91, 114, 144, 180
Corey, M. S., 20, 91, 180
Cormier, L. S., 67
Cormier, W. H., 67
Csikszentmihalyi, M., 95

Darwin, Charles, 39, 107
DiGiovanni, I.S., 178
Della Corte, M., 141–142
Denver, John, 142
Dewey, John, 31, 39
Donleavy, J. P., 249–250
Doster, J. A., 143
Dostoyevsky, Fyodor, 92, 194
Dyer, W. W., 91, 144, 164, 185, 234, 248, 253, 255

Edgerly, J. W., 251
Egan, G., 67, 285
Einhorn, J., 231

Einstein, Albert, 94, 107
Ellerbrock, W. C., 118
Ellis, Albert, 37–38, 71, 91, 101, 102, 126, 129, 246–247
Epstein, N., 178
Erickson, Erik, 65
Erickson, Milton H., 46, 58, 73, 100, 126, 231, 238–240, 259

Festinger, L., 13
Fey, W. F., 190
Fish, Jefferson, 64
Fiske, John, 39
Foley, W. J., 21
Foster, J. A., 253, 254
Frank, Jerome, 64
Frankl, Viktor, 246, 247
Freud, Sigmund, 37–38, 68, 73, 91, 107, 162, 238, 252, 264
Frey, D. H., 54
Frost, Robert, 228

Galinsky, M. D., 113
Galloghy, V., 178
Gauron, E. F., 174
Gershenfeld, M. K., 113, 245
Gesell, Arnold, 59
Getty, C., 185
Gide, André, 107
Gill, S. J., 255
Glossop, R. J., 26
Goertzel, M. G., 14, 96
Goertzel, V., 14
Goldberg, C., 114
Goldberg, M. C., 114
Goldfried, A. P., 78
Goldfried, M. R., 78
Goodman, J., 101
Gordon, David, 239, 240
Gorsuch, R. L., 54
Gottman, J., 85, 146, 165
Greenberg, Dan, 245
Greenwald, H., 246
Grieger, R., 152, 170–171
Grinder, J., 60, 101, 102, 112, 126, 165, 231, 240

Haley, J., 68, 136, 229, 259
Haney, J. N., 279
Hansen, J. C., 21, 54–55, 114
Harper, R., 102
Hartley, D., 151
Havighurst, R. J., 173
Hayakawa, S. I., 118, 122–125
Heller, Joseph, 72, 246
Hemingway, Ernest, 107
Hertzler, J. O., 244
Hill, W., 143
Hitler, Adolf, 18
Holmes, Oliver Wendell, 39
Hopper, G., 166–167
Horney, Karen, 143
Hull, R. F., 180
Huppe, B. F., 119, 121

313

Subject Index